To
Gilbert T. Stephenson

From

I D Willcock
of Gray's Inn
London

Dec. 1944.

LEGAL ESSAYS
AND
ADDRESSES

CAMBRIDGE
UNIVERSITY PRESS
LONDON: BENTLEY HOUSE
NEW YORK, TORONTO, BOMBAY
CALCUTTA, MADRAS: MACMILLAN
TOKYO: MARUZEN COMPANY LTD

All rights reserved

LEGAL ESSAYS
AND
ADDRESSES

by

THE RIGHT HON.
LORD WRIGHT OF DURLEY

DR. NORMAN A. WIGGINS

CAMBRIDGE
AT THE UNIVERSITY PRESS
1939

PRINTED IN GREAT BRITAIN

To
MY WIFE

CONTENTS

	Preface	page ix
	Table of Cases	xxix
	Table of Statutes	xxxv
I	*Sinclair* v. *Brougham*	1
II	Restatement of the Law of Restitution	34
III	Public Policy	66
IV	The *Liesbosch Case*	96
V	The *Northwestern Utilities Case*	124
VI	Gold Clauses	147
VII	Judicial Proof: A Review	174
VIII	Some General Aspects of Law	186
IX	Williston on Contracts	202
X	Some Developments of Commercial Law in the Present Century	252
XI	Ought the Doctrine of Consideration to be Abolished from the Common Law?	287
XII	The Common Law in its Old Home	327
XIII	The Study of Law	387
XIV	*In Memoriam:* Right Hon. Sir Frederick Pollock	411
	Index of Matters	437

PREFACE

THE function of this Preface is to explain and if possible to justify the issue of this book. It is obvious that I am breaking the old rule that the shoemaker must not go beyond his last. It is my business as a judge to decide cases and write judgments. The work of writing judgments is in a sense the work of the miniaturist in law. He works with limited and definite facts and with limited and definite authorities and legal rules. Everything is directed to the particular result and everything not directly relevant should be excluded. The theory of economy forbids digressions into cognate rules of law or the enunciation of wider principles than are necessary for the particular case, or the attempt to reconcile and synthesize rules and achieve a more abstract and overriding principle. There is the further difficulty that the judge speaks with authority. He is a magistrate. He must look into the future and consider how the words he uses are susceptible of being applied to other facts and conditions, and he must guard against tying the hands of a future court which may have to determine what extensions are proper and what distinctions should be drawn. Thus the judge must neither speculate nor theorize. The essayist or writer on legal topics is in a position of greater freedom and less responsibility. In our Common Law system he is still bound to regard the course of the decided authorities, but he is not concerned with the determination of a particular issue. His horizon is wider.

Preface

He can criticize and theorize, he can analyse and classify. The legal writer may work on a large canvas; he make take for his theme the complete treatment of one of the great divisions of common law or equity, e.g. contract, tort, restitution, trusts. Or he may as an essayist work to a more limited objective and examine some restricted, though perhaps fundamental, topic, such as consideration or contributory negligence or mistake of law. Thus the essayist may seem to approximate to the judge, because he, like the judge, is working within narrow limits. But there is a real difference between the two types of work. The essayist is not concerned with the decision of a case, but with general problems of law, however limited the actual topic, whether that topic is a special rule or an authority, or whether it is some abstract but still limited question.

In these extra-judicial writings I deal in the main with limited objectives, or, if the objective may at times appear to be of wider import, only in a limited fashion. These writings are occasional. They have been produced in odd moments of leisure, outside my proper work; they are essentially *parerga*. I can in each case point to the occasion, or particular personal request. Thus the essay on *Sinclair* v. *Brougham* was originated by the request of Professor Winfield that I should give an address to his Cambridge University Law Society, the Review of the American Restatement of the Law of Restitution was written at the request of Professors Scott and Seavey, the Reporters for the American Law Institute of the branch of that law. Then came four lectures which I delivered at Harvard at the request of Dean Landis: the idea of the essay on the Common Law

Preface

in its Old Home was due to Dean Roscoe Pound. Professor Goodhart must take responsibility for the review of Williston on Contracts and for the "In Memoriam" article on Sir Frederick Pollock, which on my side was a labour of pious affection. The essay on Ought Consideration to be Abolished? came from a promise lightly given at the *Law Quarterly Review* Jubilee dinner to the young and persuasive student editor of the *Harvard Law Review* of that day. I had to keep my word, though with some present cost of labour and subsequent reproach from the legal world. The paper on Commercial Law was for the Holdsworth Society at Birmingham University (which bears the honoured name of my friend, Sir William Holdsworth), and was delivered because I was asked to do so by Professor Smalley-Baker. The slight review of Dean Wigmore's important work on Judicial Proof was done at the request of the literary editor of the American Bar Association. The other addresses explain their origin. But the friends on whose suggestion I wrote the essays contained in this book must not be taken to be in the least degree responsible for what I have written, or even to agree with it. The errors, whether of omission or commission, are my own and must be visited on my head.

It is clear that the articles are somewhat of a mixed bag. I should not, I think, of my own motion have thought of collecting and publishing them. But my friends Professor Goodhart and Professor Winfield advised me that it might be useful to do so, and I yielded to their judgment and experience. Professor Winfield has rendered me the great service of seeing the book through

Preface

the press and has entirely taken that labour off my shoulders. I have to thank Mr G. V. Carey, M.A., for preparing the Tables of Cases and Statutes and the Index of Matters.

In this miscellaneous collection of disconnected fragments are there any central or nodal ideas? Let me first refer to two topics, that of quasi-contract or restitution and that of consideration. It did not occur to me at first that I was to some extent aligning myself after a long interval of time in these matters with that great judge, Lord Mansfield, perhaps the greatest of the English judges. Nor did I appreciate what criticism and opposition my humble extra-judicial expression of opinion would provoke. On the subject of quasi-contract I went so far as to say that in England it was generally accepted that there were three principal categories, contract, tort, and quasi-contract. I was perhaps misled by the views which I found or thought I found in Pollock and other English writers of eminence. It may also be that such acquaintance as I had with the Common Law as understood in the United States made me look at the question through distorted glasses. In the review which I wrote of the Restatement of Restitution, I sought to explain to English lawyers that not only was restitution (or quasi-contract) a separate main category of the Common Law, but that it was one capable of as strict analysis and constituted a logical whole as susceptible of integrated exposition as any other branch of law. For the proof of the statement I refer to the Restatement itself. And I may here digress to make a passing observation on the Restatements of different branches of law which have been prepared and

Preface

published under the auspices of the American Law Institute. The work in each case is that of a body of distinguished United States lawyers and is an admirable survey of the branch of law which forms its subject. Each Restatement has taken years of study and consultation. Each Restatement forms a sort of code though it has not the force of law. I cannot say that the actual sections are light reading, any more than are the sections of any other code, but the explanations and discussions and the illustrations which form the larger part of each volume are admirably written and are most illuminating. The whole series is not yet complete, but so far as they are published the volumes should be in every English Law library so that use can be made of them with the help of the excellent indexes which they contain. I am satisfied that English lawyers will never fail to get help from the Restatements on any problem with which they have to grapple.

No doubt on some points American Law is not in accord with English Law, though there is in the main a close unison. But the time is past for English lawyers to pride themselves on an insular self-sufficiency. In Blackstone's day the Common Law was the law of a few million people in England and Ireland, and, if the colonies, plantations and settlements were added, perhaps a quarter of a million more. Now in these islands there may be perhaps forty millions living under English Law, but the Common Law has long passed its old boundaries. Under its sway live the teeming millions of the United States, the greatest nation living within a ring fence that the world has ever seen. Then there are Canada, Australia, New Zealand, great now but with

Preface

unforeseeable potentialities. The enormous sub-continent of India has adopted, except for family and other racial or religious law, the Common Law which there regulates the great mass of dealings between man and man. In each of these great collections of mankind there are judges enunciating the law and schools teaching it, and professors meditating upon it, seeking to criticize and reform it. England cannot have a monopoly or even a primacy in this great and widespread development. Indeed it is a commonplace that the United States from very early days were in advance of the English in their legal education and study. Nor can any English common lawyer pretend to underrate the great work which has been achieved in legal thought in Canada, Australia and New Zealand.

I was led into this digression by observing that in the United States, as I understand, it is generally accepted that quasi-contract, or restitution as the Restatement calls it, is a separate category in the law. Williston in his great work clearly so treats it, almost indeed as a matter of course. Why, I wonder, is the view so strongly held in England that in the Common Law there are not three but only two categories of civil liability, contract and tort? That view has recently received its most complete expression in a recent article by Sir William Holdsworth in the *Law Quarterly Review,* but, with all the respect that I feel for that great lawyer, I cannot in this matter agree with his arguments. I do not repeat what I have said in these essays. But I sometimes wonder when I read some discussions if there was ever a Judicature Act, or even a Common Law Procedure Act. And I am tempted to ask if the law ceased to grow

Preface

after the third edition of Bullen and Leake, which was published in 1868. That excellent digest was my constant companion when I was a Junior Counsel, though after I became a leader I found it of little help in the wider questions with which I then had to deal. But not only has there been the Judicature Act, but there have been the formative labours of judges like Esher, Bowen, Blackburn, Macnaghten, Watson and a host of others, dealing with the new conditions of the last seventy years, a period of extraordinary development on all sides. But I ought not to be too hard on Bullen and Leake, who could not foresee what was going to happen; and even they stated that the fictitious *assumpsit* was become obsolete. I hope that English Law will, before many years have passed, forget about the forms of action and about contracts implied in law and will evolve, as America has done, a reasoned exposition of quasi-contract or restitution.

I have perhaps unduly emphasized this matter because it illustrates an attitude of mind which perhaps more than anything else it was the object of these essays to exorcise or at least discourage. I mean a devotion to form, and to antiquated form, rather than substance. But then it is said that the continuity of English Law must be preserved. Let us however be careful what we mean by continuity. We sometimes personify our English Common Law, and picture her as a lady. If we do, we must also picture her as old in years, many centuries old, but ever young and vital in spirit. "Jam senior, sed cruda deae viridisque senectus." Might we not hear her say "It is not in implied *assumpsits* that my continuity is to be sought. That was a brief and

Preface

evanescent phase. Holt, one of my devoted servants, protested against the introduction of the idea about 1700, when I was many centuries old; it lasted only until it was abolished about a century and a half later. As well foist upon me as part of my essential being that excrescence, imposed from without after the Restoration, the Statute of Frauds. I was quite capable of evolving a reasonable theory of when a transaction should be embodied in writing. But the continuity of which I boast is something much more vital and essential, as you all well know. It is furthermore a continuity which subsists in the midst of constant change, because of an inherent capacity of adaptation to changing conditions"? So our lady, though in less stilted language, might speak.

> cedit enim rerum novitate extrusa vetustas
> semper, et ex aliis aliud reparare necesse est.

This is as true of the Common Law as of every other good thing. I have often wondered how this perpetual process of change can be reconciled with the principle of authority and the rule of *stare decisis*. Without this latter, it is difficult to see how our law, in the sense of a body of binding rules, could, outside the now extensive portion covered by statutes, exist at all. Yet if we compare the body of Common Law to-day with that of a century ago, it might well seem that it has changed beyond recognition. Still more so, if we go back to Blackstone's day, or Coke or Edward I. Yet we claim and truly claim that all these centuries the Common Law has had a continuous existence. In fact the process of change is so gradual as to be almost imperceptible to the contemporary observer. There is a

Preface

perpetual erosion of authorities. The system of case law may in one aspect tend to militate against change, but in another aspect it favours change. A judge, intent on deciding the dispute before him, is able to see where exactly the cases cited differ from that present to him, and where that difference may be taken to point to a different conclusion, which he then can adopt, at least if that conclusion accords with what justice requires. In addition there is the constantly recurring *novitas rerum*, as conditions of life change and as moral and social conceptions change. For all this novelty precedents have to be modified. We are all legal historians now, since we have at our service the great works of Pollock and Maitland and of Holdsworth and others. The history of law tends on the whole to develop an open-mindedness in regard to change rather than the reverse. When we examine the accidents of procedure or judicial or social intolerance or prejudice out of which so many dogmas and rules originated, and see to what different conditions and circumstances they were adapted, we are less likely to view them all with superstitious veneration; we are freer to consider how far, with modern conditions of life and thought, they fit in with reason, justice, and convenience. This last term "convenience" I use as meaning not a mere opportunism or narrow practicality, but a wise regard to practical consideration, as contrasted with a cramped or formalistic logic. Perhaps it was something like this which Holmes had in mind when he said that experience and not logic was the life of the law, or when he said that judges must think facts, not words. He may have meant that law is not a self-contained system of rules

Preface

and concepts, "bombinans in vacuo", but a function of human life, only capable of justifying itself in so far as it meets the requirements of men and affairs. It often helps in the application of this pragmatic test to see how a particular rule first arose. The working lawyer is generally too much concerned with the task of ascertaining the actual scope and implications of a rule to have opportunity to examine its origin. But however excellent the logic which has developed the process, the excellence of the logic will not justify the rule if that is based on a fundamental premiss which is bad. Probably to-day no one would defend the doctrine of contributory negligence. The modern Admiralty rule which apportions the liability in accordance with the degrees of blame is surely juster and more logical than the Common Law rule of "all or nothing". The Common Law was logical enough in a sense in originating its rule. It said that the defendant must be guilty or not guilty; the plaintiff cannot be like the curate's egg, good in parts. But a wider and more equitable view sees how imperfect the rule is. It is characteristic of the history of such a rule that it has led to constant technicalities and refinements in order to mitigate its inequities. Only the other day the question arose in the House of Lords which at one place in these essays I said was problematic. It was whether the defence of contributory negligence applied in a claim for breach by the employer of statutory duty causing injury to a workman. The Australian High Court held that it did not. They held that the breach was the breach of an absolute or strict obligation and that though a man who had been guilty of improper conduct of so serious a nature that it could be treated as sub-

Preface

stantially causing the injury could not recover, the rule of contributory negligence did not apply. I feel that this ought to be the rule in England also, but I feel constrained by the course of English authorities to hold that an English Court must apply the rule of contributory negligence, though the rule must be suitably adapted to the peculiar facts of a case of that type. Again, the rule of common employment originated in the prejudices of Lord Abinger and in the narrow view of public policy taken by Shaw C.J. And the distinction between mistake of law and mistake of fact, which has led to so many unsatisfactory distinctions, originated in a hasty and ill-considered utterance of Lord Ellenborough. In these and in so many like instances the dead hand of the past fastens on the living present. What I have often wondered at is the reverence and even affection with which such old rules are regarded. Let me give an instance. The rule in *Shelley's Case* was abolished in 1925. Most people now perhaps remember it for the sake of the wit and wisdom of Lord Macnaghten's judgment in *Van Grutten* v. *Foxwell* [1897] A.C. at p. 668. Some time after that judgment was delivered, the editor of a well-known text-book was asked why he had not referred to *Van Grutten* v. *Foxwell*. He replied that he could not bear to think of a judgment which spoke disrespectfully of the rule in *Shelley's Case*. I wonder if some such feeling does not lurk in the minds of many lawyers when reform of any familiar legal rule is mooted.

But whatever merit may be ascribed to judicial courage in interpreting and applying the law and thus developing it, and whatever scope may be attributed

Preface

to the flexibility and adaptiveness of the Common Law, there are definite limits beyond which no judge would go. Not only is a definite decision of the House of Lords final in every English Court as to its *ratio decidendi*, but in addition there are rules which have not been definitely affirmed by the House of Lords which that tribunal would not be likely to alter because of the prolonged and consistent judicial practice of following them. This was the case recently of the instance I have given in connection with breaches of statutory duty and contributory negligence. I do not mean that the members of the House who sat on that appeal would necessarily, if not bound by authority, have come to a different decision. In such cases the law is taken to be finally fixed, just as in the case of a direct decision of the House of Lords; the law so fixed can be changed only by Parliament. From time to time the legislature does intervene in this way. Recent cases of such intervention have followed recommendations of the Law Revision Committee. But the recommendations of that Committee in reference to the rule of consideration have not received any effect from Parliament, either in respect of the general rule or of the particular defects to which I drew attention in the article which is published in this volume. Perhaps this matter is not considered of sufficient practical importance to deserve the attention of Parliament. It may be regarded as concerned rather with theory. Or it may be that any change in so inveterate a rule may be more than legal conservatism would endure. Yet both the general principle and the ancillary and subsidiary rules which I ventured to criticise do frequently work injustice. The origin of the

Preface

rule is haphazard. It is said that the bargain theory is the true theory of contract. It is true that consideration is present in most cases of contract. But I venture to criticize such a term as the "bargain theory of contract", if that means, as I suppose it does, that every simple contract is based, in fact or in theory, on consideration. There can be only one true theory of contract, and that is the theory which defines the conditions of deliberate mutual consent. To substitute for such a theory a bargain theory is to substitute an ancillary or concomitant or evidentiary matter for the element of consent, and to substitute matter of inducement for the contract itself. I dare say it will be long before either in England or in the other regions where the Common Law prevails consideration is rejected as being the sole and universal condition of a valid simple contract, but I question not that in due course this and various other like adventitious imperfect ideas will pass away. Meantime judges, as in duty bound, will enforce the law as they find it, whatever they may think.

In my paper on the Common Law in its Old Home I mentioned various matters where the law might be improved, though I made no attempt to be exhaustive in my summary. I gave examples. I do not resent it if it should be said that I merely instance "sundry reforms". The main body of the law consists of sundry rules, and the main object of the lawyer is to make these rules as perfect as he can, both in respect of harmony and consistency among themselves and of fitness to subserve the requirements of individuals and society. I also commented on and criticized what may be called the many instances of "make believe" in English Law,

Preface

or fictions. One very prevalent fiction, perhaps more prevalent in comparatively modern times though recently somewhat discredited, is that of implying a term or an intention in contracts, in order that the court may decide what justice requires in circumstances which the parties never had in their contemplation when they made the contract and still less had they any intention about them. It may be said that such criticisms go merely to the theoretical accuracy of the law and have no practical value. Then it may be said that the implied *assumpsit* in quasi-contract is harmless, because it merely shifts back the real question, which is in what circumstances the implication may be made; and similarly in cases of the repudiation or frustration of contracts which are said to depend on implied terms or intentions. The court however has to decide on the facts what the legal position is. The implication is merely a fashion of speech. But its absence is preferable to its presence.

Except very briefly in the paper on "Some General Aspects of Law" I have said nothing about the modern development of administrative or public law, in particular the system of tribunals which decide the questions arising under the many administrative statutes now in operation. Questions of this sort arise in many, if not all, the countries in which the Common Law prevails. No doubt there is involved to a great extent the supersession of the ordinary public tribunals. Parliament may authorize a body to legislate by means of rules which have statutory force, to act as prosecutor in respect of rules which it has thus promulgated, and sometimes to act as judge, though more often the judges

Preface

are some specially designated persons, but in any case not the King's Courts. Some such procedure is inevitable in these days of social, industrial and commercial legislation and control. The questions to be decided are such as in general are not suited to adjudication by the ordinary process of the King's Courts, which are, except to a very limited extent, ousted. But I think the good sense of the English people will see that the system which is clearly convenient is fairly and properly worked.

The most lengthy review in this volume is that on Williston's Contracts. When I contemplated the massive volumes, in serried array, which constitute that great work, I was somewhat appalled and disposed to decline the task. I had however met Professor Williston at Harvard and conceived a great regard for him. But primarily I was impressed by the complete and comprehensive scale on which the work was planned and the ability with which it was executed. I felt that it should be introduced to English lawyers beyond the circle of those who already knew of it. Not only would this promote the study of that branch of law in England, but in addition it would advance the mutual interchange of ideas and affinity of sentiments between English and American lawyers to the advantage of the Common Law. I observe that the only three book reviews which I include in this volume are by American lawyers. Dean Wigmore's treatise on Judicial Proof I have so far merely mentioned. It is, as it were, a supplement to his classical work on Evidence. It deals with one side of the judicial process, the evaluation of evidence and the logical principles which underlie it. I found it very

Preface

interesting to understand the principles which I have been unconsciously applying all my working life in dealing with issues of fact. It made me wonder whether some day some ingenious and learned writer would not seek to lay bare the logical processes implicit in judicial reasoning when it deals with the law of the case. It is, I think, clear that English or Common Law legal reasoning has its own special methods. These inevitably follow from the empirical methods of the Common Law and its reliance on a mass of authoritative decisions, according to which the judge must proceed. Sir Frederick Pollock has referred to what he calls "judicial valour". That may mean courage in distinguishing earlier cognate decisions and thus extending a rule so as to decide the particular case. A judge can seldom, if ever, concern himself with the broadest generalisations of jurisprudence. These are not calculated to aid in the decision of the particular problems in the case. Such generalisations as those in the judgment of Lord Macnaghten (to take them as examples) in the *Nordenfelt Case* or in *Lloyd* v. *Grace, Smith & Co.* merely supersede by a simpler rule a mass of detailed narrower and often conflicting rules to be found in earlier decisions. A judge in coming to his decision will be influenced by what may be called the subconscious effect of his long experience of fact and law. It is this mental background, often implicit rather than explicit, which leads to the comment which has sometimes been made in regard to able judges that they were less conversant with some branches of law or equity than were other judges equally able. Again, it would be interesting to analyse important decisions in order to ascertain how far they were the result of

Preface

mere logic and how far the result of temperament or social predispositions. It has also been recognized that commercial cases are best decided by those judges who have practised in such matters and who are familiar with the processes of business and its requirements. This specialization illustrates the practical and concrete character of the judge's work. I have already noted the importance of tracing back to their ultimate motivization some of the fundamental rules of law which later generations have simply used without further question as the basis of logical development. Another problem which has often exercised my mind is how it comes to pass that there have been from time to time cases of marked divergences of opinion between distinguished and competent lawyers. To take a few recent illustrations, let me refer to the differences of opinion which emerged in the decisions in the House of Lords in *Bell* v. *Lever*, *Banco de Portugal* v. *Waterlow*, *Donoghue* v. *Stevenson*. This could scarcely happen if law were a science. But judging is a practical matter, and an act of the will. Notwithstanding all the apparatus of authority, the judge has nearly always some degree of choice. Many currents of thought and feeling may determine how he decides the choice. The higher the court, the less is the decisive weight of authority and the freer the choice. This may explain what has often been said, I hope with some truth, that the House of Lords does generally or frequently take a broad and common-sense view of the law. I may refer as one striking instance of this to the general course of the decisions of the House in the Workmen's Compensation Act. But I must not proceed farther in what is only a series of marks of interrogation

Preface

on the subject of the logical and psychological characteristics of the judicial process in matters of law. Some day work analogous to what Dean Wigmore has done in regard to matters of fact and proof may be done on this other aspect of judging.

I do not intend here to say much of the four lectures which I delivered last year at the Harvard Law School. These represent extra-judicial attempts to focus attention on some cardinal problems of the Common Law. Thus I discussed the scope in modern times of that dispensing power which judges have exercised or may exercise under the name of public policy, which I regard as something within the general principles of the Common Law, not something outside and above them. Then I touched on one aspect of the extremely difficult and interesting topic of damages. Then I had something to say on the relations of *culpa* and liability. The lecture on the Gold Clauses may be regarded as a study based on a rather special instance of the methods of interpretation of commercial documents. These lectures are neither pontifical nor comprehensive nor exhaustive. They will have served their purpose if they stimulate enquiry and further study.

My address on the Study of Law had for its main theme a plea for "the scientific and systematic study of law", to quote again Pollock's words. Thus that essay closely connects with the brief "In Memoriam" notice of Sir Frederick Pollock. That was not merely a labour of esteem for a man for whom I personally felt the highest regard, but a tribute of admiration to a great man who devoted his life and his powers to the study of law and, both as professor and writer, did great service in its

Preface

teaching and advancement. Incidentally also he was a living example of that intimacy and co-operation which should exist, and I hope does and will increasingly exist, between the English and American lawyers. I refer to his lifelong association of close friendship with that other great lawyer, Mr Justice Holmes. The careers of the men were in many ways different. Both were professors, but Holmes, when comparatively young, left the professor's chair for the judicial bench, first as a judge and later Chief Justice of the Supreme Court of Massachusetts and then as an Associate Justice of the Supreme Court of the United States. It is a proof of the correlation between the theoretical study of law and its practical pursuit in America that such transitions from College to Bench are not uncommon there. A recent instance is the universally applauded appointment of Mr Justice Frankfurter from the Harvard Chair of Public Law to the Bench of the Supreme Court of the United States. Both Pollock and Holmes lived to overpass the age of ninety years. Holmes's *Common Law* is known wherever the Common Law is known. But the greatest part of his work is embodied in his judgments, which in the Supreme Court he delivered during more than thirty years of service there. Pollock, though a man of wide and diverse experience and interests, devoted himself to study, teaching and writing on law. He is a great modern instance of a life devoted to law as a matter of theory, not as a practical pursuit. His work remains in his writings, in many respects epoch-making. He is also an outstanding illustration of how the study of law may have value and importance as a career and as the occupation of a highly gifted life.

Preface

The advancement of legal studies in a country must depend, not on machinery or, as I have heard it called, "educational plant", but on the quality of the men who make that advancement the object of their life work and of their ambition. It may be true that England has fallen behind America for a century or more in legal education and study. But it seems to me that England has advanced in these respects and is advancing, and when I think of my friends who have made the pursuit of legal learning the occupation of their life, and of the work which they have done and are doing, I have pride in the present and hope for the future.

WRIGHT

August, 1939

TABLE OF CASES

Acebal v. Levy, 258 n.
Addie & Sons v. Dumbreck, 367 n.
Adelaide Electric Supply Co. v. Prudential Insurance Co., 151–155, 169, 171, 172
Admiralty Commissioners v. S.S. Amerika, 351, 425
Admiralty Commissioners v. S.S. Chekiang, 108 n.
Aikens v. Wisconsin, 371
Alison v. Wallsend, 274 n.
Arcos, Ltd. v. Ronaasen, 272 n.
Argentino Case, 109, 112
Armement Adolf Deppe v. Robinson & Co., 280 n.
Arnhold Karberg & Co. v. Blythe, Green, Jourdain & Co., 270 n., 271 n.
Ashby v. White, 97
Aslan v. Imperial Airways, 281 n.

Baerlein v. Chartered Mercantile Bank, 252 n.
Baily v. De Crespigny, 256 n.
Baird v. Williamson, 140 n.
Baker v. Bolton, 351, 425
Baker v. Courage & Co., 21, 24
Baker v. Snell, 431
Baldry v. Marshall, 274 n.
Balfour v. Balfour, 216, 291
Banco de Portugal v. Waterlow, xxv, 121–122, 149–150
Bank Line, Ltd. v. Capel, 257 n.
Barwick v. English Joint Stock Bank, 263 n.
Batchellor v. Tunbridge Wells Gas Co., 137 n.
Bates' Case, 67 n.
Baylis v. London (Bishop), 23, 25–26
Beamish v. Beamish, 18–19
Beck Case, 179

Bell v. Lever Bros., xxv, 214, 261 n., 379 n.
Bentall v. Burn, 270 n.
Beresford v. Royal Insurance Co., 78–79, 85–90
Berg v. Sadler and Moore, 91
Bilbie v. Lumley, 43, 359
Blake v. Woolf, 138
Bowman v. Secular Society, Ltd., 94
Box v. Jubb, 132 n.
Bristol Tramway Co. v. Fiat Motors, Ltd., 273 n.
British Mutual Banking Co. v. Charnwood Forest Ry. Co., 263 n.
British Steamship Owners' Association v. Chapman & Co., 268 n.
Brooke v. Bool, 144 n.
Brooks Wharf and Bull Wharf, Ltd. v. Goodman, 29
Burger v. South African Life Insurance Society, 89

Cammell Laird & Co. v. Manganese, Bronze & Brass Co., Ltd., 273 n.
Cantiare San Rocco, S.A. v. Clyde Shipbuilding Co., 258 n., 359
Carmichael v. Carmichael's Executrix, 322
Chandler v. Webster, 257 n., 350 n.
Charing Cross Electricity Co. v. Hydraulic Power Co., 133 n.
Chesterman's Trusts, 158 n.
Christie v. Davey, 372
Civil Service, etc., Socy. v. General Steam Navigation Co., 257 n.
Clark v. Lindsay, 256 n.
Cleaver v. Mutual Reserve Fund Life Association, 87

Table of Cases

Clippens Oil Company v. Edinburgh and District Water Trustees, 115
Cobb v. Great Western Ry., 105
Collingwood v. H. & C. Stores, 137 n.
Commissioners of Taxation v. English, Scottish and Australian Bank, 275 n., 277 n.
Conradie v. Rossouw, 292, 298–299, 302, 324
Cooper v. Phibbs, 260 n.
Coronation Seat Cases, 248, 256
Couldery v. Bartrum, 317
Couturier v. Hastie, 260 n.
Cox v. Prentice, 212
Craven-Ellis v. Canons, Ltd., 29
Crowhurst v. Amersham Burial Board, 137 n.
Cundy v. Lindsay, 260 n.
Currie v. Misa, 317

Dahl v. Nelson, Donkin & Co., 255 n.
Dalton v. Angus, 142
Darlington District Bank; re Riches, etc., 276 n.
Davies v. Mann, 340
Dawsons, Ltd. v. Bonnin, 282 n.
Derry v. Peek, 247, 364, 425, 432
Dominion Natural Gas Co. v. Collins, 137 n., 141 n., 365 n.
Donoghue v. Stevenson, xxv, 26, 340, 364 n., 365 n., 381, 385, 431
Drummond v. Van Ingen, 426
Duke of Norfolk's Case, 70
Dunlop Pneumatic Tyre Co., Ltd. v. Selfridge & Co., Ltd., 289, 296–297, 324 n.

Earle v. Oliver, 312
Eastern and S. African Telegraph Co., Ltd. v. Cape Town Tramways Co., Ltd., 137 n.
Eastwood v. Kenyon, 312, 315, 316 n.
E. Clemens Horst Co. v. Biddell Bros., 271 n.
Edelstein v. Schuler & Co., 267 n.

Edmunds v. Bushell & Jones, 262 n.
Egerton v. Brownlow, 71–73, 75
Entick v. Carrington, 67
Erie Railroad Co. v. Tompkins, 205 n.
Everet v. Williams, 91 n.
Excelsior Wire Rope Co., Ltd. v. Callan, 367 n.

Fairman's Case, 366 n.
Fauntleroy's Case, 88, 90
Feist v. Société Intercommunale Belge d'Électricité, 155–158, 159
Fender v. St John-Mildmay, 75, 76, 78, 79–85, 250
Finlay & Co., Ltd. v. Kwik Hoo Tong, etc., 116
Firth v. Bowling Iron Co., 137 n.
Fitch v. Sutton, 317
Flight v. Reed, 312
Flower v. Ebbw Vale Steel, Iron & Coal Co., 363 n.
Foakes v. Beer, 223, 293–296, 377
Ford v. Cotesworth, 258 n.
Frost v. Aylesbury Dairy Co., 273 n.

Geddis' Case, 133 n.
Geo. Whitechurch, Ltd. v. Cavanagh, 263 n.
Gilbert v. Sykes, 73, 75
Goodwin v. Robarts, 162, 267 n.
Goss v. Withers, 283 n.
Grant v. Australian Knitting Mills, Ltd., 273 n., 366 n.
Grant v. Norway, 263 n.
Great Western Railway v. London & County Bank, 275 n.
Grébert-Borgnis v. Nugent, 122
Green v. Chelsea Waterworks Co., 133 n.
Greenock Corporation v. Caledonian Ry., 132 n.
Greta Holme Case, 111
Grill v. General Iron Screw Colliery, 283 n.

Hadley v. Baxendale, 101, 104, 122, 243

xxx

Table of Cases

Hale v. Jennings, 137 n.
Hallett's Case, 7
Hambro v. Burnand, 262 n., 263 n.
Hampstead Guardians v. Barclays Bank, Ltd., 276 n.
Hawkes v. Saunders, 310
Heaven v. Pender, 340, 365 n., 431
Hick v. Raymond, 258 n., 259 n.
Hillas & Co. v. Arcos, Ltd., 258 n., 259 n.
Hirji Mulji v. Cheong Yue Steamship Co., 25, 255 n., 257 n., 380 n.
Hole v. Sittingbourne and Sheerness Ry. Co., 143
Hollywood Silver Fox Farm, Ltd. v. Emmett, 372 n.
Honeywill and Stein v. Larkin, 144
Hong Kong & Shanghai Bank v. Lo Lee Shi, 278 n.
Howard v. Sheward, 262 n.
Howell v. Coupland, 256 n.
Hulton v. Jones, 370 n.
Hunt v. Hunt, 84 n.

Ilott v. Wilkes, 368
Indermaur v. Dames, 340
Inland Revenue Commissioners v. Duke of Westminster, 377 n.
Inland Revenue Commissioners v. Raphael, 378 n.
Ionides v. Universal Marine Insurance, 283 n.

Jackson v. Union Marine Insurance Co., Ltd., 257 n.
Jacobs v. Crédit Lyonnais, 170–172
Janson v. Driefontein Mines, Ltd., 76, 93
Jayawickreme v. Amarasuriya, 302
Jones v. Festiniog Ry., 137 n.
Jones v. Waring & Gillow, 11, 23, 359 n.

Kelly v. Solari, 3, 21, 23, 359 n.
Kennedy v. Broun, 308

Kennedy v. Panama, etc., Mail Co., 253 n.
Kleinwort, Sons & Co. v. Assoc. Automatic Machine Corp., 264 n.
Koechlin & Cie v. Kestenbaum Bros., 278 n.
Krell v. Henry, 256 n.
Kylsant Case, 182–183

Lampleigh v. Brathwait, 307–308
Lee v. Muggeridge, 311–312, 315
Le Lièvre v. Gould, 364 n.
Liesbosch Dredger v. Edison, 96–123 pass., 264 n., 374 n.
Lindsey County Council v. Marshall, 366 n.
Littlefield v. Shee, 315
Lloyd v. Grace, Smith & Co., xxiv, 146, 263 n., 361 n., 381 n.
Lloyds Bank v. Chartered Bank of India, Australia and China, 277 n.
Lloyds Bank v. Savory & Co., 275 n., 276 n.
Lochgelly Iron & Coal Co., Ltd. v. M'Mullan, 361 n.
London, Chatham & Dover Ry. v. South Eastern Ry., 352
London Joint Stock Bank v. Macmillan, 277 n.
Lowery v. Walker, 367 n.
Lumsden v. Barton & Co., 256 n.

McCall Bros., Ltd. v. Hargreaves, 278 n.
McDonald & Co. v. Nash & Co., 278 n.
M'Naghten's Case, 337
Madras Official Assignee v. Mercantile Bank of India, 270 n.
Maritime National Fish, Ltd. v. Ocean Trawlers, Ltd., 256 n.
Marshall (or Miller) v. Robert Addie & Sons' Collieries, 137 n.
May v. Burdett, 140
Mayor of Bradford v. Pickles, 371–372

Table of Cases

Merryweather v. Nixan, 48, 49, 352
Metropolitan Water Board v. Dick, Kerr & Co., 257 n.
Missouri Case, 205
Mitchel v. Reynolds, 69, 70, 92
Mogul Case, 372
Morelli v. Fitch & Gibbons, 273 n.
Moses v. Macferlan, 20
Moule v. Garrett, 22
Mount Albert Case, 165–172
Mourton v. Poulter, 367 n.
Mtembu v. Webster, 292

Nash v. Inman, 23
National Sales Corporation, Ltd. v. Bernardi, 278 n.
National Telephone Co. v. Baker, 137 n.
Nicholls v. Ely Beet Sugar Factory, 97, 374 n.
Nichols v. Marsland, 132 n.
Nichols v. Raynbred, 306 n.
Nickoll & Knight v. Ashton, Edridge & Co., 256 n.
Noble v. Harrison, 139
Noice v. Brown, 81
Nordenfelt Case, xxiv, 70, 92–93, 426
Norman v. Baltimore and Ohio Railroad Co., 159
Northwestern Mutual Life Insurance Co. v. Johnson, 88
Northwestern Mutual Life Insurance Co. v. McCue, 89
Northwestern Utilities v. London Guarantee & Accident Co., Ltd., 124–146, 369 n.
Norwich Union Fire Insurance Co. v. Price, 261 n., 379 n.

Official Assignee of Madras v. Mercantile Bank of India, Ltd., 370 n.

Paddock v. Robinson, 81
Palmer v. Wick and Pulteneytown Shipping Company, Ltd., 352
Palsgraf Case, 118, 120
Paterson Steamships, Ltd. v. Canadian Co-operative Wheat Producers, Ltd., 284 n.
Pecke v. Redman, 306 n.
Phoenix Life Assurance Co. Case, 17
Pickard v. Smith, 143
Pillans and Rose v. Van Mierop and Hopkins, 309, 315, 325, 376
Pink v. Fleming, 283 n.
Pinnel's Case, 295, 305
Polemis v. Furness Withy & Co., 116, 120, 264 n.
Polurrian S.S. Co. v. Young, 283 n.
Ponting v. Noakes, 137 n.
Pordage v. Cole, 232
Pownal v. Ferrand, 20
Priestley v. Fowler, 340, 362
Printing and Numerical Registering Co. v. Sampson, 68
Provincial Insurance Co. v. Morgan, 282 n.

Quarman v. Burnett, 142

Rann v. Hughes, 310
Rex v. International Trustee for Bondholders, 158–165, 170
Rhodes v. Rhodes, 22, 23
Rickards v. Lothian, 138
Ritter v. Mutual Life Insurance Co., 89
Rodriguez v. Speyer Bros., 94
Rose and Frank v. Crompton, 216, 292
Rose v. Ford, 351 n.
Ross v. Fedden, 137 n.
Ruben v. Great Fingall Consolidated, 263 n.
Rylands v. Fletcher, 124, 129, 130–131, 133, 134–140, 143, 340, 369 n., 401

Scholfield v. Earl of Londesborough, 277 n.
Scotson v. Pegg, 319
Scott v. Brown & Co., 91 n.

xxxii

Table of Cases

Scott v. Coulson, 260 n.
Scott's Case, 15
Shadwell v. Shadwell, 319
Shelley's Case, xix, 343
Sinclair v. Brougham, 1–33, 358
Slade's Case, 20, 306
Slingsby v. District Bank, Ltd., 278 n.
Smith v. Great Western Ry., 137 n.
Smith v. Hughes, 214, 261 n.
Smith v. Kenrick, 140 n.
Smith v. London & South Western Ry., 117–118, 120
Smith v. Weguelin, 162
Sorrell v. Smith, 345 n., 372
Spencer v. Hemmerde, 221
Spiers v. Hunt, 80
S.S. *Plata* (Owners) v. Ford & Co., 280 n.
Starke v. Cheeseman, 20
Suffell v. Bank of England, 278 n.
Sullivan v. Constable, 274 n.
Swadling v. Cooper, 355 n.
Swift v. Tyson, 205

Taff Vale Case, 199
Tarry v. Ashton, 143
Tate v. Wilts & Dorset Bank, 275 n.
Taylor v. Caldwell, 253 n.
Taylor v. Plumer, 6, 7
Tinline v. White Cross Insurance Association, Ltd., 87 n.
Tweddle v. Atkinson, 231, 316, 321

Vandepitte v. Preferred Accident Ins. Corp., 322 n., 378 n.
Van Grutten v. Foxwell, xix
Volturno Case, 244
Vortigern Case, 280 n.

Wallace's Case, 75, 182
Wallis v. Pratt, 274 n.
W. Angliss & Co. (Australia), Proprietary, Ltd. v. Peninsular and Oriental Steam Navigation Co., 280 n.
Watteau v. Fenwick, 262 n.
Weld Blundell's Case, 99, 103
Wennall v. Adney, 314
West v. Bristol Tramways Co., 137 n.
West Yorkshire Darracq Agency, Ltd. v. Coleridge, 318
White v. Bluett, 291
Wilkes v. Wood, 67 n.
William Barker (Junior) & Co. v. Agius, Ltd., 273 n.
Wilson v. Carnley, 81–83
Wilson v. Owners of Cargo per the *Xantho*, 283 n., 284 n.
Wilson v. Wilson, 84
Wilsons & Clyde Coal Co. v. English, 145 n.
Woodley v. Mitchell, 284 n.
Woolmington v. Director of Public Prosecutions, 338 n.

TABLE OF STATUTES

Air Navigation, 1920, 125

Carriage of Goods by Sea, 1924, 265–266, 279–280
Civil Procedure, 1833, 265 n.
Coinage, 1870, 156
Common Law Procedure, 1852, xiv, 20, 30, 31, 32, 207, 356
Companies, 335, 342
County Courts, 15

Directors' Liability, 1890, 364

Factors, 1889, 370
Factory, 70, 125, 198, 363
Fatal Accidents, 351, 397, 399
Frauds, 1677, xvi, 45, 50, 62, 212, 225–231, 243, 265, 350, 377, 397

Gaming, 1845, 73

Harter (American), 239, 279

Indian Contract, 1872, 35, 419
Infants Relief, 1874, 231, 311

Judicature, 1873, xiv–xv, 20, 31, 32, 190, 207, 330, 335, 339, 359

Landlord and Tenant, 1927, 346
Law of Property, 1925, 335
Law Reform (Married Women and Tortfeasors), 1935, 353

Law Reform (Miscellaneous Provisions), 1934, 244, 351, 399 n.
Limitation, 1623, 45, 48, 57, 62, 223, 311, 350, 397

Marine Insurance, 1906, 73 n., 265, 282–285, 397
Maritime Conventions, 1911, 355

Rating, 342
Revenue, 342

Sale of Goods, 1893, 22, 212, 230–231, 234, 258 n., 265, 268–274, 377, 397, 426
Settled Land, 1925, 335, 397

Town and County Planning, 373
Trade Disputes, 1906, 199
Truck, 70
Trustee, 1925, 335, 397

Uniform Negotiable Instruments, 237
Uniform Sales, 237
Uniform Warehouse Receipts, 230, 237

Water Carriage of Goods (Canada), 279
Workmen's Compensation, xxv, 125, 200–201, 336, 342, 344, 362, 398

I

SINCLAIR v. BROUGHAM[1]

THE case of *Sinclair* v. *Brougham*[2] has been generally regarded as an authority of first-rate importance. I think it has been properly so regarded, though my reasons for so thinking may not altogether agree with the reasons emphasized by some lawyers. I regard the case as primarily significant as embodying the leading principles on which the Court acts in exercising its equitable jurisdiction to give relief in order to prevent unjust enrichment, or to achieve restitution, if we accept the useful term which has been employed in the recently published American Restatement of the Law of Restitution. The word itself is only an echo of language which will be found in English judgments, indeed, in this very case of *Sinclair* v. *Brougham*. The case shows how the Court can do justice by applying equitable principles where the common law would have been powerless. But since every Court is now bound in the same proceeding to apply either law or equity or both as the circumstances may require, the distinction between law and equity is now only important in the sense that the differences of method and rules must be observed. In the case we are considering a company had borrowed money for purposes for which it was *ultra vires* for it to borrow.

[1] An address to the Cambridge University Law Society, 26 November 1937. Published in 6 *Cambridge Law Journal* (1938), 305–326.
[2] [1914] A.C. 398.

There could in law be no claim for money lent and no claim in law for the repayment on the ground of quasi-contract or, to use the now obsolete phrase, contract "implied in law", because to allow such a claim as a merely money claim would be to sanction an evasion of the public policy forbidding *ultra vires* borrowing by companies. Further, as the money lent or its products could not be identified in the company's possessions, a claim in law could not be maintained. But the powers of the Court were not exhausted. The problem was further complicated by the conflicting claims of the shareholders. The moneys lent had become inextricably mingled with other moneys in the course of myriad transactions. The Court solved the difficulty by a sort of rough justice, in the form of a tracing order, so as (in the words of Lord Dunedin, at p. 437) "to give full effect to the doctrine of *ultra vires*—for the person receiving is not ordered to pay as a debt the equivalent of what he originally got, but ordered merely to surrender what he still has as a superfluity, an enrichment which, but for the original reception of the money, he would have been without". As I read the judgments, if the money borrowed had been either in the original form or its products, still capable of identification, the claim would have been properly brought as a claim in law. The aid of equitable principles had to be invoked because the identification had become impossible. It might also have been necessary to invoke the aid of equity on account of the company's insolvency to give the claimant the benefit of an equitable charge on the identifiable property or its products in the company's possession. The importance of the case is that it demonstrates a category of claims

Sinclair v. Brougham

distinct from contract, or tort, or trust (express or resulting), the essential principle of which is that the defendant should not be unjustly enriched at the expense of the plaintiff. The test of recovery is not the loss to the plaintiff, but the gain to the defendant, though in general the loss fixes a limit. Emphasis is to be placed on the word "unjustly". There are many positions in which a defendant may be enriched at the expense of the plaintiff and yet it may not be unjust for him to retain that benefit. It is, therefore, important not merely to recognize the existence of this separate head in the law (in which word I include law and equity), but to enumerate, to classify and to distinguish as the American Restatement of the Law of Restitution has sought to do, the different positions which may arise, bringing into one conspectus both legal and equitable rights and remedies. The fundamental principle may also be stated in the words of Lord Parker (at p. 444), which are capable of being applied beyond the special facts of the case he was dealing with. "The equity lay in this that it would be unconscionable for the society to retain the amount by which its assets had been increased by and in fact still represented the borrowed money." This language may be compared with Baron Parke's expression in *Kelly* v. *Solari* (1841) 9 M. & W. 54 when speaking merely as a common lawyer of the right to recover money paid by mistake "it is against conscience to retain it" (at p. 58), which is explained by Lord Sumner as depending on the fact that the payer had no intention in such a case to enrich the payee. Whether the remedy given is legal or equitable or both, the underlying principle is the same. In this particular case, Lord Parker points out at the outset that it was already settled law that an *ultra vires* borrowing by a society does not give rise to indebtedness either at law or equity on the part of the society. But that forms merely the starting-point for the inquiry how justice may be done and unjust enrichment prevented. Incidentally that may be, as it was in this case, a very different thing, when looked at from the plaintiff's point of view, from complete restoration to him. The governing consideration is the superfluity in the defendant, which may differ from the expense to the plaintiff.

The facts of *Sinclair* v. *Brougham* were simple. The Birkbeck Building Society had no power to carry on a banking business. It did so, along with its legitimate business as a building society, and accepted large sums from depositors for the banking business. Thus there was borrowing which was *ultra vires*. Heavy losses were incurred and the society went into liquidation. Its assets were insufficient to meet the claims of the outside creditors, and to repay the shareholders and the depositors. It was conceded that the outside creditors came first. As to the depositors, as I have already said, their Lordships held they could not on the facts of the case claim to rank in law or equity as ordinary creditors. A conflict of claims arose as between shareholders and depositors. One possible view was that the shareholders were entitled in the liquidation to share in all the assets remaining after outside claims enforceable at law were paid, which would have given them five times the amounts of their subscriptions. But the assets beyond question represented in some part the sums which had been paid to the society by the depositors. These were many times larger in total amount than the share capital

Sinclair v. Brougham

paid up by the shareholders. The House of Lords held that it would be unconscionable that the shareholders should be enriched at the expense of the depositors. As all the funds had been inextricably mingled together in the actual transactions of the society, it was impossible to identify in the assets found on liquidation in the society's possession what represented contributions which had come from the shareholders and what represented sums paid by depositors. Neither shareholders nor depositors could claim priority, as both sets of persons must equally be deemed to have been cognizant that the funds were being utilized to carry on the *ultra vires* business. It was held that justice could best be done by a rough sort of tracing order, which took the form of dividing up the assets which remained after paying outside creditors and preferred shareholders among all the claimants, shareholders and depositors, *pari passu*, in the proportions of the sums which they had severally contributed. If the net assets had been sufficient to repay all these claimants, the matter would have been simple. But there had been a loss. That loss, it was held, should be borne equally by those whose equities *inter se* were equal. The House of Lords reversed the Court of Appeal, who by a majority, Fletcher Moulton L.J. dissenting, had held that the shareholders were entitled to repayment in full. The decision of the Court of Appeal was clearly illogical, though apparently based on authority binding that Court. Logically the shareholders if entitled to priority would have been entitled to divide up all the remaining assets of the society. Fletcher Moulton L.J. held that the depositors were entitled to priority over the shareholders. The House of Lords, while agreeing with his reasoning up to a point, held that there was no ground for giving priority to depositors over shareholders, or shareholders over depositors.

There were four speeches delivered in the case in the House of Lords, two by equity lawyers, Lord Haldane (with whom Lord Atkinson agreed) and Lord Parker, one by Lord Dunedin, one by Lord Sumner. I shall deal first with the constructive portions of these judgments, in which the conclusion arrived at is justified. I shall later refer to the negative or critical portions, in which they deal with the matter, for them already a *chose jugée*, viz. that in the facts of the case there was not a debt either at law or in equity.

Of the four speeches, I have found those of Lord Parker and Lord Dunedin most illuminating. I shall primarily examine their reasoning, adding at times parallelisms from their colleagues, though the reasoning of all the Lords agrees in substance. I find in the speeches of Lord Parker and Lord Dunedin references more or less complete to almost every main principle of unjust enrichment or restitution, which latter term is actually used by Lord Dunedin. The most obvious and common claim in a case of unjust enrichment is in debt, but that is put aside as inapplicable in the facts of the case. I shall reserve that aspect for discussion later. But I may here observe that an action at law is recognized by the Lords to be competent even in cases of *ultra vires* loans, so long as the money lent or its products are identifiable. This is based on the doctrine of *Taylor* v. *Plumer* (1815) 3 M. & S. 562, an aspect which is more fully dealt with by Lord Haldane. When, however, identification ceases to be possible at law, then equity can still carry the matter

Sinclair v. Brougham

farther, for instance, it can apply the principle of *Hallett's Case* (1880) 13 Ch.D. 696. In thus proceeding, equity imposes what has been usefully called a constructive trust, to distinguish it from an express or resulting trust. In an express or resulting trust there is an actual intention of the settlor to create a trust, the intention being either expressed or to be inferred from the facts of the case. Cases of that character where the trust depends on the intention of the settlor to create it are distinguishable from those trusts or rather quasi-trusts which are imposed by the Court in order to prevent unjust enrichment, and which are called constructive trusts because they do not arise from the intention of a settlor, but are declared by the Court *ab extra*, irrespective of actual intention. But there are cases in which equity cannot find a constructive trust of the property, because that property represents in part only the property which is the subject of the unjust enrichment. It is the product not of that property by itself, but of that property combined with the defendant's own property or with that of a third person. Equity in such cases gives a partial right, which has been called an equitable lien, on the total property to the extent that the total property represents the plaintiff's property. Lord Parker in one passage speaks of all these rights as being themselves a species of property which equity has created. In such cases there cannot in general be equitable property unless there is legal property in the defendant, only the equitable property being in the plaintiff, whereas in the *Taylor* v. *Plumer* type of case, the legal property remains in the plaintiff. When the property has passed in law to the defendant, the plaintiff can only claim as beneficial owner in equity of the property, claiming either on the ground of a constructive trust when the whole property is the product of the plaintiff's property, or on the ground of an equitable lien when the property is only in part the product of the plaintiff's property. The extent to which the Court may carry this equity is strikingly illustrated by the tracing order in *Sinclair* v. *Brougham*, where the properties of two sets of claimants had, as already stated, become inextricably mingled as the result of an immense number of separate transactions over many years, so that only the roughest apportionment of the residual property could be attempted. But in effect each individual claimant was given an equitable lien in his proper proportion. Lord Sumner seeks to illustrate what was done by the analogy of a familiar case at common law where material chattels, bales of cotton, belonging to different owners, had become mixed up in a ship's hold as the result of a maritime casualty, and had become incapable of identification because the marks indicating ownership had become obliterated. The Court held in that case that the several shippers or consignees were tenants in common of the indiscriminate bulk. It is a similar principle which equity applies in the more esoteric atmosphere of financial transactions. But the point here to be noted is that equity does not stop where law must do. It will follow the plaintiff's property up to the ultimate limit of its identification in any form or in any amalgam, even into the hands of third persons, so long as they are not purchasers for value without notice, and even as against persons who have no higher title in equity than the original transferee, such as his ordinary creditors or his trustee in bankruptcy. I may here note the third or

Sinclair v. Brougham

alternative form of relief which may in proper cases be given, that is, where a person's money has been used to discharge the obligations of the recipient, but where the person can have no direct recovery as for a debt. An illustration of such a case is where money has been borrowed *ultra vires*. This third method is also noted by the Lords in *Sinclair* v. *Brougham*, and is described as subrogation. The *ultra vires* lender (if he may be so called) is put to stand in the shoes of the borrower's creditor, at least as regards the personal debt. In that way, it is said, the *ultra vires* borrower's total indebtedness is not increased, but unjust enrichment is at least in part obviated. Lord Parker put another case somewhat analogous, namely, where money borrowed to the lender's knowledge for an illegitimate purpose has been in fact used for a legitimate purpose in whole, or in part, and he indicates his view that such money would be recoverable as a debt though the borrowing was *ultra vires*. It was strongly urged in *Sinclair* v. *Brougham* that in the facts of that case subrogation was the utmost and only remedy that equity could give. It would have assuredly been futile since in the inextricable flood of transactions no depositor could have shown that his money had been used to pay any particular debt of the society. But no such limitation on the powers of the Court in equity was admitted. Lord Dunedin is particularly instructive on this aspect. After adducing parallels from Roman law and from Pothier, he went on to say (at p. 435): "I have made these citations to show that other great systems of law have not been unable to solve the problem arising where the equity of restitution comes in contact with the doctrine of nullity of contract. Is English equity to retire defeated from the task which other systems of equity have conquered? Let us for a moment examine what the argument on the other side is. There being no contract, it is impossible, it is said, to have any obligation on the part of the society to restore what it has taken from the depositors. The only right of the depositors is a right to vindicate property, or, in other words, when you have a *ius in re* you can enforce it; but if the thing has so disappeared that a *ius in re* is no longer to be found (and this must practically always be so in the case of money), then your remedy is gone. The sole relief which equity can give is that if you can show that your money has paid a just debt, in that case you shall have action. This comes to this, that having got hold of property which does not belong to you, if only you are wise or lucky enough to change its form you may enjoy the proceeds unmolested. Such a plea on the face of it seems only worthy of the Pharisee who shook himself free of his natural obligations by saying Corban. In the words of technical equity it is unconscionable." A little later (at p. 436) he proceeds: "But further, the whole strength of this argument lies in the idea that the *ius in re* represents the depositors' only right: that there can be no obligation on the other side at all. It is here that I think the importance of the action for money had and received comes in. That cannot be founded on a *ius in re*, for you cannot have a *ius in re* in currency. It shows that both an action founded on a *ius in re*, such as an action to get back a specific chattel, and an action for money had and received are just different forms of working out the higher equity that no one has a right to keep either property or the proceeds of property which does not belong

Sinclair v. Brougham

to him." This statement is, I think, in full accord in substance, though the line of approach may be somewhat different, with what Lord Parker enunciated. I may also quote a brief passage in which Lord Dunedin stated the practical result of *Sinclair* v. *Brougham*. "The position therefore comes to this. The shareholders are entitled to share among them the proper assets of the society. But they are not entitled to be made rich at the expense of the depositors, by swelling the assets of the society by means of the proceeds of moneys which they themselves never contributed. There is a mixed mass of assets as to the precise composition of which as to source it is impossible to pronounce. Had the assets never shrunk there would be enough to pay both in full. But they have shrunk, and someone must bear the loss." He finally concluded that the only equitable means was to let each party bear the shrinkage proportionately to the amount originally contributed.

I do not pretend by these brief excerpts to produce the full richness of the reasoning of the Lords in the constructive aspects of their judgments. This elaboration which has explained or indicated the full positive reach of the doctrine of unjust enrichment was rendered necessary by the negative circumstance that there neither was nor could be a contract to repay the sums deposited. The essence of the remedy was not compensation to the plaintiff, but the restitution by the defendant of what would be, if not restored, an unjust enrichment. Lord Haldane puts the remedy of law as being based on the fact that no property in the money had passed. A similar view was in a later case (*Jones* v. *Waring & Gillow* [1926] A.C. 670) suggested in regard to the recovery of money paid under mistake by Lord Sumner. Lord Haldane said (at p. 420): "[The common law] looked simply to the question whether the property had passed, and if it had not, for instance, where no relationship of debtor and creditor had intervened, the money could be followed, notwithstanding its normal character as currency, provided it could be ear-marked or traced into assets acquired with it. And this appears to me to be, on ground of principle, as true of money paid under mistake of fact or on an *ultra vires* contract, under which no property could pass or relation of debtor be constituted, as it is true in the case of a broker or bailee.

"But while the common law gave the remedy I have stated, it gave no remedy when the money had been paid by the wrongdoer into his account with his banker, who simply owed him a debt, so that no money was, or could be, in the contemplation of a Court of law, ear-marked. Here equity, which had so far exercised a concurrent jurisdiction based upon trust, gave a further remedy."

This way of looking at the matter which is reflected in the other speeches, particularly that of Lord Dunedin, eliminates any reference to contract, express, implied in fact, or implied in law, and puts the position simply on what Lord Dunedin calls "superfluity", the traceable possession in the defendant of the plaintiff's property or its products. In other words, simply unjust enrichment. On this basis the concept of debt, though convenient in practice, becomes logically otiose. The property concept obviously would apply to the great mass of cases of restitution, but would not cover that important category of cases where a defendant is enriched (or advantaged) because the plaintiff under legal compulsion has paid in

Sinclair v. Brougham

money or chattels or other property a debt, or has discharged a liability, which is properly the debt or liability of the defendant. The defendant has thus been enriched because his liabilities have been decreased and it would be unjust that the burden should be left on the plaintiff. There must be restitution. Analogous principles apply in other types of cases. But it is not easy to apply to such circumstances the rubric of a right of property as in cases of *ultra vires* borrowing or money paid by mistake or under duress. It may, however, be that all cases fall under the higher equity enunciated by Lord Dunedin, that no person has a right to keep either property or the proceeds of property which do not belong to him. The man who has obtained the release of his liability by means of another's property, cannot keep the proceeds of that property, the release from liability, without making restitution. However, in *Sinclair* v. *Brougham*, the Lords were not, it seems, thinking of these particular questions.

This line of reasoning seems to assimilate cases of *ultra vires* borrowing to other cases of restitution, such as money paid by mistake and so on. In one aspect that may be true. But there may be a further aspect peculiar to *ultra vires* borrowings. The directors of the society who receive the money do not in strict law receive it as agents of the society, because the society cannot in law borrow the money. If in fact it goes into the coffers or funds of the society and can be identified there, it is even more manifestly (if it were money paid by mistake), not the society's but the lender's money. Lord Parker, touching on this aspect of the case, puts the case of such money being used to carry on the *ultra vires* business. If, he says, the business is a success, the society could not be entitled to anything except the profits, or surplus; it could not be entitled to the assets and exempt from the liabilities on the plea of *ultra vires*, and for that purpose the borrowed money would be a liability of the business. This would seem to recognize a right in such circumstances to a money claim in law, as for borrowed money, though the money was borrowed *ultra vires*. In truth, a money claim, whether based in property, or in debt, comes in all these cases to the same thing. But there is, I think, in the case of moneys borrowed *ultra vires* an important distinction which emerges in Lord Parker's judgment and elsewhere in the case. The *ultra vires* lender can only recover *in forma specifica* if he can show that the borrowed money is actually in the possession of the borrowing society, that is, that the society is enriched. If the directors acting *ultra vires* have disposed of the borrowed money in any way, it may truly be said that it has never reached the society. The mere borrowing is not the act of the society and apart from remedies in the way of subrogation, the only cause of action either in law or equity, in respect of the borrowed moneys is by showing that at the date of claim they are *in specie* or in the form of traceable products in the society's possession. So to hold is not to evade the doctrine of *ultra vires* or to legitimize *ultra vires* borrowing. Lord Parker's view in this context is, I think, clear from the passage I have already cited. In the normal cases, it is the original reception of the money (to quote again Lord Dunedin's phrase) which carries the liability of restitution. But that idea is *simpliciter* inapplicable to *ultra vires* borrowing. The society is merely ordered "to surrender what he still has as a superfluity".

Sinclair v. Brougham

Lord Parker is careful to point out that the receipt of money in the course of a transaction which is in its general character *ultra vires*, as contrasted with the special case of *ultra vires* borrowing, may, and I gather in his opinion generally does, give rise to a debt at law. For this he cites *Scott's Case* (1884) 9 App. Cas. 523. This case, he thinks, is sufficiently explained as depending on failure of consideration, which seems to me to be a typical case of unjust enrichment. In a case of that type the society does actually receive the money, so that the liability can be put on the original reception. The Lords differed from the admirable dissenting judgment of Fletcher Moulton L.J., which well repays study, simply on the ground that he did not recognize this particular and vital distinction, which illustrates the true nature of the doctrine of unjust enrichment. All this makes it abundantly clear that unjust enrichment has no relation as a juristic conception with contract at all. Now it is pertinent to observe that at one time during last century it was said that there were only two classes of action known to the common law, contract and tort. This classification is no doubt retained for certain statutory purposes, for instance this classification is found in the County Courts Act in regard to questions of costs, and leads to frequent difficulties. But the dichotomy does not correspond to any juristic classification, and is of no significance for common law decisions. It has been recognized by distinguished writers, as, for instance, Pollock, that quasi-contract is a separate head from contract. From this it follows that even if the term "contract implied by law" is retained as meaning quasi-contract, and if the equitable rights and remedies are ignored, still "contracts implied by law" signify a third head apart from contract and tort. The specific character of restitution as a legal category may be disguised but cannot be destroyed by confusing and inappropriate terminology. But clear as this might appear, even from a mere reading of *Sinclair* v. *Brougham*, certain parts of, or observations in, the judgments have been taken in some quarters to deny the existence of any such body of principles, whether described as quasi-contract or restitution. It is necessary to examine this aspect of the judgments, because there has been a tendency to sterilize or petrify this branch of English law and equity, with the result that even to-day there is in England no separate or systematic treatise on this most important branch of law and equity, which is recognized as such in most, if not all, civilized laws.

The trouble has arisen because the Lords, as I think, unnecessarily, reverted to legal antiquarianism in order to explain why an *ultra vires* borrowing did not give rise to any indebtedness in law or equity. The explanation was unnecessary because, as Lord Parker pointed out, the proposition had been already settled by the cases he cites, two of which were in the House of Lords. It was unnecessary to go farther, and new and separate reasoning would be merely matter of *obiter dictum*. But all four Lords do refer to the old form of action for money had and received as based upon an implied promise to repay, which would be a promise which the society could not lawfully make. Lord Sumner puts the matter broadly (at p. 452). "The depositors' case has been put first of all as consisting in a right enforceable in a common law action. It is said that they paid their money under a mistake of fact, or for a consideration that has wholly

Sinclair *v.* Brougham

failed, or that it has been had and received by the society to their use. My Lords, in my opinion no such action could succeed. To hold otherwise would be indirectly to sanction an *ultra vires* borrowing. All these causes of action are common species of the genus *assumpsit*. All now rest, and long have rested, upon a notional or imputed promise to repay. The law cannot *de iure* impute promises to repay, whether for money had and received or otherwise, which, if made *de facto*, it would inexorably avoid."

Lord Dunedin says (at pp. 433-434): "I confess that for a person not bred to the common law to express an opinion as to the true meaning and extent of the common law action is to handle *periculosae plenum opus aleae*. But to the best of my comprehension and notwithstanding the case of *Phoenix Life Assurance Co.* (1862) 2 J. & H. 441, I have come to the conclusion that the action for money had and received cannot be stretched to meet the situation. It is not, however, necessary that the claim should be one capable of being made good by an action at law. It will suffice if there is an equitable remedy." He then proceeds to discuss the principles of unjust enrichment. He concludes that the doctrine of *ultra vires* was introduced in order to let societies keep their own, not to appropriate other people's money. For him, it seems, the introduction of argument on the old forms of action (which he seems to approach with some distaste) does not carry the matter very far.

Lord Haldane is much more thoroughgoing as regards the forms of action. He says that actions arising *quasi ex contractu* are actions based on a contract which is imputed to the defendant by a fiction of law. "The fiction can only be set up with effect if such a contract would be valid if it really existed" (at p. 415). He proceeds to an historical disquisition, terminating with a passage from Ames' well-known lecture on the history of *assumpsit*, in which that distinguished professor ends by saying that *assumpsit* competed with equity in the case of the essentially equitable quasi-contract growing out of the principle of unjust enrichment" (p. 417), which certainly seems to indicate a development far beyond any original idea of *assumpsit*. Lord Haldane concluded that the depositor's claim cannot be *in personam* and must be *in rem* to recover property with which in equity at all events they have never really parted. He puts the claim therefore on property.

I cannot help regretting the importance which has thus been ascribed to the old forms of action. I have already shown that the doctrine of *ultra vires* does make a real difference in any claim for unjust enrichment. That was settled by the House of Lords long before *Sinclair* v. *Brougham*. Why plunge into this unnecessary discussion, which seems to me to be rather a debating point than the exposition of any juristic conception? It is true that while the forms of action existed the appropriate form applicable to a claim for money had and received or quasi-contract was, since about 1700, the *indebitatus assumpsit*. So that what is said about the fiction of a notional contract or a contract implied in law is true enough so far as it goes. But a disquisition on legal history does not as such constitute a *chose jugée*. It may in fact form the ground of an actual decision, which as we know is a *chose jugée* though based on or explained by wrong legal history, as, for instance, in *Beamish* v.

Sinclair v. Brougham

Beamish (1861) 9 H.L.C. 274. But it is the decision which is the precedent. Here no decision was based on the Lords' views about legal history or about the old forms of action. It was already settled that in such a case as that before them the legal claim did not lie. The importance of the substantial and affirmative decision and of the actual discussion in the judgments lies in the exposition of the equity of restitution. But Lord Parker, for instance, pointed out that an action at law would lie in respect of money paid under an *ultra vires* borrowing if the claim were made before the money or its products had ceased to be capable of identification, and could be brought if the money lent is used for the legitimate purposes of the society. I am not sure whether in such cases he meant that such an action would lie (if old forms are to be regarded at all) as for money had and received. Lord Dunedin says that the action for money had and received "cannot be founded on a *ius in re*, for you cannot have a *ius in re* in currency. It shows that both an action founded on a *ius in re*, such as an action to get back a specific chattel, and an action for money had and received are just different modes of working out the higher equity that no one has the right to keep either property or the proceeds of property which does not belong to him" (at p. 436). The fictional contract, after there has been a certain lip service accorded to it, seems to be vanishing more and more, indeed, even the ghost of the form seems to have disappeared. The peculiar rules which apply to the claim in respect of *ultra vires* borrowing are not determined in any sense by reference to the fictional contract. Indeed, I repeat, contract has nothing to do with the matter.

But there seem to me to be many reasons why references to the fictional contract should now be eliminated even on grounds of history. The fiction of the contract implied in law was adopted for procedural reasons of convenience which were quite sufficient while the old forms of action continued. The old common lawyers were a robust people, and if a fiction was convenient under the old rigid forms of pleading they did not worry about its correspondence to reality or to juristic concepts. But it does not follow that they did not realize the true nature of the concept.

Before the Common Law Procedure Act, 1852, and the Judicature Act, judges naturally referred to the contract implied in law, because the convenience of the writ of *indebitatus assumpsit* outweighed the logical absurdity which Holt C.J. emphasized when he said it was a metaphysical idea, because the Court could not make a contract for the parties, but contract depended on the will or consent of the parties (*Starke* v. *Cheeseman* (1699) 1 Ld. Raym. 538). Lord Mansfield about sixty years later in a passage in *Moses* v. *Macferlan* (2 Burr. 1005, 1008), often quoted and often unfairly criticized, uses the term debt implied by law, which is more accurate and accords with *Slade's Case* (1604) 4 Rep. 92 *b*, according to which the fictitious *assumpsit* is implied from the debt. Even since the two Acts of reform, judges speak of the contract implied in law. But when judges are defining the characteristics of the claim, as contrasted with the procedural form, they drop a reference to the idea of notional contract and state the liability in objective terms. For instance, Lord Tenterden C.J., in *Pownal* v. *Ferrand* (1827) 6 B. & C. 439, said, in regard to a claim

Sinclair v. Brougham

for money paid under compulsion of law to the defendant's use: "I am of opinion that he is entitled to recover upon this general principle, that one man, who is compelled to pay money which another is bound by law to pay, is entitled to be reimbursed by the latter" (at p. 433). My comment is not affected by the fact that his two colleagues spoke of a contract being implied by law. Again Parke B., the greatest of the classical common lawyers, in his famous statement of the law (in *Kelly* v. *Solari* (1841) 9 M. & W. at pp. 58–59) as to money paid by mistake does not mention the notional contract: the substantial ground and the only substantial ground is that "it is against conscience to retain it". As I shall show later this is accepted as the ground by Lord Sumner in a case nearly a century later. Parke B. goes on to add that a demand may be necessary in these cases where the party receiving may have been ignorant of the mistake. Some have found in this observation a veiled reference to contract as the idea underlying the cause of action. I cannot see the force of this. What I think is meant is that as the receipt of the money is innocent, the recipient should not be vexed by an action until he has had notice so as to have the opportunity of making repayment: it is the retention, not the receipt, which is the wrong. But even this qualification of the cause of action was not accepted by Hamilton J. in *Baker* v. *Courage & Co.* [1910] 1 K.B. 57, at p. 65. He held that notice of the mistake which was common to both parties was not necessary to complete the cause of action, which was complete independently of any notification of the discovery of the mistake.

Lord Tenterden's statement of the law was repeated

by Cockburn C.J. in 1872 in *Moule* v. *Garrett*, L.R. 7 Ex. 101, at p. 104.

I do not intend any complete citation, and pass now to 1890, to *Re Rhodes* (1890) 44 Ch.D. 94, where the claim was for necessaries supplied to a lunatic. It had been said that the party supplying became a creditor by implied contract. Cotton L.J. said (at p. 105) that the term implied contract was a most unfortunate expression because there cannot be a contract by a lunatic. "It is asked, can there be an implied contract by a person who cannot himself contract in express terms? The answer is, that what the law implies on the part of such a person is an obligation, which has been improperly termed a contract, to repay money spent in supplying necessaries." Lindley L.J. (at p. 107) says the doubt as to the lunatic's liability "has arisen from the unfortunate terminology of our law". The term "implied contract", he said, had been used to denote "not only a genuine contract established by inference, but also an obligation which does not arise from any real contract, but which can be enforced as if it had a contractual origin. Obligations of this class are called by civilians *obligationes quasi ex contractu*." This case does not seem to have been cited in *Sinclair* v. *Brougham*, but its principle has received the sanction of the Legislature, so far as relates to goods which are necessaries, in the Sale of Goods Act, 1893, s. 2, where it is in terms said that the liability is not affected by reason that the person is, by reason of mental incapacity or drunkenness, incompetent to contract. I do not believe that the Lords in *Sinclair* v. *Brougham* had any intention of overruling these authorities, which still apply in regard to necessaries other than goods. To the

Sinclair v. Brougham

same effect I may refer to *Nash* v. *Inman* [1908] 2 K.B. 1, a case relating to infants. Fletcher Moulton L.J. (at p. 8) agrees with the views expressed in *Rhodes* v. *Rhodes* that the language about the implied contract is somewhat unfortunate, and adds: "An infant, like a lunatic, is incapable of making a contract of purchase.... The consequence is that the basis of the action is hardly contract. Its real foundation is an obligation which the law imposes on the infant to make a fair payment in respect of needs satisfied. In other words the obligation arises *re* and not *consensu*." In *Baylis* v. *London (Bishop)* [1913] 1 Ch. 127, at p. 140, Hamilton L.J. says of claims for money paid by mistake: "The question is whether it is conscientious for the defendant to keep the money, not whether it is fair for the plaintiff to ask to have it back." This does not put the case on contract, which is reciprocal. Lord Sumner (as he had become) again discusses the claim for money paid by mistake in *Jones* v. *Waring & Gillow* [1926] A.C. 670, at p. 696. He takes *Kelly* v. *Solari* as the leading case. He points to the peculiar character of coin or currency. If goods, he says, are delivered to the wrong person, they do not become the property of the receiver, "for passing of property is a question of intention, and obviously the tradesman never meant in such circumstances to make his goods the property of the wrong man". Equally, he proceeds to say with reference to *Solari's Case*: "The executrix of Solari ought to have known, and probably did, that the company had cancelled the policy, and was making a mistake in paying again. If so there was no real intention on the company's part to enrich her." I cite this passage not on the topic whether either or both parties knew of the mistake, but as taking the essential basis of the claim to be property. The same great judge in *Baker* v. *Courage & Co.* (at p. 66) refers to the case where the defendant is required to return something which has come into his possession, but which he is not entitled to keep. There is no reference to contract implied in law. The property concept has superseded the implied contract concept, as I think it did throughout *Sinclair* v. *Brougham*, when the forms of action had receded out of sight.

I have already pointed out that the House of Lords cannot have intended to overrule the established authorities relating to infants, lunatics, drunkards, a category to which before the modern Acts married women were added. So that we must not take too absolutely the epigrammatic phrase: "The law cannot *de iure* impute promises to repay, whether for money had and received or otherwise, which, if made *de facto*, it would inexorably avoid." It is old law that even if a lunatic promised by word of mouth to pay what was in fact a reasonable price for necessaries actually supplied, his liability would rest not on the promise, but on the actual supply of the necessaries. It is thus just a case where valuable things or services are received by a person from another who has no intention of bounty. However, I feel a difficulty in limiting the concept to the ideas of property. The cases of services rendered or debts discharged certainly afford frequent examples of unjust enrichment. I think it is safer to state the claim for unjust enrichment in such cases as depending on an obligation imposed by law in all the circumstances of the case in order to satisfy the requirements of justice, that is, to avoid what is unconscionable or unconscientious in the words of Parke B.,

Sinclair v. Brougham

Lord Sumner and, I think, all the Law Lords in *Sinclair v. Brougham*. Such a criterion is said to give the go-by to precedent and to reduce everything to the *liberum arbitrium* of the particular judge, and promote a sloppiness of thought. I do not know why such things are said. I hope the object of the law is to seek and ensure justice. Lord Sumner puts the matter in a nutshell in *Sinclair v. Brougham* (at p. 458) when he is describing his final conclusion: "In my opinion, if precedent fails, the most just distribution of the whole must be directed, so only that no recognized rule of law or equity be disregarded." Precedent must come first, recognized rules of law and equity must be regarded, otherwise all certainty of law would disappear. But the underlying purpose is justice. In *Sinclair's Case*, it is clear that in order to achieve justice, old limitations (at least assumed if not expressly laid down by the ultimate Court) were passed over and new precedents or at least new extensions of precedent were established. There is another illuminating phrase of Lord Sumner's which occurs in *Hirji Mulji v. Cheong Yue Steamship Co.* [1926] A.C. 497, at p. 510, where he speaks of the doctrine of frustration of contract as "a device by which the rules as to absolute contracts are reconciled with a special exception which justice demands".

I cannot understand why it is not more generally recognized that quasi-contract or restitution involves a definite system of rules, just like the rules of contract or tort. Hamilton L.J., in *Baylis' Case* (at p. 140), said that both the equitable and legal considerations applicable to the recovery of money paid under a mistake of fact have been crystallized in the reported common-law cases. It was with this in view that he added: "We are not now free in the twentieth century to administer that vague jurisprudence which is sometimes attractively styled 'justice as between man and man'." But he did not mean that the rules applicable to claims for money had and received or restitution were not subject to the same development to fit new circumstances as that found in other regions of law and equity.

It has also been said that the fictional or notional or imputed contract is the only thing that can constitute a relation such as to justify the claim for restitution. I find this difficult to understand. Perhaps underlying the statement is the idea of privity, which at one time figured so large in the law of tort. It was obscure what exactly privity meant, but it seemed to bear a vague relationship to privity of contract. In tort this idea led to the conflict of opinion in *Donoghue* v. *Stevenson* [1932] A.C. 562, but there the idea was finally put to sleep. There was there held to be a duty or a liability arising from the circumstances of the case. A careful study of the English reported cases at law or in equity will, I think, show that the basis of the doctrine of unjust enrichment is, as has been so often here stated, that the defendant has received some property of the plaintiff or received some benefit from the plaintiff, for which it is just (as shown in the precedents) that he should make restitution. That is sufficient to establish the liability, which the law imposes. If this is all that is meant by privity, the term is innocuous. But it is an unnecessary term and may mislead by suggesting some sort of contractual relationship.

When it is said that the law of Restitution is the sphere of sloppiness of thought, I cannot help thinking of the

Sinclair v. Brougham

Restatement of the Law of Restitution recently published in America. I can only here refer to the scheme of that work in the baldest outline. I am not here writing a treatise, but merely maintaining a thesis, which is that Restitution is a distinct branch of law capable of, and worthy of, careful study. The Restatement is based on the American cases, which are very numerous and in some ways appear to differ from the English authorities. But they seem to present a substantial agreement with our decisions. The Restatement falls into two main divisions. Part I deals with what have been called Quasi-Contracts, but is not limited to situations where there may be recovery at law, but also "situations in which there is a remedy in equity for the payment of money, for the return of a specific thing or for the establishment of a lien" (p. 4). Part II is devoted to considering the right of a person who has been deprived of property to follow it or its proceeds by means of a constructive trust or an equitable lien. As to the actions at law, it is stated (at p. 9) that "for many years the actions upon the common counts not based upon an agreement were said to be actions upon contracts implied in law, to distinguish them from actions brought upon promises. The fiction that such actions were based upon implied promises was misleading, and of late the phrase has largely fallen into disuse, the more descriptive term quasi contracts being substituted." The underlying principle is defined to be that a person who has been unjustly enriched (that is, received a benefit) at the expense of another is required to make restitution. The appropriate proceeding in an action at law for the payment of money in States which have statutes providing for the abolition of the distinctions between forms of action is an action in which the facts entitling the plaintiff to restitution are set forth. This seems to correspond with the rule in England since the Judicature Act. There are, of course, States in which the forms of action have not been abolished.

All I can do in this paper is to summarize the different divisions and headings of the Restatement. The first, of sixty-nine sections, deals with restitution where there has been payment under mistake. The next deals with payments under coercion, which includes the various rules and distinctions applicable to duress and undue influence, money paid under compulsion of law, contribution, indemnity and so forth: it also deals with non-officious services rendered voluntarily and also benefits tortiously acquired by the defendant, as for instance conversion, regarded not as a tort but as a case of unjust enrichment. Under all these headings will be found analogous cases which, however, require separate discussion. Part II deals with constructive trusts and other analogous equitable remedies. It is in general an essential condition in these cases that the property should have passed to the defendant, leaving to the plaintiff a claim for a beneficial interest in equity. Constructive trust and equitable lien are distinguished, according as the plaintiff's property has or has not been commingled with the property of others. The various and complicated rules which govern the following of property into its products are explained. Special cases of the transfer of property, as for instance the acquisition of an interest in land under an oral agreement, are discussed. This outline is merely to indicate in the most inadequate form the scheme of the work, which I hope will form a stimulus to a com-

Sinclair v. Brougham

plete and detailed survey of the subject as it has been developed in the English Reports.

I must now refer to two decisions in the English Court of Appeal which illustrate the inapplicability to quasi-contract of the theory of the contract implied in law, that is, if the term has any real significance. One is *Craven-Ellis* v. *Canons, Ltd.* [1936] 2 K.B. 403. The plaintiff had rendered services to a company under what was regarded as a contract, but was in fact a nullity because the directors who signed it were not qualified. It was contended that he could not recover, because there could be no question of an implied contract when the parties had proceeded in the belief that they were acting under an express contract. The argument was rejected. It was held that the law imposed an obligation to pay a reasonable remuneration from the fact of the acceptance by the company of the valuable services, which were clearly not rendered officiously or by way of bounty. In *Brooks Wharf and Bull Wharf, Ltd.* v. *Goodman* [1937] 1 K.B. 534, the plaintiffs had discharged a liability for customs dues under compulsion of law for which the defendants were primarily liable, because it attached to the defendants' goods. There was a contract of bailment of the goods which contained no term applicable to these circumstances. The Court held that they could not imply a term because they could not say what the parties would have agreed. But they proceeded to give judgment for the plaintiffs on the basis that the defendants would be unjustly benefited at the cost of the plaintiffs if the latter, who had received no extra consideration and made no express bargain, should be left out of pocket by having to discharge what was the defendants' debt. The test was the unjust enrichment of the defendants at the expense of the plaintiffs.

The true ground might have been expressed in Lord Dunedin's words in *Sinclair* v. *Brougham* (at p. 431): "It is clear that all ideas of natural justice are against allowing A to keep the property of B, which has somehow got into A's possession without any intention on the part of B to make a gift to A. Where there is contract the solution is according to the contract, or you might say the position truly does not arise. Such are the cases of a bailment of a chattel or of a loan of money. But there are many cases where the position does arise and where there is no contract."

Others more learned or more industrious than myself may produce a case under the old forms of action in which the fiction of a contract has been used in order to defeat a claim for restitution. I am at present not aware of any. As I have said, the old common lawyers did not always take their fictions seriously. They used them for their practical value. The fiction of trover in trover and conversion, if scanned too narrowly, might sometimes have had curious results. But in truth the trover like the *assumpsit* was not traversable. But these and other forms were peaceably interred by section 49 of the Common Law Procedure Act, 1852, which says "all statements which need not be proved...the statement of losing and finding and bailment in actions for goods or their value; the statement of acts of trespass having been committed with force and arms, and against the peace of our lady the Queen; the statement of promises which need not be proved as promises in indebitatus counts...and all statements of a like kind, shall be omitted". Thus the

Sinclair *v.* Brougham

common *indebitatus* count for money received is stated in Bullen and Leake, *Pleadings* (3rd ed.), in 1868 to be "money payable by the defendant to the plaintiff for money received by the defendant for the use of the plaintiff" (p. 44). As these authors say, the rule before 1852 was that: "In *assumpsit* the declaration stated the debt and then averred the promise by the defendant to pay the debt (*indebitatus assumpsit*) and a breach of that promise, such promise being one which would be implied by law from the debt and not requiring proof as a fact" (*ibid*. p. 35). But Bullen and Leake go on to say that these distinctions had been removed by the operation of the Common Law Procedure Act, 1852. The authors refer to various sections of the Act, including section 49, and proceed (at p. 36): "There is now therefore but one form of *indebitatus* count which comprises all the advantages of both the forms (*sc*. debt and *indebitatus assumpsit*) under the old procedure; and the action of *indebitatus assumpsit* is virtually become obsolete." Why then should the corpse have been disinterred in 1914? The enactment cannot be dismissed as a mere pleading change. It rendered the fiction otiose. The claim was equiparated to the claim in debt which was not originally based on promise or breach of promise, but rather on property, and was proprietary in character. In this connection reference may also be made to the rules of 1863, which declared that in the *indebitatus* counts the plea of *non-assumpsit* was not admissible. However, the matter is carried still farther by the Judicature Act, 1873, which abolished the forms of action altogether. A pleader now must plead and the plaintiff must prove the facts (not the *fictions*) necessary to support his cause of action. I cannot with all respect see any justification now (if there ever was one) for paying regard in considering matters of substance in law to fictions or doing otherwise than applying to the actual facts the appropriate juristic rules and remedies. This view of the Court's duty has been expressed by the Court of Appeal (differently constituted) in two cases as I have explained. It is now accordingly, I think, the established law of England, unless or until the House of Lords declares the contrary. I do not think that on a true reading of *Sinclair* v. *Brougham* the Court of Appeal in so deciding has infringed the principle of *stare decisis*, the proper application of which is fundamental in English law. Decisions, I repeat, are decisions. Views on legal history are not legal decisions. They may form the basis of decisions, though they did not in *Sinclair* v. *Brougham*. They are simply matters of fact, which change from time to time as knowledge grows. But let it be assumed that it has been stated that the common law not only was, but even now is, that quasi-contract is based on the fiction of a promise and that the statement is intended to be a binding declaration of what the law is, and that it does not matter that it ignores the Common Law Procedure Act and the Judicature Act, and that it confuses legal substance with procedure; still in *Sinclair* v. *Brougham* the statement is merely *obiter dictum*, and I may venture to recall Lord Sumner's warning against the will-o'-the-wisp of the *obiter dictum*. Furthermore the *dictum* is limited by the context, if not by the express language to the special case of *ultra vires* borrowing. Lastly, it does not touch the real reach and scope of the doctrine of unjust enrichment or restitution.

Sinclair *v.* Brougham

It may be said to be merely a matter of words; the phrase, if unfortunate, is innocuous; the law can analyse and develop the doctrine of contract implied in law just as well as if the more accurate terms of quasi-contract or unjust enrichment are used. It may thus be said that the doctrine is the same and capable of the same beneficent application in the service of justice, whether or not people talk of the fiction of a contract implied by law. But I should prefer to do without any such unfortunate and misleading terminology. The room of the fiction is better than its company. Not only is it undesirable that English law should be defaced by superfluous solecisms and illogical phrases, but the ghost of this fiction has, I fear, actually delayed and hindered in England the systematic and scientific study of this important branch of law. I should like to see it forgotten for good and all here and now. But it is certainly doomed. Another generation of lawyers will have forgotten it, or if they ever remember it, will wonder why people troubled to discuss it except as a matter of obsolete history.

II
RESTATEMENT OF THE LAW OF RESTITUTION[1]

AS an English lawyer, I particularly welcome this new volume of the Restatement. It deals with a branch of the law which has been neglected in England, and of which a distinguished Lord Justice in the English Court of Appeal said (no doubt in his haste) that it was characterized by "sloppiness of thought". This comprehensive work with its elaborate organization and its exact analysis must dispel any such idea, if it still exists. England has been less fortunate than America in the study of this branch of law, which has been illustrated in America by some excellent treatises, for instance, Keener on *Quasi-Contract*,[2] of which I was fortunate enough to become possessed some years ago. No such work has been published in England on this subject. In the elaborate text-book, Leake on *Contracts*, the first edition of which was published in 1867 and the eighth in 1931, the index does not refer to quasi-contract. But there is a chapter dealing with Contracts Implied in Law which includes in its heterogeneous collection of causes of action many types of quasi-contractual obligation, distinguishing "contracts arising from agreement and contracts implied in law independently of agree-

[1] A review of the American *Restatement of the Law of Restitution* (1937, St Paul: American Law Institute Publishers). Published in 51 *Harvard Law Review* (1937), 369–383.   [2] 1893.

ment". Pollock in his *Principles of Contract*[1] refers to the fiction of an implied previous request or an equally fictitious promise, as resting on a compromise between the forms of pleading and the convenience of mankind. He suggests the term constructive contract, but adds that "the term quasi-contract is now generally recognized". He adds in another place that quasi-contract is outside the scope of his *Principles of Contract* and gives a reference to Keener's book. In the Indian Contract Act[2] there is a chapter dealing with Relations Resembling Those Created by Contract, but in a very unsatisfactory manner. Professor Winfield in his *The Province of the Law of Tort*[3] has a valuable and suggestive chapter on Tort and Quasi-Contract which is the only, or at least the most complete, attempt by an English lawyer to deal with this subject as a whole and to state the true nature of the concept involved. But it is only a single chapter, combining polemics with exposition. I imagine the general failure of the English lawyers to appreciate the nature of quasi-contract is the use of the self-contradictory term "contract implied by law", the unfortunate character of which has been adverted to by great judges. It is said, however, that the liability must be based on a relationship between plaintiff and defendant and that the contract implied by law constitutes the relationship. But it is clear that this is a mere fiction. If we put aside mere words, the substance of the matter is the definition of the types of relationship from which the liability flows. I feel some hope that the Restatement will induce English lawyers to produce a reasoned treatise on the

[1] 10th ed. 1936. [2] Act IX, Laws of 1872.
[3] 1931. See also R. M. Jackson, *History of Quasi-Contract* (1936).

subject, and to classify, analyse and rationalize the large mass of authority in English case law. They will find an admirable model and example in the Restatement.

The general title Restitution is well chosen but may need explanation. It indicates the essential feature of this branch of law, which distinguishes it from the other main branches. Restitution is not concerned with damages, or compensation for breach of contract, or for torts, but with remedies for what, if not remedied, would constitute an unjust benefit or advantage to the defendant at the expense of the plaintiff. Hence (to state the matter very broadly) an action for restitution is not primarily based on loss to the plaintiff but on benefit which is enjoyed by the defendant at the cost of the plaintiff, and which it is unjust for the defendant to retain. The benefit may consist of money or property of the plaintiff which the defendant is unjustly retaining, or it may be that the plaintiff has under particular circumstances discharged a liability primarily resting on the defendant or has supplied necessary services or goods to the defendant which would unjustly enrich the defendant if the plaintiff were not reimbursed. It is this unjust retention of what should be restored to the plaintiff which constitutes the relationship in which the remedy is based. This way of looking at the position may overlap other relationships, such as conversion, contract, agency, suretyship; and restitution may also be an alternative to damages. But the essence of restitution is the different line of approach. Restitution covers the area of what is often called quasi-contract, which again covers the area of what under the old pleading were called contracts implied by law. The Restatement which

Restatement of the Law of Restitution

has in Part I, as its subhead, Quasi Contractual and Kindred Equitable Relief, has also Part II dealing with Constructive Trusts and Analogous Equitable Remedies. But the common basis of all these facts is still the remedy at law or in equity for unjust enrichments.

The Restatement contains 215 sections, and I have found it difficult to decide what course to take in a short notice. I cannot aim at a critical commentary. I assume, and am entitled to assume, that the Restatement fully and accurately gives the effect of the American decisions on the subject. No less could be expected from a committee which has for Reporter on Part I Professor Warren A. Seavey and for Reporter on Part II Professor Austin W. Scott, and for its other members a body of distinguished lawyers of whom I shall mention only Samuel Williston. Nor am I familiar with the American authorities, which seem to be very numerous and to cover the subject with great detail. It would not be helpful to attempt a comparison with the English authorities, which are numerous though never fully analysed or classified in any English text-book, and which seem, on the whole, to agree with the American law. What I can do is to state briefly the architecture or construction of the work. The Restatement embodies a single coherent design, a harmonious plan, artistically carried out in detail. It may be useful to picture, even in outline, the reach and scope of this branch of law, of which some people seem to deny even the existence. Perhaps in England, the subject has been obscured by the old forms of action, the *indebitatus* or common money counts. The Restatement puts aside these procedural difficulties, by laying down rules that the appropriate proceeding in law for the payment of money by way of restitution is an action of general *assumpsit* in States retaining common-law forms of action, an action of contract in States distinguishing actions of contract from actions of tort, and finally in States which have statutes abolishing the forms of action, an action in which the facts entitling the plaintiff to restitution are set forth. This third rule is in my opinion that which applies in England since the Judicature Acts, with the qualification that there are certain statutes which provide only for contract and tort actions, so that the quasi-contractual actions have for that purpose to fall within the former. But the Restatement is concerned with substantive rights, and with remedies only to the extent that the existence of the remedy may determine the existence of the substantive rights.

The 215 sections which expound the particular rules are accompanied by introductory notes, with explanations and with concise illustrations of typical facts. Any one who has learned by experience the extreme difficulty of expressing briefly, precisely, and sufficiently propositions of law will appreciate the skill represented by these sections and their accompanying notes. More than three years were spent on the work. Sections, comments, and illustrations, read together, give a most illuminating and satisfactory presentment of the subject. There is a very full Index covering 155 pages, each page containing two columns, which, so far as I have tested it, is most practical and should be invaluable to the student and working lawyer, whether at the Bar or on the Bench.

I shall proceed to attempt a very brief résumé of the contents of the Restatement. Part I forms by far the larger portion and contains an exposition in eight chapters of the rules on which rights to restitution depend. There is one chapter dealing with underlying principles, viz. the broad general principle that restitution should be made where there has been unjust enrichment, the denial of restitution to an officious person, and the liability to account for a profit tortiously obtained at the expense of another as an alternative to a claim for damages. The final chapter of this part deals with defences to a claim for restitution, such as change of circumstances or the intervention in certain cases of a third person who purchases in good faith. It also deals with the measure of recovery. The six central chapters of Part I contain the main body of the substantive law, analysed into six Titles: (1) Mistake including Fraud, (2) Coercion, (3) Benefits Conferred at Request, (4) Benefits Voluntarily Conferred without Mistake, Coercion, or Request (e.g. necessaries supplied under certain conditions), (5) Benefits Lawfully Acquired which are not conferred by the person claiming restitution (e.g. where the plaintiff's property has been lawfully appropriated to satisfy the defendant's debt, as in distress or legal attachment), (6) Benefits Tortiously Acquired (e.g. the alternative claim in quasi-contract in cases of conversion). It is interesting to compare this list of Titles with the types of claim enumerated by Lord Mansfield in his famous sketch of the action for money had and received.

Mistake, because of its importance and its complex ramifications and qualifications, fills more space by far than any other Title. It extends from section 6 to section 69 inclusive. There is the fundamental distinction to be made between mistake of fact and mistake of law. But it is emphasized that mistake, to be operative, must have caused the conferring of the benefit. A useful distinction is drawn between doubt and suspicion. Again it is pointed out that a compromise may by bargain exclude the right to rely on mistake, though such a bargain like other contracts may be rescinded on the ground of mutual mistake if basic, while, on the other hand, payment of money made by a person as a result of his individual mistake may not *prima facie* be recovered. Following these general statements comes the enumeration of special instances. The first of these deals with the situation where money has been paid under the mistaken belief that there is a contract, whereas there is no contract either for want of mutuality or for want of consideration or for some other such reason. Then comes the special case where money is paid under a contract which the payer does not know is voidable for mistake (apart from fraud, etc.), which here means basic mutual mistake; if the contract can be avoided by the payer, he can claim the money so paid as money paid by mistake. The same principles are applied in case of payments to third party beneficiaries, with the distinctions proper to the distinction between donee and creditor beneficiaries. There is of course no direct counterpart to these last rules in English law. There follows a list of special types of mistake causing payments to be made, each possessing some peculiar features which lead to rules peculiar to that case. I can only touch on these. Thus there may be partial mistakes, involving overpayments, in regard to which only the excess is recoverable. Or the wrong person may be paid by mistake. The case of mistakes in respect of payments made by way of gift involves some peculiarities. If there is the intention to give, the right to recover is very limited. It is generally confined to cases of fraud or material misrepresentation and to cases of mistake as to the identity or relationship of the donee or as to other basic fact, but it extends in some cases to error as to the amount. The curious case is mentioned where a man intends to pay money to a person, but by some slip of the pen the payment is expressed to be a gift, whereas it was intended to settle a debt. It is explained that the payer may then be entitled to restitution because the expression of intention is not in itself conclusive. On the other hand, if payment is made to a person who honestly believes that it is due to him, the money is not recoverable merely because the payer erroneously believed that the evidence to disprove the claim did not exist or was not available. It is obviously inconvenient to reopen such transactions. The payer should protect himself by reserving the right or should leave the other party to enforce his claim strictly. Finally the rules as to restitution where money is paid by reason of fraud or material misrepresentation are summarized.

Under this head of Mistake, negotiable instruments, bills of exchange, and notes call for special treatment; the general rules apply subject to modifications consequent on the quality of negotiability and on commercial usage, in particular on the desirability of finality in the payment of such instruments. This desire for finality is illustrated by the familiar rule that the holder of the bill or note is entitled to know at once on presentment if he is going to be paid. Hence if he receives payment, being a holder for value in good faith, restitution is not granted even though the payer's name has been forged or, if the payer is drawee, the drawer's name has been forged. A more complicated rule applies in the case of raised instruments. Two cases are next noted in which, in the absence of notice, there is no duty of restitution in favour of the holder; that is where the payer relies on an accompanying security which is spurious, or where the drawee pays because he erroneously thinks that he has sufficient funds of the drawer or is otherwise under a duty to pay. But in all cases the holder is under a duty of restitution if he is guilty of misrepresentation causing the payer's mistake, or if he suspected the mistake, or if after receiving payment he failed to give due notice to the payer of facts subsequently learned. A holder under a forged indorsement, if paid, must make restitution either to the payer or to the true owner. So also, if the payer is mistaken as to acts of diligence having been duly performed. The position of a person who pays a bill for honour of a party to the bill, but under mistake, is also defined.

The next Topic deals with restitution where the transfer is not of money but of land, chattels, negotiable instruments or choses in action; in general the same rules here apply in the event of mistake as in the case of payments of money. But the rendering of services or the incorporation of improvements on another's land or chattels by mistake gives rise, for obvious reasons, to special rules, and the right to restitution, if any, is more limited. In particular, they are not like cases of the overpayment of a specified sum of money which can be refunded. The Restatement carefully analyses and distinguishes the typical cases of this class in their character and results. There is an interesting discussion of such cases as occur when a person by payment discharges a debt or releases a lien erroneously thinking it is his own debt, whereas another benefits.

I must pass on to the important questions next discussed in the Restatement relating to mistake of law as contrasted with mistake of fact. In England up to Lord Ellenborough's time, no distinction was made between such mistakes: in effect the same principle was applied, that one who had benefited by another's mistake should return the benefit. Lord Ellenborough, however, stated as a dogma that every man must be taken to be cognizant of the law. Whatever force may be given to this in criminal law, it is clearly not true as a general proposition. It is not only against principle and early authority but against common sense, and has been consistently disavowed by great judges, though often repeated by some who should have known better. The result has been a great confusion in the law relating to transfers by mistake of law, so that the actual position in England would be difficult precisely to define. The Restatement has dealt with the whole question logically. It begins by laying down the general principle that a mistake of law does not give a right of restitution where a mistake of fact would not. It then states the general rule that there is no right of restitution where owing to a mistake of law payment or transfer is made in satisfaction of an honest claim which was in truth unfounded in law. This was the effect of the decision in *Bilbie* v. *Lumley*[1] which as a decision on the facts has always been

[1] (1802) 2 East, 469.

recognized as sound, because of the principle that settlements honestly made should not be reopened save for very special reasons. The Restatement then goes on to deal with contrasted cases, for instance, payment under a judgment afterwards reversed, or payment under an agreement actually void in law or becoming, in various ways, nugatory, or payment under a mistake in law which was induced by fraud, or payment for an interest in property which was believed to exist but was non-existent. Special rules are applied to the case of conveyances of interests in land and to the rendering of services or the adding of improvements to another's property. For the full analysis under these heads, which seems to me very complete and logical, I can only here refer to the actual text. It will be very useful if the English cases are some day examined in the light of the rules laid down in the Restatement.

There is still another Topic under the head of Mistake. This is entitled Unrealized Expectations. The most typical case of this character is a transfer made expressly either as an offer of a contract or for a particular purpose. If the offer is refused or the purpose not carried out, the transferor can claim restitution from the other person, if the latter has possession and control of the property transferred. That however is true only if the benefit is capable of being restored *in specie*. But merely officious service gives no title to restitution. On the same principles, a person who renders a benefit manifesting that he does not expect compensation but really expecting some advantage in return, such as a gift or a contract, cannot claim restitution if his expectation is not realized. Similarly gifts made in expectation that a personal relationship will continue or commence, but not made conditionally, cannot be reclaimed if the expectation fails.

The final Topic of this chapter in regard to Mistake deals with some general principles, and is headed Defences and Conditions. These may be summarized very roughly: (1) Lack of care by the transferor is not a defence. (2) If there is an enforceable duty, at law or in equity, to transfer, mistake or fraud does not entitle one to restitution. The transferor has done what he was bound to do. (3) So also there is no claim for restitution in the absence of fraud, misrepresentation, or duress if there was a moral duty to transfer, which is not enforceable only because of legal pleas such as Statute of Frauds, Limitation, discharge in bankruptcy, infancy, or coverture, the mistake being as to the enforceability in law of the duty. (4) There are also cases where public policy denies a right to restitution, which would otherwise exist. Under this head come cases of *ultra vires* borrowing by corporations, to which special rules apply, and cases where a contract is not merely unenforceable, but prohibited, so that to allow restitution would be to sanction evasion of a peremptory law. (5) There is the further rule (which is now well established in England) that an action for restitution for mistake is not maintainable until the defendant has notice and an opportunity of making restitution. This rule is based on obvious reasons of fairness. (6) Delay in claiming restitution may have involved an injustice to the defendant if restitution is granted. (7) Restitution is not granted save on the terms of returning benefits received by the transfer or as part of the transaction; that rule is subject to obvious qualifications. (8) A right to restitution is lost if the transferor has affirmed the transaction, unless he did so under the influence of fraud, misrepresentation, or duress. (9) There may be such a change of circumstances as to render an order for restitution inequitable.

The category of Mistake is the largest and most complicated in the law of quasi-contract. But there are the five other categories mentioned above. I shall attempt a brief general summary of the treatment of these in the Restatement.

Coercion is dealt with under four divisions: (1) Duress and Undue Influence, (2) Legal Proceedings and Administrative Orders, (3) Discharge by One Person of Duty Also Owed by Another, and (4) Protection of Property. Coercion is thus a large subject and necessitates a full analysis covering over 100 pages of the Restatement. Duress and Undue Influence are comparatively simple: the right to restitution is the same as in the case of a transfer induced by fraud. Legal Proceedings constitute a more complicated topic. In general, payments made to a person under threats by him of legal proceedings or the institution of legal proceedings are not recoverable, but it is different if the person, who so acted, acted without reasonable cause or without belief in his cause of action, or if he was guilty of duress. But there is a further refinement if the debt which is so paid is that of a third person; in that case, the payer is entitled to restitution from the debtor by a species of subrogation. Payments or transfers under a judgment subsequently reversed are in general recoverable, but it is not a sufficient ground that a judgment, not attacked or reversed, was improperly obtained. Payments made under threat of a levy of execution under a judgment void against the payer may be recovered. In certain cases payments of void taxes, orders, or assessments may be recovered.

More important and complex than these Topics is that relating to the discharge by one person of a duty also owed by another. The right in such cases does not depend on whether or not there are contractual relations between the two parties. This right of restitution differs in one sense from those in which the defendant has acquired something which in justice should be restored to the plaintiff. The benefit or enrichment to the defendant consists in his being relieved from a liability at the expense of the plaintiff, in cases where the defendant as between himself and the plaintiff is primarily liable. The Restatement divides this class into cases of indemnity where the right is to reimbursement of the total amount expended and cases of contribution in which there is a right to partial reimbursement. A distinction must be made to cover contracts of insurance or guarantee in respect of a payment for which the insurer or guarantor, apart from his agreement, is not liable. The right of subrogation, if any, depends on the contract in such cases. Cases of tortfeasors are dealt with separately, as will later appear. The general rule of indemnity includes consensual situations, as where an accommodation indorser has to pay a bill, and situations where the plaintiff is compelled to pay because of a breach of duty by the defendant to the third party, and other cases such as where the plaintiff has been compelled to pay taxes which primarily fall on the defendant. The right of indemnity arises at the time when payment, being then due, has been made. The Restatement goes on to deal with more complicated cases, in which many refinements may arise. Thus, a primary obligor may have a defence such as infancy or Statute of Limitation, which the person secondarily liable is not entitled to raise. In order to ascertain if the plaintiff who has paid is then entitled to restitution, various matters will need to be considered, as, for instance, whether the secondary obligation was assumed with the knowledge or consent of the person primarily liable. Sometimes the fact that payment is made under business compulsion will give a right to restitution. I cannot do more than indicate these refinements which the Restatement discusses in detail. In the cases of contribution, much the same principles apply, with the broad difference that the reimbursement is partial, not total.

The next Topic of the Restatement under this head deals with the case of indemnity and contribution between tortfeasors. The Restatement proceeds on the basis of the rule in *Merryweather* v. *Nixan*,[1] which denies *prima facie* restitution to tortfeasors. This general rule has now been abolished in England by a recent statute. The Restatement points out the difficulties involved in the rule and observes that for various reasons "courts have been increasingly astute in finding reasons which permit restitution to be granted by one tortfeasor against another" (p. 388), though less noticeably where contribution is claimed. The general rule is now stated to be that a person who has discharged a tort claim, to which he and another were subject, is entitled to indemnity or contri-

[1] (1799) 8 T.R. 186.

bution from the other, except to the extent that the character of his conduct precludes restitution. Thus a tortfeasor who has innocently done the wrongful act under the direction of or on account of another would generally be entitled to indemnity from his employer, as would an employer from his employee for whose negligence he would be required to pay. I shall not attempt to follow out these refinements which have arisen because courts have felt that the rule in *Merryweather's Case* is more honoured by being distinguished than by being applied, except as to contribution between concurrent or joint negligent tortfeasors.

The final Topic under the head of Coercion deals with cases in which a person, to prevent the lawful taking or detention of his property, or to redeem his property if taken, has discharged the duty of another in whole or in part. Such a person is generally entitled to restitution, in whole or in part as the case may be, if, as between the two, the other should have performed the duty. There are various extensions and complications of the general rule which the Restatement explains, such as the case where payment by one person not only discharges a lien on his property, but also a lien on another's property, a case to which special rules apply. But the mere fact that performance of a man's duty incidentally benefits another gives no right to contribution or indemnity.

Chapter 4 has for its Topic Benefits Conferred at Request. The guiding principle here is that *prima facie* one who requests another to perform services for, or transfer property to, him impliedly bargains to pay therefor; that is to say, there is a contractual obligation.

But the Restatement, as it says in another place, does not include, except by cross-reference to the Restatement of Contracts, the rules with reference to restitution for breach of contract, nor those defining whatever right to restitution may exist because of a failure to perform a contract unenforceable because of the Statute of Frauds, or because of illegality, or where the contract becomes incapable of performance because of an event arising subsequent to the formation of the contract. No doubt the lawyer using the Restatement of Restitution may be assumed to have at hand the companion Restatement of Contracts. But it seems to me that where a contract is rescinded for breach or illegality or supervening impossibility, the right to restitution (if any) for benefits received depends as a rule on the principles of quasi-contract, if as is generally the case the express contract is silent on the matter. The Restatement does deal with the right to restitution which even a fraudulent person may have where the other party to a contract has rescinded it; such right is defined as limited to cases in which the innocent party has been fully restored to his former position and in which a harsh forfeiture cannot otherwise be avoided. The case of the third party beneficiary involves some special rules. And so does the case of a principal who has acquired a benefit under a contract made by his agent with a third person. The principal will generally not be liable to make restitution if he is not a party to the contract, and is simply in the position of a third party.

Chapter 5 deals with a position which is of special interest, that is the position where without mistake, coercion, or duress a benefit is voluntarily conferred. In cases of this character the general rule of the common law is that there is no right of restitution. *Prima facie* a man cannot impose a debt upon another, or make him liable for a benefit which is "officious". A benefit is *prima facie* not officiously conferred in the cases discussed in the three previous chapters of the Restatement. But apart from such cases there are, it is explained, certain exceptional conditions under which it is desirable for the law to encourage persons to intermeddle in the affairs of others. These are, broadly speaking, cases in which property is transferred or services are rendered which are "necessaries", or in which there is a particular emergency. Such cases include the supply of necessaries to a person whom a third person is in law bound to support, or the unofficious rendering of services for the preservation of life or health in an emergency, generally where an expectation to be remunerated may be inferred. As an illustration, the Restatement gives the striking example of a man rendered insensible by an accident who is attended by a surgeon. The surgeon in his professional capacity performs an emergency operation on the spot, not having any opportunity of asking for authority. The man dies without recovering consciousness. The surgeon, the Restatement says, is entitled to compensation. The operation, it is true, was unsuccessful, but the patient had the benefit of the enhanced chance of recovery. I do not recall any direct decision in the English courts on these lines. There is a well-known dictum by a very distinguished Lord Justice in the English Court of Appeal contrasting maritime salvage with the common-law rule (34 Ch.D. at pp. 248–249). But the case put by the Restatement seems well within the principle of restitution, and analogous to the supply of necessaries to a person incapable of contracting, such as a lunatic or a drunken individual. The common law gave a cause of action in such cases. The Restatement goes on to define the right to restitution in the cases of services rendered to preserve another's things or credit in more limited and restricted terms.

Chapters 6 and 7 deal with a somewhat different class of cases in which the benefit conferred, for which restitution is claimed, has not been conferred by the plaintiff, but the defendant has benefited at the expense of the plaintiff and justice requires that he should make restitution to the plaintiff to avoid his unjust enrichment. There can here be no question of officiousness on the part of the plaintiff. Chapter 6, which deals with Benefits Lawfully Acquired, gives several typical cases without purporting to be exhaustive. A good illustration is afforded by a case where the plaintiff's goods have been lawfully seized by a third person to satisfy the defendant's debt, as where the plaintiff's goods, having been left on the defendant's premises, have been lawfully attached under a judgment against the defendant, or where the plaintiff permitted the defendant to use his shares as collateral security for the defendant's debt and the debt not having been paid the shares are realized by the creditors, or where a pledgee, having power to repledge the pledgor's property, and having repledged it, the property has been realized by the creditor for the pledgee's separate debt. There may in such cases be questions of contribution between different pledgors. Again a *bona fide* transferee who has not given value may be liable to return the property, or account for its value or its proceeds to the true owner. There are many similar cases. All such cases present complications which are carefully examined and distinguished in the Restatement, but which cannot be discussed here. A final instance given is the striking case of a completed gift mistakenly made to the wrong person. This person or his transferee, unless a *bona fide* purchaser, may be under a duty of restitution to the intended donee, but only if the donor died or became incompetent before the mistake became known, and if the intended donee was a natural object of the donor's bounty.

Chapter 7 deals with cases of tortious acquisition at the expense of the plaintiff. Restitution does not ordinarily or primarily depend on wrongdoing, but in these cases there is wrongdoing. For wrongdoing an action for damages lies, in which the plaintiff seeks compensation or damages for the harm he has suffered. But, as has been pointed out, the question in restitution is not what loss the plaintiff has suffered but what benefit the defendant has unjustly acquired, which is a real distinction even though often loss and benefit may amount to the same thing. It is also true that in some cases tort actions are restitutionary in effect, as in replevin, or ejectment, or some claims for fraud or duress. There may, in certain cases, be a right to elect between tortious and quasi-contractual remedies, and the latter may be more beneficial for various reasons, as in cases of death or bankruptcy. Or the alternative to quasi-contractual claims may be a claim in equity.

The most familiar case of alternative remedies is where there is conversion. It is old law that the plaintiff may waive the tort, according to the traditional phrase, and claim for money had and received, that is, for restitution of the value of the chattels or, in certain cases, of their proceeds if the chattels have been disposed of by the converter or his transferee. Liability does not depend in these cases on the innocence of the defendant, who may be a purchaser in good faith but has dealt with the goods without title and without the owner's authority. The Restatement however draws a distinction between the degree of liability of an innocent and of a wrongful converter. For instance, in the former case (it lays down) the plaintiff is not entitled to recover the value of what was received in exchange but only the value of the converted things, whereas a wrongful converter is subject to the larger liability. Complications may arise where converted property has been incorporated into the converter's property, in which event the plaintiff may also be entitled to an equitable lien on the latter. There are also cases discussed in the Restatement in which the plaintiff is entitled to claim restitution against a person who by fraud, duress, or undue influence has obtained the property from a third person, and thereby prevented the plaintiff from acquiring it. In such cases (subject to various conditions and limitations), the plaintiff may successfully claim that the defendant is unjustly enriched at the plaintiff's expense. A similar principle is illustrated where the rendering of services has been tortiously obtained, as, for instance, if a married man purports to marry a woman who is innocent of the bigamy and thereby obtains the benefit of her services on the faith of their being married, she may claim in restitution when she discovers the facts. Cases of interference with trade names and so forth, or of usurpation of office, or the acquisition of a benefit by a fiduciary by means of a breach of duty, illustrate the same principle.

The seven chapters, the general purport of which it has been sought to indicate, state the substantive grounds on which quasi-contractual claims may be made either at law or in equity. The Restatement expressly does not deal with salvage or general average as being outside its purview. I agree with this view because both seem to me to belong to a different jurisdiction and a different legal code. It is true that questions of general average have in modern times become closely involved in mercantile contracts, but general average, like salvage, is still essentially a matter of maritime equity and should be kept apart from common law or equitable ideas of quasi-contract. I have already observed that some genuine claims in quasi-contract (as I regard them) are put aside as being sufficiently dealt with in the Restatement of Contracts. I agree with the authors of the Restatement of Restitution in excluding from their consideration such claims as actions on foreign judgments or for breach of statutory duties into which no true quasi-contractual element enters. As to claims based on breach of common-law duties, such as the duties of carriers or innkeepers, the cause of action there is either for breach of contract or for negligence and is not quasi-contractual at all. Equally, claims on accounts stated are not quasi-contractual. Tacit contracts, or contracts not expressed but implied in fact, are clearly not quasi-contractual.

I have ventured on this very imperfect analysis of these chapters of Part I in order to suggest a comparison between this complicated, comprehensive, and masterly analysis of the principles applicable to this head of the law (separate from, but ranking in importance with, contract and tort) and the meagre and unintelligent exposition which it has so often received.

The remaining chapter (Chapter 8) of Part I contains two Topics: (1) Defences and (2) Measure of Recovery. The defences discussed are of a general character, those peculiar to different heads of restitution having been dealt with in their particular context. The first matter mentioned is negative, viz. that incapacity to contract is not in itself a defence in an action for restitution. The common law on this point (in England now largely statutory) is specific. Reference, however, has been made to enactments which impose conditions or prohibitions on grounds of public policy, which the law will not permit to be evaded. Similarly, criminal or illegal transactions do not create a right to restitution, or do so only under special circumstances. Some changes of the law in this respect have been made recently by statute in England. The Restatement re-enunciates, in so far as is material to its subject, the rules relating to what is called title paramount, which constitute in certain cases a defence of limited application. But a right to restitution may in certain events be terminated or diminished by a change of circumstances; this question is copiously elucidated and illustrated. An application of the same principle is next discussed in reference to transfers made to a fiduciary, as, for instance, an agent, under such circumstances that he is normally expected to pass the property to his principal in ordinary course; he cannot be made liable in restitution if he has done so before notice of the transferor's claim. But the case of an agent for an undisclosed principal is distinguished, and is explained as being a survival of the older view that change in position does not prevent restitution. Questions of election, merger, *res iudicata*, laches, and Statutes of Limitation are examined, and finally the circumstances are enumerated which will discharge a cause of action for restitution. But the death of either party is not such a circumstance, even in jurisdictions where an action in tort is terminated by that event.

The second Topic of Chapter 8 deals with Measure of Recovery. The main principle is that as actions of restitution are not punitive, but have for their primary object the taking from the defendant and restoring to the plaintiff of something to which the plaintiff is entitled or the paying of an equivalent in money, the basis of restitution is not the value of the loss to the plaintiff but the value of what the defendant has received. But if the defendant has acted tortiously, he will have to pay what the plaintiff has lost though it is more than the defendant has benefited, and if consciously tortious the defendant may also be deprived of any profit derived from subsequent dealing with the subject-matter of the claim. If, however, the defendant was not more at fault for the mischance than the plaintiff, he is not required to pay for losses in excess of the benefit he received, and is permitted to retain gains resulting to him from his dealing with the property. These are the general principles set out in the Restatement with a proviso that justice may require modifications in particular cases. The general principles are elaborated and illustrated in this Topic, as are also, in particular, the rather complicated rules as to the measure of restitution where property or services have been acquired by consciously tortious conduct.

A different set of rules is laid down for cases of non-tortious receipt of benefit, in which cases the measure of restitution is the value of what is received, with a further limitation that if the defendant is not more at fault than the plaintiff, the measure of recovery is its value (subject to a further qualification in cases of a mere mistake as to price) in advancing the purposes of the recipient (this seems similar to the Scots measure *quantum lucratus*). These rules are explained by copious and varied illustrations. Further rules are laid down as to accounting for the direct product (e.g. dividends on shares) and compensation for use of the property restored while in the defendant's possession. Questions of recovering interest are also dealt with, the general rule being that interest is recoverable. It is further explained that where a person seeking restitution is bound to restore the property which on his side he received in the transaction, or its value, he is bound to pay interest or profits or the value of the use of the property, and is entitled in general to compensation for sums expended on the property while in his possession. The plaintiff, if entitled to specific restitution of property, may be entitled only on condition of compensating the defendant for expenditure on the property to the extent that justice between the parties requires.

Part II deals with the equitable remedies of which in certain cases a person entitled to restitution may avail himself. These form the subject of the remaining chapters of the Restatement. Topic I of Chapter 9 summarizes these equitable remedies as being (1) Constructive Trust, (2) Equitable Lien, and (3) Subrogation. The exposition of these equitable rights is proper and indeed necessary in order to give a complete picture of the machinery at the command of the court for the purpose of preventing unjust enrichment, and in order to present the full scope of Restitution. In countries like England and, I believe, most States in America, every court of competent jurisdiction is empowered to give relief in the same action both at law and in equity as circumstances require. I am therefore averse to references in modern times to what may be done by a court of equity. I prefer to talk of the powers of the court in the exercise of equitable jurisdiction. The two systems are complementary. A working lawyer in dealing with any practical problem must consider the rights and remedies available in the case under both systems in order to ascertain how justice is to be secured. Hence the need of Part II if the Restatement of Restitution is to be fully expounded. But the two systems though complementary still present their different characteristics, and Part II is a separate part because of that difference. It begins with constructive trusts. These form a separate class of trusts, and like other trusts are governed by equitable rules, though the circumstances under which they come into existence are for the most part the same as, or at least analogous to, those which have been discussed in connection with quasi-contract. A constructive trust is a special category in the law of trusts. I shall take the definition from the Restatement of Trusts (which was the work of a Committee of which Professor Scott was Reporter): "A constructive trust is a relationship with respect to property subjecting the person by whom the title to the property is held to an equitable duty to convey it to another on the ground that his acquisition or retention of the property is wrongful and that he would be unjustly enriched if he were permitted to retain the property."[1] The Restatement of Trusts leaves the full discussion, with certain exceptions, of the constructive trust to the Restatement of Restitution which is the subject of this notice. The constructive trust, it is pointed out, is a different concept from the express or resulting trust, not a species of the same genus. This Restatement, while giving in effect the same definition of a constructive trust, both contrasts it with express and resulting trusts and compares it with quasi-contractual relationships. It differs in effect from express and resulting trusts much in the same way as a quasi-contractual obligation differs from a contractual relation. The constructive trust differs from the other species of trust in that in the latter there is a manifestation of intention to create a trust, either expressly or tacitly, that is to say, as a probable inference of intention from the circumstances. A constructive trust is imposed by the court irrespective of any intention to create it, and it is so imposed as a remedy to prevent unjust enrichment, just as a quasi-contractual obligation is imposed for the same purpose irrespective of contractual intention. But the fundamental difference between constructive trusts and quasi-contractual obligations is that in the latter the plaintiff is seeking "to obtain a judgment imposing a merely personal liability upon the defendant to pay a sum of money, whereas the plaintiff in bringing a suit to enforce a constructive trust seeks to recover specific property" (p. 642). It is pointed out that the peculiar feature of the duty in such cases to convey the property is that it is

---

[1] 1 *Restatement, Trusts* (1935), pp. 5–6.

based on unjust enrichment. The equitable remedy is brought into play where the remedy at law is inadequate. Thus, for instance, in a case of money paid by mistake, if the payee is insolvent, the equitable remedy may enable the plaintiff to obtain specific recovery of the money paid by mistake or of its product, even in certain cases if it has passed into the hands of third persons. But to constitute a constructive trust there must be property on which it can be fastened, and that property must be held by the constructive trustee. Hence there can be no constructive trust where the defendant has merely obtained possession (as in conversion), no property having passed.

An equitable lien is also a means used by the court in order to prevent unjust enrichment, in some cases as an alternative to a constructive trust, in other cases where a constructive trust is not competent. Thus where a person is entitled to claim for improvements made by him on another's land, he cannot claim to enforce a constructive trust of the land but only an equitable lien. An equitable lien, like a constructive trust, is cut off by the intervention of the rights of *bona fide* purchasers for value, but, being an interest in property, takes precedence in insolvency over the rights of creditors.

The third remedy is the right to subrogation which is enforced when the property of one person is used in discharging another's debts or liens on his property under such circumstances that otherwise the other would be unjustly enriched; the former is then subrogated to the position of the obligee or lien holder. The conditions necessary to constitute unjust enrichment are in the main such as have been described in Part I. Thus if the plaintiff has paid off the debt, the payment must not be "officious" in the sense already described.

The Restatement develops these principles in regard to mistake, fraud, duress, and undue influence, in various aspects and with valuable comments and explanations. The position of a *bona fide* purchaser for value is fully elucidated. It is further pointed out that restoration of benefits received by the plaintiff may be a condition of enforcing a constructive trust, and that the right may terminate as a result of the defendant's change of position, and that there may be other defences such as those based on Statutes of Limitations or laches.

Chapters 10, 11 and 12 deal with three special types of circumstances under which constructive trusts may be imposed. Chapter 10 discusses cases where an interest in land may be acquired under an oral agreement. Constructive trusts are excepted from the operation of the Statutes of Frauds, and are enforceable though not evidenced by a writing. Hence though an agreement to transfer land is unenforceable by reason of the Statute, a constructive trust may arise out of the transaction. Thus if land is conveyed under an oral promise to convey land in exchange and the transferee refuses to carry out his promise, the law in order to prevent such unjust enrichment will compel him to reconvey the land. Similarly, there are certain cases of a transfer of land on an oral undertaking to reconvey to, or to hold for, the transferor or for a third party. I cannot here do more than state the general principle.

The next chapter (Chapter 11) deals with certain questions which arise in regard to property in cases of wills or intestacy. Notwithstanding the Statutes of

Wills, which provide for the invalidity of testamentary dispositions if the statutory requirements are not complied with, a constructive trust may be imposed because of the fraud, duress, or undue influence of the beneficiary, if it is proved that the disposition was the actual result of such conduct. The person so acquiring the property holds upon a constructive trust, provided adequate relief cannot otherwise be given in the probate court. Similarly a constructive trust will be imposed on a person who has procured a devise or bequest, or an intestacy, by promising to hold the property for, or to convey it to, a third person, or has prevented or induced a change in the beneficiary of a life policy. And a constructive trust will be imposed where the beneficiary has by murder caused the accrual or enlargement of his interest. These are all instances of the court taking steps in order to prevent unjust enrichment. So also in the final class of cases discussed by the Restatement in Chapter 12, which develops and illustrates the general rule that if one in a fiduciary relation to another, in violation of his duty as fiduciary, acquires or retains property, he will hold it on a constructive trust for the other. The chapter deals in some detail with the various applications of this principle, all with the object of preventing unjust enrichment, for instance, purchases by a fiduciary for his individual benefit of property entrusted to him for sale, or a renewal for his benefit of a lease held by him as fiduciary, and other similar cases. Cases in which a fiduciary is held liable to account for a bonus or commission or secret profit obtained by him in fiduciary matters furnish a further exception to the *prima facie* principle that the liability for unjust enrichment is limited by the amount of loss to the beneficiary. On the general principle laid down in this chapter, a constructive trust in favour of the beneficiary is imposed where the fiduciary has acquired property through the use of confidential information. In all these cases the trust is imposed on third parties to whom the benefit has been transferred if they gave no value or had notice. There is a comprehensive definition of a fiduciary which includes trustees, agents, guardians, attorneys, and persons in other similar positions.

Chapter 13, the final chapter, contains an admirable survey, with comments and illustrations, of the rules, so far as material in cases of unjust enrichment and necessary to effect restitution, for following property into its product and after it has become mingled with other property. I need not detail these rules. The same distinction is drawn between the liability of conscious wrongdoers and of innocent converters. This chapter also deals with improvements on a wrongdoer's property, with the liabilities of third persons, with the various and complex questions which arise in regard to the mingling of funds. It is finally pointed out that, except in some cases of securities which can be regarded as equivalent and capable of substitution, the equitable remedy is cut off and the personal claim alone exists where property has been wrongfully disposed of and it is impossible to trace it into any product.

In conclusion I wish again to express my gratitude for this most admirable work, which has illuminated the whole range of this branch of law. It will be impossible in the future to refuse to recognize its character and importance, or to speak of it as other than logically and precisely elaborated on case law and precedent. This brief survey of the detailed rules which the Restatement expounds at length and in full is certainly incomplete and must be inaccurate, where the subject admits so many subtleties, distinctions, and complications. But it is merely intended to afford a bird's-eye view of the general lay-out. For the details the Restatement itself must be studied, and I refer all who are interested in law to its careful study. A code is never light reading, but in this Restatement the reader will find relief in the perusal of the lucidly and elegantly expressed comments which form in bulk the larger part of the book. For working purposes, as I have said, the Index will be invaluable.

III

PUBLIC POLICY[1]

I INTEND to deal with this principle of English law mainly in connection with the law of contracts, though also to some extent in its kindred application to the law of dispositions of property. It is first necessary to give a definition or at least some limitation of the term. It is clear that it may be used in many contexts and with many connotations.[2] Let me without seeking to be exhaustive give a few instances. Public policy may describe the actual course of conduct or the actual objectives of a nation in its international relations, or again the term may be used to describe what to a particular individual or class of individuals appears to be the best and wisest course of national conduct. It may describe the line of political or social conduct being pursued in internal affairs by statesmen, or again a view of what is best on such matters. In this and kindred senses, the phrase is used to denote matters of statesmanship or public or national administration, conduct actual or desiderated in public affairs. These questions as such have no contact with law courts, which are concerned with the civil or criminal rights or liabilities of individuals, and are concerned with affairs of state only when relevant to such rights. In a narrower sense public policy has been called into play to defend executive acts of the

[1] A lecture delivered in the Harvard Law School, 26 September 1938.
See Knight, *Public Policy in English Law*, 38 *Law Quarterly Review* (1922), 207–219. Winfield, *Public Policy in the English Common Law*, 42 *Harvard Law Review* (1928), 76–102.

Public Policy

state which have gone outside the course of the common law, as for instance when it was sought to justify the legality of general warrants, or search warrants, on the ground of public policy, which, it was said, demanded that Magna Carta and the right of personal liberty could legitimately be violated, and justified the exercise of arbitrary powers by public officers if such violations of right were alleged or assumed to be necessary for the good government of the realm.[1] This as you know was the theory of Star Chamber government, but even after the Star Chamber was abolished claims of this nature were advanced in Courts of Law to justify what was *ex facie* contrary to the common law. This was a positive not a negative use of the idea of public policy, as meaning the convenience of the common weal, the allegation being that such powers were necessary in the interests of good government. I need not remind you, though perhaps in these days it is not entirely without some practical value to remind ourselves, how these doctrines so contrary to the fundamental conception of the common law were swept away by Lord Camden in *Entick* v. *Carrington*, in the year 1765.[2] Let me quote a very few words: "And with respect to the argument of state necessity, or a distinction that has been aimed at between state offences and others, the common law does not understand that kind of reasoning, nor do our books take notice of such distinctions."

We are here concerned with a much narrower and

---

[1] The doctrine, though not the phrase itself, was considered in *Wilkes* v. *Wood* (1763) 19 St. Tr. 1154 and *Entick* v. *Carrington* (1765) *ibid.* 1030. Fleming C.B. in *Bates' Case* (1606) 2 St. Tr. 371, 390, had referred to the "absolute power" of the king as "properly named Policy and Government".

[2] 19 St. Tr. 1029, 1073.

more limited use of the words "public policy" in the sphere of litigation. In one sense, obviously, every legal decision and every legal rule is based upon the purpose of securing justice as between man and man and promoting order in the state. That is a prime object of public policy in one of its wider connotations as denoting an essential element in good government. But a universal concept or ideal of that type is not serviceable in actual judicial proceedings, though it is true that a sense of justice must help the judge when precedent fails. Judges, however, are sworn to administer the law and not to direct themselves on their individual views of what law ought to be. The days are long past when a judge could say that he was not bound to enforce an Act of Parliament which he thought contrary to the common law. What then is meant by public policy as a part of the common law, not something outside the common law, but a body of rules and principles within the common law? Even here a distinction is necessary. As we shall see, public policy has in general a disabling or limiting effect, because in general its effect is to restrict freedom of contract, to which may be added freedom of a man to make dispositions of his property. Hence it has been said that public policy may come into conflict with another, and it is sometimes suggested, higher policy of freedom of contract. Thus it was said by Sir George Jessel in *Printing and Numerical Registering Co.* v. *Sampson*,[1] in words which I may quote here: "It must not be forgotten that you are not to extend arbitrarily those rules which say that a given contract is void as being against public policy, because if there is one thing which more

[1] (1875) L.R. 19 Eq. 462, 465.

than another public policy requires it is that men of full age and competent understanding shall have the utmost liberty of contracting and that their contracts when entered into freely and voluntarily shall be held sacred and shall be enforced by Courts of Justice. Therefore you have this paramount public policy to consider—that you are not lightly to interfere with this freedom of contract." This is a significant passage from many points of view, but I quote it here to suggest that it comprises two different ideas which I think it important to distinguish. There is the public policy in the general sense of what good government and justice require. This is no doubt in a general sense what the Court seeks to ensure. It is the duty and object of the Court in general to enforce bargains, though no doubt, as we shall see, the idea of the essential sacredness of freedom of contract does not stand in England where it did. There is no constitutional guarantee. But the words public policy are obviously also used in a different sense, as meaning the action of the Court in declaring in certain circumstances that a contract is void and in refusing to enforce it. This latter is the narrow and technical meaning of public policy and it is that meaning which forms the subject of this lecture. This is in fact a branch or section of the rules of the common law according to which a Court will refuse to enforce a contract or disposition of property on the ground that to do so is against public policy. It is a body of doctrine of respectable antiquity. I shall leave historians to trace its origin and its early development. But let me point out at once *Mitchel* v. *Reynolds* in 1711,[1] which laid the foundations of the modern doctrine of restraints of trade,

---

[1] 1 P. Wms. 181.

and about twenty-five years earlier the *Duke of Norfolk's Case*,[1] which was a leading case on the rule against perpetuities. These are both true instances, the one at law and the other in equity, of public policy in its repressive or disabling sense. The one was a case of contract, the other of a disposition. We can trace the succession from *Mitchel* v. *Reynolds* to the *Nordenfelt Case*,[2] which puts the rule in its modern form. It will at once be asked by what justification and within what limits can the Court justify its refusal of the ordinary rights of persons to make such contracts as the parties desire or to dispose of their property as they think fit, by will or deed. If that is to be done, is not that, it will be asked, the function of the legislature and not of the judge? The legislature can no doubt prohibit any contract or disposition. In recent times, it has done so in many directions. Truck Acts have limited the freedom of employers and workmen to make such bargains as they think fit, by prohibiting in general payment of wages otherwise than in cash. I need not refer to numerous acts regulating the production and marketing of products or imposing compulsory insurance as a condition of the employment of workmen, or the Factory Acts which limit the hours of work and conditions of employment. But these are all the work of the legislature, which in a democratic state represents the common will of the people after full public discussion and which can revise and alter what it has done if that does not work. All these considerations point the contrast presented by the position of the judge, who has to act on his own responsibility and whose primary interest and duty are to settle private disputes between civil

---

[1] (1685) 3 Ch. Cas. 1.   [2] [1894] A.C. 535.

Public Policy

litigants and who is bound by precedent. Thus it is prima facie anomalous that a judge should attempt in settling private disputes to introduce into law the principles of state policy, or to depart from the rules of the common law in order to invent doctrines of what is good for the common weal. Modern judges, I think, neither desire nor are qualified to fill such a rôle. Yet in England in 1853 there was a serious question on this matter brought to an issue in *Egerton* v. *Brownlow*, 4 H.L.C. 1. The issue can be summarily stated thus. The Earl of Bridgewater had left his estates (I disregard the complicated settlements and remainders) to certain persons subject to the condition that the devise should fail if the devisee should not within a specified time acquire the title of Duke or Marquis of Bridgewater. It was certainly an objectionable condition and might have been decided, as it seems, by a legitimate extension and application of previous authorities, which had held that a condition or limitation was void if it aimed at or actually tended to exercise a corrupt influence on the government in regard to the appointment to a high dignity in the state. That is the recognized principle against the trafficking in honours or offices. But it led to a full-dress conflict of judicial opinion. Eleven judges were summoned to advise the Lords; nine were of opinion that "public policy", though a head of the common law, did not give the judges the right to decide suits according to their own views of what was good for the state. Two judges took the other view. The Lords themselves held the condition void by a majority of 4 to 1. Whatever the merits of the actual decision, I think it is clear that the views of the nine judges on the general question of principle have prevailed and are now accepted as law in England. Let me quote what Baron Parke (afterwards Lord Wensleydale) said in *Egerton* v. *Brownlow* (cf. p. 123): "'Public policy'...is a vague and unsatisfactory term, and calculated to lead to uncertainty and error, when applied to the decision of legal rights; it is capable of being understood in different senses; it may, and does, in its ordinary sense, mean 'political expedience', or that which is best for the common good of the community; and in that sense there may be every variety of opinion, according to education, habits, talents, and dispositions of each person, who is to decide whether an act is against public policy or not. To allow this to be a ground of judicial decision, would lead to the greatest uncertainty and confusion. It is the province of the statesman, and not the lawyer, to discuss, and of the legislature to determine, what is the best for the public good, and to provide for it by proper enactments. It is the province of the judge to expound the law only; the written from the statutes: the unwritten or common law from the decisions of our predecessors and of our existing Courts, from text-writers of acknowledged authority, and upon the principles to be clearly deduced from them by sound reason and just inference; not to speculate upon what is the best, in his opinion, for the advantage of the community. Some of these decisions may have no doubt been founded upon the prevailing and just opinions of the public good; for instance, the illegality of covenants in restraint of marriage or trade. They have become a part of the recognized law, and we are therefore bound by them, but we are not thereby authorized to establish as law everything which we may think for the public

Public Policy

good, and prohibit everything which we think otherwise." This I regard as the classical statement on the point. Baron Parke recognizes "public policy" as a description of a certain branch of the common law but protests against the idea of any independent power of the judges to declare what public policy requires. Such a protest was necessary at that time, because judges had been going outside common-law principles or precedents in order to give effect to their own views under the name of public policy. Let me give two instances. It had been held that an insurance by seamen of their future wages which depended on their ship earning freight was void because it tended to relax their effort to bring the ship safe home. This rule, which seems far-fetched and almost absurd,[1] prevailed for many years till it was abolished by Act of Parliament.[2] Again, as the common law did not prohibit wagers and Parliament had not passed the Gaming Act rendering wagers void, the judges wishing (no doubt with the best intentions) to stop gambling invented strange and almost ludicrous reasons of what they called public policy for refusing to enforce bets. One instance will be enough. In *Gilbert* v. *Sykes* in 1812[3] the Court of King's Bench held that a bet on the life of the Emperor Napoleon was unenforceable because it might on the one hand tend to induce a British subject to relax his effort to defeat the common enemy or on the other hand to induce him to promote the assassination of the tyrant. The word "tendency" has figured largely even in modern times in discussions on public policy, but

---

[1] Arnould, *Marine Insurance* (11th ed.), § 244.
[2] Marine Insurance Act, 1906 (6 Ed. 7, c. 41), s. 11.
[3] 16 East, 150.

Parke B. would seem to have given it its death-blow or at least to have reduced it to its proper proportions when he pointed out what consequences would follow from its logical applications; for instance, insurances on life or against fire might be declared void as tending to murder, suicide or arson. "In short", he adds (at p. 128), "there are few contracts in which a suspicious mind might not find a tendency to produce evil; and to hold all such contracts to be void would, indeed, be an intolerable mischief." These wise words are not without value even to-day: indeed somewhat similar language was used by Holmes J. in a case to which I shall later refer in the Supreme Court of the United States. A different view was expressed by the majority in the House of Lords. Lord Lyndhurst, referring to the case of seamen insuring wages, which he seemed to approve, and other cases, said (at p. 161): "The inquiry must, in each instance, where no former precedent had occurred, have been into the tendency of the act to interfere with the general interest. The rule, then, is clear. Whether the particular case comes within the rule, it is the province of the Court in each instance, acting with due caution, to determine." Pollock C.B. thus expressed his opinion (at p. 151): "It may be that Judges are no better able to discern what is for the public good than other experienced and enlightened members of the community; but that is no reason for their refusing to entertain the question, and declining to decide upon it. Is it, or is it not, a part of our common law, that in a new and unprecedented case, where the mere caprice of a testator is to be weighed against the public good, the public good should prevail?" Then, again, Lord Brougham referred

Public Policy

(at pp. 175–176) with approval to the case I have mentioned about the bet on Napoleon's life (*Gilbert* v. *Sykes*), and said the judges were right in refusing to take into account the remoteness of the risk that assassination would be committed, or the policy of the state be interfered with. I prefer Baron Parke's description of such reasoning. It seems to me far removed from common sense, or law.

It is clear that on such views there would be a serious risk of apparently unexceptionable rights at common law being frustrated by this objection to the fanciful ideas of judges as to what is required by public policy or the good of the common weal. *Egerton's Case* itself was peculiar and did not, it seems, call for the interference of the legislature, and many years later, in *Wallace's Case*,[1] the Court refused to apply the ruling in *Egerton's Case* to a similar condition in a testamentary disposition which made the vesting of the property depend on the devisee obtaining a baronetcy. Parliament, however, restrained the constructive imagination of judges in inventing dangerous tendencies by rendering gaming transactions unenforceable, and also, as I have said, abolished the prohibition against seamen insuring their wages. If the principle were accepted as stated by Pollock C.B. there would be a large field of possible exception to the doctrine of *stare decisis* because of the uncertainty of how the judge might regard the particular case. It was this feeling that led judges to refer to public policy as an unruly horse or as slippery sands on which to build. But I think it safe to say, especially after the views expressed in *Fender* v. *St John-Mildmay*,[2] that the opinions expressed

[1] [1920] 2 Ch. 274.   [2] [1938] A.C. 1.

by Parke B. have prevailed. This was certainly the opinion of the House of Lords in *Janson* v. *Driefontein Mines, Ltd.*,[1] where the rule that a contract is void which involves trading with an enemy of Britain was considered. That rule is generally classed as falling under the head of canons properly describable as rules of public policy. The claim was on an insurance against belligerent capture and seizure of bullion effected before the outbreak of war by a gold-mining company which became technically an alien enemy on the outbreak of the war between Britain and the Transvaal. The seizure was clearly in order to provide the Transvaal with gold to conduct the war. The House of Lords refused to hold the contract unenforceable. The rule of public policy they held did not begin to operate until the war had actually commenced. Such had been held in the older cases and the House of Lords would not extend the doctrine. Public policy like any other branch of the common law ought to be, and I think is, governed by the judicial use of precedents. In *Janson's Case* Lord Halsbury said in terms (at p. 491): "I deny that any Court can invent a new head of public policy." Lord Atkin in *Fender's Case* thought that view might be too rigid. In the same case I said that I found it difficult to conceive any new heads of public policy. Lord Roche said (at pp. 54–55) that "to evolve new heads of public policy or to subtract from existing and recognized heads of public policy if permissible to the Courts at all, which is debatable, would in my judgment certainly only be permissible upon some occasion as to which the legislature was for some reason unable to speak and where there was sub-

[1] [1902] A.C. 484.

Public Policy

stantial agreement within the judiciary and where circumstances had fundamentally changed". This concurrence of circumstances is so improbable, as to support Lord Halsbury's view for all practical purposes. If I may quote again from Lord Halsbury, he said that the rule of public policy "does not leave at large to each tribunal to find that a particular contract is against public policy".[1] He also quoted from Marshall on Insurance: "To avow or insinuate that it might, in any case, be proper for a judge to prevent a party from availing himself of an indisputable principle of law, in a Court of Justice, upon the ground of some notion of fancied policy or expedience is a new doctrine in Westminster Hall, and has a direct tendency to render all law vague and uncertain." It is really a question of what is meant by a "new head". There are certain subdivisions of public policy which you will find classified in the text-books. Each is an application of a particular rule to the facts of the time. Within the limits of the rule there is room for changes in application as the times change. It is true that in the earlier days of the law, when it was being gradually evolved, there was a large latitude allowed to judicial invention. The basis of customary rules and authorities on which they could work was limited. They had to evolve new forms of action and consciously or unconsciously to create or apply new juristic concepts in order to decide the cases before them. Thus they evolved the doctrines about restraint of trade, the rule against perpetuities, the rule about the unenforceability of contracts which involved trading with enemies, or which involved interference with public

[1] [1902] A.C. at p. 491.

government or the course of justice, or which were immoral, and these and other categories are now recognized to constitute the body of rules which come under the head of public policy. The business of the judge now is to interpret the law, and, as Lord Bramwell said, judges are more to be treated as expounders of the law than as expounders of what is called public policy. Their duty in general in this as in other branches of the law is to proceed on the basis of authority, or when authority does not cover the precise case, they have to apply the recognized principles to the new conditions, along the lines of logic and convenience, just as they do when dealing with any other rule of the common law or equity. If it is said that rules of public policy have to be moulded to suit new conditions of a changing world, that is true; but the same is true of the principles of the common law generally. Hence, whenever a particular case comes up for decision and public policy is invoked in order to defeat what is otherwise a legal claim, the question must be, Is there any rule based on public policy which could justify avoiding the promise sued on? Or the question may be stated to be, What are the definite propositions as to what interest of the state or what public injury is supposed to be involved or how or on what principle of law the promise was unlawful? The matter must be decided on tangible grounds, not on mere generalizations.

Quite recently two cases have come before the English Courts which have required the principle of public policy to be considered; one was *Fender* v. *St John-Mildmay*,[1] to which I have already referred. The other is *Beresford* v. *Royal Insurance Co.*, in which the decision of

[1] [1938] A.C. 1.

Public Policy

the Court of Appeal is reported in [1937] 2 K.B. 197: this decision has been affirmed by the House of Lords on substantially the same lines as in the Court of Appeal, [1938] A.C. 586. These two cases offer an instructive contrast; in one the contract was enforced, in the other it was not. Both involved questions not covered in the precise form by previous authority, but the cases were decided on the lines of earlier judgments applying the principles on the basis of analogy, logic and convenience. I shall deal first with *Fender's Case*, then with *Beresford's Case*, and then add some comments by way of comparison or contrast.

The facts in *Fender's Case* were of the simplest. The plaintiff, who was appellant in the House of Lords, met the defendant, who was to her knowledge a married man, but he was unhappy with his wife. An intimacy sprang up between them and after mutual promises to marry if and when his wife divorced him sexual relations took place. His wife petitioned for divorce and obtained a decree nisi. Thereupon he promised to marry the plaintiff immediately after the decree was made absolute. Before the decree was made absolute and again after it was, the defendant repudiated his promise, and some months later married another woman. The question was whether it was contrary to public policy that a promise made between decree nisi and decree absolute should be enforceable. The trial judge held as a matter of law that it was not enforceable, the Court of Appeal affirmed that judgment by a majority, but the House of Lords by a majority reversed it, and ordered judgment to be entered for £2000, being the amount of damages found by the jury.

It is necessary to indicate the difference between a

decree nisi for divorce and a decree absolute for divorce under the English Divorce Acts. The decree of divorce is in substance made in two parts. When on the trial of the cause the petitioner has established his case and the judge has found in his favour, the decree which is made is called a decree nisi, because its operation is suspended for a period generally of six months. That period was introduced in order mainly to allow time for the King's Proctor to make inquiries whether there are facts not disclosed to the Court why the decree should not be made absolute. It is only upon the decree absolute being granted that the marriage is dissolved. The parties remain in the eyes of the law man and wife. If they come together again, the decree nisi is avoided. If the man dies before decree absolute the divorce has never become complete and the woman is his widow. The Court may refuse to grant the decree absolute if grounds are shown why the decree nisi should not have been made. But though the marriage in law continues, it is clear that for all practical purposes it is dissolved by the decree nisi. The matter has been tried in open Court, the parties have separated and are at arm's length, at that stage every hope of reconciliation is exhausted, if indeed it was not exhausted when the Court proceedings were commenced. In a word there is no married state except in mere legal form, but the law imposes a fixed period of delay, which on special grounds the Court may shorten.

It has been held in England that a promise to marry a second time made by a husband during the first wife's lifetime and while the first marriage subsists, is bad on grounds of public policy. This was decided in *Spiers* v.

Hunt,[1] and *Wilson* v. *Carnley*.[2] The latter was a decision of the Court of Appeal. The question has not come before the House of Lords, but it was conceded in argument in *Fender's Case* that such was the law and it was assumed to be so by the House of Lords. It has also been held in the United States that if the promise is given while both parties are married the promise is void: *Paddock* v. *Robinson*,[3] *Noice* v. *Brown*.[4] In the former of these cases no question of divorce was involved, in the latter the wife was prosecuting a suit for divorce but no adjudication by the Court had taken place. The question was whether the principle of public policy, which was assumed to apply to these cases, applied also to the facts in *Fender* v. *St John-Mildmay*. The question had to be decided on ordinary common-law principles, subject only to this, that the doctrine of public policy was not to be unduly extended.

The first thing was to decide whether this case was governed by such a case as *Wilson* v. *Carnley*, where the husband and wife were both living together. It is necessary to ascertain if possible on what ground of public policy that case was decided. It was not based on the well-established rule of public policy that the law will not enforce an immoral promise, such as would be the case if a promise of marriage was in consideration of immoral relations. That is clearly unenforceable, just as any promise to live in immorality is unenforceable in law, whether the consideration be money or anything else, including a promise to marry at a subsequent date.

---

[1] [1908] 1 K.B. 720. [2] [1908] 1 K.B. 729.
[3] (1871) 14 Amer. Rep. 112 (Illinois).
[4] (1876) 20 Amer. Rep. 388; 23 Amer. Rep. 213 (New Jersey).

I shall not further refer to this matter, which indeed is not suggested in the case we are considering. The grounds of public policy relied on in *Wilson* v. *Carnley* seem mainly to have been that the promise was likely to induce a breach of morality or even the crime of murder or perhaps also the procuring of false evidence to get a divorce. These grounds of public policy seem to be based on mere tendencies and to illustrate the danger of imagining remote tendencies which may be far from any practical reality. I could not agree with the decision if based on such grounds. If the decision in *Wilson* v. *Carnley* is right it must, I think, be based on a broader ground, viz. that such a promise is inconsistent with the fundamental basis of married life, of which the moral idea and legal obligation are expressed in the promise to love and cherish. A promise like that in *Wilson's Case* implies a disloyalty to the vital idea of the married state. The safeguard and promotion of the married state is a well-recognized head of public policy.

But the parallelism completely fails if it is sought to be applied to the conditions which exist when the decree nisi has been pronounced. It is true that technically the marriage still exists until the decree absolute. But a question of public policy cannot be decided on a technicality. In every other material aspect the case now being considered differs from that of *Wilson* v. *Carnley*. The consortium of married life has ceased. The married state in fact no longer exists. The parties are living apart. There is no longer any question of disloyalty if either party thinks it desirable to provide for the near future when the decree absolute will in ordinary course be granted. If the principle of public policy applies at all, it must

Public Policy

equally apply to what are called the innocent and the guilty parties. Looking at it from a practical or common-sense point of view, it might seem the best thing that as soon as possible the guilty party should be able to regularize his position by promising to make his paramour what is called an honest woman, or under other circumstances he may desire to make a new alliance for his future life. The innocent partner, on the other hand, should not be debarred from entering into engagements in anticipation of the conditions of complete freedom which will so shortly exist in fact. Indeed the promise would be equally void against a third party who in good faith but knowing of the marriage and divorce has desired to pledge himself or herself to one or other of the divorced or divorcing parties at a time between the decree nisi and the decree absolute. Why in any case such a promise should conduce to immorality, I cannot conceive. I should think that it would have just the opposite effect, especially as a definite period of time is fixed at which the new marriage is legally possible. It is not possible to dwell on the possibility of corrupt conduct in order to procure a divorce, for the divorce is already procured. There is one matter which is more worthy of consideration and that is the argument that it puts an end to any chance of reconciliation. But when matters have reached the stage of decree nisi, the chance of reconciliation is very remote and indeed negligible. On the same principle it might be said that after the decree absolute the chance of reconciliation is weakened.

Hence *Wilson* v. *Carnley* seems to be no authority in favour of the invalidity of the promise. But in addition there are well-established authorities which point to the opposite conclusion. I refer to the cases in the Courts about separation agreements. It was settled in the House of Lords in *Wilson* v. *Wilson*[1] that agreements for immediate separation or made where there was actual present separation were legal and valid and that dispositions of property under them would be specifically enforced. In a later case Lord Westbury said that such agreements were not contrary to public policy, which he defined as a consideration of such general and universal public utility as should as a matter of sound reason regulate the proceedings of a Court of Justice.[2] It is clear that such agreements legalized the cessation of the married consortium and prejudiced the chance of reconciliation and were thus contrary to the public policy which favours the married state. Though agreements for future separation which obviously prejudiced the future prospects of married happiness were held void, it was different where the parties had separated or were actually separating. The distinction drawn in these decisions strongly supports the view of the majority in *Fender's Case*. It can also be used to illustrate the help that can be derived by analogy in deciding a question of public policy, like any other question of common law. The broad public policy invoked in all these cases is the public interest in the promotion of the married state. The practical limits which good sense and convenience require are elucidated by the conflicting decisions. If, however, the demands of public policy do not clearly apply, then the contract must be enforced. The pre-

---

[1] (1848) 1 H.L.C. 538.
[2] *Hunt* v. *Hunt* (1862) 4 De G. F. & J. 221.

Public Policy

sumption should be in favour of the validity of the contract.

I now turn to the contrasted case of *Beresford* v. *Royal Insurance Co.*[1] The question was whether the personal representatives of the assured under a policy of life assurance could recover, when the assured had committed suicide being at the time of sane mind. The defence was that public policy rendered such a claim unenforceable.

It is necessary first of all to distinguish the invalidity of the contract from the enforceability of a particular claim by a particular claimant in particular circumstances. The policy, which was in the usual form, provided that it was indisputable subject to the conditions, one of which was that "if the life or any one of the lives assured shall die by his own hand, whether sane or insane, within one year from the commencement of the assurance, the policy shall be void as against any person claiming the amount hereby assured or any part thereof, except that it shall remain in force to the extent that a *bona fide* interest for pecuniary consideration, or as a security for money possessed or acquired by a third party before the date of such death, shall be established to the satisfaction of the Directors". This was construed as at least impliedly promising that, after one year, the Company would pay, even in the event of the assured dying by his own hand while sane.

The action was brought by the personal representative of the deceased man, who, as the jury said, was of sane mind and understanding when he shot himself in a taxi-cab exactly three minutes before the policy which

[1] [1938] A.C. 586.

had been in force for some years ran out. In fact he was hopelessly insolvent and could not raise funds to renew the policy. The judge held that the insurance company was liable. He said that while he agreed that the law would not enforce a contract entered into in contemplation of a man committing a felonious act, he could not see why when a perfectly legal contract had been entered into and had been observed by the parties for many years, one party to it should escape the liability which fell on him by alleging that the other had terminated it in an illegal manner when he had stipulated as part of the consideration for the bargain that he would not dispute it (as he construed the contract) after it had been current for more than twelve months even if the man insured died by his own hand being sane at the time. The Company, he said, might have inserted in their policy that they would not be liable in the case of felonious suicide whenever committed. They did so in respect of the first twelve months but not for the period afterwards. He held that there was no public policy involved except that the contract must be fulfilled. This decision was reversed by the Court of Appeal, whose judgment was affirmed by the House of Lords. The basis of these judgments is that it is the general principle of English public policy that a criminal or his representative will not be allowed by the judgment of the Court to reap the fruits of his crime. That principle rests on a broad rule of public policy. It was not necessary in this case to determine whether the same canon applies to crimes of inadvertence such as manslaughter by negligence; in fact recovery has been allowed by Courts of first instance in England under third party insurances where the

Public Policy

assured has caused death by negligent driving and has been held guilty of manslaughter.[1]

In English law suicide by a person while of sane mind, which is called *felo de se*, is in fact self-murder. In old days such a suicide was a felon and his crime was followed by ecclesiastical penalties, for instance, as we know, his body was refused Christian burial, though his lands were not forfeited nor his blood corrupted nor his wife barred of her dower. Though the penalties under the old law have been mitigated, *felo de se* still remains a felony. Thus an attempt to commit suicide is punished as an attempt at a felony, and the survivor of a suicide pact may be indicted as an accessory before the fact to murder. When it is added that a policy on an assured's life, though the policy monies cannot be collected by the assured himself and in terms are payable to his personal representative, is a contract with the assured and only enforceable as such, it follows logically that such a claim as that presented in the *Beresford Case* as being a claim on behalf of a murderer or his estate (for *felo de se* is self-murder) can be regarded only as a claim on behalf of a criminal to reap the fruits of his crime. It is curious that up to 1936 no precise authority on the point is found in the books. The Court in deciding this question of public policy had to proceed on recognized principles according to logic and convenience and according to the nearest authorities. The Court called in aid these authorities. An authority involving the principle was *Cleaver* v. *Mutual Reserve Fund Life Association*,[2] where a man, who had effected a policy on his life in favour of his wife, was

---

[1] *Tinline* v. *White Cross Insurance Association, Ltd.* [1921] 3 K.B. 327.
[2] [1892] 1 Q.B. 147.

murdered by her. It was held that persons claiming under her could not recover, though there was held to be a resulting trust of the policy rights in favour of the deceased's estate, the deceased being innocent. The decision was based on the general principle of public policy, under which rights will not be enforced directly resulting to the person asserting them from the crime of that person. A striking, but less obvious, instance of that rule is afforded by an old case in the House of Lords, *Fauntleroy's Case*.[1] That takes one back to the old days when forgery was a capital offence. There was a policy on the life of the forger, who was a banker. He was convicted and hanged. His assigns claimed on the policy. It was held that the action was upon the plainest principles of public policy not sustainable. It cannot be said in such a case that the assured deliberately willed his own death, as in the case of *felo de se*. I feel it hard to accept the decision, though it is to be treated as good law. It is scarcely necessary to mention that a suicide committed while the deceased was insane is not a crime, because the act of an insane person is not in law his act. I need not here refer to other supporting authorities in England. There are, however, certain decisions in the Supreme Court of the United States to which brief reference may be made. English Courts always aim as far as possible at securing uniformity in regard to the law of contract between the two countries. These United States cases seem to be based on somewhat different lines of reasoning from *Beresford's Case*, which turned specifically on the character of *felo de se* as a criminal act. In the latest case, *Northwestern Mutual Life Insurance Co.* v. *Johnson*,[2] the

[1] (1830) 4 Bligh N.S. 194.   [2] (1920) 254 U.S. 96.

Public Policy

decision seems to have depended on the view that it was not established that by the law of the State which governed the matter, suicide committed during sanity was a crime. The insurance company were held liable to pay. It is not, however, clear whether the suicide in question was sane when he killed himself. The case seems mainly to have turned on the question whether a policy implying that the suicide of the assured person, whether sane or insane, after a specified time should not be a defence, was invalid as being against public policy. Holmes J., while pointing out that the rule of public policy depended on State law, observed that the mere evocation of a possible motive for self-slaughter (that is, it seems, the prospect of payment of the policy monies) is at least not more objectionable than the creation of a possible motive for murder, as where a policy on a man's life is assigned to a third person. But no disapproval was expressed of the earlier case, *Ritter* v. *Mutual Life Insurance Co.*,[1] the actual reasoning in which seemed to turn on the view that the policy expressly or impliedly covered the assured's suicide while of sane mind. The Company were there held not liable to pay. In that case recovery was refused where the assured had in fact, while sane, committed suicide. And in *Northwestern Mutual Life Insurance Co.* v. *McCue*,[2] the action on the policy failed when the assured had been executed for murder. There was an interesting South African decision in the Supreme Court of the Cape, *Burger* v. *South African Life Insurance Society*,[3] where a British subject had been killed while

---

[1] (1897) 169 U.S. 139.
[2] (1911) 223 U.S. 234.
[3] (1903) 20 Cape of Good Hope, S.C. 538.

fighting in arms against the British Government and the executors were held entitled to recover the amount of the policy. The Court seems to treat the decisive factor as being whether the deceased when effecting the policy had contemplated the illegal act or had become a rebel with the object of hastening his death and securing the amount of the policy for his representative. I am not clear that the Court considered the principle that a man or those representing him should not reap the fruits of his crime by a judgment of the Court. There is, however, a clear distinction from *Fauntleroy's Case (supra)*.

It may well be, however, that an innocent assignee for value of the policy or a third party who, having an insurable interest, had effected an insurance on the deceased life, would not be barred from recovering. In any case, whether rightly or not, the decision in *Beresford's Case* has disturbed in some minds the faith in policies on debtors' lives as satisfactory securities for money or debts.

There is a closely allied rule to which I may here advert, which is that the Court will not lend its aid to a man who founds his course of action upon an immoral or an illegal act or contract. As Lord Mansfield said or quoted, "ex dolo malo non oritur actio". This may be put simply on public policy or on the inherent jurisdiction of the Court to forbid its process to be used where the plaintiff invoking the process shows, by the evidence he calls to prove his case, that his claim is based on, or arises from, a crime, fraud or immorality. There is the famous eighteenth-century case where a highwayman filed a bill in Chancery for partnership accounts against another highwayman who worked with him. The prin-

Public Policy

cipals though eventually captured and hanged kept outside the reach of justice for the time being, but the attorney and counsel were suitably dealt with by the Court.[1] Similarly, an action was dismissed when it appeared that the transaction sued on was a fraudulent conspiracy to make a market in shares.[2] A more striking case which has been somewhat debated is *Berg* v. *Sadler and Moore*,[3] where a claim for money had and received was dismissed though the defendants had in one sense no right to the money. But as the plaintiff had paid it to them in pursuance of a fraudulent scheme which had miscarried, the Court refused to enforce repayment. The decision has been criticized as infringing the principles of restitution.

My object has been not to give a digest or classification of the various cases in which the principle of public policy was involved, but to explain the nature of this branch of the law and to give some recent illustrations of its application. I regard its rules as governed by precedent, like any other branch of the common law or equity. The cases I have cited and the lines adopted in the judgments sufficiently, I think, establish this. But let me add one or two further illustrations of how the principle works. One of the oldest and most frequently invoked rules of public policy is that dealing with covenants in restraint of trade. There was a long line of authorities in which limitations were laid down within which a restraint might be justifiable. It would be absurd and mischievous to condemn every contract in

---

[1] *Everet* v. *Williams* (1725) 9 *Law Quarterly Review*, 197–199.
[2] *Scott* v. *Brown & Co.* [1892] 2 Q.B. 724.
[3] [1937] 2 K.B. 158.

which for good reason a man covenanted to limit his freedom to trade as he liked. Even in *Mitchel* v. *Reynolds*,[1] to which I have already referred, it was said that a restriction made upon good and adequate consideration might be upheld as a proper and useful contract. It was, however, held (to take one instance) that a general restraint must be bad, because it could not help anybody. "What does it signify", said Lord Macclesfield, in one case, "to a tradesman in London, what another does at Newcastle?" The modern rule was laid down by the House of Lords in *Nordenfelt's Case*.[2] The test for deciding if a covenant in restraint of trade is against public policy and void was there laid down to be whether the covenant was not wider than was necessary for the reasonable protection of the covenantee or injurious to the public. Experience of life had shown the Court that some restraints of trade were inevitable in the conduct of affairs. A firm which employed a servant and thereby necessarily placed him in possession of their business secrets and knowledge of their customers had to be allowed to impose some restrictions on the employee when he left their service to enter into competition. Similarly on the sale of a business. The public policy against a man restricting his freedom to trade had to be modified by allowing in certain cases restraints that were reasonable. There sprang up a long line of decisions in which it had to be decided in case after case what restraints were reasonable having regard to the particular circumstances. The Courts attempted to lay down precise rules and limitations, as for instance that in no event could restraint unlimited in space or in time be reasonable.

[1] (1711) 1 P. Wms. 181.   [2] [1894] A.C. 535.

Public Policy

In *Nordenfelt's Case* the restrictive covenant, which was upheld, was for twenty-five years and was world-wide. It was held to be valid. The covenantor sold his patents and business to the covenantee. The business was worldwide because it dealt in munitions and other warlike instruments, the customers for which were generally foreign states scattered over the world. The covenant was held to be reasonable because it was not beyond what was necessary for the protection of the purchasing company and was not contrary to the interests of Great Britain. Lord Macnaghten summed up the modern rule (at p. 565): "It is a sufficient justification, and indeed it is the only justification, if the restriction is reasonable—reasonable, that is, in reference to the interests of the parties concerned and reasonable in reference to the interests of the public, so framed and so guarded as to afford adequate protection to the party in whose favour it is imposed, while at the same time it is in no way injurious to the public." This case, when read in the light of the authorities over two centuries before it, is a good illustration of the way in which a doctrine of public policy changes with the times. It has to change when the times change, at least when it is a flexible rule adjusted to conditions of the day, like covenants in restraint of trade, the reasonableness of which is judged by a different test in days of rapid and easy communication as compared with old days when circles of trade and commerce were restricted to small local areas. There are, however, some rules of public policy which are not flexible but rigid, such as the rule against trading with the enemy, which, however, was not extended in *Janson's Case*, to which I have already referred.

The rule was limited to transactions during war and was not extended to transactions just before war or indeed in anticipation of a war which actually took place. But it was held in *Rodriguez* v. *Speyer Bros.*[1] that the rule that an alien enemy could not sue in an English Court during the continuance of a war was not so rigid as to debar an action being brought after the outbreak of war on behalf of a partnership between a British and a German subject, which had been dissolved by the war. That extension of the existing rule led to great conflict of opinion in the House of Lords and was upheld only by a majority of three to two. Another instance of notions of public policy varying with the times may be afforded by *Bowman* v. *Secular Society, Ltd.*,[2] where one question was whether a company, one of the objects of which involved a denial of Christianity, was objectionable on the ground of public policy. The House of Lords, deciding that there was no illegality as there was no scurrility or profanity in the denial, held that there was no public policy involved. Old cases were discussed. Lord Sumner pointed out that in the present day meetings and discussions are held lawful which 150 years ago would have been deemed seditious, and this is not because the law is weaker or has changed, but because, times having changed, society is stronger than before. In the present day reasonable men do not apprehend the dissolution or downfall of society because religion is publicly assailed by methods not scandalous. What public policy requires in the circumstances of one time may not be required in the circumstances of another age. The rule remains the

[1] [1919] A.C. 59.
[2] [1917] A.C. 406.

Public Policy

same, but its application is conditioned by the facts. *Cessante ratione legis cessat ipsa lex.*

Thus I come back again to the original proposition that public policy is not a matter depending on the personal views of the individual judge, but a body of rules in some cases fixed, in other cases flexible, but governed by precedent and authority like other branches of the common law.

IV

THE *LIESBOSCH CASE*[1]

I HAVE chosen as the subject of this lecture some aspects of the law of damages, or more accurately a small corner in that ill-defined and ill-charted region of the law. I do not wonder that it is so. It is true that the fundamental principle of the law of damages is that reparation is to be made to an injured person by the wrongdoer by means of a payment in which money will, so far as money can, put the victim in the same position as if he had not been wronged. But when I think of all the cases with which I have been concerned, and all the cases I have read in the books, I am impressed by the immense range and variety of the issues in regard to assessing damages which have to be determined and the difficulty of reducing them to precise categories and rules. Only some general principles seem to be capable of formulation. The problem in the main is to apply the general principles to the multifarious permutations and combinations of fact. My experience makes me timorous in coining epithets and adjectives which in the abstract have generally no significant meaning at all, though they may take a colour from the special circumstances before the Court which used them. I intend here to deal with concrete cases, using them to some extent to illustrate certain general principles.

Before I turn to the *Liesbosch Case*,[2] I shall venture to

[1] A lecture delivered in the Harvard Law School, 30 September 1938.
[2] [1933] A.C. 449.

The Liesbosch Case

state tentatively and summarily some general principles and distinctions in a somewhat dogmatic fashion, not attempting to define all the possible qualifications. It is at once apparent that every juridical cause of action may raise its special problems as to damages. Though I am more particularly concerned with tortious injuries to chattels, I may merely glance at some other types of injuries.

A fundamental distinction is that between cases in which, as it is said, damage is the gist of the action and those in which no damage need be proved in order to succeed. In the latter category come those cases in which if no damage is proved nominal damages may be awarded and those in which exemplary or punitive damages may be given and those in which the actual loss is alone recoverable. I had occasion to discuss these distinctions in *Nicholls* v. *Ely Beet Sugar Factory*,[1] which was a case of nuisance or trespass on the case to a several fishery in a river by fouling the stream higher up its course. That was a disturbance of an existing legal right in which, as it is said, "the law presumes damage". I quoted in my judgment *Ashby* v. *White*[2] where a man complained that he had been prevented from voting at a Parliamentary election and Lord Chief Justice Holt said "an injury imports a damage when a man is thereby hindered of his right". The jury in that case awarded substantial damages, though the plaintiff could prove no pecuniary loss and though the candidate for whom he intended to vote was duly elected without his vote. In cases like this, and in similar cases such as assault, libel, false imprisonment, substantial damages may be given

[1] [1936] Ch. 343.
[2] (1703) 1 Sm. L.C. (13th ed.), 253, 274.

for the infringement of the right, but also punitive damages may be given. By contrast, in actions for breach of contract, which also involve interference with a right, only nominal damages may be given, save in the exceptional case of breach of promise of marriage. From all such cases, the other main category must be distinguished; which consists of cases where there is no cause of action unless damage is proved, because otherwise no legal right is infringed. The most important class of this type is negligence, a tort of comparatively modern development as a separate head, but nowadays of the widest and most multifarious application. A man's negligence does not infringe another man's rights till it affects him by damaging him. A duty to be careful as against the other man is an essential element of negligence, but even if that duty is infringed the cause of action is not complete until there has been damage to the plaintiff. As I drive on the highway, every other driver owes me the duty of being careful not to collide with me, but I have no cause of action against the negligent driver who passes me and endangers my safety unless his negligence results in actual injury. I am disregarding questions of criminal liability. The rule is not justified merely because it is based on the old form of action in case, but on common sense and practical reasons. It is based on a juristic conception, not on a form of action.

I shall in the main be concerned with negligence. There are, however, other causes of action in which the cause of action is incomplete in the absence of damage, such as malicious prosecution, deceit, and conspiracy.

There are also many other torts which do not involve

The Liesbosch Case

physical injury to chattels or persons which have their own problems in the matter of damages. I shall not refer except incidentally to them. But there is one principle of universal application which I cannot do better than state in the words which Lord Sumner used in *Weld-Blundell's Case*.[1] He is dealing with a claim for damages for breach of contract in not keeping secret a libellous letter written by the plaintiff, which in consequence of the defendant's carelessness was put by a third party, who had accidentally come upon it, into the hand of the defamed party, who brought an action in libel against the plaintiff and recovered damages. The question was whether the plaintiff could recover what he had to pay in this way as damages for the defendant's breach of contract in not keeping the letter safely. It was held that the defendant was not liable for what had happened, because the repetition was the voluntary act of a free agent, just as much as if it had been stolen, so that the breach of contract was not the legal cause of the damage. Lord Sumner said: "The object of a civil inquiry into cause and consequence is to fix liability on some responsible person and to give reparation for damage done, not to inflict punishment for duty disregarded. The trial of an action for damage is not a scientific inquest into a mixed sequence of phenomena, or an historical investigation of the chapter of events by which Mr Weld-Blundell, the libeller of Messrs Comins and Lowe, came to be their judgment debtor." He goes on to say. "It is a practical inquiry, the object of which is to settle" that it was the defendant's doing which caused the loss to the plaintiff.

[1] [1920] A.C. at p. 986.

Such inquiry is *ex post facto*. The plaintiff must prove that he has suffered loss and must also prove that the loss which he claims is due in the eyes of the law to the wrong which the defendant has committed towards him. It must be shown that defendant's act has changed the actual set of conditions which existed before and apart from the act and that the plaintiff is actually affected to his detriment by that change in the actual conditions. This seems simple enough, but the problems constantly arising are concerned with what is often called remoteness of damage. When an act, say of negligence, operates directly on the plaintiff's property or person and damages it, it would seem there could be no further question. Like Lord Sumner, I prefer to use the word "direct" in such a case, rather than words like proximate. If a man is negligently run over and he dies of his injuries, I should call his death the direct result of the negligent act. His death may follow at an interval of time, at a hospital to which he has been carried, and where attempts have been made to save his life, but these complications are in themselves irrelevant. What has happened has happened according to the course of nature, as a result of the negligent impact on the man, he being what in fact he was and where he was. If he is frail and delicate, it is not pertinent to say that a stronger man would have recovered, nor is it pertinent to say that if he had been struck down in a place where he could have got more immediate and efficient medical attention, the injury would not have been fatal. Nothing but confusion seems to be introduced by using words like "natural" or "probable" or "reasonable" to qualify the consequences of the wrongful act. Every-

The Liesbosch Case

thing that happens in such a case happens in accordance with the laws of nature and must be natural. To ask whether it is probable or reasonable is to introduce a wrong point of view. The *ex post facto* investigation of what actually happened necessarily excludes questions of what would have seemed probable or reasonable, to an imaginary inquirer before the event hypothetically speculating on what would probably or reasonably happen if the wrong was committed. The facts have superseded any such speculations. Nor is it relevant to discuss whether what happened was ordinary or not. It did happen, and, *rebus sic stantibus*, must have happened in the ordinary course. The use of all these epithets which Lord Sumner condemns arises in fact from one or all of three possible confusions. One is that damages to be recoverable against a tortfeasor must be limited to what he could foresee. This I think is a fallacy, which I shall discuss at greater length later. The second confusion is a failure to distinguish between negligence and breach of contract. I disregard intentional wrongs, because I imagine no one argues that a man, who intentionally inflicts an injury, can qualify his wrong by claiming that he did more harm than he intended. But the damages for breach of contract have to be approached by determining first of all what degree of responsibility the contracting party assumed by his agreement, and this may exclude, in accordance with the rules of *Hadley* v. *Baxendale*,[1] certain portions of the actual damage, because from the point of view of the parties, when the contract is entered into, they may be treated as not ordinary or probable. It is a question of contract or consent, of

[1] (1854) 9 Ex. 341.

deliberation or free choice. But the essence of negligence is that the negligent person acts without due foresight or care, and hence it is irrelevant to presuppose a purely imaginary weighing of possible consequences or a deliberation that is quite inconsistent with the idea of negligence. A third possible confusion may arise from the fact that a pre-requisite to negligence is duty to the injured person, and a man cannot be held liable for breach of that duty unless the facts were such that a reasonable man is assumed by the law to be aware that danger will follow if he is not careful. That is a purely objective criterion and does not depend on the wrongdoer's actual state of mind. In Lord Sumner's words, this inquiry goes to culpability, not compensation.[1] The duty and breach being established by considering the facts at the date of the wrongdoing, the amount of compensation or damages must depend, subject to questions of remoteness, on what actually happened, and on the injury actually suffered by the victim, either in his person or in his property, as a result of the wrong, on the principle sometimes stated as *restitutio in integrum*. But this phrase, like most Latin phrases, needs much qualification. Apart from the rare cases, such as those in which specific restitution of chattels can be ordered, *restitutio* is by way of money payment, which is often far from giving adequate compensation; for instance, how can money compensate for the loss of health or a limb or life? But there are also certain limiting questions, generally referred to as questions of remoteness of damage. I have already indicated that injuries following directly from the act of wrongdoing are not remote,

[1] [1920] A.C. at p. 984.

The Liesbosch Case

because unanticipated, nor because distances in time and space are interposed, so long as the wrongful act is still in operation as the legal cause; thus the injury consequent on the negligent preparation of a drug may eventuate at the other side of the Atlantic and a month or months after it was delivered, so long as the person who suffers is the person or belongs to the class of persons contemplated or intended to use it and the character of the drug has not been affected by extraneous conditions. The course of events follows in fact from the act of negligence. But there may be new operative elements introduced by outside persons which may come between the tort and any effect on the person affected. These elements may in some cases simply co-operate, in which case they may not affect the responsibility of the original wrongdoer, whose tort remains still in effective operation. In other cases, the new elements may supersede the operation of the original act, so that it cannot be deemed to be a cause of the damage. Hence in the *ex post facto* investigation of the sequence of events, it may be necessary to define for purposes of the judicial inquiry the true cause of the damage, that which may be called the legal cause. Thus in *Weld-Blundell's Case* the original publication of the libel was not the legal cause of the subsequent publication, which was independent of the first publication, and was by independent persons in breach of their separate duty to the writer of the letter.

But there is another aspect of remoteness of damage, which relates to what are sometimes described as consequential damages. Where a thing or a person is tortiously subjected to physical destruction, loss or damage, there may be and perhaps generally is, in addition to the material injury, some disturbance or injury to the plaintiff's trade or occupation, or other activities causing financial or other loss; this loss, subject to certain limitations to be indicated later, may be a proper subject of compensation. I should like to describe such consequential loss as remote, to distinguish it from direct damage and further in order to divide it into two classes according as it is "remote" or "too remote", the latter epithet being used when it lies outside the compensation which the law allows. I need not point out that in certain torts such as deceit or conspiracy the damage is generally pecuniary, whereas in defamation the direct damage is to reputation.

It is sometimes said that the measure of damages in tort is the same as that in contract, taking the latter as fixed by the two rules in *Hadley* v. *Baxendale*,[1] but rejecting as inapplicable to cases in tort the second rule which requires notice to be given at the date of the contract of any special or peculiar circumstances which will involve enhanced damage to the plaintiff if the contract is broken. It is obvious that as a general proposition it cannot truly be stated that the measure of damage is the same in tort as in contract, because there is a large area of the law of tort which has no analogue in contract, such as libel, conspiracy to injure, interference with absolute rights and many other torts, including a vast number of cases of negligence. The statement, if true at all, can be true only of those claims in tort which may seem to overlap with, or to be alternative to, claims in contract, of which instances are claims against carriers of goods or passengers, where the action may be framed in

---

[1] (1854) 9 Ex. 341, 354.

The Liesbosch Case

contract or in negligence or conversion. And it is true that in many such cases the measure of damage would be the same whether the claim is framed in tort or in contract, as for instance in *Cobb* v. *Great Western Ry.*,[1] where the damage claimed would have been too remote in whatever form the cause of action was alleged because the wrongful act was not on the facts of the case the legal cause of the damage, which I think was what was meant by the epithets "direct and natural" applied to "consequence". But the starting-point for the two obligations, i.e. that in contract or that in tort, is different. In contract the question is what obligation has been assumed by the contractor, what is the extent of his duty? That depends on the terms of the contract, on the voluntary choice of the contractors, to be ascertained by the Court as a matter of objective construction. This may operate in two directions, to cut down or to extend the liability for damages. In contract, apart from express terms, there is the question of what may reasonably be held to have been in the contemplation of the parties when the contract was made. But this idea of contemplation is, I think, inapplicable in general to tortious acts, whether intentional or negligent, at least where the duty which is infringed is not based on contract, but arises under the general law in the facts of the case. The wrong being established, the only inquiry, which as I have said is *ex post facto*, is what is the direct damage, or the damage which is not too remote, *rebus sic stantibus*, taking the victim *talem qualem*, so that the contemplation of the parties, if it exists at all, is irrelevant. The wrong being established, the inquiry is not into what damage could be

[1] [1893] 1 Q.B. 459.

described as reasonable or probable as a matter of hypothetical foresight as at the date of the wrong, but when the event has happened, what damage has been actually caused, subject to the proviso that the causation must be what is called legal.

In stating these general principles, I feel at the back of my mind a sense of the infinite diversities of fact which have presented themselves, and will continue to present themselves, in case after case and affect the assessment of damages in each particular case. Nor do I here discuss such questions as assumption of risk, mitigation of damage, the victim's personal fault, or many others.

I can now turn to the subject of this lecture, the *Liesbosch Case*.[1] The facts in some respects were curious, but up to a certain point were sufficiently covered by authority. The *Edison*, owned by the defendants, was proceeding to sea out of the port of Patras in Greece, when she fouled the moorings of the *Liesbosch*, which was a dredger, and did not free them till she had carried the *Liesbosch* into the open sea, where, being without crew on board, she filled with water in the heavy sea that was running, sank and became a total loss. It was an unlucky coincidence that there was no one on board the *Liesbosch* at the time, but the *Edison* had to take her victim as in fact she was. There was no question that the loss of the dredger was directly caused by the negligence of the *Edison*, so that her value was recoverable. But beyond that there was the consideration that the loss of the dredger had interfered with the profitable contract with the port authorities on which her owners were employing her, and consequential damages were claimed under

[1] [1933] A.C. 449.

The Liesbosch Case

that head. In other words, the dredger was not merely a structure of steel, but a profit-earning chattel. Her value had to be determined not merely as scrap metal, but as a mechanism capable of profitable employment, and with the further element that she was at Patras at the date of the casualty and was actually being employed by her owners on a profitable contract. The judgment thus states the fundamental question (at p. 459): "The substantial issue is what in such a case as the present is the true measure of damage. It is not questioned that when a vessel is lost by collision due to the sole negligence of the wrongdoing vessel the owners of the former vessel are entitled to what is called *restitutio in integrum*, which means that they should recover such a sum as will replace them, so far as can be done by compensation in money, in the same position as if the loss had not been inflicted on them, subject to the rules of law as to remoteness of damage."

There was a novel point raised in the case which I shall reserve to be considered later, but up to a point the matter was clear, notwithstanding the contentions of the owners of the *Edison*, the respondents to the appeal. At this stage the contest can be thus stated, it being premised that in fact it was possible to buy on the market a dredger to take the place of the *Liesbosch*, though inevitably besides the purchase price there would be the cost of transport to Patras and some delay. Subject to the special point I have reserved, the conflicting views advanced were on the one hand by the wrongdoers that all that was recoverable was the market price of the dredger, together with the cost of transport to Patras, and on the other hand by the owners of the dredger that they were also entitled to damages in addition for loss due to interruption of the work during the period of inevitable delay before the substituted dredger could arrive and start work at Patras. That conflict was settled by what seems to me to be clear authority, though there had been some confusion in earlier cases, arising, I think, from the great variety of types of vessel in respect of which the question of damages might arise, and the different circumstances affecting them at the time of the accident, and also whether the case is one of total loss or of mere damage capable of repair but involving delay while repairs were being effected. Again, the vessel at the time of the accident might be neither in employment nor likely to secure employment in the near future, or might be a public ship like a ship of war or a lightship, not earning profits in the normal sense, though its user might have an ascertainable value reducible to terms of money. The multiplicity of circumstances which may have to be considered in any particular case makes it impossible to lay down any universal formula, though as Lord Sumner said in an earlier case "the measure of damages ought never to be governed by mere rules of practice, nor can such rules override the principles of law on this subject".[1] As I ventured to add in the *Liesbosch* judgment,[2] "the dominant rule of law is the principle of *restitutio in integrum*, and subsidiary rules can only be justified if they give effect to that rule", subject of course to rules as to remoteness and so forth. On that footing it is clear that the contention of the appellants was entitled to prevail, so that they were entitled to

[1] *Admiralty Commissioners* v. *S.S. Chekiang* [1926] A.C. 637, 643.
[2] [1933] A.C. at p. 463.

The Liesbosch Case

compensation for delay in performing their contract. In addition to the cases cited in the judgment, there is an illuminating judgment of Bowen L.J. in the *Argentino*,[1] afterwards affirmed by the House of Lords.[2] The importance of the case lies in the comparison of the dissenting judgment of Lord Esher M.R. with that of the judgment of the Court delivered by Bowen L.J. That was the case of damage to a ship, and consequent loss of her use for the time, but, as Bowen L.J. points out, there is no difference in principle between such a loss and that of the loss of any serviceable instrument consequent on its wrongful damage or detention. Lord Esher takes a narrow view of what is involved in *restitutio in integrum*. The conflict was whether damages could be recovered for the ship being compelled by the damage to abandon an engagement to load on the berth at Antwerp for Batoum. Lord Esher took the view that the loss of the future employment was not recoverable; he said,[3] "the existence of the agreement as to the future voyage is a circumstance which might or might not happen as joining the damage relied on to the act complained of, so that the condition as to the damage being the direct and immediate result of the act complained of is not fulfilled". Lord Justice Bowen rejects this criterion of what is the direct result, viz. a hypothetical or abstract ordinary vessel, and fixes on the actual circumstances of the particular record as fixing the compensation. He says:[4] "A ship is a thing by the use of which money may be ordinarily earned, and the only question in case of a collision seems to me to be, what is the use which the

[1] (1888) 13 P.D. 191.   [2] (1889) 14 App. Cas. 519.
[3] 13 P.D. at p. 199.   [4] *Ibid.* 201.

shipowner would, but for the accident, have had of his ship, and what (excluding the element of uncertain and speculative and special profits) the shipowner, but for the accident, would have earned by the use of her." Lord Justice Bowen is taking the actual facts of the case, the actual position of the vessel, so far as that is capable of ascertainment and is not too remote or speculative, that is, incapable of ascertainment, as he discusses later. The ordinary is the actual. He explains "special" later when he talks of all uncertain and special profits which might or might not be reaped in a particular speculation. But he is there concerned with the qualification of the element of damage, not with the definition of these elements. I think that Lord Herschell in the House of Lords is using "ordinary" in the same sense.[1] As is pointed out in the *Liesbosch* judgment it is impossible to talk of an ordinary vessel or the ordinary employment of a vessel, or indeed of a person or chattel. The actual characteristics of the particular subject-matter must be ascertained. I refer to all this simply as illustrating concretely what may be relevant to consider in assessing damages.

The actual facts were considered in the *Liesbosch Case*. The judgment points out that[2] "the *Liesbosch* was not under charter nor intended to be chartered, but in fact was being employed by the owners in the normal course of their business as civil engineers, as an essential part of the plant they were using in performance of their contract at Patras. Just as in the other cases considered, so in this, what the Court has to ascertain is the real value to the owner as part of his working plant, ignoring

[1] 14 App. Cas. at p. 623. [2] [1933] A.C. at pp. 465–466.

The Liesbosch Case

remote considerations at the time of loss. If it had been possible without delay to replace a comparable dredger exactly as and where the *Liesbosch* was, at the market price, the appellants would have suffered no damage save the cost of doing so, that is in such an assumed case the market price, the position being analogous to that of the loss of goods for which there is a presently available market. But that is in this case a merely fanciful idea. Apart from any consideration of the appellants' lack of means, some substantial period was necessary to procure at Patras a substituted dredger; hence, I think, the appellants cannot be restored to their position before the accident unless they are compensated (if I may apply the words of Lord Herschell in *The Greta Holme*),[1] 'in respect of the delay and prejudice caused to them in carrying out the works entrusted to them'. He adds: 'It is true these damages cannot be measured by any scale.' Lord Herschell was there dealing with damages in the case of a dredger which was out of use during repairs, but in the present case I do not think the Court are any the more entitled to refuse, on the ground that there is difficulty in calculation, to consider as an element in the value to the appellants of the dredger the delay and prejudice in which its loss involved them; nor is it enough to take the market value, that is, the purchase price (say, in Holland), even increased by the cost of transport, and add to that 5 per cent interest as an arbitrary measure. It is true that the dredger was not named in the contract with the Patras Harbour authority, nor appropriated to it; but it was actually being used, and was intended to be used, by the appellants for the contract work."

[1] [1897] A.C. 596, 605.

Legal Essays and Addresses

Hence the eventual decision (at p. 468) was that "the value of the *Liesbosch* to the appellants, capitalized as at the date of the loss, must be assessed by taking into account: (1) the market price of a comparable dredger in substitution; (2) costs of adaptation, transport, insurance, etc., to Patras; (3) compensation for disturbance and loss in carrying out their contract over the period of delay between the loss of the *Liesbosch* and the time at which the substituted dredger could reasonably have been available for use in Patras, including in that loss such items as overhead charges, expenses of staff and equipment, and so forth thrown away, but neglecting any special loss due to the appellants' financial position." But the last words referring to the financial position of the owners of the dredger involve the point by reason of which the decision is a leading case. Up to that stage it proceeded on well-recognized principles embodied in decisions like the *Argentino* and others cited. But the owners were short of funds and instead of doing what a solvent firm would have done, that is going at once into the market and buying a dredger in substitution for the *Liesbosch* and bringing it to Patras and resuming the contract work without unnecessary delay, they took a different course. They delayed in order to get financial help from the Harbour Authorities and eventually hired a dredger on very onerous terms. The registrar of the Admiralty Court and the judge both held that they could recover their actual loss on the basis of the wasteful procedure adopted because of their impecuniosity. The Court of Appeal and the House of Lords held that they could recover only such loss as would have been sustained by a prudent and solvent firm, which is what

The Liesbosch Case

was summarized as stated above. To this extent it may be said the actual position was disregarded and an artificial state of things assumed. The ordinary was substituted for the actual. How was this departure from the actual to be justified? Why was the owners' delicate financial position to be disregarded any more than the delicate physical state of a man run over and injured by negligence? The answer adopted by the House of Lords was that so far as loss was due to insolvency it was due to a cause which could be isolated from the other conditions and which was not a legal cause of the damage. In the practical *ex post facto* inquiry which the Court undertakes to assess damages, it necessarily abstracts from the complicated facts of the world a special segment, limited both in space and in time, and disregards everything else, or, more precisely, in a case like this it cuts out an actual happening or complication and substitutes a hypothetical state of affairs as that which would have prevailed if the actual complication had not existed. This is done in the interests of justice, because if the right to damages is clear, it would be unjust to deprive the plaintiff of what is fair merely because there have supervened conditions aggravating the damage which the law excludes from the category of legal causes. It is not possible to give any logical reason why the law disregards this particular element of financial incapacity which is part of the plaintiff's circumstances and substitutes the hypothetical for the actual. It does so in various other connections; thus where a payment of a debt is withheld, the creditor may be in such a difficult financial situation that he may be driven into bankruptcy, but all he can recover as damages is interest on the amount during the period of delay. I have never heard it suggested that the position is any different even if when the debt was contracted the debtor was informed of the creditor's position. Similarly, if a seller defaults in delivering the goods sold, the buyer, if there is a market, can recover only the difference between the contract and the market price if the market has risen, and only nominal damage if the market has fallen, even though he can show that want of money or credit would have prevented him from availing himself of the market and covering the default. It seems that in this way the common law for convenience, I suppose, will only deal with the damages on the footing that the plaintiff has access to sufficient funds and treats that as a necessary basis. As I said in my opinion (at pp. 460–461): "The respondents' tortious act involved the physical loss of the dredger; that loss must somehow be reduced to terms of money. But the appellants' actual loss in so far as it was due to their impecuniosity arose from that impecuniosity as a separate and concurrent cause, extraneous to and distinct in character from the tort; the impecuniosity was not traceable to the respondents' acts, and in my opinion was outside the legal purview of the consequences of these acts. The law cannot take account of everything that follows a wrongful act; it regards some subsequent matters as outside the scope of its selection, because 'it were infinite for the law to judge the cause of causes', or consequences of consequences. Thus the loss of a ship by collision due to the other vessel's sole fault, may force the shipowner into bankruptcy and that again may involve his family in suffering, loss of education or opportunities in life, but no such loss could

The Liesbosch Case

be recovered from the wrongdoer. In the varied web of affairs, the law must abstract some consequences as relevant, not perhaps on grounds of pure logic but simply for practical reasons. In the present case if the appellants' financial embarrassment is to be regarded as a consequence of the respondents' tort, I think it is too remote, but I prefer to regard it as an independent cause, though its operative effect was conditioned by the loss of the dredger. The question of remoteness of damage has been considered in many authorities and from many aspects, but no case has been cited to your Lordships which would justify the appellants' claim." Logic must yield to convenience in this as in other legal rules. A simple and uniform rule which generally works well may be preferred to having special rules to fit unusual cases. I ought, however, to notice certain not very clear observations of Lord Collins in *Clippens Oil Company* v. *Edinburgh and District Water Trustees*.[1] Lord Collins is there dealing with the plaintiffs' duty to minimize damages and is putting the case where the plaintiff was unable to avail himself of remedial measures because of lack of funds. He indicates a possible view that as "the wrongdoer must take his victim *talem qualem* and if the position of the latter is aggravated because he is without the means of mitigating it, so much the worse for the wrongdoer, who has got to be answerable for the consequences flowing from his tortious act". This is obviously a different line of approach. It does not consider whether the impecuniosity is a separate cause to be abstracted from the actual conditions, but treats the damage as having accrued irrespective of the impecuniosity

---

[1] [1907] A.C. 291, 306.

which is only relevant to the question of mitigating damage. The duty to do so is only to do what is reasonable, as for instance in *Finlay & Co., Ltd.* v. *Kwik Hoo Tong, etc.*,[1] and did not extend to enforcing a legal right which would damage the plaintiffs' business reputation because it would be contrary as the facts stood to business fair dealing. It may be that Lord Collins' view may be justified on some such ground, but the House of Lords did not think it affected their judgment in the case before them. There is in my opinion a real difference between impecuniosity and physical weakness of the plaintiff, which as I have already indicated may aggravate the loss caused. The relationship between the injury and the result is in the latter case direct; the act operates immediately on an actual state of material conditions; an instance is *Polemis* v. *Furness Withy & Co.*[2] A steamer was totally destroyed by fire caused by a heavy plank being allowed by the negligence of stevedores to fall into a hold laden with tins of benzine which had leaked on the voyage. The facts were stated in an Award, in particular that the fire was caused by a spark produced by the board, the falling of which was due to the negligence of the defendants' stevedores, and that the causing of the spark could not reasonably have been anticipated, though some damage to the ship might reasonably have been anticipated. The case accordingly raised precisely the question whether a man could be held liable for consequences neither intended nor probable. It was held by the arbitrators, the judge and the Court of Appeal (despite my arguments as counsel) that the defendants were liable. It was held to be relevant to the

[1] [1929] 1 K.B. 400.   [2] [1921] 3 K.B. 560.

The Liesbosch Case

question whether an act was negligent to determine whether a reasonable man would foresee that the act would or might probably cause damage. That goes to culpability or liability. Once it is found there is negligence, then the fact that the exact operation of the negligent act was not foreseen is immaterial, so long as the damage is traceable directly to the act. That goes to compensation. Indeed, with respect to the distinguished names who have taken the opposite view, I do not see how foreseeability matters once a duty to be careful towards the victim is made out, and the damage sustained is within the principles of legal cause. I am not clear what foreseeability means. The question does not arise in respect of intentional torts. In the case of negligence, it cannot mean the state of mind of the actor, because negligence implies lack of foresight and care. It would not help to postulate the hypothetical reasonable man, even if we also endow him with knowledge of the actual conditions on which the act operates, and then being *ex hypothesi* a reasonable man he would see that the consequences which followed were natural and ordinary and thus the natural or ordinary and the actual mean the same thing. So far as authority goes in England, the principle was established in the sense I have stated in *Smith* v. *London & South Western Ry.*,[1] which indeed involved this further complication that the negligent act was one which did mischief only when operated on by another event, the danger of which, however, was probable. The plaintiff's cottage was destroyed by fire, which had spread to it from a heap of dry grass left near the railway line where it was liable to be ignited by

[1] (1870) L.R. 6 C.P. 14.

sparks from passing locomotives and was so ignited. It was held that the danger should have been apparent to the defendants' servants when they left the heap. There was negligence and the spread of the fire was the direct consequence in the actual conditions of that negligence. This clearly involves a further complication: a plaintiff cannot complain of negligence unless the defendant owes to him a duty of due care. In *Smith's Case* the Court held there was such a duty, I suppose because of the relative position of the cottage, though it was separated from the heap of grass by a field over which in fact the fire spread. In cases of this character a question must always be whether the plaintiff can reasonably be regarded as within the range of the act of negligence. In considering if there is negligence towards the plaintiff the question must always be decided on the basis of what a reasonable man would understand as distinguished from the extent of damage for which there may be responsibility. Whether there is a duty to a particular plaintiff may be difficult to decide. Such a difficulty is illustrated by a case cited by Professor Goodhart in one of his excellent essays on the law of damages.[1] It is the *Palsgraf Case* in the New York Courts.[2] A railway guard in assisting a passenger to board a train knocked a package from his arms. In fact, though the porter did not know, it contained fireworks which exploded. The explosion caused a disturbance of the air which knocked over some scales some considerable distance away, and these in falling injured a woman who was on the station premises in order to travel by the defendants' line. It was held by a majority of the Court that the plaintiff

[1] *Essays in Jurisprudence*, ch. VII.   [2] (1928) 248 N.Y. 339.

The Liesbosch Case

was outside the radius of the duty. Cardozo C.J. said: "One who seeks redress at law does not make out a cause of action by showing without more that there has been damage to his person. If the harm was not wilful, he must show that the act as to him had possibilities of danger so many and apparent as to entitle him to be protected against the doing of it though the harm was unintended." The essential words here are "as to him". I remember a Petition for special leave to appeal coming before the Privy Council when I was sitting. An unfortunate man happened to step on board a barge lying alongside the quay at a port on one of the Great Lakes for some quite irrelevant purpose, such as speaking to a friend. The barge had been used for carrying petrol and had been washed out, leaving an inflammable vapour in the hold. This by some chance exploded and the man was terribly injured. The Canadian Courts decided that there was no duty owed to him and the Privy Council refused to give leave to appeal. It seems pretty obvious in such a case that whatever negligence in other directions there may have been, no duty was owed to that plaintiff. But it is clear that many difficult questions may arise in cases of this character. An instructive illustration may be taken from the American *Restatement of the Law of Torts*, Volume II, p. 1176, sec. 435. I may thus summarize it. B is a workman engaged in repairing the pilings of a bridge. He is seen by the captain of a steamer approaching the bridge to be so engaged. Hence arises the duty of the captain towards the workman to take due care in navigating the steamer so as not to throw down or injure him. The steamer, being navigated negligently, runs into the bridge and the man is killed. The manner of the accident causing death was not however foreseeable by the captain. The plank on which the man was working had been in fact held in position by being forced in between the pilings. The impact of the vessel caused the pilings to spring apart. This caused the plank to fall and B with it. The plank being removed, the pilings came together and crushed B to death. This was the direct damage due to the breach of the duty. The duty was apparent, but the damages, though not foreseeable, were direct and were recoverable. There are so many cases of such infinitely varied character which can be imagined and in which it may be asked whether there was a duty to any one and if so whether there was a duty to the plaintiff, or again in which it may be asked whether the kind of damage which ensued was so far removed from any kind of damage that could reasonably be imagined that *quoad* such risk or damage it could not properly be said there was any duty to take care. I should not like to dogmatize. My experience has taught me to hesitate to lay down absolute formulae. The case of *Polemis* was one dealing with a dangerous explosive condition in which anything might happen in the way of fire if a spark were anyhow let loose. The *Smith Case* also dealt with fire. (The *Palsgraf Case* also dealt with explosives.) I do not wish to water down the rule which distinguishes culpability or liability from compensation, but I feel that there may be refinements which may need special consideration, particularly in the direction of questioning the existence of any duty or of limiting it, so that there may be a duty in respect of certain matters but not in respect of others.

The Liesbosch Case

A small act may produce the most momentous results, as when a town is burnt down because an old woman upsets a cooking stove, or a light blow may in certain physical conditions cause a person's death. An act may propagate itself over a wide area and a prolonged sequence, and the damage which follows in the "ordinary" or "natural" course may because of extraordinary conditions appear most staggering. As a single illustration let me mention *Banco de Portugal* v. *Waterlow & Sons, Ltd.*,[1] which was a case of breach of contract. The defendants were a firm of printers of international repute as printers of bank notes. The plaintiffs employed them to print notes for them. They were induced by an extremely ingenious fraud to print and deliver to the criminals, who, they believed, were acting for the Bank, a batch of 580,000 notes exactly similar to an existing issue which they had printed for the Bank. The criminals put the false notes into circulation. The true issue and the false issue were identical in form. The fraud was discovered and no one in Portugal could be sure whether the notes of that denomination which he held were genuine or false notes. To save the credit of the currency the Bank called in all the notes of that issue, genuine or false, and gave in exchange other notes of another issue of the same face value, on which the Bank of course were liable. All Courts in England held unanimously that the breach of contract in printing notes without the Bank's actual authority was the legal cause of the damage. The circumstances were most extraordinary. No one could in advance have dreamt of such a strange series of events. In one sense the Bank created the damage by calling in all the notes of that character. But it was

[1] [1932] A.C. 452.

necessary to do so in order to save their credit. The Bank's action might be compared to that of a man cutting off a limb in order to save his life endangered by a wrongful injury, which would generally be held to constitute damage directly caused by the injury inflicted on him. In other words what are ordinary or natural or proximate consequences of a wrongful act may appear most extraordinary until the actual conditions are realized. Similarly, in a not unusual action for breach of contract for the sale of goods, the measure of damages may seem surprising. If there is a market, there is the conventional measure of the difference in market price which generally does justice. If there is no market, there remains only the standard of actual loss, subject to the second rule in *Hadley* v. *Baxendale*.[1] But in ascertaining such actual loss where there has been at the date of the contract no notice of special circumstances which will aggravate the damage in the event of breach so as to bring home to the seller that he is assuming that risk of damage of the defaults, the Court takes account of actual circumstances and treats them as ordinary for purposes of the contract and breach. Thus in *Grébert-Borgnis* v. *Nugent*,[2] the plaintiff had bought goods for resale in France as the sellers knew. They made default and the plaintiff recovered both his loss of profit and the damage he had to pay to their sub-buyers. That was not a special risk of which special notice had to be given when the contract was made. It was deemed to have been in the reasonable contemplation of the parties to the contract. The same result may follow where there is no reference as between buyer and

---

[1] (1854) 9 Ex. 341.
[2] (1885) 15 Q.B.D. 85.

The Liesbosch Case

seller to the fact that the purchase is for resale, if the buyer is a merchant who normally buys for resale.

But I must not pursue the ramifications of this subject any farther. All I have attempted to do is to discuss one small corner of the subject and a very few cases. So far as I have stated general propositions, I feel that each one needs qualification and that though I have sought to state the law in accordance with the authorities and judicial observations, I have not given effect to every refinement or sought to harmonize every inconsistency. I can only hope that the general survey may be a guide to closer study.

V

THE *NORTHWESTERN UTILITIES CASE*[1]

BEFORE I proceed to examine the decision which I have chosen as the text of this lecture, I ought to preface some general observations which will help to explain it. A maxim has been frequently repeated that there is no liability without *culpa*. That may be regarded as a statement of an ideal of what the law should be, or of the existing law. In the latter sense it is demonstrably inaccurate, whether we look at the old or the modern common law. As to the old law it is enough to say that the writ of trespass was not based either on intention or on negligence. It was prima facie enough to found liability, apart from certain special defences, that there had been, for instance, a trespass by the defendant on the plaintiff's land or an assault on his person. An absolute right of property or some other absolute right had been interfered with. So also in nuisance or in trespass to goods. In modern law, there is a wide range of cases in which negligence on the part of the defendant is not an essential element for recovery in tort, and if negligence in this context is taken to mean not only the personal negligence of the defendant but also his vicarious liability for the negligence of others, the range is enormously greater. Then there is the wide field covered by the rule in *Rylands* v. *Fletcher*,[2] which will be

[1] A lecture delivered in the Harvard Law School, 3 October 1938.
[2] (1868) L.R. 3 H.L. 330.

The Northwestern Utilities Case

examined later, and by the liability to employees which the common law has superimposed on statutory provisions enacted wholly or in part for their protection, such as those under the Factory Acts for the fencing of dangerous machinery, supporting roofs of mines, and many others. These forms of liability have been created by the common law, but in addition modern legislation has imposed duties the non-performance of which cannot be excused by saying that it was not due to negligence, and liabilities where compensation is payable for accidental injuries to particular persons, irrespective of negligence, as in the Workmen's Compensation Acts. A more recent illustration is afforded by the Air Navigation Act, 1920,[1] which makes the owner of aircraft absolutely liable for all damage done by it while in flight, in taking off or in landing, to person or property, without proof of negligence or intention or other cause of action as though the same had been caused by his wilful act, neglect or default. Thus we see both by statute and under the common law a tendency to enlarge the sphere of liability irrespective of intention or negligence. This tendency has been deplored in certain quarters. It has been said to be unmoral, and contrary to the spirit of the law because, it is said, the object of the civil law is to punish an offender by compelling him to make pecuniary compensation and that it is futile to punish any one who has not a guilty mind. But this attitude has been rejected by the law in civil cases. What the law aims at in the area of torts is compensation, not punishment. I disregard the limited class of cases in which not merely compensatory but punitive damages may be

[1] 10 & 11 Geo. 5, c. 80, s. 9.

given, where indeed in assessing the damages a moral element may be imported. But in tortious actions of the very extensive and important classes which I have indicated, the state of mind of the defendant is, generally speaking, immaterial. The liability is the same whether he personally acts or not, or whether he, or his agent, acts with intention or with negligence. The maxim "no liability without *culpa*" can be squared with the actual law which operates over a wide range, only if *culpa* is interpreted as meaning legal liability, which makes the phrase meaningless and tautological. It is in one sense curious that in the modern law there has been so enormous a development of the law of negligence, especially now that it is regarded as a substantive tort and not merely as an ingredient in specific torts. It is obvious that though the forms of action have been abolished in England and, as I understand, in a large part of the United States, the cases decided before this abolition are still precedents, many of the greatest value, but they are not precedents because of the forms of action, but rather in spite of them. They are precedents because they embody a juristic principle of permanent value, such as trespass, deceit, defamation or nuisance. But no one now distinguishes trespass or nuisance from trespass on the case or nuisance on the case. These distinctions, which were all-important when the forms of action prevailed, are now meaningless. I think when Maitland said that though the forms are dead, they rule us from their graves,[1] he was lamenting that it should be so because he was thinking that they might prevent the ascertainment of the true juristic conceptions. In that sense I agree

[1] *Forms of Action* (1936), 2.

The Northwestern Utilities Case

with what he said. But negligence, which began to be developed as an independent tort about the end of the first quarter of the nineteenth century, has become now one of the most widely used and flexible instruments in the hands of the law. The juristic conception is simplicity itself. Did the defendant owe a duty in the matter to the plaintiff, did he break the duty, did the plaintiff thereby suffer damage? These three elements sum up the doctrine. All the plaintiff has to do is to allege in his pleading and to prove the material facts on which he relies; he need specify no form or formula. The diverse circumstances in which this cause of action may be applied are almost as infinite as the possible varieties of fact. There is now a tendency to bring almost every case (that is of course excluding particular matters like fraud or deceit, or libel) within the range of negligence. Hence the disposition to look askance at cases of strict or absolute liability (that is, where negligence is immaterial) and if possible to bring them within the fold of negligence, and to that extent the tendency to moralize the law is apparent. But the opposite tendency is also strong. Take the vicarious responsibility of an employer or master for the negligence of his employees or servants. The recognition of this principle (which is to be found as early as the time of Lord Chief Justice Holt) and its modern wide extension are necessary in view of modern conditions. A large part of the affairs of the world is conducted by corporations or large employers, so that the actual operations must necessarily be performed by employees of various grades. Hence the inevitability of the rule that the employer must answer for the defaults of his or its employees, so long as they are committed in the course of the employment. Otherwise the person injured would mostly have no effective redress against any one. The justice of this principle is explained on the ground that the employer, who for his own benefit extends his activities and the scope of his operations by employing his subordinate instruments, should bear the loss of injuries suffered by those wronged by the action of those agents so long as what they did was done in the course of the employment, which depends on the objective character of what they did, not on their intention to serve the employer. This is true in many cases where the law would not permit the employer to do the work himself, where he must act through servants or agents, e.g. his ship must by law be navigated by a certificated shipmaster, his mines must be managed by a certificated manager. In fact also, and apart from the law, the great mass of operations in a modern industrial or commercial business can be performed only by expert or highly qualified employees and are quite outside the capacity of the owners of the business. In all these and other cases, though performance of the operation neither is nor can be personal, the obligation for due discharge of it is personal to the employer. He may, perhaps must, delegate the performance, but he cannot delegate the liability. This conception that the liability for injury should rest on the shoulders most able to bear it and most able to discharge obligations to compensate, and on the person who profits by the multifarious activities which he or it has called into operation, is also extended beyond the case of employers in the ordinary sense, so as to place liability on the employer or undertaker for the acts of independent contractors in regard to activities or operations

The Northwestern Utilities Case

which are inherently dangerous. This conception is also at the bottom of the doctrine that he should be liable who has created for his own purposes a special set of conditions on land, which may spread or escape beyond the land even without negligence and thereby damage others. This is what is called the *Rylands* v. *Fletcher*[1] principle. In other words the law imposes the obligation on purely objective considerations, without considering the personal state of mind, the carefulness or want of care, of the defendant himself or itself (if it is a corporation). It comes by a different process of development to the same general principle of liability that in old days it arrived at in such cases as cattle trespass, nuisance, trespass or conversion. This development has followed naturally and inevitably from modern conditions, especially industrial and commercial conditions. This is obvious if we compare for one moment with the simple rural or small trade life of old times the modern complex world, particularly in industrial matters.

Northwestern Utilities v. *London Guarantee Company, Ltd.* [1936] A.C. 108, is a good illustration both of the limits of the *Rylands* v. *Fletcher*[1] doctrine and how the doctrine, where it fails, may be supplemented by the concept of negligence so as to impose liability.

The facts in the case can be shortly stated. The Northwestern Utilities Company was a Canadian Company, which distributed natural gas under a franchise in the City of Edmonton in Alberta, Canada. In the course of their operations, acting within their powers, they laid a 12-inch gas main within the City, carrying gas under pressure. The main was laid at a depth of 3 ft. 6 in. At

[1] (1868) L.R. 3 H.L. 330.

one place it was necessary to lay the pipe with three welded joints, each in the space of an excavation, into which sections of the pipe had been pushed or pulled through the tunnel, the earth being back-filled. This was done in 1923. In 1932, it was noticed that gas was escaping from the pipe into the Corona Hotel. The gas ignited and the hotel was burned down and adjoining premises were damaged. On opening up the ground it was found that one of the welds on the pipe had given way, and that the pipe had sagged $6\frac{1}{2}$ in. The gas had thus escaped and percolated through the soil and found its way into the hotel basement. The sagging of the pipe was traced to the operations of the City in constructing a new storm sewage system immediately beneath the main and in the way of the joint. This was in 1931. The Court held that though these operations were underground, it was obvious to the outside world that they were being conducted, because they were necessarily done from the surface and the nature of the workings was apparent. The claim in the action was primarily based on the principle laid down in *Rylands* v. *Fletcher* (1868) L.R. 3 H.L. 330, affirming *Fletcher* v. *Rylands* (1866) L.R. 1 Ex. 265. The precise nature and limits of this doctrine may be considered rather more closely later in this lecture, but in effect it imposes a strict or absolute liability, not dependent on negligence (still less on intention), on a person who maintains on land a dangerous thing or substance. It is not unlawful so to do, but if it escapes from the limits of the land and does damage to another, then, subject to certain defences, the cause of action is complete. The liability is in some ways analogous to liability for nuisance where also negligence is

The Northwestern Utilities Case

not essential, but it is different in its legal character and history and in many of its incidents and applications. Thus, for instance, nuisance covers a wider range, including things like noise or smoke, to which the doctrine of *Rylands* v. *Fletcher* does not extend, and also such wrongs as interference with light. That doctrine of *Rylands* v. *Fletcher* is based on the fact that the subject-matter is likely to be dangerous and to do damage if it escapes. Here, beyond question, the gas was in that sense dangerous, because of its inflammable and explosive character. Nor is the doctrine limited to things maintained by a person on his own land, or on land of which he is tenant. Thus in the present case, all the interest, if it may be so called, which the Company had in the soil was the licence to lay and use the pipe line. It was not disputed that damage was caused by the escape of the gas from the pipe, operating on the actual existing conditions, that is, by percolating through the soil and so reaching the hotel basement, where it was exposed to the risk of meeting a naked light. When that occurred, there resulted a fire which spread to, and destroyed, the hotel and adjoining premises.

So far the liability of the Company might seem plain. But there were various complications to be considered. It has been held that the doctrine of *Rylands* v. *Fletcher* is not to be extended. Judges felt, not perhaps quite logically when analogous doctrines of strict liability are remembered, that the effect of the doctrine was likely to be oppressive. I suppose the feeling was due to a prejudice against liability without negligence, though as I have explained there are in the old law many classes of liability without negligence. Hence the Courts have introduced many qualifications of the liability, which a defendant may set up by way of defence. The defences relied on by the defendants in this case were (1) that the escape of the gas was due to the conscious act of a third party, that is, the City Corporation, in disturbing the adjacent and subjacent soil and thus causing the pipe to sag. Such a defence has been recognized as good in certain cases. Thus it has been held that the escape of water from a reservoir maintained by the defendants did not render them liable, if the escape was due to the act of a stranger in diverting a stream into it.[1] The same would be true if the casualty was due to the act of God, such as a flooding caused by a torrential rain of such a character that it would not be negligence to fail to foresee and guard against it.[2] The act of the third person in such cases need not be malicious in the sense that the person intended to produce the damage that ensued from his act. It is enough that it was his conscious and deliberate act, done for his own purposes without any thought of ulterior consequences to others. Thus in the present case the City had no idea of damaging the Company's pipes. Though their action may have been negligent as against the Company, that was immaterial as between the Company and the owners of the property destroyed. But (2) there was a further defence *prima facie* available. The Company laid their pipes under statutory powers given by a Canadian Utilities Act. In a number of cases it has been held that a person maintaining a dangerous thing under statutory powers may plead these powers as a

---

[1] *Box* v. *Jubb* (1879) 4 Ex. D. 76.

[2] *Nichols* v. *Marsland* (1875) L.R. 10 Ex. 255; the decision (but not its principle) was criticized in *Greenock Corporation* v. *Caledonian Ry.* [1917] A.C. 556.

The Northwestern Utilities Case

justification for what he does, but only so long as he is exercising these powers without negligence. Whether this is so depends on the construction of the statute giving the powers.[1] The *prima facie* presumption is that he is not to be liable if in exercising the powers he does so with due and reasonable care. He is thus not subject to the strict duty under *Rylands* v. *Fletcher*. The statute gives the authority to do the act but the authority does not generally extend beyond doing it in a proper and reasonable manner unless it is clearly provided that even negligence is not to impose liability. I question if that has ever been done.[2] It accordingly became necessary to consider the special statute under which the Company acted. The Court held that the authority of the Utilities Company was subject to the obligation to use reasonable care.

I disregard a contention which was raised by the Company but rejected by the Court, namely, that as the hotel people were supplied with the gas they had a common interest with the Company in the operations necessary to supply the gas and that they must be taken to have consented to the risk. The Court, while recognizing that in particular conditions a plaintiff may be found to have consented to take the risk of a potentially dangerous installation, held that this was not so where there was on the one hand a commercial undertaking supplying the utility for profit to the whole township, and on the other hand individual consumers merely taking the supply offered them in common with other townsfolk.

So far as the argument has now gone the Company

---

[1] Cf. *Green* v. *Chelsea Waterworks Co.* (1894) 70 L.T. 547 with *Charing Cross Electricity Co.* v. *Hydraulic Power Co.* [1914] 3 K.B. 772.
[2] So Lord Blackburn in *Geddis' Case* (1878) 3 App. Cas. at pp. 455-456.

then were entitled to defend themselves on the grounds that the trouble was due to the act of the City and also on the fact that they had statutory authority to carry the gas as they did in the pipe. But that still left the issue whether they had acted without negligence. If they were guilty of negligence in not observing and guarding against the act of the City in disturbing the soil in which the pipe lay, neither defence would avail them. Hence came the final and crucial issue on which the Company was held responsible for the damage, which amounted to something like $300,000, on the ground that they had been negligent. It was not that there was any negligence in laying the pipe. The negligence was held to be this. The gas being carried at high pressure was dangerous if it escaped and was likely to damage neighbouring premises, hence a duty to the owners or occupiers of these premises to take care in order to prevent such damage. The degree of care required must correspond to the degree of risk involved if the duty were not fulfilled. This liability is obviously different from the strict liability under *Rylands* v. *Fletcher*, because it was based on proof of want of due care. The Court held that the Company, by their engineers, ought to have observed the obvious signs that the City were working underground in the vicinity of their pipes, and ought to have examined the soil and the pipes likely to be affected so as to see that no disturbance had been caused to the pipes. They did nothing at all. Thereby they were guilty of negligence. Thus after a devious process of argument, their liability was established.

I turn now to consider *Rylands* v. *Fletcher*[1] itself. The

[1] (1868) L.R. 3 H.L. 330.

The Northwestern Utilities Case

facts were simple enough. A mill-owner constructed on his land a reservoir. Under the land where the reservoir was constructed there were some disused mining passages, both vertical and horizontal. The water of the reservoir escaped through these passages and flooded the mines of an adjoining owner. The mill-owner was not guilty of any want of care, though it was found that the independent contractors whom he employed were so guilty. The mill-owner was held to be liable for the damage, irrespective of any proof of negligence. The principle is not merely that expressed in the old maxim " Sic utere tuo ut alienum non laedas". English law has not accepted the doctrine that harm caused by one person to another is even prima facie sufficient, though Lord Cranworth seems to state that view, where he says: "When one person, in managing his own affairs, causes, however innocently, damage to another, it is obviously only just that he should be the party to suffer."[1] This is not a correct statement of English law, which requires more to found a cause of action, because it requires a duty and a breach of that duty. The peculiarity of the *Rylands* v. *Fletcher* rule is that, like other duties which I have referred to, it is an absolute or strict duty, irrespective of negligence. The difficulty has been to define the exact limits and definition of this exceptional duty. The case is not a case of abuse of rights. There is no question of malice. The landowner is doing only what he is entitled to do and is free from offence so long as the mischievous thing or animal[2] does not escape from his

---

[1] (1868) L.R. 3 H.L. at p. 341.
[2] The rule in *Rylands* v. *Fletcher* is often taken to include liability in tort for (i) cattle trespass and (ii) savage animals. But both these forms of

control and from his borders and do damage. He rightfully does what he does on his own land (apart from any criminal responsibility) but only subject to the duty to his neighbours that the thing or animal does not escape to his neighbour's detriment. That defines both the duty and the persons to whom it is owed. It is an exceptional duty. The difficulty is to define the conditions under which it comes into effect. It is clear that the thing (or animal) must be of such a nature as to be likely to cause the damage. This is obviously true of the water collected in the reservoir; it is also true of savage animals, whether or not they are *ferae naturae*. But it is clear that more is wanted to constitute the necessary conditions of liability. The difficulty is to define what that is. If Lord Cairns had been challenged to say how far he would go when he gave judgment on *Rylands* v. *Fletcher*, he might have retorted "as far as this case". In doing so he would follow the practice, so often criticized as the mark of English judges, of preferring a finding of fact to a comprehensive or dogmatic statement of principle. But Lord Cairns does attempt a further definition by using certain epithets, by way of exclusion or negative limitation. Thus he speaks of natural user of the land or use for any purpose for which the land might in the ordinary course of its enjoyment be used as a circumstance excluding the principle. But the difficulty of using such adjectives is that they are relative. "Ordinary" is meaningless unless a standard can be applied to define what is extraordinary; if natural refers to the product of merely

liability are distinct in historical origin and frequently in practical application from liability under *Rylands* v. *Fletcher*. Cf. Winfield, *Text-Book on Tort*, 539–540, 550–551.

The Northwestern Utilities Case

natural processes, it may afford some negative help, but there may be artificial uses to which the rule does not apply and some natural products to which the rule has been applied, as I shall illustrate in a moment. The rule has been applied to gas,[1] electricity[2] and water[3] when carried in bulk, fire,[4] oil,[5] rusty wire from a decayed fence,[6] a sort of revolving swing-boat at a fair,[7] poisonous vegetation,[8] noxious fumes,[9] but not to water, gas or electricity when carried in pipes or tubes in tenement buildings in the manner which is now normal in modern life. Thus where the tenant of lower premises in an apartment house was damaged by the escape of water from a cistern or lavatory in the upper part of the building the rule of liability was not applied:[10] and the same result has followed where an adjoining tenant in the same premises has had a fire caused in his premises by the escape of electric current from his neighbour's electric installation.[11] This distinction seems to turn on considerations of common sense, for instance that water, gas,[12] or electricity are normally carried in the premises

[1] *Batchellor* v. *Tunbridge Wells Gas Co.* (1901) 84 L.T. 765. *Dominion Natural Gas Co.* v. *Collins* [1909] A.C. 640.
[2] *National Telephone Co.* v. *Baker* [1893] 2 Ch. 186. *Eastern and S. African Telegraph Co., Ltd.* v. *Cape Town Tramways Co., Ltd.* [1902] A.C. 381.
[3] *Rylands* v. *Fletcher* (1868) L.R. 3 H.L. 330.
[4] *Jones* v. *Festiniog Ry.* (1868) L.R. 3 Q.B. 733.
[5] *Smith* v. *G.W.Ry.* (1926) 135 L.T. 112.
[6] *Firth* v. *Bowling Iron Co.* (1878) 3 C.P.D. 254.
[7] *Hale* v. *Jennings* [1938] 1 All E.R. 579.
[8] *Crowhurst* v. *Amersham Burial Board* (1878) 4 Ex. D. 5. *Ponting* v. *Noakes* [1894] 2 Q.B. 281.
[9] *West* v. *Bristol Tramways Co.* [1908] 2 K.B. 14.
[10] *Ross* v. *Fedden* (1872) L.R. 7 Q.B. 661.
[11] *Collingwood* v. *H. & C. Stores* (1936) 155 L.T. 550.
[12] *Marshall* (or *Miller*) v. *Robert Addie & Sons' Collieries*, 1934 S.C. 150.

of each tenant in such quantities as are necessary for his ordinary use. Thus the element of reciprocity may be invoked, and also it has been said that the risk is a normal and ordinary incident which every one so situated may be taken to accept. The standard of what is ordinary is supplied by the usual habits of mankind in such circumstances. In *Blake* v. *Woolf*,[1] the judge said of the *Rylands* v. *Fletcher* rule: "That general rule is, however, qualified by some exceptions, one of which is that, where a person is using his land in the ordinary way and damage happens to the adjoining property without any default or negligence on his part, no liability attaches to him." He was using "ordinary" in the sense I have indicated, but I should prefer to say of such a case not that the rule is qualified, but that its conditions do not exist. Hence Lord Moulton in *Rickards* v. *Lothian*[2] says: "It is not every use to which land is put that brings into play that principle. It must be some special use bringing with it increased danger to others, and must not merely be the ordinary use of the land or such a use as is proper for the general benefit of the community." These words, not very precise in themselves, get their colour from the context in which they are used, which was one of the many cases of water carried in pipes in a tenement or apartment house escaping to a lower floor without negligence on the part of the defendant. The same principle, as I have said, has been applied to electric current under similar circumstances. With these cases may be contrasted the cases where the rule has in principle been applied where gas or water or electricity has been carried on a large scale for industrial purposes or purposes of

---

[1] [1898] 2 Q.B. 426, 438.   [2] [1913] A.C. at p. 280.

The Northwestern Utilities Case

profit, as for instance in the mains of gas or water or electric companies. In such cases the rule has been held to apply, subject to the recognized exceptions. On the other side of the picture may be mentioned *Noble* v. *Harrison*,[1] where the plaintiff proceeding along a highway was injured by a branch falling on him. The branch, which overhung the highway, belonged to a tree on the border of the defendant's park. The Court refused to apply the *Rylands* v. *Fletcher* doctrine upon which it was sought to rely. It was clear that the defect which caused the branch to fall was latent, so that no negligence could be attributed to the landowner. The Court held that such a branch was not a dangerous thing, that it was an ordinary incident of the countryside in no way unusual, and the result of natural growth.

The constituent elements of the rule may be stated to be (1) that the thing is dangerous if it escapes from the land of the party who kept or maintained it there, (2) that the keeping or maintenance is of an exceptional character, having regard to the usual practice of the common run of mankind. This is very far from precise, but read with the decided cases it gives a working guide to the Court. Things of natural growth are not generally of an exceptional character, but even such things may bring the rule into operation, when either planted by or maintained on his land (that is allowed to grow) by the defendant, such as poisonous weeds or trees. On the other hand some natural objects, such as ferocious animals, which are essentially products of nature, involve the rule.[2] It is not wrong for a man to keep them on his

---

[1] [1926] 2 K.B. 332.
[2] At any rate according to some judges and writers.

land, but if they escape he is under the strict or absolute liability. Of such animals, long ago Sir Matthew Hale in 1 *Pleas of the Crown*, 430, stated the rule to the effect that the keeper of a ferocious dog, if he knows it to be ferocious, is in exactly the same category as the keeper of a naturally wild animal. As to a naturally wild animal it had been laid down more than twenty years before *Rylands* v. *Fletcher* in *May* v. *Burdett*,[1] that the owner must at his peril keep it safe from doing harm, for though he use his diligence to keep it in, if it escapes and does mischief, damage is presumed without express averment. To say that damage is presumed is to say that it is not a necessary part of the cause of action. This states in special reference to dangerous animals, *mutatis mutandis*, the principle of *Rylands* v. *Fletcher*. That was indeed no novel doctrine. It had long been applied to fire; a man may light a fire on his own land, so long as he sees that it does not escape and damage his neighbour. In *Rylands* v. *Fletcher* reference was made to the ancient action for cattle trespass. Two cases were also cited in the House of Lords in *Rylands* v. *Fletcher* to illustrate the difference between natural and artificial processes;[2] both were cases where a mine had been flooded by water coming from adjoining premises. The effect of these cases is that if the water came by natural flow or percolation there is no liability; but that if the invading water has been pumped up in large quantities by the adjoining mine-owner in order to work his own mine, he is liable.

[1] (1846) 9 Q.B. 101.
[2] *Smith* v. *Kenrick* (1849) 7 C.B. 515; *Baird* v. *Williamson* (1863) 15 C.B. (N.S.) 376.

The Northwestern Utilities Case

The liability is said to attach to the escape of the noxious subject-matter from the defendant's land. It is true that escape from one piece of land to another is a condition of the rule, but it does not mean that the defendant is either owner or occupier of the land. He may be a mere licensee, as in the *Northwestern Utilities Case*, and in the various cases where the defendants were utility companies carrying gas, water or electricity under public highways in the course of their undertakings.[1]

It has been objected that the term "absolute" liability is not appropriate because, as we have seen, there may be several defences, such as *vis major*, act of God, act of a third person, exercise of statutory powers; hence the liability is in that sense not absolute, but subject to be qualified in one or other of these ways. That is true, but I am not sure that the suggested substitute "strict" is really better, though it is now generally used. Whichever adjective is used, the meaning to be conveyed is that liability does not depend on negligence. In this respect, the failure in keeping secure a ferocious animal, preventing the escape of water or gas and so forth, and the breach of a statutory obligation which causes damage to a person for whose protection the obligation is enacted, are on the same footing.

There are, however, peculiarities special to the different classes.

I turn now for purposes of comparison to a different category of cases, which depends on the dangerous character of the operation. This is a special rule of vicarious responsibility, that is, of an employer for the act of his employees. The general rule is that an employer is not

---

[1] See also *Dominion Natural Gas Co.* v. *Collins* [1909] A.C. 640.

liable for the negligence of independent contractors or their servants in the same way as he is liable for the negligence of his own servants or agents. It is difficult here not to use the word employer in two senses, in the one case as meaning a person who engages his own servants or agents, in the other as meaning a person who contracts with another person to do a piece of work for him, to construct a reservoir, or to build a wall, or to take a photograph, or to do a myriad other things. It may sometimes be difficult to determine in any particular case which is the category which applies. But the distinction is generally stated to depend on whether the actual employer not only determines what is to be done, but retains the control of the actual performance, in which case the doer is a servant or agent; or whether on the other hand the employer while prescribing the work to be done leaves the manner of doing it to the control of the doer, in which case the doer is an independent contractor. The general rule is stated by Lord Blackburn in *Dalton* v. *Angus*:[1] "Ever since *Quarman* v. *Burnett*[2] it has been considered settled law that one employing another is not liable for his collateral negligence unless the relation of master and servant existed between them. So that a person employing a contractor to do work is not liable for the negligence of that contractor or his servants. On the other hand, a person causing something to be done, the doing of which casts on him a duty, cannot escape from the responsibility attaching on him of seeing that duty performed by delegating it to a contractor. He may bargain with the contractor that he shall perform the duty and stipulate for an indemnity

---

[1] (1881) 6 App. Cas. 740, 829.   [2] (1840) 6 M. & W. 499.

The Northwestern Utilities Case

from him if it is not performed, but he cannot thereby relieve himself from liability to those injured by the failure to perform it: *Hole* v. *Sittingbourne and Sheerness Ry. Co.*;[1] *Pickard* v. *Smith*;[2] *Tarry* v. *Ashton.*"[3]

Now the duty arises, so far as is relevant to this lecture, when what is contracted to be done is of an inherently dangerous character, that is, calculated to cause mischief unless special precautions are taken. The principle is that if a man for his own purposes procures the doing of things by the independent contractor which from their inherent character involve danger to others unless special precautions are taken, he cannot delegate responsibility for failure to take such precautions if others are damnified. The differences between this rule and that in *Rylands* v. *Fletcher* are too obvious to require to be explained at length. The resemblances are that the person who has caused a dangerous state of things for his advantage has to bear the loss inflicted on others as a consequence. But the distinction is that here the gist of the cause of action is negligence. It is in fact an extension of the general rule of vicarious responsibility. The duty is in effect a duty that no damage should be caused to others by the operation in consequence of negligent performance. Its special feature is that the duty remains even though the performance is delegated to persons who are neither servants nor agents of the employer.

It has been questioned whether there is a logical distinction between things or actions inherently dangerous and those which are dangerous only if negligently performed. It may be said that there is scarcely any opera-

---

[1] (1861) 6 H. & N. 488. [2] (1861) 10 C.B. (N.S.) 470.
[3] (1876) 1 Q.B.D. 314.

tion which does not become dangerous if negligently performed, e.g. driving a motor car. But the distinction is clearly recognized by the law, and has, it seems to me, a sound justification in fact. What the classes of operations are to which the rule applies have been defined, at least in general terms. Illustrations are readily available. Such acts as the causing of fire or explosion are established instances of operations inherently dangerous. Familiar instances are where the dangerous acts are done near a highway. But the rule extends to operations which may be done on premises or land not in the occupation either of the employer or the independent contractor. Thus if the contractor has undertaken on behalf of the employer to correct a gas leak and his servants proceed to locate it with the help of an open light so that an explosion follows, the employer will prima facie be liable for the negligent acts of the contractor and his servants.[1] The rule has been recently examined and applied by the English Court of Appeal in *Honeywill and Stein* v. *Larkin*,[2] where the plaintiffs had engaged the defendants as independent contractors to photograph the interior of a theatre in which the plaintiffs had executed certain works. The plaintiffs were not in occupation but had a licence to photograph. The taking of the photograph involved the use of a flash light, which was a dangerous operation in its intricate nature, because liable to cause fire, though the degree of danger was not very striking. But it did involve creating a fire and an explosion. Through the carelessness of the contractors' men, certain curtains were burnt and damaged. The

---

[1] Cf. *Brooke* v. *Bool* [1928] 2 K.B. 578.
[2] [1934] 1 K.B. 191.

theatre proprietors sued the employers, who accepted liability and paid them, rightly as the Court held. The employers then claimed an indemnity from the contractors for what they had thus paid. They defended on the ground that the employers' payment was a voluntary payment, because they were not liable for the negligence of the contractors. That defence failed because the Court held that the operation was intrinsically dangerous. Hence the employers were liable for the negligence of the independent contractor. The plaintiffs accordingly succeeded.

Here again it may not be possible to give an exact and exhaustive definition, but the broad general definition is clear enough for all practical purposes of judgment, when considered in the light of the decided cases.

In recent years there have been certain cases in which another head of liability is exemplified, that in cases in which an Act of Parliament has imposed an absolute statutory duty on an employer, that is a duty which attaches to the employer personally, though he does not and indeed often cannot perform it himself, but is compelled by circumstances or sometimes by law (as when the law requires the employment of certified mine managers or shipmasters) to perform it by others. Here he may or perhaps must delegate the performance, but cannot delegate the duty, that is, he remains liable. The duty, not the performance, is personal.[1] In certain of such cases the common law has engrafted on to the statutory duty (to which criminal penalties are generally attached, and which is primarily a public duty) a further personal duty in favour of the workmen, whose protection is one of the

[1] *Wilsons & Clyde Coal Co.* v. *English* [1938] A.C. 57.

purposes of the law. There again, in general, the workman's cause of action is not based on negligence, but on the breach of a strict or absolute duty arising in favour of the man out of the statute.

Before leaving the subject of vicarious liability, I should like to mention the extension in modern times of the employer's liability for the fraudulent or tortious act of his servant. It was held at one time that the master was not liable if the servant, though apparently acting in the course of the employer's business, was in truth acting for his own purposes, which he was seeking to advance by a fraudulent act. That limitation was swept away by the House of Lords in *Lloyd* v. *Grace, Smith & Co.*,[1] where a solicitor's clerk left in charge of the business defrauded a woman client who thought she was dealing with the clerk as the employee acting for the solicitor. The transaction was within the apparent scope of the business. It was held that it was not relevant that the clerk was committing the fraud for his own purposes. His employer had placed him in the business in such a position that he could hold himself out as acting in such matters for his employer, with the consequence that when in the particular case he did so for his own gain, but the other party dealt with him in good faith on the basis that he was acting about his employer's business, the employer had to answer for the fraud as if the clerk had really intended to act for the employer's benefit. The Court being satisfied that his action could be described as within the course of his employment (which refers to ostensible as well as to actual authority), the solicitor was held liable to the woman who was defrauded.

[1] [1912] A.C. 716.

VI

GOLD CLAUSES[1]

IN this lecture I shall explore some side issues in the law of contract, relating to money or currency, and involving some limited glances at private international law, or the conflict of laws as it is often called. What is money for the lawyer? It was once fashionable to speak of the Commodity theory of money and to approach questions relating to it as if it were a species of chattels or goods. Presumably that dates back to the older and simpler days when people thought of money as being some tangible precious metal, silver or gold. In England we have the pound sterling. The word sterling which has come into popular parlance as something genuine, as we speak of a man of sterling character, has not been satisfactorily derived or explained, but it is clear that it was the description applied from about the twelfth century to the English silver coinage, because of its consistent fineness. The word "pound" which is so familiar is of even more ancient date. It was used in Saxon times, and meant exactly what it means now, in its ordinary usage, a standard of weight. It meant a weight of silver, consisting of 240 pennies, each of which originally weighed 24 troy grains, but later a smaller weight was substituted. But if we pass from Saxon times, through Norman to English days, the pound still continued to denominate the monetary unit, and the silver penny remained the only coin. Sterling silver became

[1] A lecture delivered in the Harvard Law School, 28 September 1938.

the silver of commerce in a great part of the world. We have pictures of the sheriffs bringing to the Exchequer the taxes due from their counties in silver, and the Treasury Officials weighing the silver so brought to see that the tale was correct. Until the eighteenth century the pound was based on a silver standard. Gold was, however, found necessary for international trade in the Middle Ages, and gold coins were minted in England from about the fourteenth and fifteenth centuries. It was not till 1816 that the sovereign was established by Act of Parliament as a gold piece coined at the Mint of a specified weight and fineness, and was defined as the sole standard measure of value and as legal tender for payment without any limitation of amount. But in the preceding centuries a system of banking and credit had developed, though it remained for more recent times to see the full development of that system. Until the Great War, in England the Bank of England note issue which was legal tender was convertible into gold. A holder of Bank of England notes of £5 and upwards, which were legal tender, could demand from the Bank the equivalent amount of gold sovereigns of the standard weight and fineness. On Bank counters, there were still scales to weigh the sovereigns. During and since the war, gold went out of circulation and finally in 1931 the pound as a monetary unit ceased to be convertible into gold. England went off gold. Bank of England notes are now the legal currency. But even notes are now used only in a limited class of cases, in effect principally for small change. Commercial and financial transactions are conducted by means of credits, by credit documents, bankers' drafts and ordinary cheques, and no currency

Gold Clauses

is used. Hence the commodity theory of money, if ever theoretically true, is now an anachronism. No one would refer to Bank notes as a commodity, because the only commodity involved is the piece of paper, which is in itself valueless. The pound has ceased to mean a weight of silver or of gold, and has become a unit of account in which credits are granted and liabilities are incurred. So far as it represents anything tangible it represents a unit of the currency, the value of which is ascertained only by its purchasing power. For keeping of accounts and making of bargains and granting of credits it is necessary to have a unit of account of a fixed denomination. What that denomination means at any given time or place is determined first by defining what is the currency and then describing what it is worth either for domestic use in the country or for exchange in international transactions. The distinction between a unit of account and what it denominates and is worth is the clue to many problems. Hence in law the credit theory of money must supplant the commodity theory. It will be convenient here to refer to a decision of the House of Lords, *Banco de Portugal* v. *Waterlow & Sons, Ltd.* [1932] A.C. 452. The Bank had become entitled to damages from Waterlows, who by a breach of contract had unwittingly caused to be brought into circulation a large mass of spurious notes of a particular issue, and thus had destroyed the credit of the notes of the whole of that issue of the Bank, including the genuine notes. In consequence the Bank had been compelled to call in the whole of the issue, and to replace the notes by notes of another issue, which was free from any taint. The notes of the Bank were inconvertible into gold, that is, if a holder brought notes to the Bank and required payment, the Bank could discharge the liability by paying out other of its notes. On the one hand it was the opinion of two members of the House of Lords that the damages were merely nominal, that is, the price of printing the notes which were issued in place of the notes which had been called in, and it was said that the Bank had parted only with bits of paper so that its damage was completely covered by the cost of printing the paper. The other view, which prevailed with the majority, was that the Bank was entitled to recover, not for the value of the bits of paper, which no doubt was all the notes were worth while in the cellars of the Bank and before they were issued, but their value as currency once they were issued by the Bank. They then became not bits of paper but bits of currency, on which the Bank was liable for their face value, a liability which could be enforced against its assets on default. The damage was that they had increased their liabilities without any corresponding increase of assets to the extent to which they had been compelled to redeem the bad notes put into circulation as a consequence of Waterlows' breach of contract. The measure of damage for the wrong was the value of the thing, that is, the market value, at the date of the accrual of the damage. Its value was determined by the fact that it was currency. The notes issued by the Bank could be tendered to the Bank in settlement of a debt due to the Bank or for the purchase of foreign currency or of goods. The Bank had been compelled by Waterlows' breach of contract to assume liability without getting anything in return.

I refer to this view, which affirmed a decision of my

Gold Clauses

own, as embodying the credit theory of money and not the commodity theory, which I regard as inconsistent with the facts of modern life. The curious will find it interesting to read the conflicting judgments in the House of Lords and perhaps also the numerous discussions both from the standpoint of law and of economics, which the case has aroused.

I can now pass to the case of the *Adelaide Electric Supply Co.* v. *Prudential Insurance Co.*[1] and the allied authorities. The Adelaide Electric Supply Co. was an English registered company incorporated in 1905 with its registered office in London, though it carried on its business in South Australia. Its issued capital was expressed in pounds in the documents of incorporation and so were the rates of dividends. Before 1921 the Company paid its dividends in London according to its original constitution in pounds sterling, but thereafter the constitution was changed by a Resolution of 1921 so that in future all dividends should be declared and paid in Australasia. The real question was whether dividends declared since the Resolution of 1921, which made them payable in Australia, were payable in Australian currency or were payable in, or on the basis of, British currency. The former was substantially depreciated as compared with the latter. It was not disputed that if the Company being an English Company were wound up it would be wound up in England, and that in such an event any distribution of assets to the shareholders would be in British currency. The issue in the action, which involved substantial sums of money, related to the payment of dividends and to the effect in that regard of

[1] [1934] A.C. 122.

the Resolution changing the place for paying the dividends from London to Adelaide or Australasia. It is clear that the currency in which dividends were payable might be different from that in which the assets would be distributed on a winding up of the Company. Some confusion was introduced into the discussion by a controversy whether the pound in Australia was the same as the pound in England. It was clear that before the war the pound was the same. In both places, before the war, the pound was convertible into gold, the monetary gold unit being the sovereign, which was minted both in London and in Australia by the same Royal Mint, branches of which had been established in Australia. There was accordingly no difference in value for exchange purposes, if trifling differences and bank commissions were disregarded. But during the war, according to my opinion, the two currency systems fell apart. England and Australia each developed its own currency system by a series of separate enactments. Eventually, in 1931 both countries had gone off the gold standard. The notes in each country, while still bearing the denomination of pound notes, were severally issued by different banking systems in each country, and had no common basis of convertibility, because each issue was convertible into the notes of the issue of its own country and was subject to the legislation of its own country. The currency legislation in England in fact followed different lines from that in Australia. In this way the respective values of the two currencies fell apart. This indeed was the cause of the dispute, because the shareholders were getting less if paid the face amounts of the dividends in Australian currency than if they had been paid in

English sterling. There was some difference of opinion in the House of Lords whether logically the Australian pound and the British pound were the same pound, but the point was really technical, the difference in value of the two currencies not being in dispute. There was it seems some confusion between the pound as a unit of account and as meaning the currency whereby an obligation to pay so many of such units is to be discharged. Some expressions used in places in the opinions delivered in the House of Lords fostered, it may be, this tendency to confuse different concepts. For instance, phrases like "money of account" or "monetary unit" were used as if they meant the same as unit of account. But the distinction between these two ideas underlay all the opinions which agreed in the result. Later authorities have clearly proceeded on the basis that the word "pound", though it was the same word and was identical as a denomination, might denote different currencies; and in that sense, which is the practical sense, the pound, though originally it meant the same thing, had come to mean different things, that is, different currencies. We speak of Australian pounds or New Zealand pounds, just as we speak of Egyptian or Turkish or Cyprus pounds, and there are separate exchange quotations for each.

It had therefore to be decided in which sense the word "pound", whether British or Australian, was used in the Resolution of 1921 dealing with dividends. The Company was an English company. It was not controverted that the documents embodying its constitution were as a whole to be construed as governed by English law. It is, however, clear law that different parts of the same instrument may be governed by different laws. The question was what as a matter of construction was meant by the word pound in the Resolution whereby payment was required to be in Australia. It was held that according to rules of private international law it is *prima facie* to be presumed that the Australian pound was intended because the manner and incidents of performance, i.e. the currency in which payment was to be made, would *prima facie* be governed by the law of the place of payment. The payer would naturally pay in the currency in use at the place of payment, and not in a foreign currency. The question may indeed be regarded as simply one of construction, the word "pound" being construed according to the context as meaning English or Australian as the case may be. Or if the word is treated as *ancipitis usus*, the currency in which payment is to be made is treated as the manner of performance, to be determined by the law of the place of performance. There were a number of authorities cited in support of this view, including a case in the Irish Privy Council in the time of Elizabeth. It is obvious that such issues are not likely to arise except when, in the period after the contract date, the values of the different pounds in question have changed in relation to each other. Where the difference existed at the date of the contract, the contract would generally by express words define what pound was intended.

In the converse case where payment was to be in London, the law was declared to be that payment was to be in English currency.

But more complicated questions of conflict of laws have arisen where the legislature of the place where pay-

Gold Clauses

ment is to be made has purported to change the obligations of a contract, which is governed *prima facie* by another system of law, as for instance where it had been enacted that the rate of interest on mortgages or debts arising under a foreign contract should be altered. Similarly, provisions have been enacted in order to affect the operation of gold clauses in contracts. I shall now deal with what has been called the gold clause, reserving till a later stage what I have to say about enactments affecting gold clauses, rates of interest and so forth.

The general idea or purpose of a gold clause in a contract may be obvious, but the difficulty has been to say what exactly it means in each particular case, a difficulty mostly due to bad drafting or imperfect appreciation by the parties of their actual intention. In general a gold clause is inserted in order to protect a creditor against depreciation in the currency. It is therefore peculiarly appropriate in the case of long-term loans or indebtedness. So far as I know it was not in use in England until in the years after the war, when currency conditions were uncertain and disturbed, and fluctuations in the value of the currency had arisen or might be expected to arise. But the system of inserting gold clauses had been adopted after the Civil War in the United States and such clauses were the subject of decisions of the Supreme Court in 1868. In the English Courts the clause came up for consideration in *Feist* v. *Société Intercommunale Belge d'Électricité*.[1] The House of Lords unanimously reversed the judgments of the trial judge and of the Court of Appeal. The clause was found in a series of bonds and was in identical terms in each. The bonds

[1] [1934] A.C. 161.

were issued in 1928 by the defendants, a Belgian Company, through an issuing house in London and were payable in London in 1963, and were for various amounts. The bond sued on was on its face for £100 and provided that on presentation of the bond, the Company's agent in London, England, would pay the sum of £100 in gold coin of the United Kingdom of or equal to the standard of weight and fineness existing on 1 September 1928. It similarly provided that the interest, which was at the rate of $5\frac{1}{2}$ per cent per annum, would be paid in gold coin in the United Kingdom of or equal to the standard of weight and fineness existing on 1 September 1928 by half-yearly payments. The interest coupons were expressed to be for £2. 15s. in sterling gold coin. At the relevant date England was on the gold standard, but gold coin was for practical purposes no longer in circulation. The Coinage Act of 1870 which was still in force specified as the weight of the gold coin or sovereign 123·27447 grains and specified also the appropriate standard of fineness. It was not contested that this weight and fineness were what was referred to by the clause. Of the rival views put before the Courts that adopted by the lower Courts started from the description on the face of the bond that it was for £100, and went on to construe the words of the clause literally and then held that its sole intention was to obtain payment in one particular form of tender only, viz. gold, which was still legal tender; that that intention was defeated by the law under which the paper currency, which was depreciated in relation to gold, was made legal tender; and that it was unlawful to provide for payment otherwise and so to abrogate the enactment which enabled the debt to be so discharged. The House of Lords rejected this contention as to the effect of the currency Act and as to the construction of the clause. It was pointed out that this view in truth gave no effect at all to the clause and left the contract merely a contract to pay in any legal currency. It was also pointed out that the stipulation for payment in gold coin could not be literally construed, because there were no gold coins in which a payment of £2. 13*s*. (which was the amount of the half-yearly interest, less income tax) could be made. It was also observed that gold coins could never have been found of the exact standard weight and fineness, because in practice there must always be some variation or allowance from the standards. The House of Lords accordingly held that the words could not have been used by the parties in their literal sense as requiring payment in gold coin of the standard weight and fineness, because no such mode of payment was or had ever been possible. They held therefore that the clause did not prescribe a mode of payment. But they decided that the clause which the parties had deliberately inserted should if possible be given some intelligible meaning. Having regard to the various provisions of the bond and to its obvious intention to secure to the long-term lender a specific sum free from uncertainty and depreciation, they construed the clause so far as it related to the capital sum as if it ran thus: "Pay in sterling a sum equal to the value of £100 if paid in gold coin of the United Kingdom of or equal to the standard of weight and fineness existing in the United Kingdom on 1 September 1928." In other words they construed the clause as defining not a mode of payment but a measure of liability. The same construction was applied to the interest payments. It is true that this construction involved some remoulding of the precise language used, and had the effect of making each payment a payment of an uncertain amount depending on the precise value of fine gold, at the due date of each payment, which would vary with the amount of currency necessary to purchase the specified weight. The House of Lords held that this construction gave effect to what the parties intended. They preferred it to the only other possible alternatives, namely either attributing no meaning at all to the gold clause, or attributing to it a meaning which from other parts of the document and the surrounding circumstances the parties cannot have intended it to bear.

It had been held some years earlier that a contract to pay so many pounds when the country was on the gold standard could not be construed as a contract to pay in gold or in gold coins, but merely as a contract to pay in whatever might be the currency of the country when the money fell due. To achieve any other obligation than to pay in whatever might be currency at the relevant time a gold clause was necessary.[1]

The question of conflict of laws was not raised in this case, but it did arise in *Rex* v. *International Trustee for Bondholders*.[2] There were three main questions in that case. The first was as to the construction of the gold clause, the second was as to the proper law of the contract and the third was as to the effect of the legislation in the United States on the gold clause. I shall consider the first question and postpone for the moment the

[1] See *In re Chesterman's Trusts* [1923] 2 Ch. 466.
[2] [1937] A.C. 500.

Gold Clauses

other two. The bonds in question, which were issued in New York by the British Government in February 1917, were described as twenty-year $5\frac{1}{2}$ per cent coupon gold bonds, payable 1 February 1937, and were issued in denominations of $100, $500 and $1000 to a total amount of $143,587,000. Interest was payable half-yearly. According to one option both interest and principal were payable at the option of the holder in the city of New York at the office or agency to be maintained in the said city for the service of the bonds of the issue—then follow the words of the gold clause, "in gold coin of the United States of America of the standard of weight and fineness existing February 1917". The alternative option entitled the holder to claim payment in the City of London in sterling money at the fixed rate of 4.86\frac{1}{2}$ to the pound and had no gold clause. As the plaintiffs in the action claimed on the basis of the New York option, the London option may here be disregarded. The trial judge held that the gold clause meant payment in actual gold coins of the United States. The Court of Appeal held that it did not mean a payment in gold coin but imported a measure of value as was held in *Feist's Case*. The House of Lords did not find it necessary for reasons which will appear later to give a final decision on the point but indicated their opinion that the clause should receive the same construction as that given to the substantially identical clause in *Feist's Case*[1] and so far agreed with the Court of Appeal. A similar construction had been applied to a similar gold clause by the Supreme Court of the United States in *Norman* v. *Baltimore and Ohio Railroad Co.*,[2] and other cases: the

[1] [1934] A.C. 161.   [2] (1935) 294 U.S. 240.

Supreme Court held that such clauses were intended to afford a definite standard or measure of value and thus to protect against a depreciation of the currency and against the discharge of the obligation by a payment of less value than that originally prescribed. A similar construction has been applied to practically similar clauses by the Court of International Justice sitting at the Hague and other Courts. The clause, which is an international clause widely used in international finance,[1] has in this way received a uniform construction and it is most important that the uniformity should be maintained in the absence of compelling reasons to the contrary. Its purpose is clear and has been generally recognized, that is, to prevent the lender from having to accept payment in the currency (however depreciated) which is circulating at the due dates at the place of payment, as he would be bound to do if there were no gold clause. The difficulty which has been felt in some quarters is caused by the curiously bad draftsmanship of the clause. If it is, as has been held, a money clause, providing a measure of value to be discharged in current money at the due dates, it involves only an ordinary banking calculation. If it is said that even gold changes in value as compared with other commodities, that is no doubt true in a sense, but such changes are relatively remote, and if they do occur some risk must be taken by a long-term lender. The position may be summed up as follows. The clause might be construed in any one of four possible senses. (1) It might be dismissed as meaningless or misleading, leaving the stated amount to be discharged in whatever is at the due date legal tender.

[1] Arpad Plesch, *The Gold Clause* (2nd ed. 1936).

(2) It might require payment in actual gold bullion as a commodity. (3) It might require payment in actual gold coin. (4) It might refer to gold as a measure of value and the specified gold coin as a specification of the standard and fineness of gold referred to. (1) is rejected because it would treat the clause as having no effect at all. (2) is rejected because the contract is a money contract, not a commodity contract. (3) is rejected because it is in fact impossible to give effect to it, and also because it involves treating the gold coins as chattels. (4) makes good sense and gives effect to the intention of the parties. It may be said that it would have been easy for business men to express this meaning in simple and precise language. That is true enough, but I think the clause has settled down in its present shape as a traditional or conventional clause, which business people use without criticizing the exact phraseology, because they know what they mean. Many such instances of conventional forms are to be found in commercial documents. In practice business men are rather afraid to change the accepted verbiage.

So much for the gold clause. I turn to the other questions debated in the *Bondholders' Case*, which turn upon the effect of a Currency Joint Resolution passed by Congress in June 1933. This Resolution, which had the force of law, declared that any provision contained in any obligation which gave the obligee a right to require payment in gold or in a particular kind of coin or currency or in an amount of money of the United States measured thereby was against public policy and prohibited such provisions in the future; and it also enacted that debts should be dischargeable in whatever was legal tender, dollar for dollar. It was also clear that at material times it was illegal according to the law of the United States to pay a dollar debt in gold coin.

The trial judge held that, as in his judgment the bond stipulated it, the New York option was exercised for payment in gold coin in the United States and, as that had become illegal, the English Court, though the proper law of the contract was English, could not enforce such payment, so that the gold clause became inapplicable and the bond was to be discharged in currency. The Court of Appeal agreed with the Judge in holding that the proper law of the contract was English, but held that the Joint Resolution did not render it illegal in the United States to discharge the bond on the basis of the gold clause according to its true construction, that is as a measure of value clause, and that the rights of the bondholder to enforce the clause were unaffected. The House of Lords held that the proper law of the contract was American, and therefore it was to be construed in accordance with American law, but that American law included the provisions of the Joint Resolution, which, at the material time having the force of law, governed the transaction and so disentitled the bondholders to claim payment otherwise than dollar for dollar in the coin or currency which was at the time of payment legal tender.

The vital difference in the two views was as to what was the proper law of the contract. The Court of Appeal thought they ought to follow certain dicta of Lord Romilly in *Smith* v. *Weguelin*,[1] approved by Lord Selborne in *Goodwin* v. *Robarts*,[2] which laid down that

---

[1] (1869) L.R. 8 Eq. at p. 213.
[2] (1876) 1 App. Cas. 494.

where a foreign government contracts a loan in another country, its law governs the transaction: "If the English government were to negotiate a loan in Paris or in New York, the English law must be applied to construe and regulate the contract." So it was said by Lord Romilly in 1869. If that rule could be disregarded, the Court of Appeal were prepared to hold that the transaction was most closely connected with the law of the United States or of New York State. It is now unnecessary to discuss the reasoning by which the rule might be justified, because the House of Lords were of opinion that the rule, though it indicated an element to be taken into consideration, was not decisive on the issue what was the proper law of the contract, and they held that if the whole position were considered the bond was governed by American law.

I need not here explain that where an action is brought, say in an English Court, on a contract, it may have to be construed and receive effect, in whole or in part, according to some law other than the English law. The English Court, in order to decide the case, must then acquaint itself by appropriate evidence with the material provisions of the foreign law and give effect to it. There is here said to be a conflict of laws, that is a conflict as to which system is to prevail as determining the decision of the Court. This may arise under various circumstances. The contract may have been made outside England, or it may have to be performed in whole or in part outside England, or it may have related to foreign immovables, or the parties may have stipulated that it should be governed by the foreign law, or there may be other matters to be taken account of, such as the domicile of the parties. When such questions arise, the Court before which the case comes must first determine what is the proper law of the contract (as the phrase is), that is, what law, or laws, must be applied to the contract in whole or in part, because different laws may have to be applied to different stipulations. The principles adopted by the English Courts have been crystallizing over a number of years, partly as the result of decisions and partly as the result of expositions by text-writers, such as the late Professor Dicey. The decision of the House of Lords in the *Bondholders' Case* may be said to lay down these principles in their latest and most authoritative form. Lord Atkin (at p. 529) said the proper law of the contract is "the law which the parties intended to apply. Their intention will be ascertained by the intention expressed in the contract if any, which will be conclusive." I think Lord Atkin means "*prima facie* conclusive" and I think this appears from his statement read as a whole. He goes on to say, "If no intention be expressed the intention will be presumed by the Court from the terms of the contract and the relevant surrounding circumstances. In coming to its conclusion the Court will be guided by rules which indicate that particular facts or conditions lead to a *prima facie* inference, in some cases an almost conclusive inference, as to the intention of the parties to apply a particular law: e.g., the country where the contract is made, the country where the contract is to be performed, if the contract relates to immovables the country where they are situate, the country under whose flag the ship sails in which goods are contracted to be carried. But all these rules but serve to give *prima facie* indications of intention: they are all capable of

Gold Clauses

being overcome by counter indications, however difficult it may be in some cases to find such. The principle of law so stated applies equally to contracts to which a sovereign State is a party as to other contracts." As to the particular dicta on which the Court of Appeal proceeded, he says (at p. 531): "It appears therefore that in every case whether a Government be a party or not the general principle which determines the proper law of the contract is the same: it depends upon the intention of the parties either expressed in the contract or to be inferred from the terms of the contract and the surrounding circumstances, and in the latter case the inference may be drawn that the parties intended a foreign law to apply. The circumstance that a Government is a party is entitled to great weight in drawing the appropriate inference, but it is not conclusive and is only one factor in the problem." More recently, in a case where the conflict was between the law of New Zealand and the law of Victoria, Australia, the Privy Council stated the principles in much the same form, in the *Mount Albert Case*.[1] I shall later discuss this case, but I here cite the statement of general principle which is expressed in the following terms in a judgment which I delivered as the judgment of the Judicial Committee of the Privy Council. "The proper law of the contract means that law which the English or other Court is to apply in determining the obligations under the contract. English law in deciding these matters has refused to treat as conclusive, rigid or arbitrary criteria such as *lex loci contractus* or *lex loci solutionis*, and has treated the matter as depending on the intention of the parties to

---

[1] [1938] A.C. at p. 240.

be ascertained in each case on a consideration of the terms of the contract, the situation of the parties, and generally on all the surrounding facts. It may be that the parties have in terms in their agreement expressed what law they intend to govern, and in that case *prima facie* their intention will be effectuated by the Court. But in most cases they do not do so. The parties may not have thought of the matter at all. Then the Court has to impute an intention, or to determine for the parties what is the proper law which, as just and reasonable persons, they ought or would have intended if they had thought about the question when they made the contract. No doubt there are certain *prima facie* rules to which a Court in deciding on any particular contract may turn for assistance, but they are not conclusive. In this branch of law the particular rules can only be stated as *prima facie* presumptions. It is not necessary to cite authorities for these general principles. Sometimes their application involves difficulty; but not in this case. It has been already pointed out that there are, in their Lordships' opinion, such circumstances as lead to the inference that in the present case the proper law of the contract is the law of New Zealand, and accordingly that law should *prima facie* govern the rights and obligations to be enforced under the contract by a Court before which the matter comes, *a fortiori* a New Zealand Court. It is true that, when stating this general rule, there are qualifications to be borne in mind, as, for instance, that the law of the place of performance will *prima facie* govern the incidents or mode of performance, that is, performance as contrasted with obligation. Thus in the present case it is not contested that the word

Gold Clauses

'pound' in the debenture and coupon is to be construed with reference to the place of payment, and as referring to the 'pound' in Victorian currency. Again, different considerations may arise in particular cases, as, for instance, where the stipulated performance is illegal by the law of the place of performance. But there is no question of illegality here, since the Victorian statute is not prohibitory."

These statements, like all general statements of principle, leave many difficulties of detail and require modifications adapted to particular circumstances. Nor do they deal explicitly with the fact that different laws may have to be applied to different aspects or portions of the contract. Again it may be said that what they emphasize is the intention of the parties, which can only mean intention in an objective sense which has to be presumed by the Court; not an actual state of mind at the time of contracting. This is true enough, but it is equally true in reference to the ordinary process of construing a contract. Then it is said that the English rule involves uncertainty. It may be impossible to forecast what view will be taken by the Court as to what is the proper law of a contract until all the circumstances have been explored and the decision of the final Court delivered. It is said that it would be much better to have arbitrary rules, such as that the law of the place of contracting or of the place of performance may apply, or the law of the flag in the case of ships, and other definite rules which can be precisely stated and automatically applied. But experience of particular cases shows that these general rules, if rigidly applied, will at times produce absurd and irrational consequences. The English law does not fail to give effect to these definite rules as guides or *prima facie* presumptions, and in the majority of cases they will settle the matter. But the general purpose of contract law is to effectuate what was the parties' intention so far as it can be objectively ascertained and within the limits of the law, and there seems to be no sound reason of law or business convenience why this should not be the guiding principle in cases of conflict of laws. It has been pointed out that, even so, a rule *prima facie* so obvious as that the expressed intention of the parties should receive effect may admit exceptions. This would be rather on grounds of public policy or legality, though it might be because the expressed intention is insensible. But I am lecturing on only a few particular cases, not writing a treatise on this subject.

I may, however, refer in rather more detail to the *Mount Albert Case* as dealing with the effect of a change in the law of the place of performance when that law is not the proper law of the contract. The contract or covenant was in a mortgage by a New Zealand Local Authority under an act called the New Zealand Local Bodies Loans Act. The money which was expressed in the denomination "pounds" was lent by an Australian Insurance Company carrying on business in the State of Victoria; it was secured by a charge on real property situate in New Zealand, but was repayable at the Company's Office in Melbourne in Victoria. It was held that the proper law of the contract as a whole was New Zealand law, but that the word "pound" in the obligation was to be construed as meaning the currency of Victoria, because that was the place of payment. This

Gold Clauses

latter followed from the *Adelaide Case*.[1] But the real difficulty in the case arose from the fact that the Victorian legislature had passed an Act reducing the interest payable on mortgages to a rate equivalent to 4*s*. 6*d*. for every pound of such interest. The question was whether the interest stipulated for in the mortgage, which was higher than 4*s*. 6*d*. in the pound, was affected by this Victorian statute. The Local Authority paid the interest at 4*s*. 6*d*. in the pound. The Victorian Company then brought their action in New Zealand for the balance of interest short paid by the Local Authority, the mortgagor, which had claimed that it was liable to pay only at the reduced rate. The Victorian Company on the contrary contended that the stipulated rate was not affected. The Courts in New Zealand and the Privy Council on appeal held that the Victorian statute did not apply and that the Victorian Company were entitled to succeed.

The main ground on which the New Zealand Court of Appeal (reported in 1936 *New Zealand Law Reports*, p. 54) proceeded was that though the place of performance so far as payment of interest went was in Victoria and though the Victorian law had been changed so as to reduce the rate of interest, yet as the proper law of the contract was the law of New Zealand, the Victorian law could not affect or change the obligations under the contract, though admittedly the Victorian law as the place of performance governed the currency in which payment was to be made.[2] The distinction was drawn between the

---

[1] [1934] A.C. 122.
[2] This is true at least in the sense that it determined what construction was to be given to the word "pound".

substance of the obligation and the mode or manner of performance. If the contract had been a Victorian contract, it would have been affected by any change in the law of Victoria, even though that affected the obligation, just as in the *Bondholders' Case* the Joint Resolution abrogated the gold clause, the contract being an American contract. The Victorian statute became in such a case part of the relevant law, according to which the contract was to be construed and enforced. But the position was different as soon as it was held that the proper law of the contract as a whole was that of New Zealand. The essential distinction was drawn between manner or mode of performance and obligation. The currency in which the debt payable in Victoria was dischargeable went to the incidents of performance, whereas to change the covenanted rate of interest was to change the contractual obligation. It was to strike out the figure of the rate of interest set out in the covenant and to substitute the statutory figure. The Court thus distinguished performance from obligation. They particularly relied on *Jacobs* v. *Crédit Lyonnais*, a well-known English authority.[1] The question arose in a contract for the sale of esparto grass made in London in 1880, to be shipped f.o.b. Algeria. Only partial deliveries were made and the plaintiffs sued for damages for short delivery. The defence relied on the fact that the sellers' agents had been prevented from shipping by an insurrection in Algeria. This was alleged to constitute *force majeure* within the French Civil Code, which was the law of the place of performance, and was said to govern the contract as to the matters to be there performed. The Court of Appeal

[1] (1884) 12 Q.B.D. 589.

Gold Clauses

rejected that contention. They held that the contract was an English contract, and that the mere fact that it was partly to be performed in Algeria did not put an end to the inference that the contract remained an English contract, and was to be construed according to English law and according to the obligations and liabilities which English law attached to the non-performance of contracts; English law did not recognize *vis major* in such a case as a defence. The Court conceded that the parties might have intended to incorporate the foreign law to regulate the method and manner of performance abroad without altering any of the obligations which attached to the contract according to English law. This case proceeded on the distinction between obligation and performance, which is also emphasized in the American Restatement on Conflict of Laws, §§ 332, 358. The Restatement points out that there is no logical line which separates the obligation of the contract which is to be determined by the place of contracting (for which I should according to English ideas venture to substitute "the proper law of the contract") from the performance which is determined by the law of the place of performance. In the *New Zealand Case* the Court of Appeal had no difficulty in saying that the change in the rate of interest went to the obligation of the contract and in distinguishing that from such a question as the currency in which performance was to be effected, the construction of the word "pound" being regulated by the law of the place of performance as was held in the *Adelaide Case*. There are many other matters which have been held to go to the manner and mode of performance, in addition to currency, such as days of grace and similar requirements in the case of negotiable instruments, legal hours for making tender or giving notices, and many other matters. It was argued that the House of Lords in the *Adelaide Case* had used language which laid down that the law of the place of performance applied to all purposes relating to performance, even to the extent of changing the substance of the contractual obligation. The Court rejected that contention and pointed out that the House of Lords were dealing only with the single matter of currency and the language used should be construed in accordance with that view. They certainly evinced no intention of reversing or differing from the leading case of *Jacobs* v. *Crédit Lyonnais*, which was not cited or mentioned. The Privy Council did not in any way dissent from the views on this point of the New Zealand Court of Appeal, though they expressly decided the case finally on another ground also taken by the Court of Appeal. This was that the debentures were mortgages of realty situated in New Zealand and were governed by a special statute in New Zealand, which provided remedies for enforcing the security in the New Zealand Courts, and hence the Victorian statute ought not to be construed as extending to obligations of that character or as varying the specific New Zealand law.

Similar questions as to the effect of statutes varying the obligations of a foreign contract have also arisen in Australia and have been decided substantially on the same lines. It may seem curious that these questions have arisen all at once in so many parts of the world about the same time, but that fact may be explained by reason of the peculiar financial and trade conditions which have led to the interference with obligations by legislatures. Where, however, the statute enacted at the place of performance makes it positively illegal there to perform the contract, it seems that an English Court would not enforce the doing of acts in a foreign country contrary to the positive law of that country, on the principle that to do so would be contrary to the comity of nations.

I must here conclude my observations on these very interesting questions of law.

VII

JUDICIAL PROOF: A REVIEW[1]

DEAN WIGMORE'S monumental work on Evidence, which is known with gratitude to every working lawyer, was published in 1904. The present very substantial volume on the Science of Judicial Proof, published in its first edition in 1913, in its second in 1931 and in its third and present edition in 1937, does indeed in some part overlap with the work on Evidence, but its scope and purpose are different. The former deals in the main with what may be called Admissibility, the practical rules adopted by Courts in order to decide what facts are to be brought in evidence before the jury or considered by the judge. The present work has a different object; it deals with the scientific principles which should regulate the use of the admitted evidence in order to decide the issue in the case. Hence the name Science of Judicial Proof. To a person like myself who was a Common Law Judge for seven years, and had for many years previously practised as counsel in contentious cases of fact, but who had never applied his mind consciously to the logical categories and processes which underlay his practical work, this work has come as an absorbing interest. It has made explicit what has been implicit in working practice. Just as M. Jourdain was astonished

[1] A review of *The Science of Judicial Proof*, by John Henry Wigmore. Third Edition. Revised and enlarged. 1937. Boston: Little, Brown & Co. Pp. 1065. The review was published in *American Bar Association Journal*, vol. XXIV (1938), 478–480.

Judicial Proof: A Review

to find that he had been speaking prose all his life, so I am astonished to find that I have been applying these scientific principles. I realize my misfortune in that I was not a pupil of Dean Wigmore, so that I could have learned from him the principles and practised under his guidance their application in planned experiments and in the study of reported cases. In this latter aspect, the book is a mine of wealth, full of instructive illustrations of every type of judicial reasoning, accurate or fallacious. The mere logical analysis may seem a little tough sometimes, but the illustrative specimens are intensely interesting.

I have asked myself whether I should have done my work any better if I had studied this book in earlier days, not merely for information, but for living mastery of the principles so as to apply and use them. I think the answer should be in the affirmative. Rule of thumb is all very well, especially in a subject like legal proof, where the subject-matter is mainly the stuff of common life, and the logic is generally inexact and directed to probabilities rather than certainties. Besides, as Dean Wigmore points out, the actual course of proof in a court of law is in a very human atmosphere, often charged with emotion and excitement. But all the same, the logic is there. A workman is all the better if he knows and understands his tools as scientifically as he can. On the other hand, I observe with interest how often Dean Wigmore is able to illustrate some rule by quotations from the directions of English or American judges, who may not have known of the rules but certainly could apply them correctly.

It is impossible in a brief notice to do more than refer

to the most salient topics contained in this book of more than one thousand pages. The first two chapters are perhaps the most fundamental. They repeat to a certain extent what in substance is found in the earlier general work on Evidence. They define certain elementary distinctions which underlie every judicial inquiry. At the outset there is the *factum probandum* as contrasted with the *factum probans*. The former is the central question which is found in every case. As Dean Wigmore points out in an appendix, the ultimate question is fixed at the start of the trial, whereas in detection, as we know from reading detective novels, the question has to be defined as we proceed. Contrasted with the *factum probandum* is the *factum probans*, the material elements which go to establish the *probandum*. But though there is in the last resort the single *factum probandum*, there is also the *interim probandum*, which has to be separately proved, so as to combine with its fellows in pointing to the final conclusion, and there may be several *interim probanda*. The main logical method in use here is inference, by which from particular facts a conclusion, interim or final, is reached. From certain facts we infer others; the inference is the process, the proof the result. In ordinary cases, the inference is probable, not certain. We have to select that inference out of the possible alternative inferences which is most probable according to common sense and experience. We cannot expect in legal inquiries that thoroughgoing investigation of a wide range of contrasted or identical instances which science would employ in order to infer a law of nature. As compared with inference the deductive form of reasoning is less important for the lawyers. Dean Wigmore classifies evidentiary facts as falling under (1) what he calls "autoptic proference", an alarming term which means things *oculis subiecta fidelibus*, such as knives, documents, garments, *et hoc genus omne*, (2) testimonial evidence, that is, narrative evidence, (3) circumstantial evidence, where the proof is achieved by way of inference from particular circumstances, not by the narrative of an observer of an occurrence. But it is clear that classes (1) and (3) must both be supplemented by (2). The thing produced has no significance until it is connected by testimonial evidence with the event, and the same is true of the circumstantial facts. Then Dean Wigmore propounds the four "probative processes" which, he says, lie at the basis of all legal reasoning. He distinguishes the "proponent", whom he represents as P, and the opponent, whom he represents as O. Dean Wigmore is fond of symbols, and in the later and more complex part of his book gives specimens of elaborate diagrams to illustrate the conflict of harmony, the dependence, the interaction of the different stages of proof. I have never been able to use diagrams or symbols with any ease or confidence and, though I admire this part of Dean Wigmore's work, I find I can handle the problems better without the aid or perhaps embarrassment of his very ingenious charts. But by these symbols he does show simply his elementary processes. Let P denote the proponent. The opponent, O, may either deny what P alleges, that is figured as OD, or he may explain it away, for instance by giving an innocent explanation of his possession of an incriminating object, this is figured as OE, or he may set up a rival view, a process denoted by OR. I suppose an alibi is a good instance of this last. The prosecution alleges that the accused did an act, he rebuts the charge by showing that at the relevant time he was somewhere else. This analysis of the four processes sounds elementary and obvious, but all the same, as Dean Wigmore points out, it is exhaustive of the processes of proof and brings to consciousness the underlying principles. Of course, some other rule may be helpful in practice, such as the methods of similarity and difference, or the explanation or refutation of an inference by inconsistent instances or by dissimilarity of conditions.

The great bulk of the work falls into two main parts, the part dealing with circumstantial evidence and the part dealing with testimonial evidence, followed by a comparison of the relative values of the two. The author refuses to say that one of these is more valuable or truer in results than the other. He is able to show by a great mass of instances that either may be fallacious. There are both in England and in the United States only too many cases in which either class of evidence has led to erroneous decisions. History shows a sad number of cases where people have been hanged for murders which were never committed, as was conclusively shown by the person supposed to have been murdered turning up alive. These were largely cases of circumstantial evidence, apparently most convincing. Dean Wigmore is justified in saying that the proverb that facts cannot lie is not true as generally understood. As he points out, what we are dealing with is testimonial evidence of certain facts and then the inference from these facts that the crime was committed as charged or the acts done. Either class of evidence, testimonial or circumstantial, may be mistaken. Indeed, as he says, a Court is not con-

Judicial Proof: A Review

cerned with facts in the real or objective sense, but facts as reflected in the evidence and intelligences of men. He also gives a series of startling instances of mistaken identity, apparently based on the most conclusive evidence, yet in the end found to be fallacious. We had in this country, not so many years ago, the famous Beck Case. In history there was the Lyons Mail Case. The curious should turn to Dean Wigmore's book, a great bulk of which is devoted to illustrative instances drawn from the widest possible range, and brought under every head of rule or analysis. I wish I had the opportunity of giving a selection. The reader may find pleasure and instruction in reading and comparing in detail the instances cited and considering how they justify and explain the text. After reading the book, I find myself picking out and re-reading and comparing typical classes of illustration. A striking case is that of a man charged with bigamy, who was confidently identified by the woman with whom the bigamist went through the ceremony and with whom he lived for some time as her husband. But there seems to be no doubt that she was mistaken.

The defects of testimonial evidence are very fully discussed and exemplified. What is involved is the result of perception, recollection and narration. Under each of these heads there may be defect or failure. Dean Wigmore has made practical experiments in order to investigate possibilities of error. He has staged a happening and then taken and compared the accounts given by the different spectators, whom he has classified. He has given percentages of error. I think I am right in saying that even in the most intelligent members of the audience there was no perfect account. Certainly every judge who has tried cases of fact has been compelled to realize the defects of oral testimony, even when tested by cross-examination and checked by putting one witness against another. He welcomes, whenever he can get it, a written statement made at the time with no idea of recording evidence, before processes of forgetting, of prejudice, self-sophistication, sophistication by discussion with others, and other disturbing factors have done their work. So much for those constituents of oral evidence which fall under the heads of perception and recollection. Then the third stage, narration: that is, the oral evidence of men in the course of a trial, in the witness-box under conditions which most people find trying, introduces further tendencies to error. With all these defects it is not astonishing that legal history contains many instances of wrong decisions based on oral testimony. Apart from my forensic and judicial experience I have noticed in myself instances of defective observation. To give one instance, I remember one summer evening when motoring in France, a cyclist, who was proceeding ahead of us on his wrong side, swerved right across the road without warning, crossing in front of us to his proper side. By luck and my chauffeur's skill there was only light contact and no harm worth mentioning. I observed that I wondered why the man had swerved across as he did. My mother said it was to avoid the girl cyclist who was coming on her proper side in the opposite direction to the man and who came and spoke to her after the collision. Neither my chauffeur nor myself had seen her at all, though we were sitting in the front of the car and it was broad daylight.

No doubt much can be done by what Dean Wigmore

Judicial Proof: A Review

describes as forensic methods of detecting testimonial error—by demeanour, cross-examination, by comparing the evidence of a witness with that of others either on the same or opposite sides, or even by the self-contradictions of a witness. Any one who has not done so should read the illustrations which Dean Wigmore gives under this head; many examples of ingenious, simple, and effective cross-examination. He has also a chapter on scientific methods which have been suggested as likely to enable a Court to decide whether a man is speaking the truth. These he describes as "methods of experimental psychometry". For instance, there are the machines for registering changes of blood-pressure or respiration. I am afraid that I am old-fashioned and sceptical on these matters, and was glad to find that Dean Wigmore thus sums up the position: "The conditions required for truly scientific observation and experiment are seldom practicable. The testimonial mental processes are so complex and variable that millions of instances must be studied before safe generalizations can be made. And the scientist in this field is deprived (except rarely) of that known basis of truth by which the aberrations of witnesses must be tested before the testimonial phenomena can be interpreted." He sanely concludes: "No wonder then that the progress of testimonial psychometry must be slow." This is a different matter, of course, from the help which science affords in the discovery of truth, for instance, especially in criminal cases. Thus some help can be obtained in paternity cases from comparing types of blood; medical jurisprudence is constantly called in; and in murder cases scientific evidence constantly helps in establishing clues. I remember a set of cases in which

I was counsel where the question was whether certain steamers had been accidentally sunk or had been deliberately scuttled to enable the ship-owners to recover the excessive insurances. An important part of the evidence in these cases consisted in elaborate plans of the complex pipe arrangements of the vessels, and of the means by which they could be flooded and sunk by sea-water by manipulating particular valves, and calculations as to the rate of inflow and the effect on sinking the vessel. Indeed in these days of mechanism and of scientific applications, evidence of an expert character is constantly necessary to decide a case. Sometimes such evidence is the essentially material or decisive evidence in the case, sometimes it is only one element in the complex mass of evidence, dealing with *interim probanda*, the central *probandum* (to refer to the illustration just given) being whether there was the intentional casting away of the vessel; other *interim probanda* would be questions of motive, subsequent conduct, and other matters of circumstantial evidence, and also matters of single narration, with the various inferences following on the actual evidence, whether oral, documentary, photographic or other. Dean Wigmore gives some models of the methods of analysing mixed masses of evidence, sometimes according to the narrative method and sometimes according to what he describes as the chart method. He gives a very full list of criminal trials as recorded in various publications, so that the student may practise upon them his skill in analysis. I find in these lists two criminal cases of the many that I tried as a judge, the Wallace Case and the Kylsant Case. I regard them both as significant cases of complex evidence. The former was mainly interesting as presenting a series of *interim probanda*, the total effect of which was said by the prosecution to be to establish the final *probandum* of guilt: but at each stage of the prosecution's case there was the opponent's alternative explanation, so that, as I thought and the Court of Criminal Appeal thought, the final inference of guilt could not safely be drawn from the complex mass, and the prisoner was finally acquitted by the Court of Criminal Appeal, which quashed the jury's verdict of guilty. In the Kylsant Case the raw material of the evidence consisted of a mass of accounts, but the final *factum probandum* was the fraudulent intention of the accused man in issuing a prospectus which, true in what it stated, was misleading because of what it omitted, a lie that was half a truth. In the last resort, the issue depended on the decision of the jury on a broad common-sense matter of human intention: that is, on a question of personality. This emphasizes the thesis developed in one place by Dean Wigmore, that the ultimate determination is not to be explained in the last resort by mere logic, but is an act of the will. He gives a striking metaphor. He figures the parallel of a man in a bath chair, getting pushes as a result of the *interim probanda* sometimes in one direction and sometimes in another, till the ultimate push takes him at last into the doorway, or, as the event may be, finally away from it. This is so not merely in criminal trials, but in many civil actions, where the evidence is complex and conflicting.

I ought also to refer to the elaborate and fully documented analyses which form a large part of the chapters on circumstantial and testimonial proof. This I can only touch on very briefly. As to the former, Dean Wigmore distinguishes the three categories of evidentiary data, concomitant, prospectant, and retrospectant. The "concomitant" data are the accompanying conditions, supposed to attend at the time and place of the *probandum*. Thus, for instance, if the *probandum* is the doing of an act, such would be tools, personal and material conditions. "Prospectant" data are matters such as threats, motives, design and so forth, which are taken as antecedent to the act. "Retrospectant" data are matters subsequent to the act (such as conduct evidencing a consciousness of guilt), which raise a probable inference of guilt. These categories may to a great extent run into each other, but the general distinctions help to clearness of thought. There must always be the single inference from the evidence to the existence of the fact, and then there may be the second or double inference from the existence of the fact to its significance. For instance, if consciousness of guilt is in question, there is the inference from the evidence that certain things were done, e.g. the flight or attempt to conceal what might be regarded as incriminating traces. Then the second inference is as to whether such conduct does really evidence guilt or whether an alternative explanation is possible. Dean Wigmore has further heads of analysis according as the *probandum* is the doing of a human act, a human trait or condition, or an event or cause, etc., of external nature. There is a very instructive chapter on identity as a *probandum*.

The analysis of testimonial evidence covers no less than five hundred pages. This is not so alarming as might appear, because a large space is occupied in illustrations from recorded cases. His analysis deals with the three main elements to which I have already referred:

perception, recollection, narration. On this, as indeed on the whole of the work, I can here only refer the reader to the actual text.

I am conscious of the inadequacy of this summary notice. While apologizing, I must excuse myself by referring to the wide scope of the subject and the closeness and intricacy of the detailed analysis. I can only wish that I had known of it and been able to study it at an earlier stage of my legal career, rather than now when my appellate work seldom gives real occasion for analysing and deciding on evidence of fact. It would, I am confident, have often helped me to clear my mind and understand what I was doing. Dean Wigmore's reputation is so well established that I need say nothing about it. I can only say here that I regard this work as a most valuable and original addition to legal thought.

VIII

SOME GENERAL ASPECTS OF LAW[1]

WE seldom consciously realize how intimately law touches each of us from the moment of birth to the moment of death. Law requires surgical aid (by doctor or midwife) at birth; the birth must be registered; soon law imposes educational requirements; household arrangements are in many respects subject to Public Health rules; if we work in factories Factory Acts come in; health and unemployment insurance obligations and benefits apply to most occupations; the currency in which we pay or are paid is fixed by law; if we marry the law fixes the procedure and some of the consequences; if we have a motor car it must be registered and duty must be paid; if we drive on the roads we must obey the Road Acts and police regulations; we are rated and taxed by law and required to license our dogs; even when we die, law requires registration and a certificate to be sure that we have not died by our own act or by that of another. We are so accustomed to this omnipresence of law that we take it for granted and scarcely think of it. Then again there is another branch of law, which we see figuring in the daily press but hope to keep clear of ourselves, either actively or indirectly; I mean the criminal law. Then

[1] An address given to the Students' Union of the London School of Economics, 24 November 1938.

there is the law of the everyday dealings of business life, the law relating to property, to contracts, to liabilities towards others for damage due to wrongful acts, which are called torts, such as injuries to persons, as by negligence, or to reputation, as by defamation, and a host of others. It has been said by people who should know better, even by judges, that every one is presumed to know the law. This led to the ironical definition by Bentham of lawyers: "The only persons in whom ignorance of the law is excused." But in truth there is in general no such legal assumption. A person accused of a criminal offence is not allowed to say that he did not know he was doing wrong. There are good practical reasons why this should be so. If such ignorance were a defence it would be raised by every criminal and that might make it impossible to convict any offender. But when we contemplate the immense range of law, especially in modern times with all its administrative rules, regulations and impositions, no one can be expected to know it. It is not, however, so hopeless as it seems. It is generally easy at each step in life to find out what the law is. The expectant bridegroom can ascertain what he has to do to be married according to law; an intending testator can discover or take advice how to make a will; a man buying or leasing a house can get a solicitor to see that the conveyance or lease is in order; there are rating experts and income-tax experts to help in these painful episodes of life and so on *ad infinitum*. In most cases, it is easy enough to find out what the law requires. When we talk of the uncertainty or, in Bentham's phrase, incognoscibility of the law, we are thinking of these nice questions of law which go to the Court of Appeal or to the

House of Lords. These form an infinitesimal proportion of cases, though it may be a reproach to law that they exist at all. In the vast majority of cases an ordinarily prudent person may shape his acts according to law with certainty and without much trouble or expense, even if he has at times to pay a small fee to a deserving solicitor or other legal expert.

So it seems that law amounts to a vast collection of rules which everybody is bound at his peril to obey. At the back of them is the power of the State to compel obedience. I speak of the internal law of the country which in this sense entirely depends on overt or latent power to coerce. Here we see an essential difference between internal law and international law. The latter depends generally on moral sanctions. There is no central international police to enforce that law or to punish a breach of it. If one state infringes the rules of international law, the other state which is injured may seek to punish the infringer by reprisals or by war. But that is merely a resort to brute force, to taking the law into one's own hands. That is the negation of law, which aims at substituting for combat an impartial arbitrament based on the idea of right. No doubt if state and individuals were anxious only to do right and as soon as the right was pointed out were anxious without more to give effect of it, law could dispense with a backing of coercive power. But we know that such is not the case. Hence the weakness of International Law. The strength of national law depends on the power and will of the State to enforce it. This is clear enough in criminal law, where the police are a present force to prevent crime and to bring the offender to the Court and to see to the carrying out of the punishment decreed by the Court. But it is equally true in civil cases. If the Court orders that the wrongdoer should pay a sum by way of damages, the State can put into operation the machinery of what is called execution. If the Court by injunction orders the wrongdoer to abstain from doing the wrongful acts, and the injunction is disobeyed, the Court may commit the offender to prison. But I do not mean that laws do not also involve moral sanctions for their due operation. A law which is contrary to the force of public opinion is always liable to be evaded, as for instance prohibition in the United States and in England some aspects of our Gaming Laws.

Thus Law seems to consist of regulations of different kinds, for instance prohibitions of criminal acts, burglary, murder and so forth, or mandatory provisions breach of which is subject to penalties, such as those under Factory or Public Health Acts, Registration and Licensing Acts, rules prescribing how valid acts in the law are to be carried out, such as the formalities necessary for a will, which is a unilateral transaction, or a disposition of property, or a contract which takes two (at least) to make it, or rules which determine what is a wrongful act giving a right to compensation or damages. This very bare statement clearly involves a distinction between public and private law, which partly corresponds to that between statute law and judge-made law. I say "partly" because in fact the two categories largely overlap. But let me make it clear that in England all law is subject to Parliament. We have no written constitution, no code of guaranteed rights which the Legislature cannot override by its ordinary law-making power, which can only be changed by the nation itself by some procedure which is taken to represent the voice of the people. On the other hand it is not true to say that Parliament is the only law-making body. There is a large scope for what is called judge-made law. In theory all the judges do is to declare the law embodied in the customs of the realm, which originate from and flow from the customary law of the Anglo-Saxons, which again may be said to flow from the customs of the ancient Teutonic or Scandinavian tribes. This is the Common Law. But Edward the Confessor would find it hard to recognize the Common Law of to-day as being what he knew. In truth, the Common Law as we have it now is the product of the decisions of a long line of judges. It is in fact judge-made law. Alongside of it is another branch of judge-made law, called Equity. That began at a much later date. It was administered or invented by the Lord Chancellors, and later by the Masters of the Rolls and the Vice-Chancellors. Its original aim was to temper the rigour or injustice of the Common Law and it went on as a separate system of a remedial character until the Judicature Act, 1873, effected what was called a fusion. In effect the two systems, so far as they are still separate, are complementary. They constitute the judge-made law, so far as the rules laid down by the judges have not been superseded by being embodied, with or without amendment (as they have been to a very large extent), in Acts of Parliament. It may seem curious that all law should not be embodied in Acts of Parliament. It is sometimes demanded that the whole law should be codified by Parliament. This is an ideal which has often appealed to reformers. It is said that a code is simple and intelligible and that it would prevent the uncertainty and difficulty with which law is often reproached. Napoleon is said to have required a Code so simple and precise that any Court could settle any dispute with the same ease and certainty as a simple mathematical calculation by looking at the code. That is an impossible idea because most disputes which occupy the Law Courts are concerned with questions of fact, which the Judge or Jury has to decide on conflicting, and often very complicated, evidence. Legal problems are not as a rule so numerous or exacting. When they do arise as often as not, perhaps more often than not, they turn on construing Acts of Parliament, and fitting in the words of an Act to the facts of a case, which often the draftsmen never contemplated. Still there has been a great deal of codification in England. Criminal Law is mainly codified, large portions of Commercial Law (such as Bills of Exchange, Sale of Goods, Partnership, Company Law, etc.), Real Property Law and the law of Trust Settlements have also been codified. The remaining portions of common law and equity might be codified, though it would be a difficult and laborious task. But if that were done it would be necessary to devise some system which would secure flexibility. No code nor any Act of Parliament can foresee all future problems or changing conditions. It would be necessary to have a revising body to report to Parliament what changes appear from time to time necessary or desirable. Common Law and Equity have the merit of being to some extent flexible, though they are also rigid. That latter quality may be said to be inevitable because of the principle that judges must act in accordance with earlier decisions or precedents. This has led to the reproach that the past governs the future and prevents progress, which, so far as it is true, is unfortunate. But if precedent did not govern there could be no certainty in law and people could not regulate their conduct to comply with law. Precedents are intended to give that certainty, just as the provisions of the code do in their sphere. Parliament can change judge-made law just as it can alter statutory law, if it cares to do so. The difficulty is to get Parliament to find time to do it. The problem can perhaps be solved only by having some established revising body which at stated intervals should report to Parliament. Here again is the difficulty that many lawyers are opposed to changes in the rules of law (which are sometimes more like rules of thumb) to which they have become habituated. Thus at every proposal to change or amend, the cry is raised that the law is being destroyed or revolutionized. Yet all through the long history of English Law, Parliament has intervened to reform, or at least to change, the law which the judges have declared. Such changes, when they have been established for a century or so, have become dear to the hearts of lawyers, who protest against any change there, even though the old Acts have long since lost whatever value they had. At the same time there have been some very valuable co-ordinating or amending Statutes like the great Acts of 1925 dealing with the Land Law, Trusts and Settlements. But in the main these reforming Acts have dealt with some limited matter.

I may here refer to another matter which arises in connection with what I have been saying about the relation of Statute Law and judge-made law. We have been familiarized with a legal or at least a political principle, the separation of the powers; that is into executive, legislative and judicial, each supposed to be independent of, and separate from, the others. This principle is true in the sense that it defines separate functions in government, and is valuable as indicating that these functions should generally be exercised by separate persons or bodies. In England we have always had, or claimed to have, the reign of law, which means that every person except the King is subject to law, and, as to the King, though he can do no wrong, he can act only through agents and they cannot rely on his command to justify a breach of law. In that sense, the executive, which operates in the name of the King, is subject to law. Again the executive can determine the constitution of the Courts and their functions, though in modern times that prerogative has been superseded by Legislation. But still the executive, that is the government of the day, appoints the judges, though when appointed they cannot be removed except for bad behaviour or on an address by both Houses of Parliament to the Crown, and they have their independence guaranteed. This is the basis of the independence of the judiciary. But it is not true to say that the legislative functions, that is law-making, are exercised only by Parliament. I have already pointed out that from the earliest times the judges have really made laws, that is legislated, even though they pretended to be merely declaring law which already existed. In another sense also they exercised important functions of a legislative character; what I refer to is the duty of the judges to construe Acts of Parliament. Some one said that the real legislators are the judges, because though Parliament passes Acts it is only the judges who say what they mean. This is a paradox, but it has some element of truth; because when disputes arise about what a Statute means, for instance between Local Government bodies, or between individuals or companies and the State, e.g. in tax matters, or local authorities, such as rating authorities, the judges have to settle the dispute by saying what the rights are, and that can be decided only by construing the Statute—a matter which is sometimes or frequently obscure and uncertain until decided by a Court of Law. In that way also judges have a share in law-making.

But conversely it is not true that the judges have a monopoly of judicial functions. There is now well established a system of what is often called administrative law. The effect of this in a large area of affairs is to remove decisions as to rights and duties from the province or supervision of the judges. This is due to the growth of statutory functions, duties and rights which has followed from the regulation by the State of industries, of trade, of modes of conduct in many departments and also from ameliorative social legislation, such as Health Insurance, Unemployment Insurance and Old Age Pensions and so forth, all which lead to disputes. These questions are in the main wholly unsuited to decision by the ordinary process of law, partly because of the immense number of cases to be decided and partly because there are technical questions which can be easily decided by those who are expert in the matter, but which, if dealt with according to ordinary procedure of law, would require long and elaborate explanations to lay judges. Thus we have delegated jurisdiction, just as we have delegated legislative powers, expressly given in either case by Act of Parlia-

Some General Aspects of Law

ment. This system has been criticized as a sort of new despotism, leaving the subject at the mercy of the executive, and inconsistent with the division of the powers of legislative, executive and judiciary, which has been said to be an essential of a good constitution. But new problems require new remedies. What was adapted to the old individualistic system of life is not suited to the more complex conditions produced by modern social legislation. In truth the modern system of administrative law in its proper place has worked well. If it created abuses, modes of remedying them could be devised.

Nor is it in essence inconsistent with the ancient doctrine of the Common Law of the freedom of the individual. The liberty of the subject is still maintained, but it is liberty according to law. Even in the great days of this doctrine in its most unqualified form, the days of *laissez-faire* and freedom of contract, and freedom from regulatory legislation, there were many restrictions, some good, some bad. Take for instance the law relating to trade unions and trade combinations. The condition of liberty and of individual freedom is that it should respect the equal rights of others and should obey the regulations and obligations legally imposed by the State in the public interest. What these regulations are at any time must depend on the current views of what the good of the State requires, and in a democratic country these current views must have the assent of a majority of the nation. The essence of democracy is not merely that it is government by the people, of the people, for the people, but also that the minority must be bound by the will of the majority expressed in constitutional form. In this way each individual is in law deemed to have consented to whatever restraints on his freedom are constitutionally imposed. The law on recognizing the legality of these restraints is not abdicating, but exercising, its functions.

Hence I find any reference to despotism inapt. The Common Law is, as it has been described so often, still the law of free people. That idea has both been nurtured by and has in turn nurtured the idea of the importance of the individual. In the totalitarian State the individual has no rights against the State, the State is an entity in which the individuals are merged. The Common Law conception treats the State as a collection of individuals each of whom has a value of his own, though each individual does not exist *in vacuo*, but as a member of a community and subject to the obligations, as well as the advantages, which flow from that membership. The function of law is to see that each man performs his obligations and enjoys his rights. So far as I understand, there is no law in totalitarian States except the will of the despotic power. No individual rights are secure against that will. There is no judicial machinery to declare, or at least to enforce, any individual rights against the State. Even rights as between individuals are not enforced if the State thinks they should not be. Thus the individual is a nonentity as against the State; but no State however despotic can absolutely or in the long run flout all individual rights, though the long run may be very long.

The totalitarian system seems to fulfil the old description of law as merely the will of the stronger. That is not the English view. We think that law exists to regulate human life in the interests of justice. But it is difficult to define justice. We think we know what it means in any particular case. But there again we are merely acting on the current sociological and moral ideas, which change from generation to generation, and indeed in every generation are different in different classes of the nation. If we look back even a century we see ideas accepted at least by authority and by law which to-day seem barbarous and unjust. Law is not an abstract science or indeed a science at all. Its rules have often been shaped by the interests of the dominant class. Rules of law are not like the rules of what we call the laws of nature, which are derived from the recording of observed sequences of cause and effect in the objective world and consist in the generalization and rationalizing of these observations. Hence has come that vast and complex system of ideas which we call science. In one sense these ideas are not absolute. Science is always progressing. But the principles correspond to and are based on observed facts. Hence science has enabled that great harnessing of natural forces to the service of man, all those marvellous mechanical inventions from which we all benefit, though sometimes we say the world would be better if there were no internal combustion engines and no wireless and no aeroplanes and so forth. But for better or worse we cannot stop progress. What I mean is that with all necessary qualifications the laws of nature are concerned with truth. But law in our sense is not concerned with truth, but with the accomplishment of justice. It deals with rules of human conduct and is imperative in that it seeks to enforce just conduct, taking that phrase in the widest sense. A man must not steal or murder or break his contracts or injure his fellow-man by careless or unregarding conduct. Hence the moral or ethical element in law. I am not saying that much law is not grounded on particular interests or prejudices, that much law is not unjust in the true sense. That, however, is not the ideal of law but its failure. The amelioration of law has been the purpose of men with humanitarian impulses, such as those who initiated the great movement which led to Factory Acts, the abolition of child labour, Health Acts and so forth. These dealt with broad national matters. But there is also another aspect of law reform which may be typified by Bentham, the reform of the details of rules of law, and the correction of defects of procedure, such as those of the Chancery Courts which were pilloried in *Bleak House* by Dickens, who was substantially accurate in what he wrote. Then there is a slow but continual process of revision and readjustment in the smaller points of the law, which interest lawyers more than ordinary people, that has been going on for a century or more. This may be called the technical reform, the removal of all the solecisms and fictions which grew up inevitably in the piecemeal, often haphazard, always empirical, process of judge-made law, confined by precedents. Lawyers are a conservative body in what they regard as their own special sphere. But even in the inner fastnesses of the law the modern idea of social service is penetrating, just as Bentham was influenced by the utilitarianism of his day. A lawyer is now called a modernist if he insists that law has to justify itself by its fitness, in broad aspects and in technical details, to subserve the public good. There have been lawyers in the past who boldly declared that law was a body of imperative principles, which did not need to be justified by results. A century or so ago a Chancery lawyer, giving evidence before a commission,

Some General Aspects of Law

indignantly repudiated the idea that the interests of clients had to be considered. What did they count in comparison with the majesty of the established system, a system which at that time embodied all the abuses which Dickens exposed?

It has been pointed out with great truth that the reform of law has followed in great measure the extension of the franchise. A good illustration in the more limited sphere of private law is furnished by the position of married women. By the old Common Law a married woman had in general no right to make a contract or to hold property of her own. Equity did indeed invent certain methods of enabling her to hold what was called her separate estate, but these cumbrous methods were only adapted to the rich with their elaborate system of trusts and settlements. It is only within the last few years that by gradual and halting steps the old law has been swept away and a married woman has all the rights as to holding property and doing business that a single woman has. In more public aspects of law the same process has taken place. Take for instance the right of workmen to combine to improve their conditions and their wages. The combination laws of a century ago are shocking to modern ideas. It is little more than 60 years since trade unions were given a kind of legal status. Even in this century we had the *Taff Vale Case* [1901] A.C. 426, and it was not till 1906 that the Trade Disputes Act was passed. I mention these illustrations only to show how slowly laws are changed even if they are unjust, and even then they are not always completely reformed. In a narrower sphere there was an old law that, as a rule, when a man died his rights of action and his liabilities died with him. From early times this illogical and unjust rule was cut down in material respects, either by Parliament or by the Judges. It is, however, only within a few years that it has been almost completely abolished. The possibility of accomplishing this change was due in part to the growth of motor-car accidents. A negligent driver who caused serious damage, but himself died in the accident, ceased to be liable because he died, and so did his insurance company. That seemed shocking and at long last the injustice was corrected.

Such processes of amelioration work slowly and sometimes do not work efficiently. Let me take what is called the doctrine of common employment. Let me illustrate it by a simple instance. A contractor sends his lorry to a distant job. It is driven by his own driver, with him are one of the contractor's men, and also a strange workman employed by the contractor going to do a separate job, such as electric fitting on the work. By the negligence of the driver there is a road accident, both the contractor's employee and the specialist workman are killed. The widow of the latter can sue for damages, the widow of the former cannot. It is true she has a claim under the Workmen's Compensation Act, but that is much less beneficial than if she could, like the other widow, claim for damages by the ordinary law. The doctrine is an exception to the ordinary rule that an employer is responsible for the negligence of his servants while doing his work. The exception is quite illogical. Between 1837 and 1880 the injured workman had no practical redress in such cases; his fellow-workman would not be able to pay and his employer was not liable. It is interesting that instead of abolishing the rule, Parliament sought to soften the injustice by the Workmen's Compensation Acts, which indeed introduced a new idea of insurance where the right was not based on negligence. But the Acts have given rise to an enormous amount of litigation and the compensation is on a scale much less beneficial than the Common Law would give, that is, of course, if in cases where the plaintiff could prove negligence. There is, I believe, a commission sitting or about to sit to consider the working of these Acts. I have given this illustration of the vitality of a bad rule, but there are others.

I must conclude these desultory observations.

IX

WILLISTON ON CONTRACTS[1]

THIS great work[2] in eight volumes and 7725 pages does indeed deserve the appellation "monumental". Dominie Sampson would have called it prodigious. Bulk and merit are not necessarily antithetical. They are certainly not so in the present case. I do not know whether to applaud more the scope and range of the plan or the excellence of the performance. The publication of the first edition in 1920 marked a stage in the history of the Common Law. This second and revised edition, the publication of which was completed in 1938, is another landmark.

In this edition Williston has had the distinguished assistance of Professor Thompson, of Cornell. But Williston "has personally examined every section of the manuscript and either collaborated in its production or approved its form". I hope, therefore, Professor Thompson will not think I am undervaluing his share in the revised work if for convenience I refer to the authors under the compendious term Williston. However important Professor Thompson's contributions are, the earlier edition has always been known as "Williston on Contracts", and this edition is still so described. Indeed

[1] This article was published in the April number of the *Law Quarterly Review*, 1939.

[2] *A Treatise on the Law of Contracts.* By Samuel Williston. Revised edition by the author and George J. Thompson. New York: Baker, Voorhis & Co. Eight vols. Large 8vo. 2044 sections, with Forms, Index and Tables.

this work is justifiably regarded as a monument of the greatness of the Harvard Law School, and Williston, now a veteran and emeritus, is esteemed as having a place in the direct line of succession among the great lawyers who have adorned that School

When I approach the work itself I am a little daunted by its magnitude. But the work is certainly not "consili expers". On the contrary "mens agitat molem et vasto se corpore miscet". Of the eight volumes two call for separate mention. The seventh is devoted to a collection of forms appropriate to the different exigencies which arise in practice in regard to contracts. It has been prepared by Mr Edwin M. Bohm of the New York Bar, and is suited for use in conjunction with the main work or independently by itself. It has a very full index and the forms in most cases have references to the actual decisions cited in the main texts from which they are derived. But as Mr Bohm wisely observes, the forms are not the final word, but are designed and offered as suggestions and guides. So far as I can judge they should be of great value to practitioners.

Volume VIII consists of Tables and Indexes. It is on an impressive scale and is a volume of just over 1000 pages. About one-half consists of the "General Index". No lawyer needs to be reminded how essential is such an Index, which is a sort of clue to guide him in his work through the mazes of the book. Without a really good Index the practising lawyer would be almost entirely debarred from making effective use of the treatise. The Index enables him to make the book, or such part or parts of it as he immediately wants, his tool. I have tested it in many ways and have not found it to fail.

The Table of Cases next calls for notice. It is stated to contain approximately 70,000 cases, with references to the exact section in which they appear. The Table is to be a "guiding light" "in the dark labyrinth of the modern law". The utility of such a Table is enormous. I myself constantly find that, when considering some point of law, I begin by trying to remember some important case related to the problem and then using that as a starting-point. This Table is supplemented by an index to legal articles cited in the book, containing under the names of their authors references to the sections in which they are cited. The systematic reference to these articles in connection with the particular decisions round which they centre is, so far as I know, a novel feature, and it cannot fail to aid in the criticism and development of law. When we speak, as we often do, of law as being bound hard and fast by precedent, we are apt to forget that precedents may have the opposite effect and lead to advance in the law. The advocate or judge faced by an authority may realize its limitations and may see that, though it does not appear exactly to fit the facts, the rule is capable of being properly applied and modified without any breach of authority or contradiction in principle so as to meet the new case. It points the way of advance. Thus the law is constantly growing and expanding. The process is aided by the number of authorities dealing with such varieties of illustration. Their comparison and criticism and the various acute articles which are now regularly published greatly promote these developments.

The total of 70,000 cases is somewhat alarming. It does indeed include a great many English cases, some Canadian, a few Australian and New Zealand, and a

Williston on Contracts

very few Indian cases either in the Indian Courts or the Privy Council. I like to think of the Common Law as one great system covering perhaps half the inhabitants of the world, covering the United States, England, the British Commonwealth of Nations, and also the Crown Colonies and India, where systems other than Common Law are to some extent in force. I regret to see that the citation of American authorities has almost completely ceased in England. In 1889, Lord Halsbury, Cotton L.J. and Fry L.J. solemnly condemned the practice of citing in English Courts American decisions as if they were decisions of our own highest Courts (*Re Missouri S.S. Co.* 42 Ch.D. at pp. 330–331). Lord Halsbury explains that an inquiry would be involved whether the American law was the same as the English. He might have added that the law of one State is often different from that of another, on particular points, as I have observed over and over again in reading this book. I do not know if the overruling of *Swift* v. *Tyson*[1] will diminish or aggravate the differences, or whether forces like Uniform State Laws and recourse to the Restatements will tend to eliminate or reduce the differences. But I cannot help deploring the cessation of free trade in the Common Law authorities and ideas. Perhaps the most serious obstacle in the way is the great multiplication of authorities in the United States. There are, I think, forty-eight States each with its own jurisdiction. I understand that an American lawyer learns to handle this mass and can find whatever he needs from time to time. An English lawyer is not likely to master that facility and may be excused for practical reasons if he does not attempt it, but he can

---

[1] (1842) 16 Pet. 1; overruled by the Supreme Court in *Erie Railroad Co.* v. *Tompkins* (1938) 304 U.S. 333.

at least get some useful acquaintance with American legal thought by studying the current law journals and an occasional voyage of discovery in such a book as Williston.

I must not overlook another Table, that of the References throughout the book to the Restatements issued by the American Law Institute. Against each section of the particular Restatements quoted there is in the Index a reference to the section or sections of the book in which it is cited. Naturally in this regard the Contract Restatement largely predominates. Williston was the reporter for that subject. There are also references (among others) to several sections of the Restitution Restatement. Williston does not specifically or in detail discuss Restitution, but he was a member of the Committee which prepared the Restatement and is fully alive to the distinction between contract and what he calls quasi-contract, a term which he evidently prefers to unjust enrichment. He says at pp. 6–7: "The expression 'implied contract' has given rise to great confusion in the law. Until recently the divisions of the law customarily made coincided with the forms of action known to the common law. Consequently, all rights enforced by the contractual actions of *assumpsit*, covenant, and debt were regarded as based on contract. Some of these rights, however, were created not by any promise or mutual assent of the parties, but were imposed by law on the defendant irrespective of, and sometimes in violation of, his intention. Such obligations were called implied contracts. A better name is that now generally in use of 'quasi-contracts'." He emphasizes the confusion between contracts implied in law and those implied in fact. A little later he points out that the obligations imposed in quasi-contract do not depend, as in contract, on assent to making a promise. In other places he discusses the distinction between damages for breach of contract and the measure of restitution in quasi-contract. He also distinguishes as three juristic categories, contract, tort, quasi-contract. On this topic legal thought is, in my opinion, more generally advanced in America than in England, where it is still considered a mark of legal orthodoxy to deny or ignore the distinction between contract and quasi-contract and say that there are only two categories, contract and tort. This may appear strange when it is realized that in England after the Common Law Procedure Act the fictitious *assumpsit* became superfluous and obsolete, and then a little later all forms of action were abrogated by the Judicature Act, 1873. This confusion of juristic conceptions is unfortunate because it has, at least for the time, prevented the development in England of the doctrine of quasi-contract.

The bulk of the book consists of sixty chapters, comprising 2044 sections. The chapters are divided into eight parts. Part I (after certain introductory definitions) deals with the formation of Contract, Part II deals with parties, Part III deals with the Statute of Frauds, Part IV deals with performance of Contracts, Part V deals with particular classes of Contract, such as those for the sale of land and of personal property, of employment and to marry, of bailment and innkeepers, of carriers, of Bills of Exchange and Promissory Notes and of suretyship. Part VI deals with breach of Contract and remedies for breach of Contract. Part VII deals with invalidating circumstances, Fraud, Mistake, duress, illegality. Part VIII deals with the discharge of Contracts.

I may observe as to Williston's general method of exposition that it is less that of an analytical jurist than of a case lawyer. I do not mean that Williston does not examine principles throughout in a manner which is lucid, acute, broad-minded, and progressive. But his exposition is in general concrete, keeping close to decided cases in accordance with the spirit of the Common Law. I can best explain what I mean by taking Chapter XLVI, in which he discusses Mistake, sections 1535 to 1600 F, pages 4321 to 4492. The most striking illustration of the differences between Williston's method and that of analytical jurists is afforded by the brief but clear and precise summary which forms the concluding part of the chapter in which he discusses the treatment and judicial interpretation of Mistake under the Civil Law, the German Civil Code and under French Law. But even a Common Lawyer may attempt a somewhat abstract analysis, as, for instance, Pollock does in Chapter IX of his *Principles of Contract*, when he discusses the subject under three headings, Mistake in General with the subordinate distinction of mistake of fact and of law, Mistake as excluding true consent, Mistake in expressing true consent. The distinction between the two later categories is pronounced. I do not think there is anything in Pollock which is not in Williston, and in Williston with greater variety of examples and cited authorities and more ample discussion. And the leading ideas and categories can be found by going through the headings of the different sections. But there is no dissected and integrated analysis. I do not say that Williston's system is not excellent. The practitioner can find the heading he wants and can select the authorities and illustrations proper to his problem. The student can take the Civil Law systems as set out by Williston not only under this heading but in the other chapters under the respective headings, and can examine the analogies and differences as compared with the Common Law system. But he will bear in mind Williston's sound warning against borrowing from the Civil Law classifications and rules which are not appropriate to English (that is, Common) Law.

While Williston emphasizes the distinction between contracts void for mistake and contracts merely voidable, he particularly describes as a source of error "confusion as to whether mutual assent or an expression of assent is an essential element in the formation of a contract". This distinction seems to involve a theory as to the essential nature of mistake and its place in the law of contract. I shall venture to refer to this question later. Williston goes on to say that mistake "involves the effect of erroneous ideas upon legal acts or upon acts which would have been legal acts had it not been for the error. In this treatise the subject is necessarily confined to the effect of such erroneous ideas upon acts connected with the formation, performance or discharge of contracts." He then restates what he had stated earlier in the book, that it is not mental assent which constitutes the contract, but the expression of assent by the parties. If that were strictly and absolutely true and not merely true *sub modo*, I should find it difficult to see what place can be found for mistake as an effective element in the law of contract, apart from certain special cases such as those where there is no identical expression of assent, for instance, where by some mischance, for which neither party can be held responsible, offer and acceptance do not agree, or where a plea of *non est factum* would have been available. But in the ordinary cases of common or mutual mistake, if the Court simply proceeded on the objective expression of intention, it would have to treat the mental state of the parties as irrelevant.

As I suppose every Common Lawyer would accept the objective theory of interpretation and would also recognize the place of mistake not only in expression (which is dealt with by rectification) but also in substance where there is only the appearance and not the reality of consent so that there may be no contract at all, there may seem to be an antinomy which has to be reconciled. I once had the temerity when delivering a judgment of the Privy Council to suggest tentatively some sort of explanation, which with hesitation I venture to repeat. It was in effect that while intention in these matters is generally to be regarded objectively, that is, intention is to be ascertained from what the parties said or did, affirmative proof of mistake may in special cases exclude that finding of intention. But if it is to have that effect the mistake must be fundamental or basic, it must be in respect of the underlying assumption of the contract, and it may be a matter of great difficulty to determine whether it is so. Where there is such a case the parties intend to express themselves as they do in fact, and intend to bind themselves in that way by contract, but they do so under an erroneous view, shared by both, as to what the basic underlying conditions of fact are. They mean to contract on the basis that the basic facts are so and so, whereas it turns out that they are otherwise. Hence the mistake prevents true consent.

I am not sure how far Williston would agree with this bare statement, but it may be that the general idea runs through the most illuminating collection of particular cases which he sets out. It may be that the idea is embodied in his instance (3) in section 1541: "There may be an expression of agreement and the expression may conform to the intention of the parties, but a mistake as to the way the agreement would apply to existing facts may make it equitable to rescind the transaction." I do not take this as limited to what has been called technical equity because, as I understand it, the Common Law, at least after a certain date, would say in certain circumstances that an agreement was void for mistake; as, for instance, an agreement to sell a specific chattel which both parties believed to be existing but in fact had perished. Every agreement has to be construed in the light of the surrounding facts "known" to the parties; but suppose the "knowledge" is illusory and the facts are different. Williston very shrewdly protests against the use of the word "mistake" as limited to cases where it has a legal effect, which he says would be an attempt to give an artificial meaning to an ordinary English word. Williston points out that where there is such an erroneous assumption as to constitute mistake which has a legal effect, the principle should be applied as a principle of justice without any further question as to whether the mistake is intrinsic or extrinsic, or whether it affects identity or quality.

His discussion of rectification or reformation of mistake in the expression of contract is very fully documented with citations. That is a purely equitable form of relief. Indeed but for its existence the Common Law method of objective interpretation would at times have led to intolerable injustice. Equity has saved it. Williston very fully illustrates the limits of rectification. He deals very clearly with the complications sometimes introduced by the Statute of Frauds. He obviously approves of what I think is now the English practice of reforming where necessary in one action both the prior executory contract and the completed conveyance or contract and also enforcing it as reformed. His comment on the objection to that course is typical of his robust common sense. "To allow reformation, it was said, would be in effect first to reform an executory contract and then enforce it as reformed. Doubtless this is true, but it is not so clear why it is objectionable." He deals in detail with mistake as to the person contracted with, as to the existence of an essential thing or person, and also cases under the Sale of Goods Acts. I notice that he approves the view that there may be a case of effective mutual mistake as to a material fact where goods, the subject of a sale, were not at the material time in ordinary merchantable condition as the parties are to be taken to have assumed that they were. Williston also gives illustrations of mistake in regard to various types of contract. While pointing out that mistake as to collateral matters is generally immaterial, he refers to *Cox* v. *Prentice* (1815) 3 M. & S. 344, and various American cases where it has been held that there was mistake effective in law on the ground of an extreme difference between the real and the assumed quality or nature of the specific thing in question. I should have thought that here the mistake was not collateral but in regard to the substance. He observes that in this connection it may happen that the thing is better not worse than the parties believed. He instances the case of a cow assumed to be barren and in fact discovered to be a breeder. The seller was held not bound. Williston is dealing here with common or mutual mistake, which he points out may exist with a difference in each party and yet may involve an error in the basic assumptions. He gives a very striking illustration of what might appear to be a basic mistake where the State Court held that the bargain was binding. Williston is of opinion that the decision was unjust and would not be followed by the Courts nowadays. Appreciation of the legal effect of mistake has unquestionably grown both in America and England.

Unilateral mistake, he points out, is only a ground for affirmative relief, as distinguished from a mere refusal of specific performance, where the other party knew of the mistake or where the party against whom relief was sought was a volunteer. While he regards such relief as approaching to a contradiction of the objective theory of assent, he does, as I read him, favour an extension of such relief in proper cases in equity, and he questions if the equitable and legal doctrines in regard to the formation and enforcement of contract can be permanently kept in separate compartments. He discusses mistake of law at considerable length and says it is impossible to co-ordinate the cases satisfactorily because the rule distinguishing mistake of law from mistake of fact is founded on no sound principle.

I have, I think, done enough to indicate Williston's method, empirical or pragmatic rather than ideological, keeping close to the cases on the whole, but liberal and enlightened and favouring such extensions and amendments as will advance the cause of justice. I can at best give a very poor idea of an exposition that covers 170 pages. I may add two observations. In another section, that dealing with Fraud and Misrepresentation, he refers to *Smith* v. *Hughes* (1871) L.R. 6 Q.B. 597, for the rule, of law at least, that there is in general no legal obligation on a vendor to inform a purchaser that he is under a mistake not induced by any act of the vendor. This is a rule not to be commended as being of a high moral standard. But he adds the important qualification quoted from the Contract Restatement that if a fact known to one party and not to the other is so vital that if the mistake were mutual the contract would be voidable, and the party knowing the fact also knows that the other does not know it, non-disclosure is not privileged and is fraudulent. No doubt every case must depend on its facts, but I should not like to say that this qualification would be accepted by English law, however desirable it might be. Williston cites cases of what he calls snapping up of a "too-good-to-be-true offer". *Bell* v. *Lever* [1932] A.C. 161, he refers to briefly as a case which treated the mistake as not fundamental. I gather he does not approve of the final decision given by the majority of the House of Lords. In that case my judgment as a judge of first instance was eventually reversed. I think the decision turned on what in all such cases is the real problem, whether the mistake was sufficiently basic. I may here add, without developing, his wise definition of estoppel as a conclusive admission of a non-existent fact which may be essential either for a cause of action for a defence or for a replication.

Williston on Contracts

I have discussed Mistake at some length, though of necessity most inadequately, both to illustrate Williston's method of exposition and because the logic of it is both significant and interesting. Williston is an exponent of what he calls the objective theory of contract as contrasted with the subjective theory. The latter theory makes a contract depend on the meeting of the minds of the parties, what is or used to be sometimes called *consensus ad idem*. It is beyond question that when a Court has a contract before it, it does not in general attempt to examine the state of mind of the parties. To do so would indeed be an impossible task wherever the interpretation of the contract was in dispute. The parties could not at the date of the trial be expected to explain what they really intended, and if they attempted to do so their evidence would be likely to suffer from prejudice and self-sophistication and would be contradictory. The law therefore is necessarily driven to proceed on the basis of the external manifestations of the parties, words, written or spoken, or other overt acts. Evidence of intention is therefore generally held to be inadmissible. Parol evidence is excluded except in so far as it is evidence of the surrounding facts known to both parties and in contemplation of which they contracted. This evidence is merely admitted to enable the Court to put itself so far as possible in the position of the parties when they made the contract. The overt signs must be interpreted in the light of such facts. This is the Common Law principle of interpretation which is applied not only to bilateral contracts, but to unilateral obligations, such as settlements, wills, and also Acts of the Legislature. It is adopted not merely because it is the only practicable method, but also because by and large it does actually give effect to what the parties did intend. It is no form of words when a Court of Construction says that it is giving effect (that is so far as is humanly practicable) to the intention of the parties. I hesitate to accept Williston's statement that the whole objective theory of contracts is based on analogy to estoppel. The Court is dealing with the only helpful facts that are available to it to settle the dispute. It is dealing with the overt acts. But there are important qualifications before it is possible, so it seems to me, to accept the objective theory as absolute or complete. In the first place, a distinction must be drawn between the content of the contract, to be ascertained by the overt acts, or written or spoken words, which have to be construed, and the prior question, which is whether the parties did intend to make a legal bargain or contract at all. In *Rose and Frank* v. *Crompton* [1925] A.C. 445, a case which I argued up to the House of Lords, it was held that there was no contract, because the parties had expressly inserted a clause saying that there should be no contract. It was held that on the interpretation of that clause there was no contract. But surely the same problem is implicit in every contract. It seldom comes to light because nearly always people who go through the external forms of contracting do intend to contract. But it may appear to the Court, considering the external manifestations in the light of the surrounding facts and of common sense, that there was no intention to contract. Such a case was *Balfour* v. *Balfour* [1919] 2 K.B. 571, and there are some others cited by Williston, though such cases are the exception, not the rule. Estoppel is not here relevant. The question is purely objective—that is, the intention or absence of intention is to be ascertained from the facts. There is in such cases, however rare, no *animus contrahendi*, to use the old phrase. Actual intention is the decisive test here. Then there is the question of mistake which I have already discussed, where the law goes behind the external manifestations. This was done at law, though no doubt more extensively in equity, but now that law and equity are administered by the same Court, no modern theory of contract can fail to regard this matter. Much the same is true of fraud, misrepresentation, impossibility. The objective theory ceases to cover the ground in such cases. Perhaps rectification is an even stronger illustration of the same principle, though in its origin that was a purely equitable relief. It seems to me that the objective theory, true within limits, must not be driven to death. I should like simply to say that if it is not disputed or established that there was an intention to contract, the law enforces the contract on the basis of the external manifestations, unless there is positive reason shown why in the particular case it should not.

Williston discusses clearly and fully the questions which have arisen in regard to offer and acceptance, which it is natural to regard as the normal mode of making a contract. I am not clear that the analysis is not artificial. In a complicated commercial contract, preliminary negotiations result in a contract being drawn up, which both parties sign. The preliminary negotiations have become irrelevant for the construction of the contract except in the event of rectification being claimed. But no doubt many bargains are made by offer and acceptance. This is so perhaps most where the parties are at a distance from each other. Williston adopts the view that in such cases the offer speaks from receipt by the offeree, and the acceptance from the date it is dispatched by the contemplated means of communication, such as the post or telegraph. He discusses the difference between illusory promises and indefinite promises to which the law can apply the standard of what is reasonable. He criticizes the maxim that silence does not mean consent. If by silence is meant absence of words, it is clear that consent may be indicated in other ways. There may also be circumstances where by reason of the relation between the parties or by custom silence both in word and deed may mean consent. He indicates, however, a further criterion which I find it hard to accept as a general statement, namely, that if the offeree has solicited the offer, his silence may be construed as an acceptance if in the facts of the case a reasonable man would so interpret the silence.

I must turn to the important chapter on Consideration, which, with the associated chapter on Promises requiring neither Consent nor Consideration, and that on Formal Contracts, covers 350 pages, and embraces a very full statement of the Common Law, at least as understood in the United States. The statement at times includes criticism, but in the main it is a positive statement of existing rules. That he has some difficulty in regarding the rule as a wholly good rule appears from the suggestion which he puts forward that there should be a form of simple contract (that is, one not under seal) in which consideration is as much unnecessary as if the contract were under seal, though I gather the recommendation was made only for the benefit of those States which have abolished the Common Law effect of the seal. The clause recommended as drafted by Williston ran thus: "A written promise or release hereafter made and signed by the person releasing or promising shall not be invalid or unenforceable for lack of consideration, if the writing also contains an additional express statement in any form of language that the signer intends to be legally bound." If this is an advisable measure in States where the seal has been abolished, I do not see why it should not be equally good where the seal remains as an alternative form of obligation. I do not, however, like the requirement of the express statement. An intention to be bound may equally be shown by the nature of the transaction. The true question, to my mind, is whether there was an intention to be bound. The difficulty about Consideration is that it is sought to elevate it into the sole and absolute condition of a contract. In most contracts there is actually, at least on the conventional view of bilateral contracts, consideration. People bargain for an advantage in return for an advantage. Gratuitous undertakings are rare in comparison. Yet there may be such undertakings which a complete system of law should be able to enforce. In the century or thereabouts after Lord Mansfield the English judges after much uncertainty evolved what they considered to be a logical theory of consideration. It was logical enough when it defined consideration as an advantage conferred on the promisor by the promisee or a detriment suffered by the promisee at the request of the promisor, and also required consideration to be contemporaneous, not precedent or past, and therefore excluded, though with some exceptions, "moral consideration" and "past consideration" (terms which were self-contradictory on the basis of the definition) and also insisted that consideration must move from the promisee and thus excluded the third party beneficiary. But the fallacy was, I think, in the major premiss that consideration, as defined, was the essential condition of the contractual intention or the validity of a simple contract. It is this proposition which is to be disputed. I do not myself underrate the value of consideration as a proof of contractual intention. It will be forthcoming much more often than not. What I object to is the doctrine, quite modern, that it is the only necessary proof. As I have indicated, contractual intention is always a matter of fact, whether there is consideration or not. The question whether there is a contract should not be excluded from the determination of the Court merely because there is no consideration in the Common Law any more than it is in other systems of law. Indeed (apart from contracts under seal) there are recognized both in England and in the United States certain promises which are held good without consideration. These are fully dealt with in Williston's chapter. The most striking of these cases is the acknowledgment in writing of a statute-barred debt. There has been much controversy as to the true effect of this. Does it simply revive the old debt or is it a new promise to pay? If the latter there is no consideration, save what is moral or past. There was some confusion in the old procedure under which in practice the declaration was on the old debt, but, as Williston points out, where the original creditor had died and the new promise was made to his executor or administrator, the new promise had to be declared upon, and similarly in bankruptcy. And beyond doubt the new promise, which is implied from the acknowledgment, may be qualified. The nature of the debtor's obligation is determined by the new promise. It is on this latter ground that Williston, as I read him, impliedly criticizes and dissents from Lord Sumner's observations in *Spencer* v. *Hemmerde* [1922] 2 A.C. 507, where Lord Sumner seeks to avoid finding a new promise because to do so would contradict the doctrine of consideration. The observations of Lord Sumner were not necessary to the decision of the case. Williston, I think, gives convincing reasons why it is the new promise which is the cause of action. Thus there is a real survival of "moral" consideration which is not under the definition consideration at all. But in addition there has been developed, at least in some States, what Williston calls the doctrine of promissory estoppel, where there is no consideration for the promise. He quotes section 90 of the Restatement of Contracts, which is in these terms: "A promise which the promisor should reasonably expect to induce action or forbearance of a definite or substantial character on the part of the promisee and which does induce such action or forbearance is binding, if injustice can be avoided only by enforcing the promise." I do not think there is any such rule in English law, though in three cases Williston finds a recognition of what he calls a consideration of trust or a consideration of confidence on the analogy of the gratuitous bailment cases, which originally led to the doctrine of *assumpsit*. I am not at present satisfied that this is the English law. It is, however, clear from what has been said that on any view there may be some promises enforceable without consideration and that there is no theoretical obstacle to finding an intention to promise without consideration. Indeed, as Williston points out, equity has found no difficulty in enforcing gratuitous declarations of trust, without change of possession. These, he truly observes, infringe the principles that a promise is not binding without consideration and that a gift without delivery is ineffectual. It is true that this is a rule of equity, but again it shows that there is no absolute objection to enforcing gratuitous obligations. The modern English rule can only, I think, be justified on grounds of prejudice or tradition or convenience. In fact the modern theory of consideration is riddled with illogicality, fiction, and anomaly, and is only not inconvenient because the cases in which there is not actual or pretended consideration are comparatively few, partly because of ingenuity of lawyers in constructing consideration of which the parties never dreamt. But it is inconvenient in a number of cases which is not negligible, where a serious promise is intended and a serious breach of promise goes unredressed. I may add the case of Commercial Credits, for which I have never found any consideration, at least in English law, though Williston finds some in American law. I shall later revert to that. It is a curious reflection on the law of great commercial nations that they have no logical sanction for these important transactions which annually involve untold millions of money. It is no answer that bankers fulfil their undertakings in practice. I cannot examine in detail Williston's very careful and full treatment of the existing law of consideration.

I have been using the word as meaning something regarded as consideration by both parties, and also sufficient in law. Williston prefers to use the word as meaning any consideration or exchange given in fact irrespective of legal sufficiency.

He takes with apparent approval the strict view that payment of part of a debt is no consideration for a promise to accept it in satisfaction of the whole. There is, he says, in such a promise neither legal benefit nor legal detriment. He had said a little before that the law was made for man not man for the law, and might perhaps have been led to consider the reasoning of the House of Lords in *Foakes* v. *Beer* (1884) 9 App. Cas. 605, which was based on grounds of commercial expedience and perhaps even of precedent. He accepts also the conventional view that a composition with creditors is valid because each creditor contributes the agreement of the other creditors to accept the dividend. This has always seemed to me to be an artificial view, but I suppose it is the best possible. On the same lines Williston discusses promises given to a creditor to fulfil an existing obligation whether given by the original promisor himself or a third person. Here again he finds no legal benefit and no legal detriment and no binding contract. The stress here is on the word "legal". But there is clearly in fact both benefit and detriment, or why do people make such promises? In any case the repetition of a promise may have effect on the operation of the Statute of Limitation. Again, if strict logic is to be invoked, how are the mutual promises in a bilateral simple contract to be regarded? Each is said to be the consideration for the other; that is, each taken by itself is a nonentity. But two nonentities do not make an entity. The plain man has no difficulty. He regards himself as bound because he has given his word intending to be bound. So does the other man. It seems against common sense to say that the mere exertion of writing or making other manifestations to the other man is a legal detriment apart from the substance of the promise. Williston seems to find a solution of the problem in Leake's definition, which he quotes, to the effect that whatever matter if executed is sufficient to form a good executed consideration [that is, in a unilateral contract] if promised is sufficient to form a good executory consideration [that is, in a bilateral contract]. That seems to me merely to confuse the essential distinction between executed and executory. Williston recognizes that if one promise is not binding, there is no legal detriment and the other is not binding either. As Holt L.C.J. said, either all is *nudum pactum* or else the one promise is as good as the other. But it should be added "or as bad as the other". I have difficulty in appreciating Williston's attempt to resolve the dilemma. But as a practical lawyer I can say that there is no doubt about what is the existing law on this point and this particular difficulty in theory makes no difficulty in practice, because it goes to give effect to the intention of the parties. In truth in logic there is no legal consideration at all. But I must desist from further heresy. Space at least forbids. Williston accepts (as most writers do) Lord Justice Bowen's explanation of the promise to pay for a past consideration which the older lawyers coupled up with the previous request. I have never felt happy about the modern explanation. But I have already spent more than a proper allowance of space on consideration. I leave the student or the practitioner to the details of Williston's admirable and, I think, unrivalled exposition of the existing law.

I depart from Williston's order of chapters and turn to the Statute of Frauds, or rather sections 4 and 17 of the Statute, which are the material sections for Williston's subject. It is to be observed that the discussion of these two sections, which consisted of perhaps 200 or 300 words in all, occupies just over 400 pages of the book. How many thousand cases are cited I have not stopped to count. To an unsophisticated mind, this comparison may cast some doubt on the wisdom or efficacy of the legislation. It may also be that judges have often been reluctant to give literal effect to the provisions, or, more bluntly, have evaded it. Indeed the Statute, enacted in 1677, seems to have been merely opportunist and dictated by the pressure of the many groundless and fraudulent claims which emerged after the confused times of the Civil War, the Commonwealth and the Restoration.

I have sometimes in more formal moods said to myself that no contract should be enforceable unless it was a written contract; in other words, that the valid formation of the contract should be conditioned by its being reduced to writing. That would be nice in theory. But a little reflection has told me that not only everyday bargains but many most important contracts are made and done by word of mouth. I well remember cross-examining the veteran chairman of one of the great London banks about an important commercial transaction. I asked him why he had nothing in writing. He replied: "I had Mr Y's word. That was enough for me."

The Statute does not require the contract to be in writing, either at the date when it is concluded or afterwards. What it requires is a note or memorandum signed by the party to be charged or his agent made at any time before action. This is not a condition on which the existence of the contract depends. As Williston aptly says, rejecting the common statement that it is a rule of evidence, it is a condition precedent to the power of the Court to enforce it. Under section 17, but not under section 4, certain acts of part performance will supply the want of the memorandum. It is not clear why part performance should not have in principle applied to cases under section 4. The reason was, it seems, procedural. Equity did not venture to apply its doctrine of part performance to that section, and the cases were cases at law.

I do not know of any exposition of the very numerous cases and of the niceties, distinctions and anomalies which they present better than that contained in the six chapters of Williston's book which deal with the Statute. I do not expect it will ever be replaced or surpassed. I confess I found it, however ably and brilliantly done, somewhat depressing. There is no principle involved. It is all devoted to construing badly drawn and ill-planned sections of a statute which was an extemporaneous excrescence on the Common Law, imposed, as it were, from without as recently as the third part of the seventeenth century. It might well be asked why the Legislature chose the particular contracts which they did. As to the case of promises to answer for the debt of another, Williston supports the view, for which there is authority, that there was a special ground for protecting a guarantor who received, so it is said, no advantage and had no interest in the transaction save what came from his promise to guarantee. I confess I find it difficult to accept this reasoning. A guarantor is a free agent. He gives a guarantee because he wants to do so. He obtains consideration where there is no other consideration at least because the creditor, at his request, suffers the detriment of advancing the money or giving the credit. The creditor has as much right to enforce his contract against the surety as a creditor for goods supplied. He has given the value which the guarantor wanted. There is no special reason to suspect him of perjury. On this view is based a distinction drawn in regard to guarantees between those cases in which the guarantor is an absolute stranger to the transaction and those on which the "guarantor" has a "personal immediate and pecuniary interest in the transaction and is himself a party to be benefited by the performance of the promise". On this distinction have been based the series of cases in which the Courts have held the Statute not to apply. I confess I fail to see the value of this distinction, still less how it can justify the Courts in giving the go-by to the Statute, which contains no words which draw the distinction. Why should a promise to answer for the debt of another cease to be such a promise because the promisor obtains some extrinsic beneficial advantage to himself or has an interest in the performance of the principal undertaking? The words of the section do not draw any such distinction. In truth the actual words of the Statute, which appear to be simple and plain enough, seem almost to have been forgotten and to have become buried in the mass of decided cases. Williston, as in duty bound as an expositor of the existing law, seeks with great ability to rationalize and reconcile the cases, but it is a difficult task. We have here only one more example of the mischief which follows when Courts of law depart from the true principles of construing legislative Acts; that is, to interpret the actual words. Perhaps the most striking instance is afforded by the rule now accepted (and very convenient) that the promise made to his principal by a *del credere* factor to guarantee the debts arising from the factor's sales of his principal's goods is not within the Statute. As Williston observes, quoting English authority, that decision goes to the verge of the law. It might well be said to go well beyond it. However, it is well settled that such is the law. It is clearly, however, a promise to answer for the debt of another, and it seems *nil ad rem* that it forms part of a larger contract. There are, of course, cases which look at first sight like guarantees but where in fact the third party assumes the primary obligation, sometimes because he has a private interest, sometimes where he is, apart from the promise, a stranger to the transaction. But in such cases which are outside the Statute there is no promise to answer for the debt of another. The question merely turns on what was said.

Another provision of section 4 which has led to enormous litigation is that dealing with contracts not to be performed within a year. The broad rule now accepted no doubt is that what is meant is contracts which cannot be performed within that period. The question is to be looked at from the standpoint of the date at which the contract is made. Was there at that time a possibility in law and in fact that such performance as the parties intended might be completed before the expiration of the year? Thus Williston admirably expresses the test. He also points out, however, that the form rather than the substance of a contract may bring it within the Statute. He gives four illustrations: a promise to serve two years, a promise to serve two years but if the promisor dies the contract to be terminated, a promise to serve for two years if the employer lives so long, a promise to serve as long as the employer lives, not exceeding two years. It is clear that the legal effect of these four contracts is the same, yet, as Williston points out, the first and probably the second would be within the Statute, but not the last two. There are many other difficult questions, some perhaps not even yet settled. For instance, what is the position if the contract can be performed on one side within the year, but not on the other? Excellent judges have held that such a case is not within the Statute at least if on that side it is fully executed within the year. Williston, however, cites numerous decisions in which what he regards as a more reasonable construction of the Statute has been taken, and it is held that unless the contract from its inception is fully performable in the year, it is within the Statute. Such are a very few of the problems raised. It is clear that part performance is not relevant under section 4 to render the contract enforceable. This may lead, as it has done, to the gravest injustice. There are many curious consequences which flow from the fact that the contract is not void but merely unenforceable by reason of the Statute. For all these and other questions I refer the reader to Williston, where he will find the most recondite and intricate rules most clearly expounded.

So also the ingenious rules which define what the note or memorandum must be and contain.

I must, however, very briefly advert to section 17 (now section 4 in the English Sale of Goods Act, and there are corresponding sections in the different United States Acts). In England the Statute is limited to goods, a term which does not include choses in action. Thus in regard to them a contract of a million pounds in value may be oral. In at least some States I gather choses in action are included. I must advert to one point where English and American law seem to differ. Acceptance and actual receipt of the whole or part of the goods have been construed as imposing a double condition, receipt (that is, delivery) and acceptance. The question then has been what is meant by acceptance. In England, acceptance has been construed and is in fact now defined by the Act to mean any act by the buyer in regard to the goods which recognizes a pre-existing contract. Hence it is held to include acceptance of the goods not in the full sense, that is, as complying with the contract (as it means in other parts of the Act), but an acceptance with a right to examine and if necessary reject. The American Courts treat the words as having the same meaning as they have in other parts of the Sale of Goods Act, an assent on the part of the buyer to take specified goods as owner. Williston very properly points out that the English view involves a remarkable disregard of the words of section 17.

I note with interest that under the Uniform Warehouse Receipts Act, where the warehouse receipt is negotiable, its transfer constitutes delivery *ipso facto*. In England it is still necessary, except where there are special acts, to notify the warehouseman and obtain his attornment before there is delivery to, or receipt by, the buyer. It is curious that English law herein has not been changed by statute. I need not remind readers that there have been many difficulties in defining what constitutes actual receipt.

I have now, however inadequately, referred to the principal heads discussed by Williston in regard to the formation and form of contracts. He has also a valuable chapter on the capacity of parties. Williston takes the view that in general an infant's contract or transfer is voidable, not void. In England this is subject to the Infants Relief Act. The obligation of an infant to pay for necessaries does not, as Williston points out, properly depend on contract, but is quasi-contractual. This is quite clear under the English Sale of Goods Act, and the same is true in the case of the insane. As regards married women, Williston does not seem to refer to the recent English Act which has put the contractual position of a married woman on the same footing as a *feme sole*. There are valuable chapters on Agency Contracts, on Joint Duties and rights under Contracts, on the Assignment of Contracts, and on Contracts for the Benefit of Third Persons. This last I particularly commend to the consideration of my English friends, and ask them to say whether the carefully devised system in America is not preferable to the general refusal (since *Tweddle* v. *Atkinson* (1861) 1 B. & S. 393) to recognize such contracts, though in certain cases the cumbrous fiction of a trust is applied. I shall also pass over the interesting and important chapters on Rules of Interpretation (in which incidentally he sensibly dismisses as an unprofitable subtlety the distinction between latent and patent ambiguity), and on Usage and Custom. I can say little on the chapters dealing with Express Conditions, Excuses for Non-Performance of Conditions, and other questions connected with Conditions. There is an important chapter on the Dependency of Mutual Promises in the Civil Law. This is one of those valuable discussions on Comparative Law to which I have already adverted. The modern lawyer is not likely to need to study *Pordage* v. *Cole* (1668) or the notes thereon in 1 Wms Saunders, 319, but he has still to decide on less technical lines questions of that character; for instance, whether a contract is severable or not. As an instance of Williston's faculty of going to the practical root of a question I can quote a few words: "The essential test to determine whether a number of promises constitute one contract or more than one, is simple. It can be nothing else than the answer to an inquiry whether the parties assented to all the promises as a single whole, so that there would have been no bargain whatever if any promise or set of promises were struck out" (§ 863). He adds that it is a question of fact, and goes on to illustrate the difficulties which have to be solved in some cases. That leads him to a valuable discussion on the position under instalment contracts and the effect of defective performance of one or more instalments. When in such cases is the injured party justified in refusing to continue the contract as to future instalments? The test, he truly says, is the materiality of the breach which has been committed, or which the party has manifested an intention to commit. The other party may then elect to refuse to continue the contract. Williston criticizes certain English decisions which in his view make the injured party's rights depend not on the materiality of the breach, but on whether the wrongdoer's acts "amount to an intimation of an intention to abandon and altogether to refuse performance of the contract". There are certainly such expressions to be found in leading decisions. Williston, I think rightly, points out that it is a question of the materiality of the breach, not of the actual intention of the wrongdoer. I agree that the reference to intention is unfortunate, because it makes people think in terms of actual intention. But on the whole I think that what the judges meant was presumed intention, to be judged from what is done. Still the phrase leads to confusion and tends to distract from the true issue. He quotes from a judgment of my own (as a judge of first instance), where it was found that there had been no actual intention to break the contract, but it was said that the intention of the seller must be judged from his acts and the breach being substantial and persistent the other party was entitled to break the contract as repudiated. Williston cites this judgment as one in which the repudiation was found solely from a defective performance, though lip service was paid to the test of intention. I agree with the criticism that any reference to intention at all, even in words, is undesirable. I am consoled to find that he quotes with approval a later decision of a Court of Appeal of which I was a member which "deliberately rejected a subjective inquiry as to intent, and viewing the breach objectively, applied the test of materiality of the breach". I do not think there is any English authority to prevent English Courts from acting on this test, as I gather is done by the American Courts.

It is unnecessary to add that the wrongdoer cannot by his own wrongful act put an end to the contract save as founding a claim for damages. The election whether to do so or not lies with the injured party. All the chapters on Conditions, which occupy nearly 700 pages, are most practical and illuminating. Let me give one more illustration. He is discussing when time is of the essence of the contract. He concludes: "There are intermediate degrees between the latitude allowed by courts of equity in dealing with contracts to buy and sell land and the strictness which would hold that the slightest breach by the plaintiff of a promise in regard to time is fatal, even though time is not stated to be vital and is not so in fact, and though strict performance is not made an express condition of the defendant's promise" (§ 855). The English Sale of Goods Act provides that except as to time of payment which is not of the essence, it depends on the terms of the contract whether stipulations as to time are of the essence.

The fourth volume comprises what may be described as a series of separate treatises on special branches of contract law, such as negotiable instruments, contracts of carriage, maritime or by land or air, contracts for sale of land, or of goods, contracts of bailment, contracts of employment and to marry, contracts of suretyship. Except the last three, these contracts are largely governed by special statutes, which in many respects differ in America from the corresponding English statutes. In the first of these chapters, that relating to the Sale of Land, I have found the part dealing with the English rule that in equity the purchaser under an executory contract becomes the owner of the property full of suggestiveness. His criticisms, which are too long to discuss here, are marked with shrewdness and independence of thought. As to the Sale of Personal Property, the statutory law in the United States is substantially, but not entirely, the same as in England, at least in those States (the majority) which have adopted the Uniform Sales Act. In an earlier portion of the work (Chapter xviii) the provisions of the Act were discussed in reference to the section of the Statute of Frauds. I may here note that the American law does not accept the English view that a contract for the making and delivery of a particular article is a contract for the sale of goods. The view taken in America, as Williston points out, is that it is a contract for work and labour. But generally the American law is in this region substantially the same as the English. There is, however, it seems, a difference in terminology. The English Act defines a condition as a term breach of which entitles the buyer to reject if he has not waived that right. A warranty is something collateral, breach of which sounds in damages. In American law a warranty is used of a condition which may give a right of rescission. Williston seems to raise a doubt if on a sale of specific goods with a sample the buyer can reject if on examination the goods do not correspond to sample. I am not sure that I appreciate the difficulty, but I think on the whole Williston does not agree with the doubt. I should like particularly to refer again to his admirable discussion of commercial letters of credit. Bankers have in very rare cases disputed their liability on letters of credit or claimed to revoke them, and have failed, I think, in every case when they have so claimed. It is, however, certainly

Legal Essays and Addresses

difficult, as I have already noticed, to put the liability on the irrevocable letter of credit or on a satisfactory legal basis. Williston finds a solution in American law by means of the theory of the third party beneficiary, who is in these cases the seller. That explanation is not available in English law. Williston approves of the English rule that the seller's responsibility on an implied warranty (which might be called a condition in certain cases) is independent of negligence. He discusses the question carefully. Apparently in some of the States liability depends on the seller's negligence. But the general rule in the United States is in agreement with the English rule that negligence is not material. In this branch of law Williston makes frequent citations of the English cases, and in the main the two systems of law correspond.

The chapter on Contracts of Bailment and of Innkeepers contains a convenient statement of the principles applicable in such cases. Williston points out that, except in the cases of an involuntary bailment, the bailment involves a contract, express or implied, though often the terms of the bailment are largely left to be implied. As to involuntary bailments, Williston does not favour the view that the involuntary bailee is not under any duty of any sort or kind. He leaves the existence or extent of the duty rather at large and is wisely content to say that this must to some extent depend on circumstances. I do not think that the modern law would sanction the idea that even an involuntary bailee would be justified in taking no steps to avoid the certain death or destruction of the animal or thing. In general the bailee of goods on hire is bound to use ordinary care and skill in regard to them. I have already referred to the

Uniform Warehouse Receipts Act, and to its important stipulation, which might well be copied here by the general law, that the receipt may be made negotiable. The Act is set out in full in this chapter. There is a short but clear and useful statement of the law affecting innkeepers, which, except for some statutory difference, seems to be like that of England.

The law of Bills of Exchange and other negotiable instruments is governed by the Uniform Negotiable Instruments Act, which is adopted in all the States. The Act goes beyond the English Bills of Exchange Act in that it deals with negotiable instruments other than bills of exchange and promissory notes. These other negotiable instruments are in England left to be regulated by the general principles of the law merchant. Williston sets out the Act in full, with a copious citation of American cases. There are in this chapter few citations of English cases. The language of the two Acts is not by any means always identical.

On the other hand, in the chapter on the Contracts of Suretyship, there is a close community between the American and English law, and there is accordingly a frequent citation of English authorities. This chapter is very fully elaborated.

The chapter on Transportation Contracts of Carriers presents difficulties to the English lawyer, because in America these forms of contract are so largely and minutely controlled by legislation, both State and Federal, to a great extent on principles of Constitutional Law, and for reasons which have no analogue in English law, such as the differences due to there being both State and Federal legislation. The chapter is also more difficult for the English lawyer because it deals both with sea carriage and with land carriage. In England, carriage of goods by sea has been treated as a specific branch of the law because of the detailed rules which apply to sea carriage and do not apply to land carriage. It is true that both classes of contract are based in origin on the rules as to carriers, in particular common carriers, which still survive at least in principle, for instance, in the fundamental rule that a common carrier is *prima facie* an insurer of the goods he carries. But from an early period there were imported into the contract of sea carriage the forms and rules of the maritime law, which were eventually developed by the Common Law Courts when they imported as part of the Common Law the rules of commercial law. Land carriers were not affected by these maritime rules, and were little subject to legislation in England until the era of railways began, which brought with it a set of statutes and a special body of railway law. And now there is a statute dealing with carriage by air. In the United States there has been a tendency to assimilate the law of the two systems of transportation, land and sea, while in England the law is to a greater extent considered as in separate compartments. It is a small matter but symbolic that the word "bill of lading" is still used in England in general only in connection with sea carriage, whereas it is used in the United States indifferently of land and sea carriage. Even in the general law, apart from statute, there was a fundamental difference, because in England shipowners were free to exempt themselves from liability for negligence, while in the United States the law rendered such exemption void as being against public policy. And in the United States there was passed the Harter Act. It is true that English and American systems agreed in the Common Law rules in many important respects; for instance, in regard to the warranty of seaworthiness, its nature and effects. It is still called a warranty in England, though, as I have already noted, in England such a fundamental obligation is generally in other connections called a condition. Equally, the fundamental obligation not to deviate is common to both laws. But here again there is a difference. In England improper deviation abrogates the special contract, including the contract right to freight, though probably a reasonable remuneration is not excluded if the shipowner delivers the goods at the destined port. Deviation thus also abrogates the express or Common Law exceptions, so that he is liable for any loss though not caused by the deviation. The theory is that the improper deviation has changed the character of the voyage, and in particular that it can never be said after a deviation that, if the ship had not deviated, the peril would have come upon her. She would not have been at the place where she met the peril if she had not deviated, or at least not at the same time. On the other hand, in America, at least in some jurisdictions, the law seems to be that a definite causal connection must be shown between the deviation and the loss, whereas in England the ship is liable even for loss due to the act of God and the King's enemies if she has improperly deviated. But in many aspects of the law the two countries agree—for instance, in the distinction between a charter by demise and an ordinary time charter and in the rules relating to demurrage. There is, however, a difference in the law relating to advance freight. But since 1936, the two laws also agree in that both in England and in the United States The Hague Rules have been adopted. In England they were enacted as part of the law in 1924. Presumably the Courts of both countries will construe these Rules substantially in the same way, except for some specific slight differences. But there is also a mass of legislation in the United States which has no parallel in England (for instance, the State Uniform Bills of Lading Acts and the Federal Bills of Lading Acts), all of which is strange to the English lawyer.

I turn now to the remaining volumes of the work, which deal with more general aspects of law. The subject of Chapter XL is what constitutes a breach of contract. In this chapter the central feature is the doctrine of what is called anticipatory breach. Williston, I think, does not like the doctrine, but he admits that the great weight of American authority accepts it, though with some differences from the English theory. The theory may be shortly stated to be that under an executory contract, one party before the time for his performance has arrived may by word or act manifest an intention not to perform it when the time comes. In that event the other party may take one or other of two courses: he may accept the manifestation as a final repudiation and is then entitled to sue for damages, or he may ignore the manifestation, in which case the manifestation, at least in the English doctrine, has no effect; the other party may wait till the time for performance comes and the contract remains in force. It is clear that if impossibility or illegality or other like circumstance supervene, the repudiating party can avail himself of that defence. The question raised by

Williston as distinguishing the English from the American view is that under the former, if the manifestation has not been accepted as a repudiation, the other party must still go on so as to be ready with counter-performance at the due date. The American view, as I understand it, is that after the manifestation the other party is not entitled to prepare against the chance of the repudiating party changing his mind, as he has the right to do, and tendering performance, because it is said that to do so would merely aggravate the damage and loss. In my experience a case of anticipatory breach has frequently occurred in commercial transactions. The theory is that the injured party is entitled to disentangle himself from the business and not be exposed to the risk of the other party performing or not as he might think fit. Thus he can accept the manifestation as a final breach and, as it is often said, put an end to the contract save for the purpose of claiming damages, which will still be assessed as at the contract date or dates for performance. If, however, he does not do so he must still be prepared to do his part. So it seems to me as at present advised logic requires. I do not remember any English decision directly on the point. In ordinary cases it may be that the injured party was committed before the anticipatory breach; for instance, if a seller of goods, he may have covered himself, or, if a charterer, may have his cargo booked or ready. I suppose the point will some day arise in England.

Williston criticizes the whole theory, because he asks how it is possible to have a breach before the date for performance, a breach of something which at the time the party was not bound to perform: how can he be held to have broken his contract by not doing something which he is bound to do only at a future date: how can he be liable on a promise which he never made? Again, how can the other party turn into a breach at his option something which is not a breach, it being clear that unless the party so elects there is no breach? Against this the American view seems to be that the manifestation is in itself a breach, but one which may be nullified if the injured party does not sue or bring an action. It is clear that if that course is not taken the party who repudiated may repent and tender performance at the due date. The American view also seems to be that the manifestation may have the effect of excusing counter-performance at the due date or of excusing timely preparation for counter-performance by the other party. I confess I find some difficulty about this. It is true that if the injured party goes on getting ready for his counter-performance at the due date he may be merely aggravating damage in the event of the party still refusing to perform. But I cannot see any alternative, because then the position is exactly the same as if there had been no anticipatory breach at all. But out of respect for the American view I shall reserve my opinion. I do not think that the anticipatory breach is properly called a breach except in a very artificial sense. The right of the injured party to rescind does not affect his right to claim damages, the term frequently used (by myself among others) that he puts an end to the contract being, strictly speaking, inaccurate if the contract remains in force for the purpose of claiming damages.

The doctrine may be illogical but it is certainly convenient and, I think, well established, subject, no doubt, to the outstanding problem to which I have referred.

Chapter XLI deals with Damages. As Williston admirably puts it, the measure of damages for breach of contract is, ordinarily, not the value of the consideration, or of the contract as it is called, but of the defendant's performance. Williston does not treat the measure in contract as the same as in tort. He simply, but as I think accurately, distinguishes the measure in contract and in tort as being that in tort the defendant becomes liable for all proximate consequences (which I understand to mean all the actual consequences subject to the rule of remoteness), while for breach of contract he is liable only for consequences which were reasonably foreseeable at the time when it was entered into as probable if the contract was broken. That leads to a discussion of the rule in *Hadley* v. *Baxendale* (1854) 9 Ex. 341. Williston emphasizes that if damages, in addition to what would follow from the breach in what is called the usual course of things, are to be recovered because of special circumstances, there must be at the time of the contract being concluded not mere notice of the special circumstances, but something more which, I think, it is difficult to define, though in practice the difficulty is not felt. The notice must be in such terms as to bring to the party's mind not only the risk of the special damage but some intimation that the party would be held answerable for it. The difficulty here in principle is that this liability for special damage is not deemed to be strictly a part of the contract. It is constantly imposed under contracts in writing, even if within the Statute of Frauds, and the notice and intimation may be merely oral. Williston explains the anomaly as based on the principle that a court of law may deny damages for unusual consequences where the plaintiff, when he entered into the contract, was not aware how serious an injury would result from the breach. *Prima facie* he is charged with the apparent value of the performance, not with what ultimately proves to be its value; that is to say, in the absence of such notice as the rule requires. This is certainly more near to an explanation than any I have seen. At the same time, it is clear that though there has not been such notice as to found a claim for special damage, the apparent value of performance may include large consequential damage if that is held to occur in the ordinary course of things from the breach, so that no special notice is needed. The detailed rules for the assessment of damages are discussed at length in the next chapter, XLII: Application of Rules of Damages to Particular Cases. On the question of interest as damages Williston refers to the discretion now given to English judges to allow interest as additional damages by the Act of 1934 (Law Reform (Miscellaneous Provisions) Act). In the United States, Williston says that, apart from special statutes in some jurisdictions, the judicial decisions are not always harmonious. On the question of the rate of exchange for expressing in the English or United States currency damages assessed in a foreign currency, in England the law is now settled that it is to be the rate of exchange at the date of the breach, not of the judgment. There was at first some conflict of authority, to which Williston refers, but the English rule was settled by the House of Lords in *The Volturno* [1921] 2 A.C. 544, which Williston does not cite. That seems to be the American rule, at least in the case of a breach to pay foreign money in the country of the forum.

Chapter XLIII discusses the remedy of specific performance. Williston finds in the United States a distinct tendency in modern times to extend the remedy when justice requires it. He truly observes that rules of equity tend to become rigid and, like rules of law, do not always yield readily when reason makes it desirable. But while he recognizes that damages are often a wholly inadequate remedy for breach of a promise to render personal services, he accepts the rule (which is based on obvious reasons) that such promises are not enforceable by affirmative decree.

Chapter XLIV is headed "Rescission and Restitution for Breach of Contract; Quasi-Contractual Remedy". The chapter is both interesting and instructive to the English lawyer because it describes rights and remedies which are either not recognized in English law or at least not recognized as explicitly or in the same way or with the same effectiveness. Comparisons which Williston makes from time to time lead him to observe that in this as in other branches of the law the English Courts are more conservative than the American, and less ready to accept a new general rule varying from early precedents, and more wedded to formal rules. Rescission in this chapter is defined as meaning the abrogating or annulling of a contract. The term is not used as applying to cases where the contract has not been terminated in the full sense, but where one party has acquired an excuse for non-performance because of breach or repudiation by the other, and may also be entitled to claim damages. In this chapter the term "a right to rescind" is used as meaning a right alternative to a right to claim damages, though it may not be inconsistent with a right to restitution. Williston emphasizes that in this context rescission is an alternative to damages, so that the two remedies are mutually exclusive. It is a different position from that which arises when, on a repudiation, there is an acceptance of the breach as final and a claim for damages. If rescission puts an end to the contract *in toto*, there is nothing on which a claim for damages can be based. The great variety of circumstances in which rescission and restitution are possible and the variety of forms and measures which restitution may take have been developed in American law, which makes use of the quasi-contractual concept far beyond what English law does; I give but one instance of this, which Williston remarks. He observes that the policy of giving restitution to a party in default, not guilty of moral obliquity, has increased in favour in recent years in America, and is followed if a substantial net benefit has accrued to the other party. For instance, a party in default may be allowed restitution in certain cases for labour and materials.

The next chapter, which deals with Fraud and Misrepresentation, affords another instance of variation from English law. Rescission is allowed in America for innocent misrepresentation. It would be unjust, it is held in general, and apart from special circumstances, to allow one who has innocently made false representations to retain the fruits of a bargain induced by such representations. In England the right of rescission for misrepresentation of an executed contract is denied if the contract has been executed on both sides, unless there has been fraud or perhaps essential error. But certain qualifications are necessary in American law to meet cases where due restoration is impossible. Williston indeed goes farther and holds that the law in America either is or should be, if it is to be sufficient to satisfy inherent justice, that a speaker should be liable for damages for false representations though his intentions were innocent and his statements honestly intended, especially if the other party had reason to attribute to the defendant accurate knowledge of what he was talking about and the statement related to a matter of business on which action might be expected. He says that probably few Courts in the United States to-day would follow *Derry v. Peek* (1889) 14 App. Cas. 337, on its facts. His discussion of that much-criticized case is peculiarly full and suggestive. Nor, it seems, is such liability to be limited to negligent misstatements. These questions seem to appertain more specifically to Tort than to Contract. The whole of this chapter deserves close study.

The chapter on Mistake, XLVI, I have already discussed, and I shall pass at once to Chapter LVIII, which deals with Impossibility. Williston is of opinion that the defence of impossibility rests on the same fundamental principle as the defence of mistake. The defence of impossibility, he says, is based on the presumed mutual assumption when the contract is made that some fact essential to performance then exists or that it will exist when the time for performance arrives. Thus the analogy with mistake is obvious. Impossibility as an excuse for non-performance of contract is a modern idea, dating in its inception from about the middle of the nineteenth century. In judgments impossibility has generally been on the ground that there is an implied condition in the contract providing for its defeasance notwithstanding that in form the contract is absolute. This fiction is not very useful, because it does not help the Court in its problem, which is to determine in the case of an absolute contract when the condition is to be applied. Lord Sumner in one place simply said that the object of introducing in contract law this defence was to reconcile justice with the absolute contract. Williston says, much in the same way, that the Court qualifies the promise when it thinks it fair to do so. And it does so in the absence of either the express or the implied intention of the parties. Williston carefully works out the limitations of the doctrine. He treats what have been called the Coronation cases as not really involving impossibility of performance but the fortuitous destruction of the value of the contract, which depended on enjoying the view of the procession. This was obviously in the parties' contemplation the sole inducement to enter into the contract and to pay the agreed price. He adds that one consequence (*inter alia*) of impossibility may be a quasi-contractual obligation to pay the value of any partial performance which has been received whether by the party whose performance has become impossible or by the other party. This raises a number of difficult questions which cannot here be touched upon. There are, of course, many other complications.

Impossibility has to do with the discharge of contracts, whereas Mistake, Misrepresentation, Duress and Undue Influence are matters which invalidate bargains. There is a further head of matters which have this effect, that of Illegality, to which I can only very shortly advert. This topic is treated by Williston with extraordinary completeness and ability in a discussion which covers about 550 pages. A great part is not in detail of practical importance to English lawyers, such as the particulars relating to Sunday laws and to the various State statutes making wagers illegal, and the State statutes against usury. The list of illegal bargains is very long and covers matters affecting almost every aspect of life and activity. It is impossible here to examine them with any particularity. Many categories of illegality depend on specific statutes, some of which make the bargains void. Otherwise the governing factor is some rule of public policy, which often may be based on statutes. There are many heads of public policy, that is, of principles on which a Court may without legislative sanction invalidate a bargain otherwise good. The question of general importance is, how far may the Courts go in extending these inhibitions? Williston thinks that it is for the Courts to fix their own limitations, and accordingly he refuses to accept the view of Lord Halsbury that the Courts cannot invent a new head of public policy. I think the difference really depends on what is meant by a new head of public policy. The comparatively recent instances which Williston gives from English decisions of what he calls new applications or heads of public policy, which he regards as being in substance or wholly new heads of public policy, seem to me more accurately described as extensions or applications of already established heads of public policy. The rules of public policy are only part of the Common Law and, like the Common Law rules in general, admit of variation and extension and development to meet changing circumstances. But we do not say that judges can now invent a new head of the Common Law. It is, I think, for the Legislature, not the judges, to invent new heads of public policy. This is particularly true, as I think Williston recognizes, in the modern days of legislative activity. It is not, I think, the province of the judges to usurp the functions of the Legislature. But I do not imagine Williston would go so far as that or that there is any real difference in substance between his views and my own. In England there has been quite recently a full discussion of the principles of public policy in the House of Lords in a decision which was later than the publication of this edition (*Fender* v. *St John-Mildmay* [1938] A.C. 1).

I shall not discuss the various final chapters which deal with the discharge of contracts. They are characterized by the same fulness and acuteness.

I must conclude these observations, which are already too long. Life is short and leisure is even shorter, both for reviewers and readers. I have exceeded the limits, but my excuse is that my remarks, which are both fragmentary and fugitive, fall far below what my theme merits. I have inevitably passed by without comment very many instances of lucid and accurate exposition of the law, of wise criticism, of judicious indications of lines of amelioration. I must leave to others and to the future fuller and more adequate treatment. I have culled a few specimens as I went along. I cannot even pretend to have made the best selection or anything approaching to that. I end as I began, by saying that this is a great work not only in size, but in amplitude of treatment, not only in learning but in breadth and open-mindedness of view. I am inclined to agree with what Williston says more than once, that American law is at present in many respects more liberal and progressive than English law. If that is so, Williston has played a great part in making it so. The Law of Contracts which the Common Law has evolved is a wonderful product of good sense and practical utility. It has been evolved piecemeal and empirically, by constant development and adaptation to new needs. It is marvellous in its richness of content and its flexibility. But its development has not reached its final conclusion. It has still within it the potentiality of growth, of shedding excrescences and defects, of defining more logically and accurately its concepts, of fitting itself to deal with new and changing conditions, of satisfying new social demands. "Williston on Contracts" has already had a great part in the secular progression of our Common Law. This new edition will nobly continue the great work.

X

SOME DEVELOPMENTS OF COMMERCIAL LAW IN THE PRESENT CENTURY[1]

WHAT does Commercial Law include? A rough test is that it comprises those parts of the law which are commonly administered in the High Court in the "Commercial List". This special list limited to commercial cases is an improvisation to meet the difficulty which otherwise might occur of having these cases tried by any judge, who, however eminent, is not experienced in commercial matters.[2] The plan was devised in 1893, and the credit of it is due to Mr Justice Mathew. It has worked excellently ever since.

The test excludes such subjects as Patents, a form of personal property around which a complex system of specialized law and practice has grown up, and also, of course, the allied subject of Trademarks. Moreover, certain other branches of the law fall within the scope of Commercial Law only in so far as they are relevant to the law of contracts—Commercial Law being almost entirely concerned with contracts. Such branches are Bankruptcy, Partnership Law and Company Law, which are each to some extent material in regard to contractual

---

[1] The Presidential Address as President of the Holdsworth Club of the Faculty of Law in the University of Birmingham, 1934–35, delivered at the Annual Dinner of the Club on 17 May 1935.

[2] *Baerlein* v. *Chartered Mercantile Bank* [1895] 2 Ch. 488; see also Scrutton, *Charterparties* (13th ed.), 464.

matters. For instance, Company Law deals with the personality and capacity of companies, which nowadays figure more frequently as the parties to commercial contracts than natural persons do. Railway Law may also have to be considered in a case where a contract of carriage is concerned.

By the end of last century Commercial Law in England was in substance full grown. We know from our Holdsworth[1] how it was adopted, not without a certain distaste, by the Common Lawyers who wanted to bring so rich a haul into their net. It would be tempting to discuss, if time permitted, how commercial disputes were really dealt with down to the end of the seventeenth century. Lord Mansfield, following Lord Chief Justice Holt, in the eighteenth century may be said to have set this law on its legs in the Common Law Courts, and the nineteenth century saw its growth and maturity. I have noticed that until well into the nineteenth century English judges frequently relied on citations from foreign jurists, such as Pothier, Emerigon, the Civilians, and, indeed, the Digest, which Blackburn often quoted.[2] In the present century I cannot recall any instance in which a judge has had recourse to those foreign sources of law, except where they were embodied in an earlier English judgment which he was quoting. Scots judges are sometimes quoted, but in Commercial Law Scots Law is almost, if not quite, entirely based on English Law, and may be regarded as forming in effect a branch of the English Commercial Law.

---

[1] Holdsworth, *History of English Law*, 1, 568–573.
[2] E.g. *Taylor* v. *Caldwell* (1863) 32 L.J. Q.B. 164, 166; *Kennedy* v. *Panama, etc., Mail Co.* (1867) L.R. 2 Q.B. 580, 587.

It is difficult, perhaps impossible, to summarize or to analyse the great flow of Commercial Law that has come forth during this century. Since 1900 there have been thirty-four volumes of Commercial Cases, each of nearly 500 pages—say, in all, roughly 16,000 pages. But when I have turned over these pages I have felt that the great bulk of that learning and ingenuity was occupied with things that help little in the elucidation of general principles: their concern was largely with the construction of ill-drawn or obscure documents and the settlement of special matters of usage or practice, or with the decision of disputed facts. I must in this Address neglect all that.

Further, I have observed that our period covers those war and post-war years which have been so fruitful in scientific and practical advances in so many spheres. I question, however, if those years have marked any comparable advance in legal concepts.

All I can do in this Address is to select some points which appear to me to mark a progress or development. It is impossible in the short time available to me to attempt to be comprehensive.

I shall begin by adverting to some general principles of the Law of Contracts which seem of commercial importance.

CONTRACTS

Let me take first the case of what has been called the dissolution of contracts by "frustration of the adventure". This doctrine undoubtedly received some extension owing to the very special exigencies of business consequent on war conditions: since those conditions have ceased the tendency has been to limit the rule once more. But the war produced unforeseen and unforeseeable circumstances, and the difficulty of applying contracts made without anticipation of what, in fact, had happened was felt to be acute.

Lord Sumner once described the rule as one devised to reconcile justice with the absolute contract.[1] There is a contract: something has happened under it which the parties have not provided for because they did not anticipate it: it is unjust that the parties should continue bound. The Court disowns the possession of any dissolving power and proceeds on the fiction that the parties must be presumed to have had the intention that if such things happened the contract should be avoided.[2] That is a fiction, because the parties in fact had no intention, because they had no foresight, about it. If the contingency had been known to them as something which might happen, and they had not provided for it, the contract ought, it would seem on ordinary principles, to stand. It is merely because they did not and could not reasonably anticipate what happened, that the Court will declare the contract to be dissolved—that is, automatically ended without the option of either party. Neither party is any longer bound. It is not that one party is excused from performance as from the relevant date: both parties are equally released from the contractual nexus.

This idea originated in what have been called "*obligationes de certo corpore*"—such, for instance, as contracts for hire, use or purchase of chattels, which perish without

[1] *Hirji Mulji* v. *Cheong Yue S.S. Co.* [1926] A.C. 497, 510.
[2] *Dahl* v. *Nelson, Donkin & Co.* (1880) 6 App. Cas. 38, 59.

the fault or election of either party,[1] or which owing to a change of law cannot any longer be lawfully employed or disposed of in the manner which the contract requires.[2]

The doctrine was extended before the war, as it may seem to some, illegitimately, to cases where, although the corpus concerned remained intact and lawful to be used, a change of circumstances had occurred which prevented one of the parties enjoying that benefit from the use of it for the enjoyment of which, as the other contracting party well understood, the contract was made. Such were the "Coronation Seat Cases"[3] where the window which was hired was available on the agreed date, but the King's Coronation procession, for the purpose of seeing which it was hired, was cancelled because the King unexpectedly fell ill after the date of the contract. In such a case it would seem that each party was able to give or to receive all that the contract specified, and it would seem that in future any Court not bound by authority would so hold.[4]

But the cases which have been called generally the "Requisition Cases" are on a different footing, and come within the same principle as the *obligationes de certo corpore*. The feature of these cases has been that a charter party was made for the hire of a ship: before the commencement of or during the charter period the ship was validly requisitioned by the Government: it was thus

---

[1] *Howell* v. *Coupland* (1876) 1 Q.B.D. 258; *Nickoll & Knight* v. *Ashton, Edridge & Co.* [1901] 2 K.B. 126; *Maritime National Fish, Ltd.* v. *Ocean Trawlers, Ltd.* [1935] A.C. 524.

[2] *Baily* v. *De Crespigny* (1869) L.R. 4 Q.B. 180.

[3] *Krell* v. *Henry* [1903] 2 K.B. 740; *Lumsden* v. *Barton & Co.* (1902) 19 T.L.R. 53; *Clark* v. *Lindsay* (1903) 19 T.L.R. 202.

[4] *Maritime National Fish, Ltd.* v. *Ocean Trawlers, Ltd.* [1935] A.C. 524.

removed *extra commercium* without the fault of either party for a period inconsistent with the commercial adventure: thus the ship was, *quoad* that contract, in the same position as if it had been destroyed.[1] The principle is the same as if the ship had been lost or rendered unavailable for an indefinite period by a sea casualty.[2] A legitimate extension of the same rule was applied to cases where there was an interruption of the contractual work, for instance building or constructional works, by an unforeseen and unavoidable contingency for such an indefinite period as might properly be held to change the character of the obligation.[3] In all these cases neither party can give or receive *modo et forma* what the contract as between the parties requires.

When the Court in such cases holds the contract to be dissolved, it has to go on and determine what collateral results follow. English Courts have held that the loss lies where it falls:[4] no new right can accrue after the happening of the event which involves dissolution: even a contractual right of arbitration goes:[5] but accrued rights remain unaffected: payments made cannot be recovered, and payments due, but not made when they should have been made, can be enforced, even though the stipulated performance has, after the due date of payment, become impossible.[6] Scots Law has adopted a different and it seems a juster rule, and has held that

[1] *Bank Line, Ltd.* v. *Capel* [1919] A.C. 435.
[2] *Jackson* v. *Union Marine Insurance Co., Ltd.* (1873) L.R. 8 C.P. 572.
[3] *Metropolitan Water Board* v. *Dick, Kerr & Co.* [1917] 2 K.B. 1; affirmed [1918] A.C. 119.
[4] *Chandler* v. *Webster* [1904] 1 K.B. 493; *Civil Service, etc., Socy.* v. *General Steam Navigation Co.* [1903] 2 K.B. 756.
[5] *Hirji Mulji* v. *Cheong Yue S.S. Co.* [1926] A.C. 497.
[6] *Chandler* v. *Webster* [1904] 1 K.B. 493.

payments made in advance or due before dissolution can be retained or recovered only to the extent that the party claiming to retain or to recover can show that he had been out of pocket in respect of the initial outlay by reason of the dissolution.[1] English and Scots Law show a similar diversity in the case of advance freight.

This whole doctrine of frustration has been described as a reading into the contract of implied terms to give effect to the intention of the parties. It would be truer to say that the Court in the absence of express intention of the parties determines what is just. Something of the same sort happens in the many cases where what is reasonable, in a matter not dealt with by the express agreement of the parties, is so treated by the Court as to be imported into the contract. It is, as we shall see later, the incurable habit of commercial men in their contracts not to anticipate expressly or to provide for all that may happen. Thus where goods are sold and no price is stated, but it is clearly intended that they should be paid for, the Court implies, as it is said, an obligation to pay a reasonable price.[2] Similarly if something is to be done but no time for doing it is specified, the Court holds that it must be done in a reasonable time.[3] Other like instances occur where it has been held that assortment or quality not precisely defined in the contract is to be reasonable.[4] It has been stated over and over again by the Court and the Legislature that what is reasonable in

[1] *Cantiare San Rocco, S.A.* v. *Clyde Shipbuilding Co.* [1924] A.C. 226.
[2] *Acebal* v. *Levy* (1834) 10 Bing. 376; cf. Sale of Goods Act, 1893 (56 & 57 Vic. c. 71), s. 8 (2).
[3] *Ford* v. *Cotesworth* (1868) 38 L.J. Q.B. 52; *Hick* v. *Raymond* [1893] A.C. 22.
[4] *Hillas & Co.* v. *Arcos, Ltd.* (1932) 38 Com. Cas. 23.

Commercial Law in the Present Century

this connection is a question of fact,[1] that is, that it is to be ascertained in each case by a consideration of all the relevant circumstances of the case. This, perhaps, is not much help in one sense, and no further assistance is afforded by saying that it is what a reasonable man would pay, or take to be a reasonable time, or a reasonable assortment or quality, and so forth. This is only proceeding on the basis of *idem per idem*. The truth is that the Court, or jury, as a judge of fact, decides this question in accordance with what seems to be just or reasonable in its eyes. The judge finds in himself the criterion of what is reasonable. The Court is in this sense making a contract for the parties—though it is almost blasphemy to say so. But the power of the Court to do this is most beneficial, and indeed even essential, because it enables it to fill up omissions, where, but for that power, though the parties have intended to bind themselves, the Court would be forced to hold that there was no contract because it was too vague. There is a good old maxim "*verba ita sunt intelligenda ut res magis valeat quam pereat*". Without this "supplementing power" of the Court (as I choose to call it) it would often be practically impossible to make long forward contracts, such as of sale, and especially instalment contracts, because of the difficulty of seeing and providing for all possible contingencies. These contingencies must be left to a large extent to be dealt with as they arise on the lines of what is reasonable. The principles applicable in such cases have recently been elucidated by the House of Lords.[2]

[1] *Hick* v. *Raymond* [1893] A.C. 22, 29.
[2] *Hillas & Co.* v. *Arcos, Ltd.* (1932) 38 Com. Cas. 23.

A difficult branch of contract law is the law of Mistake. The typical case of mistake at Common Law, which was said to make a contract void, although in truth such mistake prevented there being any contract at all, was where the contract centred on some specific thing or person, the sale of a specific chattel or the charter of a specific ship or the employment of a particular person. If at the moment when the parties thought they were contracting the specific thing or ship or person no longer existed, though neither party was aware of it, the Common Law would say there was no contract.[1] That principle was applied to the curious and unusual cases where one party was mistaken as to the identity of the person with whom he intended to contract.[2] It was decided that in such cases the contract was not voidable, as it would be on the simple ground of fraud, though in fact in such cases there was almost inevitably some fraud involved, but was void.[3] The principle of mistake was later extended to choses in action, for instance, the sale of an annuity where the annuitant was dead at the date of the sale:[4] and still further to a promise to pay money on the footing of some right which in fact did not exist, such as for the lease of a fishery where, though the fishery existed, the lessor had no title to it.[5] By similar process of reasoning the promise to pay for the cancellation of a contract which the parties both thought was binding, though in truth it had ceased to be valid, would, it seems, be void for mistake.

[1] *Couturier* v. *Hastie* (1856) 5 H.L.C. 673.
[2] *Cundy* v. *Lindsay* (1878) L.R. 3 A.C. 459.
[3] *Ibid.* per Lord Cairns L.C., at p. 466.
[4] *Scott* v. *Coulson* [1903] 2 Ch. 249.
[5] *Cooper* v. *Phibbs* (1867) L.R. 2 H.L. 149.

Commercial Law in the Present Century

The essence of mistake which thus prevents there being a contract is that there is only the appearance and not the fact of consent. The parties use language which imports consent, but they are using that language with reference to some fact or circumstance which they both believe to exist, whereas it does not. The intention to agree is ineffective because it fails to operate on the subject-matter which both parties mutually contemplate as the object of their agreement. It is true that men are as a rule bound by what they say or write, but where there is mistake the intention which is *prima facie* to be drawn from their language fails of effect because the matter in respect of which it was intended to operate does not exist. But the matter of the mistake must be something fundamental to the intention of both parties.[1] It may be difficult to say when this is so.

It was this difficulty which, I think, led to a great difference of opinion in a recent case.[2] A large sum of money was in that case promised and paid for the cancellation of a contract which the party paying was entitled to cancel for nothing if he had known, as the fact was that the other party had been guilty of misconduct under it. The other party at the date of the bargain had not himself that fact in mind and was thus in equal error. If the contract had, without either party knowing, ceased to operate when the agreement to cancel was made, there would have been nothing to cancel and the basis of the agreement to cancel would have failed. But the contract which it was agreed to

---

[1] *Smith* v. *Hughes* (1871) L.R. 6 Q.B. 597; *Norwich Union Fire Insurance Co.* v. *Price* [1934] A.C. 455.
[2] *Bell* v. *Lever Bros.* [1932] A.C. 161.

cancel existed: it was merely voidable. The difference of opinion had reference to the problem whether the basis of the agreement to cancel was, not merely that there should be a contract, but that there should be a contract which could be cancelled only on payment of money, and not, as was the fact, one which could have been cancelled by the party, if he had known the facts, at his option and without any payment or the consent of the other party.

AGENCY

In the period which we are considering there has been some development of the law of agency. Such development is inevitable in modern conditions. If we disregard the limited doctrine as to acts done by the governing authority, a company can act only by agents, and a great deal of the business of the world is done by companies. Moreover the extensive scale on which business is done nowadays even by individual business men or firms necessitates the constant employment of agents.

The rule seems now to be established that if the principal derives or hopes to derive benefit from extending and multiplying his personality by use of agents, he should be liable for what they do in the course of that employment, that is to say, unless there is express or implied notice to the other party of some limitation.[1] The notice may be express, or may come from usage or general understanding in the trade, or may come from the special facts of the case.[2] But where there is no such notice, the third party is entitled in general to hold the

---

[1] *Watteau* v. *Fenwick* [1893] 1 Q.B. 346; *Edmunds* v. *Bushell & Jones* (1865) L.R. 1 Q.B. 97; *Hambro* v. *Burnand* [1904] 2 K.B. 10.

[2] *Howard* v. *Sheward* (1866) L.R. 2 C.P. 148.

principal liable for the agent's acts, even though the agent was acting not in his principal's interest at all, but was incurring the principal's liability for his own private ends, and, as it can thus properly be said, in fraud of the principal.[1] In matters of contract, it was old law, though it had to be restated in our period, that, if the agent was making a contract in the name of his principal within his actual or ostensible authority, the principal was bound even though the agent was making the contract not for the principal's benefit but for his own.[2] The agent thus saddled the principal with a liability which was against the faith of his agency. But in questions of fraud, it was said before our period by great judges that the principal was not liable for the agent's fraud unless the agent was acting for the principal's benefit.[3] That limitation in the doctrine of vicarious liability has now been negatived by the House of Lords.[4]

An anomaly is presented by the rule that the secretary of a company falsely certifying a transfer of shares does not render the company liable.[5] This rule, which seems both curious and exceptional, was equated to the old rule that a shipmaster does not make the shipowner liable by signing a bill of lading for goods not actually received on board.[6] The question of the false certifica-

---

[1] *Lloyd* v. *Grace, Smith & Co.* [1912] A.C. 716.

[2] *Barwick* v. *English Joint Stock Bank* (1867) L.R. 2 Ex. 259; *Lloyd* v. *Grace, Smith & Co.* [1912] A.C. 716; *Hambro* v. *Burnand* [1904] 2 K.B. 10.

[3] *British Mutual Banking Co.* v. *Charnwood Forest Ry. Co.* (1887) 18 Q.B.D. 714, per Bowen L.J., at p. 718; *Ruben* v. *Great Fingall Consolidated* [1906] A.C. 439, per Lord Davey, at p. 446.

[4] *Lloyd* v. *Grace, Smith & Co.* [1912] A.C. 716.

[5] *Geo. Whitechurch, Ltd.* v. *Cavanagh* [1902] A.C. 117.

[6] *Grant* v. *Norway* (1851) 10 C.B. 665; *Geo. Whitechurch, Ltd.* v. *Cavanagh* [1902] A.C. 117, per Lord Macnaghten, at p. 125.

tion by the company's secretary was recently again raised in the House of Lords,[1] but as nothing could be discovered to distinguish the earlier case, the House was bound to follow its previous decision. The case of the shipmaster was no doubt originally dealt with on the special position which he occupied in maritime law. Whatever, in fact, is the position of the secretary of a limited liability company, it cannot, it seems, be regarded as presenting the same features as those attributed to the shipmaster.

DAMAGES

The rules as to damages in actions of contract have not been noticeably extended, at least in principle, in our period.

In tort, in negligence, it has been held that the principal is liable for all the physical consequences of the tortious act, though the actual consequences were impossible to foresee.[2] It is enough to constitute negligence that the act was likely to cause damage: then the actual damage constitutes the measure. Where the tortious act has destroyed a chattel the wrongdoer is liable for the actual value to its owner of the chattel in all the facts, including its special value by reason of the actual use being made of it by its owner, for example for the purpose of carrying out a profitable contract; but not for special loss due to the particular financial circumstances of the owner, which is in law too remote.[3]

The peculiar rules as to recovery of interest, which

[1] *Kleinwort, Sons & Co.* v. *Assoc. Automatic Machine Corp.* (1934) 50 T.L.R. 244.
[2] Re *Polemis and Furness Withy & Co., Ltd.* [1921] 3 K.B. 560.
[3] *Liesbosch Dredger* v. *Edison* [1933] A.C. 449.

were so often criticized, have now been altered by Statute recently passed in accordance with a Report of the Law Revision Committee and have been brought into relation with commercial ideas.[1]

It may be that some changes will be made in regard to the doctrine of consideration, including the position of what is called the third party beneficiary, and in regard to the requirement that certain commercial contracts must be in writing. I refer to the rules often compendiously described as the rules under the Statute of Frauds.

These observations, though not complete, will illustrate within the limits possible in this Address the development of the rules of contract law so far as they are of special importance in Commercial Law. It will now be convenient to discuss some particular classes of contracts which fill a large space in Commercial Law. Indeed, the rules relating to these contracts are often treated as constituting the whole scope of Commercial Law.

COMMERCIAL CONTRACTS

I shall refer in particular to contracts for the Sale of Goods, to Bills of Exchange, to Insurance, and to Carriage of Goods by Sea. The law in these matters is largely codified. The Sale of Goods Act, 1893,[2] and the Bills of Exchange Act, 1882,[3] were both passed in the last century, but the Marine Insurance Act, 1906,[4] was within our period, and so was the Carriage of Goods by Sea Act,

---

[1] Law Reform (Misc. Provisions) Act, 1934 (24 & 25 Geo. V, c. 41), s. 3, repealing Civil Procedure Act, 1833 (3 & 4 Will. IV, c. 42), ss. 28 and 29.
[2] 56 & 57 Vic. c. 71.
[3] 45 & 46 Vic. c. 61.   [4] 6 Edw. VII, c. 41.

1924.[1] This last was, however, not a codifying Act, but rather an Act introducing a new law to impose uniform conditions in bills of lading in respect of goods shipped from this country: it left charter-parties unaffected.

Bills of Exchange peculiarly illustrate something which is true, though less strikingly, of all the old types of commercial contracts; I mean, that the contractual documents are bare and meagre, but there has grown up around them a great mass of detailed and complex rules which fix the duties and liabilities of the parties. Nothing could be simpler in form than a bill of exchange, even if to the mere drawing there are added the acceptance and endorsement. But the Act, and the cases before and since the Act, show how many and varied are the matters to be provided for. For example, the drawing, acceptance, endorsement, presentment, dishonour, and so on, all require precise and detailed regimentation. The same is true, though perhaps in less degree, of the policy of insurance; the simple form used by the Lombards was the basis of the marine policy, but its amplification has perhaps introduced more difficulties than it has solved. Bills of lading and charter parties were simple enough in their earlier forms, though by 1900 they had become swollen into extremely complex and voluminous instruments; yet they, even in that form, left much to be filled in by the Courts. Contracts for the sale of goods often provide for matters in detail, but in all cases only with more or less completeness, so that the Court could not decide disputes without supplementing the express terms. It is this process of supplementing the mere wording which has created the vast body of Commercial Law.

[1] 14 & 15 Geo. V, c. 22.

Commercial Law in the Present Century

This law is sometimes said to have been derived from the usage of merchants, and the Law Merchant as the custom of merchants has at times been contrasted with the Common Law as the custom of the realm. There is truth in that. Thus the law of bills of exchange and banking was originally based on the principles adopted by the Italian bankers and embodied in their codes, just as the law of marine insurance and the sea law generally were based on the Continental, in particular Spanish, codes and practices. But when the Common Law somewhat reluctantly adopted the Law Merchant it did not do so blindly—witness the decisions of Lord Chief Justice Holt, and the manner of proceeding adopted by Lord Mansfield. By the verdicts of his special juries at the Guildhall Mansfield acquainted himself with the exigencies of trade and the manner in which these were regarded and dealt with by business men, and then by a process of logic and analysis he proceeded to enunciate the appropriate rules as principles of law.[1] The same process has been followed and still is being followed by commercial judges. It is true that they can now proceed on the basis of decided cases, but if new problems arise they have still to decide them by a careful consideration of the business realities, and in construing contracts they have to remember the habits of thought and expression of business men, as well as special exigencies and conditions of the particular business. And it is truly said that the Law Merchant is not a closed door.[2] It is not, however, true that the rules of construction in the case of commercial

---

[1] Lord Birkenhead, *Fourteen English Judges*, 168–196.
[2] *Goodwin* v. *Robarts* (1875) L.R. 10 Ex. 337, per Cockburn C.J., at p. 352; *Edelstein* v. *Schuler & Co.* [1902] 2 K.B. 144.

contracts differ from those in the case of contracts generally. Apparent differences are due to the differences in subject-matter.[1]

SALE OF GOODS

The Act of 1893 was an admirable piece of codification, and the modern law on this topic was in the main laid down before 1900. It was during the nineteenth century that owing to industrial and mercantile developments what may be called the shopkeeper's point of view as to the sale of goods gave place to the point of view of the merchant and manufacturer. The rules necessary where sales took place in shops or in market overt and on actual inspection had to be supplemented by the rules necessary where sales were by description, or were of future or unascertained goods, things or goods to be manufactured, or of quantities to be prepared from larger bulks of natural or artificial products.

Perhaps the two most noteworthy questions in this modern law have been (1) when in a sale the property passes; and (2) what conditions can be implied in a sale.

Neither question presented any serious difficulty when a man bought particular things which he saw. In such cases it might well be taken that the property passed at the time of the sale, and that the goods were taken as being in the condition in which and of the quality of which they were, unless the buyer was given an express warranty of condition, quality or fitness.

Take first the passing of property. Difficult questions arose to determine when the property passed where

[1] *British Steamship Owners' Association* v. *Chapman & Co.* (1935) 41 Com. Cas. 15, 25.

things were sold by description or had to be made or manufactured: and still more difficulties were presented when goods were sold which had to be shipped to the buyer or at his direction. Before 1900 the broad rules had been established in regard to these matters, and only some special problems were left to be cleared up. I have always regretted that the Sale of Goods Act stated the general rule on this matter to be that property passes "when the parties intend it to pass",[1] because in truth the parties have in the ordinary case no definite intention on the point at all. It would be truer to say that it is the Court that decides in its judicial capacity when the property passes. Perhaps, however, the fiction of intention here does no harm.

The questions on this head of prime commercial importance with which alone I need to deal have reference to those familiar mercantile contracts called F.O.B. sales and C.I.F. sales. In both these cases the contract calls for shipment by the seller to or to the order of the buyer. In the former the goods are to be put on board a vessel to be provided by the buyer, and that is all that is included in the price. The sale is free on board and the property would pass on shipment save that generally the seller by taking and retaining the bill of lading reserves a *ius disponendi* and so reserves the passing of the property till he transfers the bill of lading to the buyer, which is generally to be against payment.[2] The C.I.F. contract is different. The price is to include the cost of the goods and of freight and insurance to the specified destination, and the seller must pay for the shipping documents, that

---

[1] 56 & 57 Vic. c. 71, s. 17.
[2] *Ibid.* s. 17 and s. 19 (1).

Legal Essays and Addresses

is, the bill of lading and policy of insurance, and it is only on the transfer of these along with the invoice that the property passes. Hence it was said that the transaction was really a "sale of documents".[1] But this is now held to be wrong.[2] There is a sale of goods in these cases involving as a necessary element the transfer of the documents which the seller has to procure and tender: but the seller has to provide the goods in addition to shipping and insuring them.

But even after 1900 a very fundamental question had to be decided. It was well established that the transfer of the documents vested the property in the buyer *ipso facto*, unlike the transfer of a warehouse receipt which required at Common Law an attornment.[3] Thus in a sense it was seen that the property passed retrospectively: the buyer took the risks of any loss or damage after shipment; if the goods were lost or damaged his rights against the shipowner or underwriter took the place of his rights against the seller in these matters. But suppose the goods which the seller had shipped arrived without sea damage, but on delivery were found not to correspond with the contract requirements. What was the buyer's position when he took delivery of the goods at the destination and found that the goods were wrong—that is, wrong owing to defects existing on shipment, not to damage or loss on the voyage? He had not been able

---

[1] *Arnhold Karberg & Co.* v. *Blythe, Green, Jourdain & Co.* [1915] 2 K.B. 379, per Scrutton J., at p. 388.
[2] *Arnhold Karberg & Co.* v. *Blythe, Green, Jourdain & Co.* [1916] 1 K.B. 495, per Bankes L.J., at p. 510.
[3] *Bentall* v. *Burn* (1824) 3 B. & C. 423; now see Sale of Goods Act, 1893, s. 29 (3); *Madras Official Assignee* v. *Mercantile Bank of India* [1935] A.C. 53, 40 Com. Cas. 143.

to inspect earlier, and yet by taking up the documents he had caused the property to be vested in himself. Could he reject, or was his right, if any, merely to claim damages? The House of Lords held that the buyer was entitled to reject, and that the vesting of the property in him was conditional, that is, subject to its being revested in the seller if the buyer on inspection in due course was entitled to reject and did reject.[1]

Another illustration of the position which may arise under a C.I.F. contract is afforded by one of the war cases. A seller who was British tendered to the buyer who was also British a bill of lading for goods which had been shipped on a German ship before the war broke out. It was held that it was a bad tender, since, if the German bill of lading had been accepted, it would have put the buyer into contractual relationship with an enemy shipowner, which would have been against public policy as involving trading with the enemy.[2] This shows that a seller's obligation is not complete on shipment, but continues till a proper tender is made.

The tender must be of documents in ordinary form. This requirement has led to many questions which I cannot here discuss.

Some development has taken place in defining the extent of the implied conditions in a sale of goods. A condition is a term the breach of which entitles the buyer to reject the goods, though if he accepts them he can claim damages on the same footing as if the term had been a warranty. One condition is that the goods must

[1] *E. Clemens Horst Co.* v. *Biddell Bros.* [1912] A.C. 18.
[2] *Arnhold Karberg & Co.* v. *Blythe, Green, Jourdain & Co.* [1916] 1 K.B. 495.

correspond with the description. The correspondence must be exact: the Court has no power to dispense with a failure in precise correspondence with description merely because the failure seems small or unimportant.[1] Thus when the contract calls for goods of specific measurement, the buyer cannot be compelled to accept goods with a deviation from that, unless, perhaps, it is so small as to be microscopic so that the maxim "*de minimis non curat lex*" can be applied. The Court cannot vary an express contract merely because it seems reasonable so to do.

The further implied condition that the goods are to be fit for the purpose for which they are sold was established in the Act, but the idea has been further specified and developed. That condition is only implied, so the section provides, when the particular purpose is so made known to the seller at the time of the contract as to show that the buyer relies on the seller's skill or judgment to supply an article fit for the purpose. But difficult cases have to be considered. Thus, suppose the seller is a manufacturer, and the contract is to construct an article corresponding to a precise plan and specification supplied by the buyer. There is then no complete reliance on the seller's skill and judgment. Such was a case where a maker of ships' propellers contracted to make a propeller for a vessel according to the drawings and specifications supplied by the buyer. The propeller when supplied and fitted worked satisfactorily save that it made such a noise that it could not be used in navigation. The dimensions were correct and the material appeared on test to be unexceptionable. But something

[1] *Arcos, Ltd.* v. *Ronaasen* [1933] A.C. 470.

must have been wrong either in the final shaping off or in the material, though what it was could not be ascertained by any test or analysis. The seller was held liable.[1] In other words, the condition is absolute, unless, it may be, the defect can definitely be proved to be due to the buyer's specification. In any case the condition extends to latent effects. The seller cannot escape by proving that he was not negligent. Further, the reliance on the seller's skill and judgment may be merely partial and yet the condition may apply.[2]

The narrower condition that the goods must be of merchantable quality has been discussed in our period, and seems to mean that the goods must be capable of being used in some way in which such goods would be normally used, even though not fit for the specific purpose desired by the buyer.[3] Both these conditions have recently been discussed by the Judicial Committee of the Privy Council.[4]

The development of the doctrine of implied conditions has led to the saying that the old rule of *caveat emptor* has now been superseded by the rule *caveat venditor*. The vendor has retorted by seeking to exclude by contract the conditions in the buyer's favour. The Courts have not been too anxious to help him in this. Such exceptions have been strictly construed. The word "warranty" has been held to be too narrow an exception to cover a condition,[5] and the words "implied conditions" have

---

[1] *Cammell Laird & Co.* v. *Manganese, Bronze & Brass Co., Ltd.* [1934] A.C. 402.   [2] *Frost* v. *Aylesbury Dairy Co.* [1905] 1 K.B. 608.
[3] *Bristol Tramway Co.* v. *Fiat Motors, Ltd.* [1910] 2 K.B. 831; *Morelli* v. *Fitch & Gibbons* [1928] 2 K.B. 636.
[4] *Grant* v. *Australian Knitting Mills, Ltd.* [1936] A.C. 85.
[5] *William Barker (Junior) & Co.* v. *Agius, Ltd.* (1927) 43 T.L.R. 751.

not been sufficient to cover an express condition such as a specific description of the goods sold.[1] But if the words of exception are wide enough, e.g. such words as "conditions expressed or implied", then the only question can be whether the exception has been made part of the contract.[2] If the buyer has signed a written contract it does not matter that he has not read it. He is bound. If he has not signed the contract, or if there is no written contract, it must be proved that the exceptions were so brought to his attention that he must be taken to have agreed to them.[3]

BILLS OF EXCHANGE

This branch of law had been very fully explored and defined before the excellent Act of codification of 1882.

The main line of development in our period has been in reference to cheques, the use of which has so enormously increased since the beginning of the century, and the principal subject of debate has related to the protection given to bankers in dealing with crossed cheques. It is well known that they were given this protection in return for the burden imposed on them when the crossing was made by statute a material part of the cheque, carrying with it the requirement that a crossed cheque should be cleared only through a bank. Banks in handling such cheques were to be protected if they did so without negligence and for a customer and they merely collected as agents and did not deal with them as holders for value.[4]

[1] *Wallis* v. *Pratt* [1911] A.C. 394; *Baldry* v. *Marshall* [1925] 1 K.B. 260. [2] *Alison* v. *Wallsend* (1926) 43 T.L.R. 104.
[3] *Sullivan* v. *Constable* (1932) 48 T.L.R. 368.
[4] 45 & 46 Vic. c. 61, s. 82.

All these points have had to be elucidated. What is a customer? When does the bank merely collect for its customer; and when is it to be held to be negligent?

A mere casual stranger is not a customer,[1] but a man may be a customer though he has not before the transaction in question had a current account.[2] The cheque in question may be the first cheque paid by the person and yet may be paid in under such circumstances as to make the payer-in a customer. A deposit account may constitute a man a customer of the bank. The determination of what is a customer must be left as a question of fact.[3]

An amending Act was necessary to provide that the mere credit of the customer's account in the bank's books before the cheque was cleared did not make the bank a holder in due course of the cheque so as to deprive it of the protection.[4] The credit may be merely conditional on the cheque being duly met on collection.

What constitutes negligence of the bank has also been elaborately discussed in our period, especially in the latest case in the House of Lords.[5] It was held that it was negligent of a bank to collect a cheque if the bank was put on enquiry as to the customer's title by something

---

[1] *Great Western Railway* v. *London & County Bank* [1901] A.C. 414.
[2] *Tate* v. *Wilts. & Dorset Bank*, *Journal of the Instit. of Bankers*, xx, 376.
[3] *Commissioners of Taxation* v. *English, Scottish and Australian Bank* [1920] A.C. 683, 688.
[4] Bills of Exchange (Crossed Cheques) Act, 1906 (6 Edw. VII, c. 17).
[5] *Lloyds Bank* v. *Savory & Co.* [1933] A.C. 201.

in the form of the cheque, or something in the circumstances of the customer in relation to it, which made it out of the ordinary course of the business of the bank to collect it for the customer without sufficient enquiry. Thus, for instance, enquiry is called for if the customer pays in for collection for his personal account a cheque payable to his employer,[1] or a partner pays in for his personal account a partnership cheque.[2] A banker, it is true, is not bound to act as a detective in such matters. But where there is an apparent irregularity he must take due precaution, and he may be negligent not merely in regard to matters appertaining to the particular cheque, but in regard to matters of a general character. Thus he may be negligent if, when opening the account, he does not acquaint himself with the relevant circumstances of the customer,[3] for instance his occupation, and if he is an employee the name of his employer. All these circumstances may be very relevant—take, for instance, the case where a stockbroker's clerk pays in for his own account a business cheque of his employer. A general method of conducting business may amount to negligence: thus where the customer keeps his account at a local branch it may be negligence on the bank's part to receive at a city branch and transmit to the local branch a cheque to be collected for the customer, because in that case the collecting branch would not know who paid in the cheque at the city branch, which may be an essential fact.[4]

[1] *Lloyds Bank* v. *Savory & Co.* [1933] A.C. 201.
[2] Ex p. *Darlington District Bank*; re *Riches*, etc. (1865) 4 De G. J. & S. 581.
[3] *Hampstead Guardians* v. *Barclays Bank, Ltd.* (1923) 39 T.L.R. 229.
[4] *Lloyds Bank* v. *Savory & Co.* [1933] A.C. 201, 234.

Commercial Law in the Present Century

Negligence in this connection has a peculiar significance: it means breach of an artificial duty imposed by the Act in favour of the true owner of the cheque.[1]

These complicated rules have been developed because of the new and complicated conditions under which modern banking is conducted. They impose a hardship, perhaps, on banks: but it must be remembered that all they do is to limit a statutory protection. If there had been no such statutory protection specially given, the bank would have no defence at all against an action for conversion by the true owner of the cheque wherever the bank, however innocently, collects the cheque for its customer who has no title under the true owner to deal with it. The cheque is a chattel; such collection is on familiar principles a conversion.

Another rule that has been established is that a customer in drawing a cheque owes a duty to his bank on which he draws it not to draw it in such a form as will facilitate forgery, for instance by enabling a possessor fraudulently to alter the amount.[2] It was held that there was no such duty as between the drawer or acceptor of a bill of exchange and the holder:[3] but as between banker and customer it has been held that the duty flows from the contractual relationship between them. But the duty is only to anticipate ordinary risks, such as the insertion of figures or words altering the amount where space is carelessly left which is convenient to the forger for that purpose. An unusual alteration of

---

[1] *Commissioners of Taxation* v. *English, Scottish and Australian Bank* [1920] A.C. 683, 688; *Lloyds Bank* v. *Chartered Bank of India, Australia and China* [1929] 1 K.B. 40, per Scrutton L.J., at p. 59.

[2] *London Joint Stock Bank* v. *Macmillan* [1918] A.C. 777.

[3] *Scholfield* v. *Earl of Londesborough* [1896] A.C. 514.

the name or description of the payee is something which it is not negligence not to anticipate.[1]

I need only mention one case where a new point has been decided on the requirements of the form of bills. The Act enables a holder to complete a bill of exchange by filling in blanks in accordance with the authority given him. Suppose the holder's title depends on the bill having been indorsed by himself before it came to the transferor from whom he received it, but that was not done. The holder can complete the bill which is imperfect when he receives it, and he can do so even if he writes his indorsement on the back in the wrong order, for instance after his transferor's indorsement.[2] These rules show the tendency of the Court to favour validity, as against mere form.

The rule, however, that any material alteration avoids a bill as against former parties who have not assented to it, has been strictly applied.[3] That is more than mere form.

An important rule of private international law which has been laid down is that the effectiveness of the transfer of a bill depends on the law of the country in which the transfer takes place.[4]

---

[1] *Slingsby* v. *District Bank, Ltd.* [1931] 2 K.B. 588; affirmed [1932] 1 K.B. 544.

[2] *McDonald & Co.* v. *Nash & Co.* [1924] A.C. 625; *National Sales Corporation, Ltd.* v. *Bernardi* [1931] 2 K.B. 188; *McCall Bros., Ltd.* v. *Hargreaves* [1932] 2 K.B. 423.

[3] 45 & 46 Vic. c. 61, s. 64 (1); *Suffell* v. *Bank of England* (1882) 9 Q.B.D. 555; but see *Hong Kong & Shanghai Bank* v. *Lo Lee Shi* [1928] A.C. 181.

[4] *Koechlin & Cie* v. *Kestenbaum Bros.* [1927] 1 K.B. 889.

CARRIAGE OF GOODS BY SEA

The law of carriage of goods by sea has undergone considerable development in our period.

The greatest change has been the passing of the Carriage of Goods by Sea Act, 1924,[1] which prescribes uniform and obligatory conditions in the case of all outward bills of lading, and excludes the complete contractual freedom which had prevailed before the Act, and which still prevails in charter-parties, and bills of lading issued abroad, to which the Act does not apply.[2]

The idea of having these stereotyped conditions was adopted at an international conference, and they were embodied in what were called the "Hague Rules". It was expected that other countries would adopt them, but that expectation has not been fulfilled. The United States had previously enacted obligatory conditions of its own to apply to all shipments from that country or in the ships of that country, and Canada, by its Water Carriage of Goods Act, has taken a similar course.

Since the English Act was passed there have been very few disputes litigated on its terms, largely, perhaps, because of the very numerous cases which had settled the law when similar questions had arisen or similar words had been used in bills of lading or charter-parties before the Act, or on similar provisions in the Harter Act, the United States Act of 1893. It has generally been considered that the Act has worked well.

Of the Hague Rules thus made obligatory in respect of shipments from these shores, it has been well said that they are like a palimpsest written over the rules

---

[1] 14 & 15 Geo. V, c. 22.   [2] *Ibid.* s. 1.

which had been elaborated before the Act and which, as already indicated, still apply in respect of charter-parties and bills of lading issued in ports outside the United Kingdom, so far as not affected by similar legislation. Perhaps the most fundamental change in detail is the abolition of the absolute warranty of seaworthiness and the substitution therefor of an obligation to use due care and skill to make the ship seaworthy.[1] In effect this means that the shipowner is no longer to be liable for latent defects. In general, this may not be of much practical value, unless perhaps where a shipowner has had a ship built for him by first-class builders and by no fault of himself or his own servants there has been a latent defect.[2] In many respects the Hague Rules leave the law as it was; for instance, as it seems, in regard to deviation.[3]

Many points of detail have been defined or elucidated in this branch of law, for instance when a ship is an "arrived ship" for purposes of reckoning demurrage,[4] and the relation of deviation and unseaworthiness,[5] and many other matters too technical for discussion here.

CARRIAGE BY AIR

I should add a brief word about carriage by air which may raise various difficulties of commercial law apart from the various statutory rules and conventions which do not concern us here.

---

[1] 14 & 15 Geo. V, c. 22, Schedule, Art. III, 1 (*a*).

[2] W. Angliss & Co. (Australia), Proprietary, Ltd. v. Peninsular and Oriental Steam Navigation Co. [1927] 2 K.B. 456.

[3] 14 & 15 Geo. V, c. 22, Schedule, Art. IV, 4.

[4] E.g. *Armement Adolf Deppe* v. *Robinson & Co.* [1917] 2 K.B. 204; *S.S. Plata (Owners)* v. *Ford & Co.* [1917] 2 K.B. 593.

[5] E.g. *The Vortigern* [1899] P. 140.

Commercial Law in the Present Century

Whether a carrier by air could fall within the category of a common carrier is a question not likely to arise. The casual carrier would obviously not be so classed, and the regular lines are careful to reserve a right to refuse to carry, and do not profess to carry for all and sundry. It would be strange to apply the old custom of the realm to transport in a strange element. It has recently been held in a very instructive judgment that the air carriers there concerned were not in fact common carriers, and that the exceptions excused them in respect of negligence or want of due care either in conducting the actual conveyance or transport or in the earlier stage of providing an airworthy craft. There was not, it was held, any absolute warranty of airworthiness or any absolute duty to carry or deliver safely.[1] The bare obligation, apart from the exceptions, seems rightly to have been equated to that of carriers of passengers at Common Law.

INSURANCE

The Commercial Law is inclined when it speaks of insurance to think first of marine insurance, which was the type to be first developed as a matter of history: but in modern days in the facts both of business and ordinary life the bulk of other classes of insurance is greater. There is scarcely any element in life or affairs that is not the subject of insurance: even at Lloyd's the volume of non-marine insurance is now very great, perhaps greater than the marine. Life insurance and fire insurance began long before our period to call for the enunciation of legal principles, and more recently this became true

---

[1] *Aslan* v. *Imperial Airways* (1933) 49 T.L.R. 415.

of various ramifications of non-marine business, such as third-party, solvency, credit insurance, and a host of other subject-matters.

The fundamental principles of these newer branches of insurance law have been taken from marine insurance, for instance the principles of indemnity (which, however, do not apply to life or accident insurance), *uberrima fides*, and many other rules, but the different characteristics of the risks insured and the different forms and conditions of the policies adopted in particular classes of insurance have led to much special case law which I cannot discuss here. I shall only mention that in these cases it has been repeated that if a term is expressed to be a condition it does not matter how unimportant it may appear: its breach avoids the policy.[1] This question has particularly arisen in defining the relation of statements in proposals to the policies which embody them.[2]

By the end of the nineteenth century a great mass of case law had accumulated about marine insurance. The codifying Act of 1906[3] has no doubt done much to simplify understanding of the law. As a codification it did not purport to change the law, but whether by accident or design it seems to have done so in places. In case of conflict the words of the Act must prevail over the effect of cases decided before it: these decisions cannot control the words of the Act, though if there is doubt what words of the Act mean such decisions may help, and where on any point the Act is silent the Common Law is still to apply. Thus the authorities prior

---

[1] *Dawsons, Ltd.* v. *Bonnin* [1922] 2 A.C. 413.
[2] *Ibid.*; *Provincial Insurance Co.* v. *Morgan* [1933] A.C. 240.
[3] Marine Insurance Act, 1906 (6 Edw. VII, c. 41).

to the Act must still be referred to as embodying the Common Law. As an instance of how the words of the Act may, whether by design or not, alter the law formerly laid down I may take the case where it was held that the language of the Act, which was that there was a right to abandon a ship as a constructive total loss if the saving of the ship was unlikely,[1] had introduced a new rule: previously the question had been held to be whether it was uncertain if the ship could be saved.[2] The difference between uncertainty and unlikelihood is obvious.

I cannot now touch upon the mass of questions, mainly of construction, which have been decided upon the Act in our period. I already draw to the end of my allotted time. There is, however, one question of general principle which I should like to mention briefly.

There is an old legal maxim "*in iure non remota causa sed proxima spectatur*". That maxim is of general application though it mostly raises the difficulty of saying in any case what is remote. But it has always been treated as of special sanctity in marine insurance, and proximate cause was often defined to be the cause which was nearest in time.[3] Thus a distinction was often drawn between the effect of an exception of perils of the sea in a contract of carriage, and the effect of the same words in a policy as defining one of the risks insured against.[4]

---

[1] Marine Insurance Act, 1906 (6 Edw. VII, c. 41), s. 60 (1) and (2) (i).
[2] *Polurrian S.S. Co.* v. *Young* [1915] 1 K.B. 922, 936; *Goss* v. *Withers* (1758) 2 Burr. 683.
[3] *Pink* v. *Fleming* (1890) 25 Q.B.D. 396, 398; *Ionides* v. *Universal Marine Insurance* (1863) 14 C.B. (N.S.), 259.
[4] *Grill* v. *General Iron Screw Colliery* (1866) L.R. 1 C.P. 600, 611; *Wilson* v. *Owners of Cargo per the Xantho* (1887) 12 A.C. 503, 510.

That was not because the words had a different meaning in the two contracts, but because the contracts are different.[1] In the one case the contract is to carry safely unless prevented by the excepted perils, but always subject, in the absence of express words, to the underlying proviso that the exception cannot be relied on if the loss be due to want of seaworthiness of the ship or want of due care and skill of the crew, so that the question is thrown back from the mere perils of the sea to these remoter matters. If the proviso operates, the exception does not apply: the carrier is liable for breach of his fundamental obligations.[2] But in insurance the promise is simply to pay when the event occurs and causes the loss, and the remoter questions of negligence and unseaworthiness are irrelevant, unless where initial unseaworthiness has avoided the policy.

But in marine insurance difficult questions have arisen as to the effect of the co-operation of causes, one later in time but the other more dominant in practical effect. Suppose a ship is torpedoed, and later sinks before she can be brought into a place of safety. Is she lost by the war peril, the torpedo, or by the sea peril, the sinking? No problem arises here if the same policy covers both risks. But if the marine policy which covers perils of the sea is subject to an exception of war risks, and these risks are covered by a separate policy, it becomes essential to determine which peril caused the loss. In the simple case I have put it was held that the war peril though earlier in time was the substantial or dominant cause to

[1] *Wilson* v. *Owners of Cargo per the Xantho* (1887) 12 A.C. 503, per Lord Herschell, at p. 510, overruling *Woodley* v. *Mitchell* (1883) 11 Q.B.D. 47.
[2] *Paterson Steamships, Ltd.* v. *Canadian Co-operative Wheat Producers, Ltd.* [1934] A.C. 538.

which the loss must be attributed so as to fall on the war policy.[1] Many jurists thought that this was a departure from the true doctrine, and that if a ship was in the last resort lost by being submerged in the sea that was a loss by perils of the sea, and nothing else was material according to the meaning of a marine insurance policy. On the same reasoning there has been criticism of a decision in which it was held that loss of a cargo through the sinking of a ship in calm waters, because the ship was too weak and leaky to keep out the sea, was not a loss by perils of the sea.[2] This was a case where there was no warranty of seaworthiness, and no fraud or misconduct of the assured. But the most serious criticism has been directed to a still larger departure from what many consider the true doctrine. Suppose a ship is sunk at sea, or deliberately run ashore and lost, because for the purpose of gain the owner has procured her master to cast her away. If the owner is the assured it is obvious that neither he nor assignees of the policy under him can recover. But what if the policy has been taken out by an innocent mortgagee? The House of Lords has held that such a loss is not by perils of the sea, which is covered, but by the fraud of the owner, which is not covered.[3] This is a big departure from what used to be regarded as the rule of proximate cause, and there has been great difference of opinion. The Act, which uses the words proximate cause,[4] gives no direct help, because the question depends on what is meant by proximate cause in any particular case, and the Act does not define

[1] *Leyland Shipping Co. v. Norwich Union, Ltd.* [1918] A.C. 350.
[2] *Sassoon v. Western Assurance Co.* [1912] A.C. 561.
[3] *Samuel & Co. v. Dumas* [1924] A.C. 431.
[4] 6 Edw. VII, c. 41, s. 55.

the words either as meaning what is nearest in time or what is nearest in efficiency.

Now I must finish. I regret that time has compelled me to ignore many interesting and important questions, and that I have been forced to deal so briefly and inadequately with such matters as I have adverted to: but that is inevitable in such a general survey as I have attempted in this Presidential Address.

XI

OUGHT THE DOCTRINE OF CONSIDERATION TO BE ABOLISHED FROM THE COMMON LAW?[1]

RULES of law, like everything else in this modern age, must be prepared to justify themselves against attacks, and cannot shelter behind antiquity or prescription. Hence it seems not improper to review the rules which under the common law define what are the essential conditions by which it is determined whether an agreement is or is not of legal obligation. It might seem *a priori* that the test which should be adopted by a court is whether there is a serious and deliberate intention to enter into obligations enforceable at law: if there are no complicating circumstances, such as of incapacity or illegality or impossibility, the law ought, it might seem, to hold that the intention of the parties should be given effect. *Pacta sunt servanda!* The lawful intentions of parties should be enforced. That is the rule adopted in very many, perhaps in all, those countries where some system other than the common law prevails, as I shall point out later. But in England, as in other countries in which the common law is dominant, it is different: there must be what is called consideration. In the words of Anson, "Consideration is not one of several tests, it is

[1] First published in 49 *Harvard Law Review* (1936), 1225-1253.

the only test of the intention of the promisor to bind himself by contract."[1]

Anson expounds the rules relating to this idea of consideration with all the assured conviction of one expounding ultimate indisputable truth. Indeed, to one who like myself has for over thirty-five years practised as Counsel at the Bar, or sat as Judge in the King's Bench Court, or in appellate courts under the common law, it requires a distinct effort to contemplate a system of contract law in which consideration does not fill the rôle which Anson so complacently regards as vital. It must be so to any one engaged in actual practice in England: the necessity of consideration is established by authorities which not even the House of Lords could distinguish or disregard. But I sit in appellate tribunals which administer laws other than the common law, such as the laws of South Africa and Ceylon where the basic law is the Roman Dutch law, or of Scotland where the basic law is the civil law: in these jurisdictions consideration has no place; nor has it a place in the laws of France, Italy, Spain, Germany, Switzerland and Japan. These are all civilized countries with a highly developed system of law; how then is it possible to regard the common law rule of consideration as axiomatic or as an inevitable element in any code of law? In these days, for various reasons, accepted rules of the common law have been exposed to criticism, as, for instance, the ancient rule of *stare decisis*. The rules of law are required to justify themselves by their fitness to satisfy the practical requirements of justice, as well as to be self-consistent and rational. Criticism comes from historical studies, from

[1] *Law of Contract* (16th ed. 1923), 130.

Ought Consideration to be Abolished?

logical analysis, from comparative law, from sociological ideals. It is clear, I think, that logically there are only two theories which can properly be applied to ascertain the test of contractual intention: one theory is that there must be something outside the contractual intention, to give it, as it were, support and substance; the other, that the deliberateness of the contractual intention is in itself the sole and sufficient test. Nothing intermediate seems to be logically possible. The common law has insisted that there must be something outside the agreement itself and has defined that as being something objective and practical, something other than motive, desire, inducement, object, all of which are matters foreign to the mutuality involved in contract; it has chosen as its test "consideration", and has defined it in realistic terms.

It is curious and significant that even now there is considerable uncertainty as to what is truly meant by that term; but I accept the definition of Sir Frederick Pollock in his work on *Contracts*,[1] a definition adopted by Lord Dunedin in *Dunlop Pneumatic Tyre Co., Ltd.* v. *Selfridge & Co., Ltd.*: "An act or forbearance of the one party, or the promise thereof, is the price for which the promise of the other is bought, and the promise thus given for value is enforceable."[2] That definition involves the idea that the act or forbearance is something of value, something to which the law, in a materialistic or practical sense, can attach value. The definition also involves that the act of forbearance is bought, that it is done or suffered by the one party at the request of the other; it is a matter of mutuality, not a motive or emotion of

---

[1] (10th ed. 1936), 164.   [2] [1915] A.C. 847, 855.

affection, benevolence, bounty or charity which from their nature must be personal to the promisor. I treat detriment to the promisee, not benefit to the promisor, as the essential factor, though I am not unconscious that in the American Restatement of the Law of Contracts[1] both are bracketed as equal, an instance of the vital uncertainty to which I have just referred. The test of contractual intention is thus external, objective, realistic. The question is, Why is any such external test needed? Why is not the contractual intention, if it is properly established, enough in itself? And the further question is whether the common law test can be logically or consistently applied; is it not rather calculated to defeat than to advance the needs of justice, is its origin to be found not in absolute truth but in historical accidents and in the creation of remedies in contract from remedies *in delicto*, and is not its development to be traced in fictions and evasions? If it is neither theoretically necessary nor practically satisfactory, is there any need to preserve the idea other than legal conservatism?

The discussion of the subject seems to ramify in so many different directions that it is difficult to decide which way to turn first. I may, however, first note that, if consideration is taken by the common law as the "sole" test of contractual intention (it being always herein understood that the formality of the deed is not in the question), it is not true to say that this test is by itself conclusive or that the necessity of deciding whether there is a deliberate intention to enter into an enforceable contract is eliminated because there is consideration. I may cite two recent cases which illustrate this. In

[1] (1932), § 75.

Ought Consideration to be Abolished?

Balfour v. *Balfour*,[1] a husband, before going abroad, had promised to allow his wife £30 a month in consideration of her agreeing to support herself entirely out of that allowance. Lord Atkin (then Atkin L.J.) said in the Court of Appeal:

...it is necessary to remember that there are agreements between parties which do not result in contracts within the meaning of that term in our law. The ordinary example is where two parties agree to take a walk together, or where there is an offer and an acceptance of hospitality. Nobody would suggest in ordinary circumstances that those agreements result in what we know as a contract, and one of the most usual forms of agreement which does not constitute a contract appears to me to be the arrangements which are made between husband and wife.[2]

He adds later: "To my mind those agreements, or many of them, do not result in contracts at all, and they do not result in contracts even though there may be what as between other parties would constitute consideration."[3] I am not sure that it is not on some such ground, that is, that there was in fact no intention to contract, that the curious case of *White* v. *Bluett*[4] may best be explained. In that case a son relied against executors on a promise by his deceased father not to sue him on a promissory note he had given the father; the son alleged as consideration that he had agreed to cease importuning his father. The court held that all that this amounted to was a promise no longer to bore his father, a matter which the court said was too unsubstantial and vague to satisfy the realistic common-law ideas: whether this is so or not, the case may readily be explained as one in

[1] [1919] 2 K.B. 571. [2] [1919] 2 K.B. at 578.
[3] *Ibid.* [4] (1853) 23 L.J. Ex. (N.S.) 36.

which there was no intention to make a legal bargain. Somewhat to the same effect is an observation which I find in *Conradie* v. *Rossouw*,[1] giving as the explanation of an earlier South African case, *Mtembu* v. *Webster*,[2] that "the only reason the defendant had for giving the promise was his wish to escape the plaintiff's importunity without any apparent rudeness to him. That shows there was no such promise as is required by our law to give rise to a contract."[3] This explanation is given on the footing that consideration is irrelevant. The promise was not binding because there was no intention to create a legal obligation.

Another recent case to which I desire to refer is *Rose and Frank Co.* v. *Crompton*.[4] In that case there was a document embodying a business arrangement for the sale of goods, with consideration on both sides, but it contained a clause, described as "the honourable pledge clause", to the effect that the "arrangement" embodied in the document was not a formal or legal agreement and was not to be subject to legal jurisdiction in court. It was held that the overriding clause in the document was that which provided that it was to be a contract in honour only and unenforceable in law. Here there was what the court held to be an express statement negativing the contractual intention: but the same conclusion may be inferred, without express words, from the nature of the transaction as a whole. It is thus clear that even at common law, consideration cannot be regarded as the conclusive test of a deliberate mind to contract: whether

---

[1] S. African L.R. [1919] App. Div. 279.
[2] 21 Sup. Ct. 323 (Cape of Good Hope, 1904).
[3] S. African L.R. [1919] App. Div. at 324.
[4] [1925] A.C. 445.

Ought Consideration to be Abolished?

there is such a mind must always remain as the decisive and overriding question. In any system of law, consideration may be introduced as evidence of that deliberate mind; but it cannot, even under the common law, be decisive: the only question is whether it can be put on a pedestal as the "sole" test.

I now turn to two cases which illustrate what effect the doctrine of consideration may have in defeating the legitimate intentions of parties in ordinary business transactions. The first of these is *Foakes* v. *Beer*.[1] The gist of that authority is concisely and accurately stated in the head note:

> An agreement between judgment debtor and creditor, that in consideration of the debtor paying down part of the judgment debt and costs and on condition of his paying to the creditor or his nominee the residue by instalments, the creditor will not take any proceedings on the judgment, is nudum pactum, being without consideration, and does not prevent the creditor after payment of the whole debt and costs from proceeding to enforce payment of the interest upon the judgment.[2]

It is clear that every one of their Lordships who concurred in this decision did so with reluctance, Lord Blackburn indeed with open dissent in principle and with acquiescence doubtfully enforced by weight of authority. Lord Chancellor Selborne pointed out:

> The distinction between the effect of a deed under seal, and that of an agreement by parol, or by writing not under seal, may seem arbitrary, but it is established in our law; nor is it really unreasonable or practically inconvenient that the law should require particular solemnities to give to a gratuitous contract the force of a binding obligation.[3]

[1] (1884) 9 App. Cas. 605.   [2] *Ibid.*
[3] 9 App. Cas. at 613

That sentence seems to justify consideration as being an evidentiary test of contractual intention, which indeed often in practice, but not universally, it is in truth. But he goes on to say:

> It might be (and indeed I think it would be) an improvement in our law, if a release or acquittance of the whole debt, on payment of any sum which the creditor might be content to receive by way of accord and satisfaction (though less than the whole), were held to be, generally, binding though not under seal; nor should I be unwilling to see equal force given to a prospective agreement, like the present, in writing though not under seal; but I think it impossible, without refinements which practically alter the sense of the word, to treat such a release or acquittance as supported by any new consideration proceeding from the debtor.[1]

Finally he adds that the term consideration does not include "that sort of benefit which a creditor may derive from getting payment of part of the money due to him from a debtor who might otherwise keep him at arm's length, or possibly become insolvent, but is some independent benefit, actual or contingent, of a kind which might in law be a good and valuable consideration for any other sort of agreement not under seal".[2] What the Lord Chancellor is there saying is that the idea of the common law of "good and valuable consideration" is something different from the sort of benefit in question. How great and practically valuable that benefit would be appears from what Lord Blackburn says: he states his "conviction that all men of business, whether merchants or tradesmen, do every day recognize and act on the ground that prompt payment of a part of their demand may be more beneficial to them than it would be to

---

[1] 9 App. Cas. at 613.   [2] *Ibid.* at 614.

Ought Consideration to be Abolished?

insist on their rights and enforce payment of the whole. Even where the debtor is perfectly solvent, and sure to pay at last, this is often so. Where the credit of the debtor is doubtful it must be more so."[1] Surely no one can question this statement. The decision is of prime importance as illustrating what is meant by consideration. Lord Blackburn traced the doctrine back to Coke:[2]

> Where the condition is for payment of £20, the obligor or feoffor cannot at the time appointed pay a lesser sum in satisfaction of the whole, because *it is apparent* that a lesser sum of money *cannot* be a satisfaction of a greater.... If the obligor or feoffor pay a lesser sum either before the day or at another place than is limited by the condition, and the obligee or feofee receiveth it, this is a good satisfaction.[3]

This had been established in *Pinnel's Case*,[4] where it was also said that "the gift of a horse, hawk, or robe, &c., in satisfaction is good. For it shall be intended that a horse, hawk, or robe, &c., might be more beneficial to the plaintiff than the money, in respect of some circumstance, or otherwise the plaintiff would not have accepted of it in satisfaction."[5] This passage may be taken as embodying the essence of the law of consideration. There must be benefit; but it must be external or extrinsic, and a narrow and materialistic view is taken of what is meant by benefit though it includes a counter-obligation. It need not be adequate, so long as it is not merely a lesser quantity of an identical quality; there must be something of value in the eyes of the law, but the law cannot enquire into adequacy: hence the solemn pretence of the tomtit or peppercorn, of nominal or

[1] *Ibid.* at 622. [2] *Litt.* *212b.
[3] 9 App. Cas. at 615. [4] (1602) 5 Co. Rep. *117a.
[5] *Ibid.*

illusory consideration. Surely it would have been simpler and juster to give effect to a deliberate bargain which the parties had intended to be binding. The agreement in question would, of course, have been enforced if a wafer had been attached and delivery made as a deed. I have regarded *Foakes* v. *Beer* as the House of Lords regarded it, that is, as a case on the law of contracts, and not merely as one of accord and satisfaction.

The other case to which I shall refer at this stage is the *Dunlop Case*, which I have already cited.[1] Dew sold to Selfridge tyres, the manufacture of Dunlop, which Dew had purchased from Dunlop; under the sale from Dew to Selfridge, the property in the tyres, which had passed from Dunlop to Dew, had been transferred to Selfridge. Dunlop, however, had sold the tyres to Dew subject to a price maintenance agreement, and on terms which required them, if they resold the tyres at a discount, to obtain from their buyers an undertaking not to retail the tyres at less than Dunlop's advertised current prices. Selfridge signed a written undertaking addressed to Dew not to sell at less than these prices, and agreeing to pay to Dunlop liquidated damages if they broke their undertaking. They did sell them at less than these prices, and were sued by Dunlop. Various points were discussed, but the majority of their Lordships held that, even if there was a contract between Dunlop and Selfridge, it was unenforceable for want of consideration. Lord Dunedin thus summed up the position:

...I confess that this case is to my mind apt to nip any budding affection which one might have had for the doctrine

---

[1] *Dunlop Pneumatic Tyre Co., Ltd.* v. *Selfridge & Co., Ltd.* [1915] A.C. 847, *supra*, p. 289.

of consideration. For the effect of that doctrine in the present case is to make it possible for a person to snap his fingers at a bargain deliberately made, a bargain not in itself unfair, and which the person seeking to enforce it has a legitimate interest to enforce.[1]

Lord Dunedin spoke as one brought up in the Scots law, which has not adopted the doctrine of consideration. But every common lawyer can remember in his experience where he might have said or did say the same.

At a later stage in this article, I shall more in detail examine some of the English authorities, but I shall at once mention, without reference to decided cases, an example which must be notorious to all—that is, the case of a firm option given to be open for a certain time. In such a case people generally do not think of consideration or of taking the option by deed. But if neither course is adopted, the offeror can at any time before acceptance withdraw the option, and the donee of the option has no redress; he may have proceeded on the faith of the option being open for the stated time, and deferred his decision accordingly; most people naturally think of the firm option as really firm: there is expressly or by implication a promise to keep it open; not to do so would in ordinary understanding be a breach of faith, and the actual loss to the other party from the breach may be serious. Yet according to the common law, the absence of consideration prevents the offeree from having any claim; the offeror may snap his fingers at a serious bargain deliberately made. This, when stated to the man in the street, is likely to appear shocking. But such is the doctrine of consideration.

[1] [1915] A.C. at 855.

By way of contrast, I now desire to refer shortly to other systems of law. I begin by quoting from a very important case from South Africa, that of *Conradie* v. *Rossouw* which I have already cited. That was the case of a gratuitous option, contained in a written document, set out in full in the report.[1] Its effect may thus be shortly stated: the Rossouws, man and wife, being owners of a certain estate, agreed that after their death their executors should transfer it to Conradie at a certain price, should he claim the same. The court held that the document was not a testamentary disposition, but a gratuitous option. The Rossouws while still alive had repudiated the option. The relevant defence was that there was no consideration. There had been a conflict on the question of consideration between the Cape and the Transvaal courts, the former adopting the doctrine of consideration, the latter rejecting it. In *Conradie's Case*, the Supreme Court of South Africa, Appellate Division, resolved the conflict by deciding that the doctrine of consideration had no place in their law. As is well known, the Roman Dutch law prevails in South Africa. The three judgments given in the Appellate Division are of first importance, not only for their carefully documented examination of the Roman Dutch and the civil law in regard to the matters which are dealt with in this article, but for their discussion of principles fundamental in the law of contracts. I cannot here recapitulate in full all that is contained in the judgments of Solomon A.C.J., Maasdorp J.A., and de Villiers A.J.A. I shall limit myself to some excerpts from the elaborate opinion of the last named. He states that the "maxim *ex nudo*

[1] S. African L.R. [1919] App. Div. 279, 298.

Ought Consideration to be Abolished?

pacto non oritur actio was not incorporated into the law of Holland, nor into that of the other leading nations of the Continent".[1] He had explained that *nudum pactum* in this sense does not mean a *pactum* or agreement in which there is no consideration from one party in return for the promise of the other. It is *nudum* because it is not clothed in the particular form or accompanied by the formal acts required to transform a *pactum* into a *contractus*; Roman Law was far "from regarding *pacta nuda* as promises for which no *quid pro quo* had been promised".[2] I may interpose to remark that the common law, when it finally adopted the maxim "*ex nudo pacto non oritur actio*", gave a different meaning to *nudum pactum* because the term was used by the common law to mean an agreement naked of consideration.

After a most elaborate examination of the authorities, de Villiers A.J.A. states the law:

> According to our law if two or more persons, of sound mind and capable of contracting, enter into a lawful agreement, a valid contract arises between them enforceable by action. The agreement may be for the benefit of the one of them or of both (*Grotius* 3.6.2). The promise must have been made with the intention that it should be accepted (*Grotius* 3.1.48); according to Voet the agreement must have been entered into *serio ac deliberato animo*. And this is what is meant by saying that the only element that our law requires for a valid contract is *consensus*, naturally within proper limits—it should be *in* or *de re licita ac honesta*.[3]

This statement of the law is in harmony with that of the other two members of the court and is final so far as South Africa is concerned.

[1] *Ibid.* at 307. [2] *Ibid.* at 305.
[3] *Ibid.* at 320.

The learned judge goes on to consider what effect should be attached to the word *causa*, and he says that the discussion of *causa* or *justa causa*, as the ground, reason, object or motive of an obligation, results "from a failure to distinguish between causa as negotium or contract and causa as the ground of an obligation".[1] He concludes:

> The way the matter is looked at from the modern point of view is this. Donation itself within the restrictions imposed by law is a *justa causa*, a *justum negotium*, a contract or transaction approved of by the law. And the same must be said of every lawful contract.... Our law may be said to have moved from the *causa obligandi* to the *causa debendi*, from *causa* in the sense of a particular ground or reason which brought the transaction into the charmed circle of contract to *causa* in the sense of *negotium*.... It was a serious mistake in English law when what was merely required as proof of a serious mind was converted into an essential of every contract. It would be equally a mistake with us to introduce for a valid contract the necessity for a *causa*, whether in the shape of valuable consideration or any other ground of obligation.[2]

This view, that the ground of the obligation is simply and solely the *consensus*, is the direct opposite to that which I have quoted from Lord Selborne, which was that beyond the *consensus* there must be some independent benefit, actual or contingent, which the law could take to be, according to its definition, a good and valuable consideration. The *causa* which de Villiers A.J.A. rejects as unessential to the constitution of a contract is, I need not say, of much wider import than the common-law idea of consideration: the learned judge quotes a

---

[1] *Ibid.* at 320–321.
[2] *Ibid.* at 322–323.

Ought Consideration to be Abolished?

description of what *causa* may mean, which it may be useful to repeat here:

> Such a "cause" assumes different forms, according to the different transactions which may present themselves in our daily life. It may be the desire, born of good will, to benefit another: on the discharge of a lawful claim which someone has against us; or the desire to ensure or promote his future well-being; or to render an equivalent for an already completed performance: or to engage to render one; or to realise any other lawful end.[1]

This enumeration, I may observe, would include, besides somewhat which the common law tacitly regards as consideration, all those motives or purposes some of which at one time it was sought to bring into the common law as moral consideration. But moral consideration, though naturally used at a certain period of our history when the word moral was popular and was used to distinguish the mental or spiritual from the physical, was really a contradiction in terms. If the idea of consideration was limited to what was objective, it could not be enlarged so as to embrace something quite different, viz. various subjective motives or purposes. The adjective contradicted the substantive. But the South African law as now declared equally rejects both consideration and *causa* as essential conditions of a contractual obligation; for contractual obligation the essential matter is the *consensus*, the *negotium*, the transaction itself.

In 1918, the question whether consideration was necessary had come before the Judicial Committee of the Privy Council in an appeal from Ceylon, where, as in South Africa, Roman Dutch law prevails. The case

---

[1] *Ibid.* at 322, from 2 *Goudsmid, Pandeckten-Systeem* (1880), § 33.

is *Jayawickreme* v. *Amarasuriya*.[1] It was laid down in that case that according to Roman Dutch law a promise deliberately made is enforceable if the motive for it was a sense of moral obligation or generosity, there being a *justa causa debendi* sufficient to sustain a promise; by that was meant something wider than that which the English law treats as good consideration for a promise. This ruling agrees with that in *Conradie* v. *Rossouw*,[2] in so far as it eliminates the common-law doctrine of consideration, but it differs in that it lays stress on the element of *causa*. The facts in the case before the Privy Council showed (I disregard a different matter also discussed) that the promise was prompted by family duty and was made under a sense of moral responsibility. In *Conradie's Case* there was no such motive: there was no family tie or moral duty involved. Hence in *Conradie's Case* it was observed in reference to what was said in the Privy Council on the subject of *causa*, that it was not necessary for that Tribunal to go to the same length as the Appellate Court in South Africa was required to go for the decision of the case before it, and it was also observed that the Privy Council had accordingly not found it necessary to make that exhaustive examination of the Roman Dutch authorities which was made in *Conradie's Case*.

In Scotland, the common-law doctrine of consideration finds no place; as my friend, Lord Macmillan, once observed, the Scotch do not need to consider whether they should perform a promise or not; they do so without consideration. Thus gratuitous promises are enforced,

[1] [1918] A.C. 869.
[2] S. African L.R. [1919] App. Div. 279.

though if the gratuitous promise is to pay money some written corroboration is required: that, however, is merely evidential and is a matter of procedure. Scots law thus puts contracts without consideration on the same footing as innominate or unusual contracts. It is a matter of proof, not of substance. The contract is good without consideration, though the court requires the additional piece of evidence: hence consideration merely assumes an evidentiary character. I may quote a short passage from one Scots lawyer—Lord Mackenzie, in his work on *Roman Law*:

In Scotland it is not essential to the validity of an obligation that it should be granted for a valuable consideration, or indeed for any consideration whatever; the rule of the civil law, that no action arises from a naked paction, being rejected, and an obligation undertaken deliberately, though gratuitously, being binding. This is in conformity with the canon law by which every paction produceth action.[1]

Bell in the *Principles of the Law of Scotland* says: "To a perfect obligation (besides the proof requisite), it is necessary that there shall be a deliberate and voluntary consent and purpose to engage; excluding on the one hand, Incapacity by nonage, disease, or imbecility, and on the other, Error, Force and Fraud."[2] He makes no mention even of *cause*, and still less includes consideration as an essential. Thus the Scots law followed the same course as the Roman Dutch law.

In French law consideration finds no place, but much controversy has arisen about the use of the word *cause* in the articles of the French Code. Let me refer to two. One is Article 1131 which is that "L'obligation sans

---

[1] (6th ed. 1886), Pt. III, ch. III, sect. II.   [2] (4th ed. 1839), § 10.

cause, ou sur une fausse cause, ou sur une cause illicite, ne peut avoir aucun effet." The other is Article 1133, "La cause est illicite, quand elle est prohibée par la loi, quand elle est contraire aux bonnes mœurs ou à l'ordre public." Article 1108 also states as one of the four conditions essential for the validity of a contract "Une cause licite dans l'obligation." The precise effect of these Articles has given rise to much discussion, but as I am concerned only with consideration in the technical sense given to it by the common law I need not determine exactly what is meant by *cause* in French law, since it is clear that it is different from what is meant by consideration. It is wider even than what used to be described as moral consideration, because for instance it would, it seems, include the motive or impulse of charity or generosity. I observe that a learned author, Dr F. P. Walton, is of opinion that the theory of *cause* no longer plays any useful part in French law and that if, in Article 6 of the *Code Civil,* provision were made to include under impossible agreements those which have an impossible, unlawful or immoral object, Articles 1131 and 1133 might be left out.[1] Professor Lorenzen in a valuable essay expresses much the same conclusion as to *cause* in French law.[2] In certain cases the French courts require some written corroboration. It is, however, enough to say here that whatever *cause* may mean, it is not the same as consideration.

Neither *cause* nor consideration finds any place in the

[1] Walton, "Cause and Consideration in Contracts" (1925), 41 *L.Q. Rev.* 306.
[2] "Causa and Consideration in the Law of Contracts" (1919), 28 *Yale L.J.* 621, reprinted in *Selected Readings in the Law of Contract* (1931), 565.

Ought Consideration to be Abolished?

German Code[1] in the portion of that Code which deals with the formation of contracts, and the same is true of the Swiss Revised Code of Obligations of 1911, and of the Civil Code of Japan.

I have referred at length to these other legal systems in order to show that the common law doctrine of consideration is one which other systems successfully dispense with, and that the doctrine is no natural or essential part of a theory of contractual liability. Modern legal thought has either adopted or is tending to adopt the simple idea that (subject to the obvious qualification that the subject-matter is lawful) "*conventio* without more = *contractus*",[2] if I may borrow the formula from Dr Walton.

How then did this peculiar doctrine find so sacred a place in the common law? I do not here intend to repeat the history of the origin of the idea or the way in which it grew up in connection with the extension of the writ of *assumpsit* from misfeasance to nonfeasance. The word "consideration" had acquired its technical meaning by the time of Coke, and its main content had been defined, as clearly appears from the quotation I made above from *Pinnel's Case*.[3] All I here seek to do is to examine some of the decisions which followed, in order to show how it was sought to adapt the idea itself to the needs of justice, though in a halting and half-hearted way, and what little success attended these well-intentioned attempts.

But I may note in passing that before Coke's time it

---
[1] *Bürgerliches Gesetzbuch* (1900).
[2] Walton, *supra* note 36, at 323.
[3] 5 Co. Rep. *117a (1602).

had been established that in bilateral contracts the promise on the one side was consideration for the promise on the other.[1] In the famous authority known as *Slade's Case*[2] it was resolved that every contract executory imports in itself an *assumpsit*, for when one agrees to pay money or to deliver a thing, thereby he assumes to pay or deliver it, and therefore when one sells any goods to another and agrees to deliver them at a day to come, and the other in consideration thereof agrees to pay so much money on such a day, in that case both parties may have an action of debt or an action on the case on *assumpsit*, for the mutual executory agreement of both parties imports in itself reciprocal actions upon the case, as well as actions of debt. It is beyond question here postulated that there was on each side a deliberate intention to make a binding contract. How simple would it have been, but for what had gone before in the history of *assumpsit*, to have omitted all reference to consideration and made everything rest on the deliberate promise. I do not revive here the controversy whether in logic it can be said that one promise is consideration for the other, and vice versa, even if both are made simultaneously; but it seems clear that neither promise is binding unless the other is binding. Thus if the question of consideration is imported, the consideration for each promise can consist only in mere words of assent, unless the words are supported by consideration from the other promise so as to become binding; that, however, can only be if the former promise is itself deemed to be binding; this results in a mere circle. On

---

[1] *Pecke* v. *Redman* (1556) *Dyer* 113 a; *Nichols* v. *Raynbred* (1614) Hob. 88.
[2] 4 Co. Rep. *92 b (1602).

this process of reasoning, which is certainly difficult to answer, the whole theory of bilateral contracts rests on no foundation of consideration; the fact that the promises are reciprocal only functions as evidence of a mutual deliberate intention. I confess I have found no satisfactory answer to this difficulty.

I shall next pass to the question of what is called "past" consideration; the leading case is *Lampleigh* v. *Brathwait*,[1] which for convenience I quote from the first edition of Smith's *Leading Cases*.[2] The rule there stated was "that a mere voluntary courtesy will not have a consideration to uphold an *assumpsit*. But if that courtesy were moved by a suit or request of the party that gives the *assumpsit*, it will bind; for the promise, though it follows, yet it is not naked, but couples itself with the suit before, and the merits of the party procured by that suit, which is the difference."[3] I have quoted this statement in full because there is no hint in it that the prior request imported a promise to pay something. On the contrary, the promise when subsequently made became binding only because of some relation back to the request. There is in fact in such cases one promise, which is subsequent to the performance by the other party; when the promise is given, the consideration is executed, that is, past; no promise was made before or at the time of the request. Hence there is in such a case no consideration in the technical sense of the common law, because past consideration is not within the technical definition of consideration, though it may well be a reason or motive which in some jurisdictions would be regarded as *causa*. Here again consideration might and

[1] (1615) Hob. 105. [2] Vol. 1 (1837), 67. [3] *Id.* at 67–68.

ought to have disappeared from view; the promisee's past services might properly have been regarded as material only as evidence that the subsequent promise was deliberate: the promise might have been described as one voluntarily given, to which the defendant was morally, not legally, compellable and might also from another standpoint have been classed as a case of moral consideration, which I shall discuss in a moment, but which as I have already remarked is a contradiction in terms. I know that *Lampleigh* v. *Brathwait* has been rationalized by some judges, as for instance by Erle C.J. in *Kennedy* v. *Broun*.[1] The theory thus propounded is that the service performed on request would raise a promise by implication to pay what it was worth, and the subsequent promise of a sum certain would be evidence for the jury to fix the amount. As I read the case, I cannot find that any such idea was present to the judges who decided *Lampleigh* v. *Brathwait*. They did not contemplate that the request when made was coupled with any promise express or implied; there was in their minds only one promise, which is thus declared: "Afterwards, *sc.* &c. in consideration of the premises [that is, the riding and journeying on request], the said defendant did promise the said plaintiff to give him £100."[2] In the words of Erle C.J. "the peculiarity of the decision lies in connecting a subsequent promise with a prior consideration after it has been executed".[3] This I regard as a correct statement, showing that a promise of this type is made without consideration.

---

[1] (1863) 13 C.B.N.S. 677.
[2] 1 Smith, *Leading Cases* (1st ed. 1837), 67.
[3] 13 C.B.N.S. at 740.

Ought Consideration to be Abolished?

Before I turn to the cases in which for a good part of a century the debate went on whether moral consideration (as it was called) was consideration at the common law, I must refer to the famous case of *Pillans and Rose* v. *Van Mierop and Hopkins*,[1] decided in 1765. White, a merchant, had drawn on the plaintiffs, who, as a condition of meeting the bill, desired a confirmed credit on a house in London. White named the defendants; the plaintiffs, being satisfied with the defendants' name, honoured the draft and paid the money and thereupon received the defendants' assent and drew upon the defendants. White failed, upon which the defendants withdrew their undertaking and refused to honour the plaintiffs' draft. There was clearly no consideration for the defendants' promise, though it would have been different if a peppercorn had been sent them. The Court of King's Bench nevertheless held that the plaintiffs were entitled to recover. Lord Mansfield said that the law of merchants and the law of the land were the same; that a *nudum pactum* did not exist in the usage and law of merchants. "I take it", he said, "that the ancient notion about the want of consideration was for the sake of *evidence* only: for when it is reduced into *writing*... there was no objection to the want of consideration."[2] Wilmot J. quoted Vinnius, Grotius and Puffendorff to the effect that either writing or certain formalities were required, but want of consideration was no radical defect; but if an undertaking were entered into upon deliberation and reflection, it had activity. He held that the promise having been reduced to writing, the rule of *nudum pactum* did not apply. Yates and Aston JJ.

[1] 3 Burr. 1663 (K.B.).   [2] *Ibid.* at 1669.

also agreed that it was not *nudum pactum*. This decision, if it had been allowed to stand, would have gone some way towards bringing the English law into line with continental laws, and would have established deliberate intention as the test of a binding contract; but the decision was too revolutionary. In *Rann* v. *Hughes*[1]—a case which came before the House of Lords not long afterwards—Skynner, Lord Chief Baron, delivered to the Lords the opinion of the Judges. He said: "There cannot be *nudum pactum* in writing, whatever may be the rule of the civil law there is certainly none such in the law of *England*.... All contracts are, by the laws of *England*, distinguished into agreements by specialty, and agreements by parol."[2] He said that the law of England afforded no remedy to compel the performance of an agreement made without sufficient consideration. The House of Lords adopted that opinion.

Thus so far the efforts of Lord Mansfield and his brethren came to naught. But there was still left to be ascertained what was meant by sufficient consideration. Lord Mansfield did not desist from his efforts to reform the doctrine of consideration. In 1782, *Hawkes* v. *Saunders*[3] was decided in the King's Bench. The defendant, an executrix, was personally sued on a promise to pay a legacy; assets more than sufficient to pay came to her hands, and being so liable "in consideration thereof she promised to pay" the legacy. Lord Mansfield objected to the view that consideration merely involved a detriment to the promisee or a benefit to the promisor; that was, in his judgment, too narrow. He said: "Where a man is under a moral obligation, which no court of

[1] (1778) 7 T.R. 350, n. (a). [2] *Ibid.* at 351. [3] 1 Cowp. 289.

Ought Consideration to be Abolished?

law or equity can inforce, and *promises*, the honesty and rectitude of the thing is a consideration."[1] It is clear that so to hold would be entirely to defeat the common-law doctrine of consideration. Yet he was able to refer to cases already established as law as particular instances in support of his view:

> As if a man promise to pay a just debt, the recovery of which is barred by the statute of limitations: Or if a man, after he comes of age, promises to pay a meritorious debt contracted during his minority, but not for necessaries; or if a bankrupt, in affluent circumstances after his certificate, promises to pay the whole of his debts.[2]

He adds that in such and many other instances "as the promise is only to do what an honest man ought to do, the ties of conscience upon an upright mind are a sufficient consideration".[3] In truth, there is in the three cases mentioned by Lord Mansfield no consideration as understood by English law: yet they still stand good in English law, save that by the Infants Relief Act, 1874,[4] the promise after majority to pay the debt contracted in nonage is avoided. In the American Restatement of the Law of Contracts, Sections 86 and 87 state the other two instances given by Lord Mansfield as promises binding without consideration; thus Lord Mansfield has been vindicated to some extent, though the logical view is to say, not that there is moral consideration, but that there is no consideration.

However, the idea and the name of moral consideration held its ground: in *Lee* v. *Muggeridge*,[5] decided in 1813, Mansfield C.J. in the Common Pleas said that

---

[1] *Ibid.* at 290.   [2] *Ibid.*   [3] *Ibid.*
[4] 37 & 38 Vict. c. 62.   [5] 5 Taunt. 36.

it had been repeatedly decided that a moral consideration was a good consideration for a promise to pay. The promise in that case was a promise made by a widow that her executors would pay a bond which for good reasons she had executed while covert. It was accordingly analogous to such cases as that of the debtor who after being discharged from bankruptcy promises to pay a debt covered by the discharge, or that of a debtor who promises to pay a debt avoided by the usury laws, after the debt had been stripped of its usurious elements. That type of case was actually referred to in *Lee* v. *Muggeridge*, and a decision on these lines was given as late as 1863 in *Flight* v. *Reed*[1] (Martin B. dissenting). All the cases of this type no doubt were in time regarded as forming a class by themselves. In 1848 in *Earle* v. *Oliver*,[2] that great lawyer, Baron Parke, stated the rule in such cases as established and added its limitation, viz. that debts of the kind in question would not support a promise to do a collateral thing, or to supply goods or to do work and labour; but it seems that he regarded the existence of a debt as being sufficient consideration to support a promise to pay it simply or by instalment or when the party is able, though the consideration was past.

But the advocates of consideration in its technical sense were on their guard. *Eastwood* v. *Kenyon*[3] had been decided in 1840, and had reverted to a stricter view of consideration. Lord Denman C.J. in that case said of the argument that all promises deliberately made should be held binding, that "the doctrine would annihilate the necessity for any consideration at all,

[1] 1 H. & C. 703 (Ex.). [2] 2 Ex. 71.
[3] 11 Ad. & E. 438 (Q.B.).

Ought Consideration to be Abolished?

inasmuch as the mere fact of giving a promise creates a moral obligation to perform it".[1] The fact that Lord Denman found it necessary to give so categorical a denial of the rule which has found favour in so many modern systems of law shows how near the common law had been getting to that doctrine. Lord Denman was logical and clear-sighted when he said that to admit "moral" consideration, as it was called, was to abrogate consideration altogether. His decision was the death blow to that idea. Yet it may be asked whether our law would have been any the worse if there and then consideration had vanished from its pages. I venture to answer "No". The only reason which Lord Denman gives for his view, apart from authority, is contained in the following passage:

> The enforcement of such promises by law, however plausibly reconciled by the desire to effect all conscientious engagements, might be attended with mischievous consequences to society; one of which would be the frequent preference of voluntary undertakings to claims for just debts. Suits would thereby be multiplied, and voluntary undertakings would also be multiplied, to the prejudice of real creditors.[2]

But none of these mischiefs could arise if judges and juries did their duty in taking care that a voluntary engagement was enforced only if it was sufficiently established as being deliberate and serious; and if the Chief Justice had looked abroad to the experience of Scotland or Holland, he might perhaps have found his apprehensions allayed. He might also have reflected on the fact that obligations by deeds were in England enforceable, though gratuitous, and that promises supported by a

[1] 11 Ad. & E. at 450.   [2] *Ibid.* at 450–451.

peppercorn or other nominal consideration were also enforceable. He was much influenced by an elaborate note appended in 1803 by the reporters, Bosanquet and Puller, to *Wennall* v. *Adney*,[1] protesting against the idea which "has prevailed of late years that an *express* promise founded simply on an antecedent moral obligation, is sufficient to support an *assumpsit*".[2]

The whole of this note is worthy of careful study as illustrating the method of reasoning of the common lawyer of that period. I can here, however, merely state the conclusion at which the authors arrive from a review of the numerous cases where promises had been enforced though without consideration in the strict sense. Their object was to explain, or to qualify, or perhaps to dispute by means of many subtle distinctions based on the decided cases, the views put forward in Lord Mansfield's court; they state by way of conclusion in favour of the strict doctrine that "Lord *Mansfield* appears to have used the term *moral obligation* not as expressive of any vague and undefined claim arising from nearness of relationship, but of those imperative duties which would be enforceable by law, were it not for some positive rule, which, with a view to general benefit, exempts the party in that particular instance from legal liability. On such duties, so exempted, an express promise operates to revive the liability and take away the exemption, because if it were not for the exemption they would be enforced at law through the medium of an implied promise."[3] Later, they say "an express promise can...give no original right of action if the obligation on which it is founded

[1] 3 Bos. & P. 247 (C.P.).   [2] *Ibid.* at 249.
[3] *Ibid.* at 251.

Ought Consideration to be Abolished?

never could have been enforced at law".[1] This statement appears to be narrower than many of the cases warrant. It was not adopted, for instance, in *Lee* v. *Muggeridge*[2] and other cases cited by Smith,[3] who refers to cases where the plaintiff voluntarily does that to which the defendant is morally, though not legally, compellable, and the defendant afterwards, in consideration thereof, expressly promises; he cites *Lee* v. *Muggeridge* and other cases, but adds: "But every *moral* obligation is not perhaps sufficient for this purpose. *See per Lord Tenterden* C.J. in *Littlefield* v. *Shee*. 2 B. & Adol. 811."[4] This was written as late as 1837.

The intensive and complete study of the numerous cases between *Pillans* v. *Van Mierop*[5] and *Eastwood* v. *Kenyon*[6] would throw much light on the attitude of the common lawyers on this question. I have here referred to only a very few, as sufficient for my purpose. The idea however, propounded by Wilmot J.[7] that a deliberate intention to contract was sufficient to create a binding obligation was never seriously entertained. It was too far removed from the traditional ideas of the common law; it was still sought to find something outside the promise which was to give it efficacy; it was still called consideration, though with an epithet, e.g. "moral" consideration. Lord Denman found no difficulty in disposing of that halfway conclusion by pointing out that consideration in its technical meaning was incon-

---

[1] *Ibid.* at 252. [2] (1813) 5 Taunt. 36 (C.P.).
[3] 1 *Leading Cases* (1st ed. 1837), 70 *et seq.*
[4] *Ibid.* at 70.
[5] (1765) 3 Burr. 1663 (K.B.).
[6] (1840) 11 Ad. & E. 438 (Q.B.).
[7] See *Pillans* v. *Van Mierop*, 3 Burr. at 1670.

sistent with the idea of "moral" consideration; he dismissed with contempt and in a sentence the idea that a legal obligation could be based on the moral obligation to perform a promise which the mere promise by itself, if seriously made, involves.[1] Thus the modern law in this matter was established. I wonder how things would have gone if the common lawyers had extended their outlook beyond the English cases to a system of law such as the Roman Dutch law or had broken loose from their close adherence to tradition and precedent, or had ever considered scientific theories of contract.

Space does not permit me to refer to more than one other case, *Tweddle* v. *Atkinson*,[2] decided in 1861. That case turned perhaps rather on privity of contract than on consideration. A son sued on a promise in writing made to his father by the defendant to give a marriage portion: the document contained mutual promises between the plaintiff's father and the defendant, who was the father of the plaintiff's wife, and expressly provided that the plaintiff should be entitled to sue on the agreement. The claim was dismissed. Wightman J. said "no stranger to the contract can take advantage of a contract, although made for his benefit".[3] Crompton J. said that the law was so settled that natural love and affection is not sufficient consideration for a promise, and that a promisee cannot bring an action unless the consideration moved from him.[4] Thus, any such doctrine as that of *ius quaesitum tertio* or of the right of third party beneficiaries was finally condemned so far as the common law of England was concerned.

---

[1] See *Eastwood* v. *Kenyon*, 11 Ad. & E. at 450.
[2] (1861) 1 B. & S. 393 (Q.B.).   [3] *Ibid.* at 398.   [4] See *ibid.*

Ought Consideration to be Abolished?

The few cases which I have cited have been selected simply to illustrate the struggles which were necessary before the rigid idea of consideration which had been invented by the hard horse-sense of the common law could survive and some of the anomalous exceptions to which it had to submit. I shall now refer to some further exceptions which have been established and to some of the practical difficulties which the doctrine presents.

In the case of bills of exchange, the consideration which is sufficient by English law for a bill is any antecedent debt or liability, whether the bill is payable on demand or at some future time. This is enacted by the Bills of Exchange Act, 1882, Section 27,[1] embodying the decisions at common law in *Currie* v. *Misa*[2] and other cases.

Compositions with creditors are unfortunately ordinary incidents of business life; but some difficulty was at first felt in reconciling these compositions with the rule of consideration because the creditors agreed to accept a dividend instead of payment in full. Thus, in *Fitch* v. *Sutton*,[3] the composition was held inoperative and *nudum pactum*. The difficulty was overcome by importing, as something collateral beyond the part payment, the agreement by the other creditors to be satisfied with the composition. In *Couldery* v. *Bartrum*,[4] Jessel M.R. gives play to an ironical mood. He says that "according to English common law a creditor might accept anything in satisfaction of his debt except a less amount of money. He might take a horse, or canary, or a tomtit

---
[1] 45 & 46 Vict. c. 61.
[2] (1875) L.R. 10 Ex. 153, affirmed 1 App. Cas. 554 (1876).
[3] 5 East 230 (K.B. 1804).
[4] (1881) 19 Ch.D. 394, 399.

if he chose...but, by a most extraordinary peculiarity of the English Common Law, he could not take 19*s.* 6*d.* in the pound; that was *nudum pactum*....That was one of the mysteries of English Common Law." Sir George Jessel then points out the obvious advantages to the creditors of accepting a lesser sum by way of composition; but it was necessary to bind the creditors, and because "every debtor had not a stock of canary-birds or tomtits, or rubbish of that kind, to add to his dividend, it was felt desirable to bind the creditors in a sensible way by saying that, if they all agreed, there should be a consideration imported from the agreement constituting an addition to the dividend, so as to make the agreement no longer *nudum pactum*".[1] It is obvious that but for the doctrine of consideration this artificial conception would not have been invented. It involves difficulties. The creditor promises the debtor to accept the dividend in satisfaction of his debt. What is in fact the act or forbearance on the part of the promisee, the debtor? It seems that the willingness of the other creditors to accept less than their debt is rather a matter of agreement between themselves and forms a consideration for the creditors *inter se* to be satisfied. But some method had to be adopted to save the validity of compositions. A modern case where difficulty was found in upholding an agreement because of the absence of consideration is *West Yorkshire Darracq Agency, Ltd.* v. *Coleridge,*[2] where directors had agreed *inter se* to forego their fees: the liquidator was a party to that agreement but had given no consideration, and yet he was held entitled to refuse to pay a director, who had gone back on his promise.

[1] 19 Ch.D. at 400.   [2] [1911] 2 K.B. 326.

Ought Consideration to be Abolished?

Another form of commercial contract which it is difficult to fit in with the doctrine of consideration is the bankers' confirmed credit. The promise is by the banker to the seller, but the real consideration comes from the buyer, who arranges the contract, and pays the commission. I cannot here discuss in detail the difficulties which are fully dealt with by Professor Gutteridge in his book on *Commercial Credits*.[1] Up to the present in England the technical difficulties have not been pressed home in any case, but that they exist is clear, and afford a further illustration of the complications which are created in this species of commercial contract by the doctrine of consideration. As Dean Roscoe Pound observes in his *Introduction to Philosophy of Law*, "the doctrine of consideration with its uncertain lines stood in the way of many things which the exigencies of business called for and business men found themselves doing in reliance on each other's business honour and the banker's jealousy of his business credit, with or without assistance from the law".[2]

Another problem often discussed and still unsolved is whether a promise to perform a duty independently existing under another contract is consideration for a new promise. I may refer to *Shadwell* v. *Shadwell*[3] and *Scotson* v. *Pegg*.[4] It is to be assumed that what is promised under the new agreement is the same as the obligation under the previous agreement. The problem arises most acutely when the two parties are the same. If the new promise is made to a person other than the original

---

[1] *Law of Bankers' Commercial Credits* (1932). See also Davis, "The Relationship between Banker and Seller under a Confirmed Credit" (1936), 52 *L.Q. Rev.* 225.   [2] (1922), 277–278.
[3] (1860) 9 C.B.N.S. 159.   [4] (1861) 6 H. & N. 295 (Ex.).

promisee, the technical difficulty of finding consideration is that the new promise is merely to do what the party is already bound to do; however, it may well be that if the same obligation is assumed to a new party, a new detriment is incurred; there are now two parties entitled to enforce performance, instead of merely one. If the new promise is to the same party and there is no change in the contents of the obligation, such as in regard to time or place or mode of performance, it is difficult to find any consideration. At the same time it seems that there must have been some practical reason for taking and giving the new promise.

Another anomalous case is that in which there is what is called waiver of a condition, where the condition, if not waived, would have excused performance. In such a case there is in truth a promise to perform a duty or contract, which owing to the actual or intended non-performance of the condition is or is about to be no longer obligatory. In the American Restatement of the Law of Contracts,[1] the case is classified as an informal contract without consideration, as in truth it is.

Another case which has given difficulty is one in which a promise has been made without consideration, but is of such a nature that it reasonably induces action on the faith of the promise or in reliance upon it. In the American Restatement, that case is dealt with in Section 90, which provides that the promise is binding if injustice can be avoided only by enforcement of the promise: instances are given, such as, "A promises B not to foreclose for a specified time, a mortgage which A holds on B's land. B thereafter makes improvements on the land.

[1] (1932), § 88.

Ought Consideration to be Abolished?

A's promise is binding."[1] It is here to be understood that there was no consideration for A's promise and that it was not by deed, and that B made the improvement on his own initiative, without there being any obligation on him to do so. I do not think that by English law such a promise would be held binding. However natural B's action may have been and however much expected by A, the promise not to foreclose is not binding, and the subsequent voluntary action of B would not be held in England to change its character. The result is no doubt unjust, that is, if it is also understood that the promise was made by A with deliberate intent, though it was gratuitous.

I may mention another illustration of the way in which the rule of consideration renders promises unenforceable though the parties intended them to be binding. I refer to promises to subscribe to charities. These are generally in writing and are often made for periodical payments. There are generally no counter-promises by the institution, such, for instance, as to lay out in particular ways money so subscribed. The subscription is not in general earmarked or agreed to be devoted to any particular object, but would normally go into the general revenues of the charity. I do not see how such a case can be brought logically even into the category of the promissory estoppel or can come under the reliance theory. Under these circumstances the promise must, it seems, necessarily be held for want of consideration. But the ordinary sense of mankind revolts against such a result.

One other matter I must advert to. It has been felt in England that the results of *Tweddle* v. *Atkinson*,[2] under

---

[1] Section 90, illustration 1.   [2] (1861) 1 B. & S. 393 (Q.B.).

which it was held that a man cannot sue on a contract unless he is a party both to the contract and the consideration, are unfortunate and unjust in many cases: it has been sought in England to minimize such results by applying the doctrines of equity. In that way the benefit of the contract is conceived as a chose in action of which the actual party to the contract is treated as trustee for the beneficiary who is deemed to be the *cestui que trust*, so that suit can be brought in the name of the trustee for the benefit of the *cestui que trust*.[1] This is a cumbrous proceeding, not always applicable, but necessary to overcome the twofold difficulty, want of privity of contract and want of consideration; either would be fatal to an action at law if brought in the name of the beneficiary. In certain insurance matters legislation has been introduced to meet the difficulty. In the United States this difficulty has been overcome by the conception of the third party beneficiary; the rules under this head are summarized in the Restatement, Sections 133 to 147, the details of which I cannot here further discuss. In Scotland, the same problem is solved by the *ius quaesitum tertio*, as to which I may cite, for instance, *Carmichael* v. *Carmichael's Executrix*.[2]

I should like further to multiply instances of the working of the doctrine of consideration, but may not do so here, nor shall I seek to repeat the various absurdities, inconsistencies, and anomalies which have emerged out of the doctrine. I have heard it defended on the ground that any person of ingenuity can devise a consideration for any transaction. Certainly the books are full of

[1] See *Vandepitte* v. *Preferred Accident Ins. Corp.* [1933] A.C. 70, 79.
[2] (1920) S.C. (H.L.) 195.

Ought Consideration to be Abolished?

strange and artificial notions which have passed muster as valuable consideration. But I have given sufficient instances where no ingenuity could avail, though the contract was one the enforcement of which was called for by justice and practical expediency.

When I review in my mind the scattered threads of argument and illustration which I have set out in this article, I cannot resist the conclusion that the doctrine is a mere encumbrance. A scientific or logical theory of contract would in my opinion take as the test of contractual intention the answer to the overriding question whether there was a deliberate and serious intention, free from illegality, immorality, mistake, fraud or duress, to make a binding contract. That must be in each case a question of fact. As I pointed out above, the doctrine of consideration does not exclude this overriding question.

But if that is the question, consideration in the technical sense, that is, something valuable in the eyes of the law, is not immaterial; its presence is strong, and indeed generally conclusive evidence that the promise is not mere ostentation but that it emanates from a serious mind. So regarded, it is not a condition of the contract, but is merely a piece of evidence. Another class of evidence may be what in England has been sometimes or in some cases called moral consideration, but in some foreign jurisdictions has been called *causa* or *cause*, that is, such matters as natural love and affection, gratitude for past favours, a sense of obligation for services rendered in the past, charity, benevolence and so forth; all such circumstances, grounds, motives or objects, in appropriate measure and degree, would serve as evidence that the promise was seriously made; other evidence might consist of writing, whether simply or by specialty. But neither consideration nor *causa* nor writing is to be regarded as the substance of the promise: all such matters are extrinsic and evidentiary, matters which go to establish and corroborate the contractual intention. The substance is the promise itself, as so well explained by de Villiers A.J.A. in *Conradie's Case*.[1]

In my opinion this is the true theory of the contract, free from theoretical or practical difficulties, and capable of application to all the complicated possibilities of the world of fact.

It is true that in the great number of contracts there is the element of bargain. In some, recompense is inherent in the nature of the contract itself, e.g. in loan, sale of goods, barter, and many others. But again, there are many other contracts in which, as I have sought to explain and illustrate, technical consideration is absent, and yet they are such that justice calls for their enforcement. I think the theory of consideration ought to find no place in our system of contract law. I do not stand alone in that opinion. I may, for instance, again refer to an essay by Professor Lorenzen to which I have already referred.[2] Dean Roscoe Pound also supports this opinion,[3] and others have expressed the same view. I have referred to Lord Dunedin's opinion,[4] and to that of the judges of the South African Appellate Court.[5] Sir William Holds-

[1] S. African L.R. [1919] App. Div. 279.

[2] See note 2, p. 304.

[3] *Interpretations of Legal History* (1923), 66; *Introduction to the Philosophy of Law* (1922), 271 *et seq.*

[4] *Dunlop Pneumatic Tyre Co., Ltd.* v. *Selfridge & Co., Ltd.* [1915] A.C. 847, 855; see pp. 296–297, *supra.*

[5] *Conradie* v. *Rossouw*, S. African L.R. [1919] App. Div. 279; see pp. 298–301, *supra.*

Ought Consideration to be Abolished?

worth says that in its present form the doctrine of consideration is somewhat of an anachronism.[1] He proposes as a practical reform that a contract should be enforced by law if either it is in writing or there is consideration. In that way a gratuitous promise would be enforced if there is written evidence. Either circumstance would be evidence of the serious intention: that is what Lord Mansfield sought to establish as the law in *Pillans* v. *Van Mierop*, though he limited his proposal to commercial transactions. And I think Sir William is prepared to accept as the true test the intention of the parties to enter into a lawful agreement affecting their legal relations.

I fear, however, that there is little prospect in the near future of the English law being completely changed in so vital a respect, though the practical reform suggested by Sir William may, perhaps, before very long be achieved. But there is a dead weight of legal conservatism to be overcome.[2]

I often wonder what practical purpose is served by the doctrine of consideration in its present form. There is no public policy that I can see against enforcing gratuitous obligations. The most vital element of public policy in this regard is that people should keep their plighted word. In some cases, certainly, the judge or jury must be more particular about proof before a gratuitous obligation is enforced. We have, however, seen that the old rule of consideration does not dispense with proof of contractual intention, though it is generally strong

---

[1] *History of English Law* (1925), VIII, 47.
[2] See the recommendations of the Lord Chancellor's Law Revision Committee, Sixth Interim Report (1937), Cmd. 5449.

evidence of that. But judges and juries can be trusted, I hope, to deal wisely where gratuitous promises are alleged. They have often to handle much more difficult questions of intention or mental state, e.g. in cases of fraud or mistake. In adjudicating on a contract, they start with the objective basis of what the parties said or did, their words, written or spoken, and their conduct: they have all the surrounding circumstances and relationships. There is no reason why they should be less successful in deciding whether there is contractual intention than courts which know not consideration in our sense. The abolition of consideration would not affect the law relating to mistake, illegality, immorality, impossibility or failure of condition. In conclusion, I see no practical objections to the abolition of the doctrine, to counterbalance the reasoning on which I have advocated that it should be abolished.

XII

THE COMMON LAW IN ITS OLD HOME[1]

I FEEL some temerity in addressing so learned an audience, as I am a mere working lawyer, who has spent thirty-six years in the active work of bar and bench, who went into law chambers without a proper academic learning in law, and who has had no leisure for the purpose of making up these deficiencies.

I want at once to say how high I rate the value of the academic lawyer. We have all at heart the improvement of the law, which in one aspect is a living organism of immense complexity, touching life at every point, but which can live and work only as the embodiment of logical principles of justice. Logic and life are for ever interacting in the law. The logic of the law is a practical logic, not concerned with the absolute, but with concrete reality; the reality however must be regulated by rule. Law has to be considered as it was, as it is, as it will be. Counsel and the judge are concerned principally with law as it is, as the tool with which the work of the law has to be done. The study of the law as it was is necessary to understand the law as it is, and the working lawyer must collect the fruits of that study from the academic lawyer. The daily work of the law as it is, is engaged on particular concrete cases, but their solution depends on

[1] A paper delivered at the Harvard Tercentenary Conference of Arts and Sciences, 1936.

the application of principles, for the analysis and comparison of which the work of the academic lawyer is essential. Perhaps even more so is that true of the improvement of the law. The judge, exercising his historic function, is constantly enlarging the area of the law by applying old principles to new cases and by limiting and redefining existing principles in the light of new circumstances, and very occasionally he will be able to establish a new principle.

I do not intend to attempt any complete definition of the term "common law" or to exhaust the various aspects from which it may be contemplated. I shall identify it for the moment by its main characteristic, that from the basis of early customary or other laws it has gradually developed by a series of judicial decisions given in particular concrete cases as precedents which are to be followed and developed in turn as principles are created. This is the living process to be contrasted with the formal analysis or classifications. The contrast may be figured on the analogue of physiology and anatomy in the living body. The method of case law distinguishes the common law from other types of law in which a complete system is embodied in a code or in institutional writers, so that the judges do not create the law but merely apply it. The common law following this method proceeds from the particular to the general. These characteristics of the common law equally are to be observed in equity in its modern form, and in the admiralty and ecclesiastical jurisdictions. Thus it is arbitrary to restrict the term "common law" to the law enforced in the old common-law courts. As I shall explain later, I think that now the general principles of common law and equity should be

The Common Law in its Old Home

treated as forming a single body of law. The academic lawyer, watching and criticizing and synthesizing this constant process, will be able on his wide survey to descry the more distant horizon to an extent not possible to a lawyer immersed in the particular. In this audience I could, if it were not a work of supererogation, dilate on what services the academic lawyer has rendered to the law which both our countries enjoy. Kent, Story, and Holmes are our common heritage, though all these three great lawyers were not merely academic but also practical lawyers; then in recent times there have been, or are, men like Langdell, Thayer, Ames, Williston, Beale, and a host of others, of whom I shall here mention only Dean Roscoe Pound, who has organized this Conference. The services of these men and many others are of supreme importance to the law. I shall not by name enumerate the many great lawyers on our side of the Atlantic, but you will readily supply the names. I should only like to mention *honoris causa* our nonagenarian, Sir Frederick Pollock.

I cannot consider the future of the common law without some very general survey of the law as it is, of the law as it has become. First a word as to the existing system of courts in England. As compared with a country like France, the most striking peculiarity is the smallness in number of the judges and their close association with each other. All are congregated in London. There are six[1] in the Court of Appeal, six[2] in the Chancery Division, twenty, including the Lord Chief Justice, in the King's Bench Division, and three in the Probate, Divorce, and Admiralty Division. The ultimate court of appeal is the House of Lords, the judicial members of which consist of

[1] Now increased to nine.   [2] At present five.

the Lords of Appeal in Ordinary and the other Law Lords, including the Lord Chancellor; that is, peers who have held or hold high judicial office. For this address, I may disregard the Probate, Divorce, and Admiralty Division, which deals with special jurisdiction: I may observe that Admiralty in this connection does not include what is generally called commercial law, because the common-law courts took to themselves the law merchant three centuries or so ago, and made it part of the common law.

The judicial body is thus in England small and compact: the assize system solved in a simple way from the earliest days the reconciliation of decentralization and centralization. The assize courts all over the country were manned by the itinerant justices, that is by the judges whose ordinary work was in London, and who left the London courts only to go on circuit. This is the normal system and it still gives satisfaction.

The division between King's Bench and Chancery reflects the duality of English law, the streams of law and equity which were, at least as jurisdictions, fused by the Judicature Act, 1873. That Act provided that the separate divisions of the High Court were created for convenience only and that, though certain causes were assigned to particular divisions, that was done for convenience only and did not mean that any division might not try any cause, or that each was not bound to apply the rules both of law and of equity as the case might require. The working common lawyer is habitually using as part of his tools conceptions and remedies provided by equity. The remedy of injunction or specific performance or declaration is a matter of course; all he need be conscious of is that these remedies are discretionary. Rectification is as familiar to him as to the Chancery practitioner; he can give effect to the difference between penalty and liquidated damages; he is constantly using the concept of the trust, remembering what difference it may make (e.g. in insolvency whether the case is one of trust or of debt); he is familiar in practice with equitable remedies for mistake or innocent misrepresentation. It is impossible to conceive what we now regard as the modern common law without these and many other like concepts which, though imported originally from equity, are as much a part of his daily work as the ideas of negligence, or conversion, or damages, and indeed are essential to the functioning of the common law: without them the common law could not have survived.

Nowadays the demarcation between the Chancery and the King's Bench lawyer is the result of specialization; the Chancery Division has annexed for a variety of reasons many special branches of law, such as patents, trademarks, administration of trusts and settlements, wills, and others which I need not enumerate. This specialization reflects itself in specialization at the bar and in a less degree on the bench, but I cannot see any reason why the general principles of law and equity should not be conceived as forming a single body of principles, available in any court, in any action; they are so in practice, and in time the division based on historical origins will, I think, be forgotten. The King's Bench deals in the main with common-law cases though it applies both equitable and legal principles. It has retained the monopoly of the criminal law, after a brief period during which the Chancery judges took their share in its administration, and the ordinary common-law actions, many of which, however (e.g. passing off, nuisance, rights of way), are now frequently brought in the Chancery Division.

The use of the jury in the King's Bench courts and the greater frequency of witness actions seem to have made characteristic differences in the mental attitude of the respective practitioners. The value of the jury is still highly appreciated in England, and that not merely in criminal cases, in which it seems to me to be indispensable. During the seven years I was a King's Bench judge I constantly sat with juries, though at other times I often tried issues of fact without a jury. I formed the highest opinion of the value of the jury in its proper function, that is for the trial of issues of fact, depending for their decision on broad common sense. Incidentally the jury makes it necessary for the judge to state the law in simple terms because the judge has to direct the jury on the law and has to state it in terms which they can understand. As to the facts, he is entitled and indeed in ordinary practice required to analyse and to summarize the evidence to the jury in order to help them in arriving at their decision. This, I think, differs from the practice in some of your States. The grand jury, which had survived for so many centuries and become practically no more than a jury for presenting offenders at assizes, was abolished, I think wisely, a short time ago. Its function had become little more than a formality, because in fact prisoners are almost invariably brought up on committal by magistrates.

I ought to add that for smaller civil causes there are about sixty county courts with limited jurisdiction, located at different places throughout the country.

The Common Law in its Old Home

I may mention one respect in which an English judge differs in his functions from a United States judge, viz. that he has not to pass on the constitutionality of legislative measures. The supremacy of law in England means that whatever Parliament enacts cannot be questioned. Problems of *ultra vires* in legislative matters can arise only in respect of regulations or orders made under statutory powers, or, on a lower plane, by-laws made by local or statutory authorities. There is, however, one court sitting in England which has to deal with questions of constitutional competence; that is the Judicial Committee of the Privy Council, which has to decide questions of that nature arising under the federal constitutions of Canada and Australia and also in relation to the laws of colonial legislatures of limited jurisdiction.

When I turn to consider the future I must assume that the present lines of development are in substance continued. It might happen that by a complete change in the governmental system, e.g. by the establishment of a Communistic government of the Soviet type, the whole of the common law was abolished, and a system of popular courts established to enforce a new system of law adapted to the Communist conscience, possibly embodied in a code, administered by judges ignorant of or hostile to common law. In such a case there would be no future of the common law, because there would be no common law.

Short of that, the whole system of law might be codified, and the administration of the code left to the judges, who on that hypothesis would be deprived of, or forbidden to use, any system of precedent to guide them. In such a case also the common law as we know it would have no future unless the code were based on the common law and interpreted by judges brought up in, and inspired by, the traditions of the common law, and continuing to apply the principles of the interpretation of statutes which now form an integral part of the common-law system. I shall revert to codification a little later.

Let us put aside these possibilities and assume that the common law goes on developing on the lines now followed. It must at once be observed how much of the law now actually enforced by the courts is statutory and not common law in its strict sense of judge-made law, to adopt a distinction often drawn between common law and statute law. Thus, most of the special branches of commercial law have now been codified; in particular, those relating to the sale of goods, bills of exchange, marine insurance, partnership, bills of lading. These statutes, however, purport to embody and do in fact embody the commercial law as it had developed according to common-law methods, and notwithstanding the codes this development still goes on. Concrete cases which arise from time to time, if they do not fall within the statutory provisions, are dealt with on common-law principles. The codes provide that the common law is to apply subject only to the express provisions of the codes. In this way the interstices of the codes are filled up much as if there were no codes and the judges were merely filling up gaps in the authorities in the old way. Thus the codes merely give rules which act as starting-points and replace the rules which would otherwise have had to be deduced from the cases. The old cases are still cited to give life to the sections of the codes. The practising English lawyer scarcely thinks of these statutes as other than a part of the common law.

Formerly a large part of the common law consisted of the land law, with its elaborate rules, which had been developed by the common-law courts. These rules fill the larger part of Blackstone; until less than one hundred years ago the Chancery courts sent a question of real property for decision to the common-law courts. But later that practice was discontinued and by the time of the Judicature Act, 1873, the Chancery court for various reasons, particularly because of the predominance of equitable principles in regard to settlements of realty, mortgages, executory interests, and so forth, came to monopolize in practice that part of the law; later it became embodied in various statutes, and now, finally, by the Acts of 1925 (Law of Property Act, Settled Land Act, Trustee Act), it has been for all practical purposes removed from the common-law courts. It affords an illustration of that specialization to which I have already adverted.

Then one great sphere of modern law, the law of companies, has in effect been removed by a process of specialization from the common-law courts. The common law had its own law of corporations, which remains in force as regards corporations other than those formed under the Companies Acts or special acts. The Companies Acts and other acts regulate the very complex and multiform details of modern joint stock and other statutory companies, by which the major part of modern business is carried on. A highly specialized body of law has accumulated round these acts and their interpretation according to common-law principles. This is mostly administered in the Chancery Division. One great principle, the doctrine of *ultra vires*, has been evolved by the judges on true common-law principles. The common law has not adopted the fiction theory of corporations. One consequence of this is that it has held companies liable for the torts, even if malicious, of their agents.

Outside the range of the common law in the ordinary sense lies the vast mass of administrative, public utility, and social legislation, which constantly occupies the time of the courts. This has developed in the last one hundred years and shows no sign of decreasing. The development of railways involved the compulsory purchases of land and other special privileges which were the subject of complicated statutory provisions; so also did the development of gas and water companies; all these statutory bodies, as they were endowed with special privileges, so also were subject to elaborate regimentation in the public interest. Then came the era of social legislation, such as the developments of the modern Poor Law (now called Public Assistance), Workmen's Compensation, Old Age Pensions, Unemployment, and Health Insurance acts. These measures have either supplanted the common law or filled up areas outside the range of the common law. Still more recently marketing schemes, road traffic acts, town and country planning acts, acts embodying schemes for combination or nationalization of commercial and industrial undertakings, occupy a large area which is subjected to statutory regulation.

It may be asked what is left of the common law in the old sense. I answer that the common law, even in these spheres, exercises a dominant influence in virtue of its principles of construction and precedent. The judges have to interpret the statutes on common-law principles, and thus the common law plays a great part in the actual effect of the statutes. It has been said that Parliament passes the statutes but the judges make them, as so much of the meaning and operation need to be supplied by the judges. But apart from this general matter, there still remain the fundamental principles of the common law, such as those of personal freedom, of freedom of speech, of the supremacy of the rule of law, of the right to trial by jury, of the independence of the judges, of the exclusion of arbitrary power. These principles are the lifeblood of the common law and justify the description of the common law as the law of free peoples. No people that has enjoyed the common law has ever voluntarily abandoned it. It was adopted and it remains because it is essential to the free spirit and genius of the people. The common law also rules in the law of contract, tort, and quasi-contract. Criminal law has indeed now been largely embodied in statutes, but some of the most serious offences such as murder and manslaughter are still left to the common law. The definition of insanity in criminal law is still as stated by the judges in *M'Naghten's Case*:[1] whether the theory there adopted that insanity involves a defect in reason will be supplanted by the theory that insanity also covers irresistible impulse due to disease of the mind, I hesitate to prophesy. The former theory is clearly unscientific, but there is a prejudice, not without practical reasons, against leaving it to a jury to find irresistible impulse. For myself, I should welcome the departure from *M'Naghten's Case*, which I think

[1] (1843) 10 Cl. & Fin. 200 (H.L.).

would be a reform. Other fundamental ideas of the common law which are in truth aspects of the principle of personal freedom, such as that the prisoner is innocent until he is proved to be guilty and that the onus remains throughout on the prosecution, have been recently reaffirmed by the House of Lords[1] and are too deeply ingrained in English ideas ever to be changed. The Court of Criminal Appeal was established by statute and has worked well: appeals are decided in a few weeks after trial, bail being almost invariably refused. A statute was needed to enable a prisoner to elect to give evidence in his own defence. The obsolete distinction between felony and misdemeanour should be swept away.

The rules of evidence are almost entirely the creation of the judges and are part of the common law, but now they might be codified. They are not likely to be changed substantially in criminal trials. In civil actions, however, they should be and probably will be modified; thus, for instance, contemporaneous documents and written statements will be accepted as *prima facie* evidence to a greater extent than at present,[2] and facts of a formal character may be proved by affidavit or otherwise without calling the witnesses.

I shall turn to two questions of a general character, viz.: (1) Is it desirable to have a complete codification of the law? and (2) Is it desirable to abandon the rule of *stare decisis*, which is so fundamental in English law, whether common law in its strict sense, or equity, or the interpretation of statutes? If I may deal first with codification, the great bulk of the *corpus iuris* enforced in

---

[1] *Woolmington* v. *Director of Public Prosecutions* [1935] A.C. 462.
[2] See now the Evidence Act, 1938 (1 & 2 Geo. 6, c. 28).

The Common Law in its Old Home

England is, as I have explained, statutory. The principal subjects that would remain for codification would be contract, tort, quasi-contract, some general common-law maxims or principles, rules of interpretation, rules of evidence, the rules of equity, and the important body of law often described as conflict of laws. Rules of procedure were in effect codified by the Judicature Act, 1873; under a very flexible system they have been and can now be altered from time to time by a statutory Rules Committee who meet frequently and make new or amended rules as they think expedient; these new or amended rules become law if not objected to after being laid on the table of both houses of Parliament for a given period. This system has worked well. A defect, however, is the unwieldy accumulation of decided cases which have collected round the rules. I think the time has come when the rules need rewriting on simpler lines and in simpler terms. It might also be better if practice cases were not reported in the regular reports. Practitioners would still have the rules and presumably some unofficial notes of how in practice they have been applied.

I question if it is now generally believed that codification reduces the decision of a case to a simple process in which, the facts being found, the judge turns up a section of the code, which he then applies like a mathematical formula. It is now generally realized, I imagine, that there are, even with a code, two difficulties to overcome; first to choose the right section, and then to decide what are its meaning and effect in relation to the facts of the case. It may be that the section merely states a general principle in wide terms, so that a judge has to define it and fill in the gaps; or it may be that there is no section which fits the case. The work of the judge under such a code is not unlike that of the judge under the common-law system, except that in the latter case the judge has to find his rule from the cases, digests, and statutes, whereas the judge using the code finds or is assumed to find the rule ready to his hand. But the apparent advantage in the latter case may obviously be delusive. I do not think a codification of what is left uncodified in the common law and equity would be of much service in England. I should prefer to see the law of contract, tort, quasi-contract, equity, etc., develop on its own lines as before. When I think of the enormous development of the common law in the last one hundred years I am glad to think it was not then codified; still more so, if I go back to Blackstone's day or Coke's day. To take a very few instances from the law of tort, we have had in the last century *Priestley* v. *Fowler*,[1] *Davies* v. *Mann*,[2] *Rylands* v. *Fletcher*,[3] *Indermaur* v. *Dames*,[4] *Heaven* v. *Pender*,[5] *Donoghue* v. *Stevenson*,[6] to quote only a few of the cases which have made new law. A code would either have sterilized progress in respect of these subjects or would have been so general in terms as to have left the development to go on with no help but rather embarrassment from the code. It is true that the acts codifying the commercial law have on the whole worked well, but these subjects had already been substantially developed and were well adapted to codification. The same is true of the criminal law, where precise and simple definition

[1] (1837) 3 M. & W. 1 (Ex.).   [2] (1842) 10 M. & W. 546 (Ex.).
[3] (1868) L.R. 3 H.L. 330.
[4] (1866) L.R. 1 C.P. 274; (1867) 2 C.P. 311.
[5] (1883) 11 Q.B.D. 503.   [6] [1932] A.C. 562.

The Common Law in its Old Home

is desirable. The codification of criminal law in an amending and consolidating act has been a matter discussed for many years, and I hope before long it will be achieved. In truth, codification is not a universal specific for all legal ills. Sometimes it is very beneficial, sometimes not. It all depends.

I now turn to the rule of *stare decisis*. I cannot see how English law could have dispensed with that rule because it had no codes and no authoritative institutional writers. Apart from such statutes as there were, it could only find settled principles in the decisions of the judges, who proceeded in characteristic style to evolve the law by experience and experiment, profiting at each stage by the work of their predecessors. It is said that the theory of *stare decisis* was not definitely enunciated until the nineteenth century, but it was substantially observed in practice from early days. The idea is so deeply impressed in the mind of an English judge that he finds it hard to approach any problem except by first turning to the authorities, though in the end he may find that justice requires some modification of the rules apparently settled by the cases, and then he has to find if the authorities leave him the latitude which he desires. A good judge is one who is the master, not the slave, of the cases. There are, no doubt, definite limits in any given case beyond which the judge is not free to decide at his own will. These limits vary according as a judge is sitting as a judge of first instance or in a court of appeal or in a final court. I have observed in myself an instinctive change of mental attitude according to the status of the court in which I happened to be sitting. But it is just by the proper use of elasticity in the authorities that the law is advanced. If that were not so, the law could never have changed. How otherwise explain the difference between the law of tort, or of trusts, or of the sale of goods as it was a hundred years ago and as it is now? In these matters statutory changes have on the whole been of minor importance, yet the law might almost be regarded as a new and different law, were it not that we can trace the development from point to point, as the judges found the requirements of justice compelled them to modify or vary or innovate on the law, creating new or partially new principles, but keeping, actually or ostensibly, within or close to the decided cases. This, apart from the decision of matters of fact, is the great work of the English judges. There was reposed on them the great responsibility of making the law, which on the whole they have worthily fulfilled. I may digress to observe that academic writers sometimes seem not to recognize the importance of this modifying or innovating process; this may be because they are mainly concerned with extracting from the existing cases positive rules, and do not feel, as the judge does, the pressure of his prime duty to do right according to law in the particular case.

But the principle of *stare decisis* is applied in England to the construction of statutes, just as much as to the ascertainment of the common law and equity rules. I question if the codification of the particular branches of commercial law, excellent as it is, has reduced the subsequent volume of reported cases. Furthermore, statutes like the Revenue Acts, Workmen's Compensation Acts, Rating Acts, Companies Acts, and a host of others have collected round them a great mass of case law in which the mere words of the statute seem to be submerged. These cases are cited as authorities for the purpose of the statute, so deeply rooted is the principle of *stare decisis* in the English law. I suppose that if it were forbidden to rely on decided cases, decisions would still be recorded and be referred to by counsel and looked at by judges: I believe this happens in practice in countries which have no ostensible system of *stare decisis*. Hence when objection is made that the common-law system leads to uncertainty in the law, to a want of that predictable quality which is necessary to enable people to shape their conduct, I am led to think that this is no more and no less true of the common law than of other systems. The objection exaggerates the area of uncertainty and underrates the area of certainty in the law. In fact, the uncertain or difficult rules form but a small fraction compared with those which are practically certain. There are comparatively few cases in which the relevant rules of law are uncertain. What is more often uncertain is what is the right rule to apply. These cases where uncertainty is experienced naturally attract attention, but the vast majority of ordinary dealings in life pass smoothly because the law is known. In fact we are almost unconscious that we are habitually directing our daily doings in accordance with law. Still, the principle of *stare decisis* may undoubtedly perpetuate a bad rule, which can be removed only by legislation. Where the rule is not obviously against a widespread social interest, like the rule in *Shelley's Case*, it may survive for centuries before Parliament abolishes it. Or if it affects conflicting social or industrial interests like the doctrine of common employment, it may indeed survive, but only by reason of some ameliorative measure, such as was the Workmen's Compensation Act. When it is realized how the rule of *stare decisis* may stereotype bad rules, the difficulty of reconciling stability with change, definiteness with reform, must be recognized. Yet most of the common-law rules admit of elasticity, e.g. the law of negligence. Many new points have been decided and new horizons opened without the aid of the legislation, merely by the judges, even in my experience. From time to time I am being faced with a problem for which there is no precise authority, or which the authorities do not exactly fit, so that some restatement or extension of principle is called for. I repeat that law must be regarded as a living organism: its rules are subsidiary to justice and must, so far as precedent and logic permit, be moulded so as to conform with justice. The judge can do much; when he can do no more, recourse must be had to Parliament, though that is not always easy and is almost always slow.

I am not impressed by the complaint that the mass of reported cases has become unmanageable. I speak only of England. I have referred to our compact and small judicature. Thus in England there does not exist that embarrassing multiplicity and wealth of reported cases which are so observable in the United States where it would seem that the growth of authorities has become unmanageable. The official law reports run in general to six volumes a year. At this rate, in fifty years they will increase only by three hundred volumes. Since the Judicature Act, there have been about four hundred volumes. Up to that date, the reprint of all the English Reports (Law and Equity, etc.) is contained in about five hundred volumes. With the help of indexes and

The Common Law in its Old Home

digests, the total is not an impossible bulk to handle. But in fact it is seldom necessary to go beyond the Law Reports. Reported cases, with comparatively few exceptions, become obsolete in fifty years. A later case in the Appeal Court or House of Lords will supersede a dozen earlier cases.

The defect that the law is in many volumes is counterbalanced by the great value of having reports of decided cases to study whenever a principle comes into question. A principle is illustrated and made real by observing how it has worked in experience. I find it difficult to think that in substance the system of *stare decisis* will be abandoned in England. Perhaps familiarity has made me conservative. But I make two practical suggestions. One is that less use should be made of *obiter dicta*, which cannot possibly have the value of the application of a rule in the decision of a case where the full sense of responsibility must be felt by the judge. Lord Sumner spoke of the "will-o'-the-wisp" of the *obiter dictum*.[1] A case is only a decision for what it actually decides. The other suggestion is that the decisions of a single judge should be more sparingly cited. Citations should generally be limited to judgments of the Court of Appeal and of the House of Lords. Decisions of single judges have at times been landmarks in the law, but for the most part they should be cited as merely of illustrative or persuasive value, as indeed they are cited now in the higher courts.

I proceed to consider in detail the great branches of the common law, viz.: contract and tort, with a third branch, sometimes inaptly called quasi-contract, and

[1] *Sorrell* v. *Smith* [1925] A.C. 700, 743.

ancillary subjects like damages. Included under these heads may come subjects which might call for separate notice, such as the law of landlord and tenant, a very technical subject full of anomalies and well fitted for amendment and consolidation by statute. Some modifications of this part of the law are already contained in the Landlord and Tenant Act, 1927. Another branch of law which has developed on common-law principles is that of conflict of laws, a subject too technical for discussion in detail here, but now fully analysed and expounded in the relevant volume of the *Restatement of the Law* under the distinguished reportership of Professor Beale. I need not here discuss as part of the common law the residual powers of the executive: i.e., what is left by statutory definition, such as the large discretion necessarily vested in the executive, the exercise of which may be called in question on the basis of common-law rules of individual freedom. But though the individual's freedom is still the cardinal doctrine, it has been curtailed by the modern conception that individual freedom must, if the nation by its legislature so decides, yield place to public good or what is considered to be the public good. So that we have now numerous statutes and statutory orders and regulations affecting men not only in private life (police, health, locomotion, and so forth) but in their commercial and industrial relations, such as factory acts, building acts, marketing acts, agricultural holdings acts, landlord and tenant acts, town and county planning acts, and a mass of others. Thus, in practice, for a great part of life, law becomes regarded as that which is to be found in acts of Parliament or in regulations or orders issued under them.

The Common Law in its Old Home

The common law, being individualistic, could not satisfy modern ideas of collectivism and of social planning. But it finds its full scope in parts of the law such as that of contract, tort, quasi-contract, and equity, subjects which from their very nature are and must be individualistic. These form a single body of rules for enforcing performance as between individuals of duties imposed by law, which may be duties arising from promises, that is, from the choice of the parties, or may be duties not arising from the choice of the parties but from the circumstances in which they are placed relatively to each other, as in tort or quasi-contract. These rules are often of most constant and pervading importance in the daily affairs of life. Their common characteristic is that they form the postulate on which conduct in modern society proceeds.

But nowadays the law is not accepted as dogma or without criticism; a spirit of inquiry is abroad, in which the general principles of law are subject to review, partly because of the growth of academic studies of law, but largely because of a sense of social and economic values, based on a more liberal standpoint than that of Bentham and the early Victorian reformers. Common law is seen to contain a good many dogmatic rules and subsidiary rules deduced by formal logic from the dogmas. This was the inevitable result of its history. Common law in its modern form may be said to have originated from Coke; he was enamoured of legal maxims and stated his rules, derived or pretended to be derived from the Year Books but recast in passing through him. He was inspired by a genuine sentiment of individual freedom and of opposition to the prerogative, but he was pedantic and formal. Many of the Stuart judges were subservient, though at no time in English history have independent judges been lacking. After the Act of Settlement there came a new generation of judges, many of them men like Holt of high character and mental power. They applied to the particular problems the hard common sense of men of the world; upright, indeed, but not inspired as a rule with liberal ideas and generally tied to precedent, so that a man like Lord Mansfield found his liberal efforts thwarted. No doubt broader and more humane views have been prevailing for the last eighty years or so, but inevitably the common law tends to find itself, particularly in the law of tort, to be out of accord with the humanitarian and social ideas of to-day. A recognition of this has in the past led to inroads by the Legislature. That process goes on. Similarly, established rules are seen to be not in conformity with scientific principles or with the requirements of justice, or to be unsatisfactory in a practical sense. To a certain extent the common law can and will correct its own determinations; that is, by its traditional method of judicial legislation by means of judgments on concrete cases; but in very many cases a change can, in England, be effected only by legislation, so long as the rule of *stare decisis* continues.

The future of the common law in England will depend on these two processes, working hand in hand, both inspired by a more philanthropic and more rational outlook on human affairs. Premises will be examined to see how far they accord with the requirements of justice, because it is realized that premises are the all-important element: if the premises are not in accordance with what is just, the better the logic, the worse will be the resulting rule. Rules will no longer be taken for granted and extended by a hard and narrow logic. At the same time law will be more realistic; fictions will be abolished; there will be adjudication based on the actual facts of the case not confined within the narrow and rigid limits of the forms of action. In this great work much must depend on the labours of the academic lawyer, who in England was often in the past discouraged by the practising advocate or judge. The scholar has more opportunity of thinking out principles at large and can examine rules of law to see how they accord with humanity or with social or economic or commercial utility. But the scholar must keep in close touch with the lawyers of practical experience and with the facts of life, just as the practical lawyer must seek to benefit by what help in his daily problems he can get from the labours of the scholar. The two must work hand in hand; otherwise the scholar will be in danger of losing himself in fanciful problems, sometimes comparable to those of the Schoolmen, and in barren distinctions, while the judge may lack the wider horizons. It may sometimes happen that the scholar exaggerates formal rules, while the ideal judge seeks to mould the rules, as far as he is free to do so, in harmony with the justice of the particular case.

A consciousness of these truths is developing in England and will inspire the development of the common law of the future. A commencement of one type of reform has been made in England by a system of recasting particular rules which appear to be ill-conceived but which can only be altered by legislation, because they are based on binding authorities. Rules which seem to be of this character are submitted from time to time to a committee called the Law Revision Committee, recently formed in England, partly of judges, partly of practising, partly of academic lawyers, appointed by the Lord Chancellor. The Committee make a report. Their proposals, if generally approved, are embodied in a short bill which passes through Parliament as a non-political measure.

The Committee have already made four[1] reports. I can do no more than refer in the most summary way to them. Each report very briefly traces the history of the rule under review and its defects, with special reference to judicial comments on the defects, and proposes how the rule is to be remedied and altered.

The Committee, of which I have been a member throughout and am now chairman, are at present engaged on the thorny questions of consideration and the contract section of the Statute of Frauds—rules of law often criticized but in regard to which it is very difficult to formulate practical rules for reform. The Committee are also reviewing the Statutes of Limitation so far as they affect the common law. The four reports so far made by the Committee relate to (1) the maxim *actio personalis moritur cum persona*, (2) interest in civil proceedings, (3) contribution between tortfeasors, (4) the liabilities of a married woman and the liabilities of a husband for his wife's torts.[2]

[1] Now eight.
[2] Four more have been issued since this address was delivered: Statutes of Limitation (1936, Cmd. 5334); Statute of Frauds and Consideration (1937, Cmd. 5449); Rule in *Chandler* v. *Webster* (1939, Cmd. 6009); Contributory Negligence (1939, Cmd. 6032).

The Common Law in its Old Home

(1) Of the maxim *actio personalis moritur cum persona*, it was observed in the First Report that its origin was obscure and its meaning uncertain; it has been made at all tolerable only by a series of exceptions made either by statutes such as the Fatal Accidents Act, or by the judges, as for instance when the wrongful act has caused an accretion to the deceased's estate. The maxim applies in the main to torts. In recent times the frequent motor-car casualties on the road made some immediate change essential. A negligent driver who caused damage might himself be killed in the accident. His liability abated or indeed perhaps never attached, and his insurance company were discharged. Again there seems no sound reason why, if a wrongdoer dies before being ordered by the court to make compensation, his estate should be relieved and the person wronged go without compensation. These and many other similar mischiefs were discussed and remedies were proposed. A statute has been passed to give effect to the proposal—Law Reform (Miscellaneous Provisions) Act, 1934. A statute of this general character must inevitably give rise to difficult points, which will require to be decided by the court, but this merely illustrates the close interdependence in English experience of statute law and common law.[1] The statute as passed did not give effect to the Committee's recommendation that the very anomalous rule laid down in *Baker* v. *Bolton*[2] and affirmed by the House of Lords in the case of the *Amerika*[3] should be abolished.

(2) The Second Report dealt with the limited but

---

[1] See *Rose* v. *Ford* [1937] A.C. 826.   [2] (1808) 1 Camp. 493 (N.P.).
[3] [1917] A.C. 38.

important question of the recovery of interest in civil proceedings. It had been pointed out by Lord Herschell in *London, Chatham & Dover Railway* v. *South Eastern Railway*[1] that where money was withheld and recovered only by means of an action, the plaintiff could generally at common law get no interest for the period during which he was kept out of his money. That was clearly unjust. The injustice had been remedied to a limited extent by certain statutes, but the general injustice remained. This injustice, which was, broadly speaking, peculiar to the common-law system, was remedied in accordance with the recommendations of the Committee by the same act as that just mentioned, which empowered the court to give interest by way of damages for withholding money due either by way of damages or as a debt, subject to the discretion of the judge, as from the time the cause of action accrued or for some less period. These recommendations received statutory effect in the Act mentioned above.

(3) The Third Report dealt with the rule that there should be no contribution between joint tortfeasors. This rule seems to have assumed definite form in 1799 in *Merryweather* v. *Nixan*;[2] it was described by Lord Herschell in *Palmer* v. *Wick and Pulteneytown Shipping Company, Ltd.*[3] as not apparently founded on any principle of justice or equity or even of public policy. The judges had engrafted various exceptions on the rule; thus it had been held not to apply when a wrong was done in honest ignorance of the facts which made the act wrongful, or when the wrongdoer could not be presumed to know

---

[1] [1893] A.C. 429, 457.   [2] (1799) 8 T.R. 186 (K.B.).
[3] [1894] A.C. 318, 324.

that he was doing a wrongful act. The Committee proposed that the rule should be abolished and that a wrongdoer should be entitled to recover contribution from a joint wrongdoer, just as much as a joint contractor held liable for the whole debt can recover contribution from the other co-contractors; I am stating the result quite broadly.

(4) The Fourth Report dealt with the position of married women in English law, in respect of liability in contract or in tort. The position was very complicated. It depended partly on rules of the old common law; in particular on the rule that on marriage a woman's identity was merged in that of her husband, so that at least in respect of personalty her property became that of her husband (realty being the subject of special rules); that her capacity to contract ceased during coverture; and that her husband was liable for her torts. This position had been in very important respects modified by statute. Equity further invented the idea of the married woman's separate estate and the restraint on anticipation. I state the position in quite general terms. The report proposed that all the complicated and refined rules, partly of law, partly of equity, partly of statute, should be swept away, and that it should simply be enacted that a married woman should have the same rights and be subject to the same liabilities as an unmarried woman, and that the restraint on anticipation should be in future void. The recommendations of the Third and Fourth Reports were given effect in the Law Reform (Married Women and Tortfeasors) Act, 1935.

I have referred at some length to the above matters because they seem to me to represent a process which will go on (as I hope and expect) and will profoundly affect the future of the common law in England. It is true that each Report deals with a limited topic, as if it were a concrete case. The Report proceeds much like a judgment, except that it deals not with fact or mixed fact and law, but law only. It states the existing law on the point with a sparing but sufficient reference to authorities; it specifies what are considered to be the defects; then, having expressed the conclusion that the rule is other than what justice requires, it sets out, as it were in a judgment, the proposals for reform. In a sense this process is a supersession of the common law by statute rather than its preservation. But statutes like these seem to become part of the common law, and their explanation and application by the judges to the new circumstances which arise afford instances of that judicial legislation to which I have referred and which is so typical of common-law methods. The reform proceeds slowly. It is piecemeal, but if it goes on for a few decades its cumulative effect will be very marked. This is a very different scheme from that embodied in the *Restatement of the Law* now being produced in your country. That, as I understand it, is intended to cover the whole range and to state what the law is in the form of a code but without the binding authority of legislation. It is intended that the judges in all the States should accept and act on the rules and thus the law all over the United States should be uniform and standardized. The English scheme is less ambitious but it creates law in the strict and obligatory sense of the term. The *Restatement* will constitute one of the greatest monuments of the common law and will have profound effects wherever the common law is practised. I constantly consult the volumes already published.

It is easy to multiply instances of various rules to which the process of law revision in England might and perhaps will be applied. I shall later discuss consideration and the Statute of Frauds. To take another illustration which can be shortly stated: the doctrine of contributory negligence has been found difficult to apply to the varieties of fact which experience, especially of motor-traffic accidents, presents. The rule has come to involve subtle distinctions, which may work serious injustice because the plaintiff's responsibility for the accident, though not negligible, may be comparatively slight, yet he may fail to recover at all. The true test should be responsibility, as a matter of substance, and if both parties are to blame, the court should apportion the damage in accordance with the relative responsibilities of the parties. Responsibility, not causation, is the true criterion. In this way the very complicated and largely unworkable rules which judges have developed as the law of contributory negligence would become unnecessary, and yet justice be done. This is the rule applied in collisions at sea, as now embodied in the Maritime Conventions Act, 1911. The apportionment of responsibility should be made in accordance with the actual facts of the particular case, and as a matter of substance, without the fetters of formal and technical rules.[1] The possible varieties of fact are almost infinite.[2]

I may seem so far to be examining the future of the

---

[1] *Swadling* v. *Cooper* [1931] A.C. 1, 9.
[2] See now on this topic the Eighth Report of the Law Revision Committee (1939, Cmd. 6032).

common law in England merely by instancing particular rules which might be changed for the better, whereas it may be said that I ought to propound some drastic and revolutionary changes. But the gradual accretion of particular amendments or developments, going on from time to time, has from the beginning, as I have already explained, been the characteristic of the common law. I hope that process, with help where necessary from legislation, will constitute its future.

I shall illustrate some of the problems which, as I think, are likely to call for decision in the future. The last one hundred years have seen an enormous growth of English common law, corresponding to the enormous changes in complexity and character of modern life, in all its aspects. This growth has been almost entirely due to the judges, though no doubt the Legislature has in places taken its share. Indeed, in many spheres the judges have so staked out the ground that further changes can be effected only by Parliament. However, much is left open for judicial definition and improvement.

Let me first refer to a most important branch of the common law generally called quasi-contract. I can only deal very shortly with that type of obligation which is enforced by the common law though it falls neither within the province of contract nor of tort. The class is generally referred to as that of quasi-contract. The term is not very apt, but it does no harm if it is understood to be a label, and to refer to the peculiarity of the action that, though there is no promise in fact, the defendant is ordered by the court to pay money just as much as if he had promised to pay it. The writ employed was that of *indebitatus assumpsit*, and by the Common Law Procedure Act, 1852, s. 49, the necessity of alleging a fictitious promise was abolished, and the common *indebitatus* count was used. In Bullen and Leake, third edition, 1868, pp. 42–50, will be found a very brief summary of the decisions up to that date under this head of liability, showing what claims could be laid under the common *indebitatus* counts for money paid or money received. The former count included cases where the plaintiff had been compelled by the wrongful act of the defendant to pay money of which the defendant got the benefit, or where the plaintiff had been legally compelled to pay a debt for which the defendant was primarily liable. It was said in these cases by way of fiction that a request to pay was implied. The more numerous body of cases were under the latter count, that is for money received by the defendant to the use of the plaintiff: the principle, as stated in Bullen and Leake at p. 44, was that the defendant had received money which in justice and equity belonged to the plaintiff under circumstances which rendered the receipt of it a receipt by the defendant to the use of the plaintiff.

I cannot here enumerate the cases which are familiar to all lawyers. What is important to note is that so long as the forms of action remained, the only form available, or at least employed, was that of *indebitatus assumpsit*, which involved the fiction of a contract, whereas in truth the whole *ratio* of the claim was that there was in fact no contract. This was described as a contract implied in law, a description which led to confusion with cases where without express words the law inferred or implied a contract (that is an actual agreement) from the acts of the parties. Other phrases used have been that of a notional or imputed contract, or a constructive contract.

As recently as *Sinclair* v. *Brougham*[1] this fiction of the implied or notional contract was used in order to defeat the claim for money received, in a case where the claim was by persons who had lent money to a company which had no power to borrow. The House of Lords held that there could not be an implied promise to repay where an actual promise to repay would not have been enforceable. The House were, however, able to do substantial justice by means of a tracing order in equity, which was a remedy in equity, essentially different from the common-law remedy, because the former proceeds on the basis of a trust, whereas the latter is simply a claim in debt.

I do not desire to criticize the actual decision in *Sinclair* v. *Brougham*, but I desire to observe that now that the forms of action have been abolished, the court ought to put aside once and for all the misleading fiction of an implied contract and look at the substance of quasi-contract. Professor Ames has summed up what that substance is, in a very few words, as "the equitable principle which lies at the foundation of the great bulk of quasi-contracts; namely, that one person shall not unjustly enrich himself at the expense of another". In certain foreign codes, the principle is expressed in this form; for instance, in the Swiss Federal Code of Obligations (art. 62) it is provided that any one who is unjustly enriched at the expense of another must restore the benefit so received. A similar principle is being administered in France. That principle so stated would cover, I think, all the known cases of quasi-contracts in English law. To take as the most obvious instance that of money paid under a mistake of fact, Lord Sumner in

[1] [1914] A.C. 398. *Ante*, pp. 1–33.

The Common Law in its Old Home

regard to such a case said "there was no intention on the Company's part to enrich her" [i.e. the payee].[1] Baron Parke had defined the ground of the action to be that it was against conscience for the recipient to retain it.[2]

It is tempting but here impossible further to debate on the topic. What I plead for is a complete resurvey of this important branch of law in England, which to my mind bears no trace of sloppiness of thought except the fiction of the implied contract. That fiction was natural enough before the Judicature Act, but now we have no excuse for its use. A scientific analysis of the different conditions of fact in which English law has applied this principle would pave the way for further extensions from time to time to new cases which call for it. The judges would have a working theory, and could apply it to the facts of any particular case untrammelled by fictions. It may be that legislation would in any case be necessary to give full effect to a scientific theory, as legislation would certainly be necessary if certain desirable reforms are to be effected. Thus the rule that there can be no recovery of money paid under a mistake of law, laid down in *Bilbie* v. *Lumley*,[3] was justified only by the maxim *ignorantia juris neminem excusat*; of that maxim we may remember Bentham's gibe when he defined lawyers as the only persons in whom ignorance of the law is excused. Again the English law should be brought into harmony with Scots law, which was discussed in *Cantiare San Rocco S.A.* v. *Clyde Shipbuilding and Engineering Company*,[4] in which it was held by the Lords that an

[1] *Jones* v. *Waring & Gillow* [1926] A.C. 670, 696.
[2] (1841) *Kelly* v. *Solari*, 9 M. & W. 54 (Ex.).
[3] (1802) 2 East 469 (K.B.).
[4] [1924] A.C. 226.

action lay to recover money paid under a contract which had become discharged by impossibility, save in so far as the payer is *lucratus*. By English law the payee is entitled to keep what he has received, so long as he received it before the contract was discharged. In Scotland it is treated as a case of unjust enrichment; in England it is treated as a case of an accrued right. The same principles are respectively applied with the same diversity in regard of advance freight.

I now turn to that most important tort, negligence. Much remains to be done in the way of developing and defining that conception. Negligence is now recognized as a separate tort, not merely an aspect of particular torts; its importance and identity were not understood till quite modern times. The fundamental idea is that it involves a breach of a duty to take care, a duty which is owed to persons who are either identifiable from the beginning or become identified by the normal course of events. The cause of action is complete only if the plaintiff can show the duty, the breach, and the damage. It has been questioned whether the future line of development will not eliminate this idea of duty and concentrate on the fact of damage sustained by the plaintiff owing to the act of the defendant; in other words, whether the concept of negligence should not simply be that a man who causes damage by his act to another is liable unless he can show just cause or excuse; this would need to be so expressed as to include omission as well as commission, nonfeasance as well as misfeasance. Much might be said for this view, but there is strong prejudice against it and it is certainly far removed from current ideas. A recent proposal in England that, following the laws

The Common Law in its Old Home

enacted in certain parts of the British Empire, in motor-car cases the defendant should be held to have been negligent unless he can prove the contrary, thus creating a statutory shifting of the onus of proof, provoked decisive opposition. But the future may work a change.

On the other hand it is now clearly established that it is not the rule that there can be no liability without fault. The rule is that there may be liability without the personal fault of the defendant. The rule is applied in different ways; there is the rule of strict liability in the case of dangerous things, animals or constructions; I shall say something about that later; there is a similar rule in the case of statutory duties which cannot be delegated,[1] and most important, perhaps, of all is the rule of vicarious liability under which a principal, not personally negligent, is liable for negligent acts or omissions of his agents. This rule has received a wide extension; its enforcement is inevitable in view of modern conditions of commerce and industry in which most of the work of the world is carried on by agents. This is equally established where the principals are limited companies or corporations. The rule is based on public policy or necessity; its justice is vindicated by the idea of social policy, that compensation to the injured person should be made by the principal who employs the agent with the object of profiting by his acts. The realistic theory of corporations facilitates this concept; the corporation is liable for frauds or malicious injuries committed by the agent in his position as agent, even though he is not intending to act for his principal's benefit.[2] The

[1] *Lochgelly Iron & Coal Co., Ltd.* v. *M'Mullan* [1934] A.C. 1.
[2] *Lloyd* v. *Grace, Smith & Co.* [1912] A.C. 716.

future is not likely to change this rule, and some cases which appear not to give full effect to it may have to be reconsidered. The future is more likely to sweep away the few limitations that are left and in particular to abrogate the illogical exception of "common employment". The reasoning of *Priestley* v. *Fowler*,[1] which was that the principal is not liable for harm done by his servant to another servant of his, would not, I think, be given to-day by any judge if not bound by authority. To read that case is to feel the great change which in about a century has taken place in the attitude of the law to the relations between employers and workmen and in the law of agency. Common employment has survived only because its effects have been ameliorated first by the Employers' Liability Act and later by the Workmen's Compensation Acts. The policy of the latter Acts is firmly established, though the form and application of the Acts could well be improved. This rule is a striking illustration of an error made by the common law, which the judges were powerless to remedy because it had been affirmed by the House of Lords; the remedy was left to the Legislature, which got round the rule by means of the Workmen's Compensation Act, and in doing so exemplified a conception of social justice beyond the reach of the common law; viz., that the state must secure that sufferers from an industrial system should be compensated, quite irrespective of their own fault or the fault of anyone else.

A similar social policy has been exemplified in health insurance, old-age pensions, unemployment insurance. All these ideas are outside the essentially individualist

[1] (1837) 3 M. & W. 1 (Ex.), cited above, p. 340.

outlook of the common law, but so far as I can see they are enduring elements in the operative law of the land. The prevailing social or philanthropic ideas which these Acts embody have repercussions in the attitude of the judges, who are and always have been responsive to current impulses, though at times within narrow limits. Thus the common law supplemented the Factory Acts by holding that a workman injured by a breach of their provisions enacted for the benefit of the workmen had an action for what has been called statutory negligence. In regard to this action it was held that the defence of common employment did not apply, though strangely enough in England it is not yet settled whether contributory negligence is a defence or, if it is a defence, what exactly is the standard. In Australia the High Court have held that it is not a defence; in England, while the Court of Appeal have held that it is, the House of Lords have expressly reserved the question. The High Court held that only gross and wilful misconduct actually inducing the injury, where the breach of statute would otherwise have been harmless, will debar the worker from recovering. This seems a wise rule.[1]

The rule that there must be a relationship of duty in order to found negligence has been much ameliorated by a wider conception of the circumstances out of which a duty may arise. Much, however, is still left for the future. Thus a negligent statement or a negligently prepared document may cause serious damage if acted upon by a particular person or a person of the class who in the ordinary course would act upon it. But it has been said that if the author owed no specific duty to be careful as

[1] Cf. *Flower* v. *Ebbw Vale Steel, Iron & Coal Co.* [1936] A.C. 206.

by contract or employment, only actual fraud will suffice to find liability. This was laid down by the House of Lords in *Derry* v. *Peek*,[1] where it was held that negligent statements in a prospectus did not involve liability for deceit on the part of directors of limited companies, who were parties to the issue of the prospectus, towards persons who subscribed on the faith of it. A special act was passed to deal with such a case (Directors' Liability Act, 1893). It is indeed difficult to defend the general application of this limitation of the law of negligence. A surveyor is employed by a mortgagor to value property; he knows that the mortgagee will lend on the faith of the valuation; the mortgagee does so and suffers loss because the valuation is negligently prepared and is wrong. But the mortgagee has no redress because the surveyor is said to owe a duty only to the mortgagor, who engages and pays him.[2] This is, I think, inconsistent with later and more liberal ideas of the circumstance out of which a duty is to be implied. It seems to be based on the narrow idea that to constitute a duty there must be "privity" as it is called, that is privity of contract. This idea has been finally laid to rest in what is called the "Snail in the Bottle Case",[3] which decided that a manufacturer or maker is liable to any one who in the ordinary and contemplated course of things uses the article, not knowing of the defect, and is injured because the article has been negligently manufactured; liability of this character may extend even to makers of component parts which the producer of the actual article has assembled. The condition of this

---

[1] (1889) 14 A.C. 337.
[2] *Le Lièvre* v. *Gould* [1893] 1 Q.B. 491, 497.
[3] *Donoghue* v. *Stevenson* [1932] A.C. 562, cited above, p. 340.

liability is that the users should have used the article in the normal way without being aware of its harmful character and that the defect should be due to careless manufacture. This duty of manufacturers to the actual user has been quite recently recognized; it is in accordance with justice and shows the adaptability of the common law. It was not indeed in one sense a new departure because such a duty has been long recognized to exist in the case of things described as inherently dangerous towards those who use them in the normal way.[1] It was not easy to see why a difference should have been made simply because the thing was dangerous only because it had been negligently made; indeed on the latter case there may be said to be a trap.[2] The distinction seems to have been drawn because the maker of the article had sold it to a buyer; but it seems clear that the contract is immaterial in principle as between the maker and the third party who uses the thing. It had also been held that persons providing scaffolding and other appliances for men to work on or with were guilty of negligence if they either had not taken due care that the things should be safe for the contemplated use, or had not at least given warning to men using them who were injured by the defects.[3]

The essential feature of these and similar cases is that the law recognizes a duty in favour of persons who stand in no contractual or similar relation to the defendant. The duty is simply based by law on the actual fact that the thing which is made to be used and is sent out into the

---

[1] *Dominion Natural Gas Co.* v. *Collins* [1909] A.C. 640.
[2] See *Donoghue* v. *Stevenson* [1932] A.C. 562.
[3] (1883) *Heaven v. Pender*, 11 Q.B.D. 503.

world for that purpose is used by some one in the natural way for which it was intended without notice of the danger. To whom the duty is owed is ascertained only by the course of events which identifies the some one who is injured by the negligence. Whether in any case the duty exists is a question of law on the facts to be decided by the judge.[1]

This conception of negligence as involving a duty for careless act or omission to persons whose identity was unknown at the time of the act or omission, and could be ascertained only by the future event, is one of great significance for the future.

What the future will also have to decide about this type of liability for manufactured goods will be its exact scope; on one view it might operate for an indefinite time and in regard to indeterminate persons. I do not know what guide the common law will adopt in these cases as a limiting condition save the principle of remoteness.[2]

It is by the application of similar principles that the difficulties of defining what constitutes negligence in regard to trespassers must be overcome. As the law stands, a distinction is drawn between invitees, licensees, and trespassers.[3] The licensee is a sort of poor relation of the invitee, and indeed might easily become a trespasser, if the license were revoked. But at least there was this resemblance, that a licensee, like an invitee, was a person whose presence was known to or anticipated by the owner or occupier, and hence the duty attached of taking some care not to injure him. But the distinction was

[1] *Lindsey County Council* v. *Marshall* [1937] A.C. 97.
[2] *Grant* v. *Australian Knitting Mills* [1936] A.C. 85.
[3] *Fairman's Case* [1923] A.C. 74, 80.

drawn that, whereas in the case of the invitee the duty was to take care in order to protect him or to warn him in respect of danger of which the owner or occupier knew or ought to have known, in the case of the licensee the duty was limited to cases where the danger was actually known to the defendant. I cannot see any justification for that distinction. The essential basis of the duty is that the person's presence was known or anticipated in fact or in prospect. A distinction drawn in some cases between the duty of owner and occupier may be relevant in some cases and not in others.

But if it be a fact that the presence of the trespasser is known, I cannot see why the trespasser should not have the same claim to be protected or warned as the invitee. The principle of law is based on humanity. It is true that the owner or occupier may not be bound to restrict his normal activities because of the known or anticipated presence of the trespasser, but he can at least warn him, unless the danger is apparent: there is no need to warn him about what is obvious, such as broken glass or spikes on the top of a wall, or the danger of going too near moving machinery. A trespasser must take the natural and obvious consequences of his own wrongful act. But it is different if a new danger is created, or if there is a hidden danger. In such cases the trespasser, as soon as his presence is known, should be entitled at least to warning. There may be nice shades of distinction on particular facts, but I think that after many fluctuations of opinion the judges are tending towards the general view which I have stated.[1]

---

[1] See *Lowery* v. *Walker* [1911] A.C. 10; *Addie & Sons* v. *Dumbreck* [1929] A.C. 358; *Excelsior Wire Rope Co., Ltd.* v. *Callan* [1930] A.C. 404; *Mourton* v. *Poulter* [1930] 2 K.B. 183.

A trespasser is not an outlaw. How far opinion has already moved is to be seen by a careful reading of the judgment in *Ilott* v. *Wilkes*[1] in 1820, where the ideas implicit in the old doctrine are exposed. But even at the time, the decision elicited public rebuke and led to an amending Act. Nor should it be held that an owner or occupier who knows of a hidden danger on his land, and sees a trespasser going directly into it, is not liable for negligence if he fails to give reasonable notice and watches the trespasser walk into the danger.

The law will, I think, have to put on a consistent and logical basis this branch of the law of negligence, and abolish formal distinctions such as those between invitees, licensees, and trespassers, substituting such differences of duty as depend on the actual facts in the sense I have indicated.

I may notice here that the common law habitually and indeed necessarily builds in regard not only to negligence but to many other categories of contract and tort on ascertaining what is reasonable in view of the facts of the particular case. This principle or test is essentially characteristic of the common law. But it may well abolish reference to the reasonable man or to what the reasonable man would do or think and eliminate the fiction of the hypothetical or abstract reasonable man. After all, it is for the judge or jury to decide what is reasonable as a matter of their judgment, and the task imposed upon them of doing so is only disguised by interposing the hypothesis of the reasonable man and his ideas: in fact the judge or jury is the actual embodiment *pro hac vice* of the reasonable man. The jury or

[1] 3 B. & Ald. 304 (K.B.).

judge decide what is reasonable from their own good sense.

Before I leave the question of negligence I may say a few words about what is called the strict liability for dangerous elements, structures, animals, fire, and so forth; if they get out of hand, and do damage, the owner is liable even though he was guilty of no negligence and though the maintenance of the danger is *per se* not unlawful.[1] For a long time this cause of action was looked upon with disfavour, and perhaps still is. But I think it is sound and is not likely in future to be discredited, because it accords with the modern social view that one who maintains a potential danger for his own benefit ought to compensate, in the absence of special reasons, those who suffer if in fact the danger evades control and does damage. The rule is subject to the condition (*inter alia*) that the mischief has not been brought about by the interference of malicious or negligent third parties.[2]

I have discussed negligence at some length because of its great importance and the wide range it covers, and also because of the scope it offers for development. There are many other matters in the law of tort which could be discussed here. I may however refer to only a few minor matters. The great increase in medical knowledge, especially during and since the War, must force the law to realize, if it does not do so already, that mental or psychic damage can be as serious a matter as physical damage, even although there may be no obvious physical injury.

---

[1] (1868) *Rylands* v. *Fletcher*, L.R. 3 H.L. 330.
[2] *Northwestern Utilities* v. *London Guarantee & Accident Co., Ltd.* [1936] A.C. 108.

Hence an intentional or negligent infliction of nervous shock should in future be a sufficient cause of action for damages, if it is not so already. *A fortiori*, the nervous or mental injury attendant on physical injuries must be fully compensated in the damages.

The law of defamation has some serious defects. In particular the defamation of a dead man should be actionable at the suit of his near relations, who are the natural guardians of his character and suffer serious pain by cruel defamation of him when he is dead. Such defamation is now only dealt with as a criminal libel. A right to claim damages should be given. Another fact to be realized is that a slander may cause grave injury though no special damage is provable; the law should be amended to extend the list of cases in which a slander is actionable without proof of special damage. On the other hand, the curious rule has been admitted that an author may be held liable for defaming a person of whom he never heard or dreamt, merely because evidence is given by persons who say they read the book or article and reasonably thought it referred to the plaintiff.[1] I think that rule works great injustice and that it should be abrogated.

The rule that no one can give a better title than he possesses ought I think to be modified, and the principle of the Factors Act should be extended. In particular it should be enacted that the pledge of any document of title to goods used in the ordinary course of business should be as effective as the pledge of a bill of lading now is.[2]

---

[1] *Hulton* v. *Jones* [1910] A.C. 20.
[2] *Official Assignee of Madras* v. *Mercantile Bank of India, Ltd.* [1935] A.C. 53.

The Common Law in its Old Home

I must refer to the difficulties which arise in respect of what is not very aptly called "abuse of rights". It is often said that a man is entitled to exercise his rights with the direct motive of injuring another person, and that motive, and in particular *animus vicini nocendi*, is immaterial. To quote Lord Watson in *Mayor of Bradford v. Pickles*: "No use of property which would be legal if due to a proper motive, can become illegal because it is prompted by a motive which is improper or even malicious."[1] On the other hand, Justice Holmes, in *Aikens v. Wisconsin*,[2] expressed his general view that the correct mode of approach is that *prima facie* the intentional infliction of temporal damage is a cause of action which requires justification.

It is not, I think, true to say in general terms that motive cannot make the difference between what is lawful and what is unlawful. It makes all the difference, for instance, in malicious prosecution, qualified privilege in defamation, and civil conspiracy. There is much in favour of framing a general rule of law by statute that (to take the Swiss precedent) the law does not protect the manifest abuse of a right, or (to take what is proposed for the Franco-Italian draft Code of Obligations) that "Any person shall make compensation if he causes harm to another by exercising a right in excess of the limits fixed by good faith or by the object for which the right was conferred on him." But any such general declaration of rights is foreign to the English method of legislation and also to our judicial methods. *Pickles' Case* embodied the common-law idea that a landowner could do what he liked on his own land, so long as he

[1] [1895] A.C. 587, 598.   [2] 195 U.S. 194, 204 (1904).

infringed no positive rights, such as rights in connection with running water, or did not commit a nuisance. Further, the question of what is the motive may in many cases be obscure. In *Pickles' Case*, the landowner's motive was not in truth a spiteful desire to injure, but a desire to induce or to compel the corporation to buy his land for their water supply. On this footing, Pickles' act might be regarded as not different in principle from that of the shipowners in the *Mogul Case*,[1] who lowered their freight charges as a step in trade competition; this was held legitimate, though its natural and, indeed, anticipated consequence was either to force the plaintiffs out of business or to compel them to come in with the others. How difficult it is to ascertain the true motive (which can be decided only by the actual circumstances and not on evidence of states of mind) is shown by the cases on civil conspiracy, which the House of Lords attempted to explain and reconcile (not very successfully) in *Sorrell v. Smith*.[2] In England, many cases of abuse of rights may be dealt with by a more liberal application of the law of nuisance, as in *Christie* v. *Davey*,[3] or as in a recent case[4] where an adjoining owner, who objected to his neighbour keeping a farm for breeding silver foxes, showed his disapproval by preventing breeding of the animals by firing off at appropriate moments, at the boundary, guns loaded with black powder. The law of trespass also might be available to prevent some abuses. But I find it difficult to foresee legislation against the unconscientious use of contractual rights, unless on some

---

[1] [1892] A.C. 25. [2] [1925] A.C. 700.
[3] [1893] 1 Ch. 316.
Hollywood Silver Fox Farm, Ltd. v. *Emmett* [1936] 2 K.B. 468.

ground of public policy, such as the measures now in existence relating to moneylenders, or restricting the rights of landlords against tenants, or dealing with trade disputes. General grievances of that type may generate a popular clamour, leading to legislation; in one aspect the various Town and Country Planning Acts, which are in part directed at preventing landowners from disfiguring the country by building unsightly dwellings, are meant to check an abuse of rights in land, but rather on aesthetic than on any other grounds. Again, Parliament might pass measures in addition to the existing legislation limiting mischievous competition or certain actions of employers or workmen in labour disputes. Marketing Acts and acts regulating production also interfere with people doing what they like with their own property. But measures of this kind are generally prompted by considerations, not of individual rights, but of public policy. However, the future may evolve means of preventing unjust conduct in the exercise of rights, though I hesitate to forecast the precise form they will take. There is certainly difficulty in applying the provisions of Continental jurisprudence in these matters, because the general background of our law of tort is different.

Very much the same difficulties apply in establishing in England what has been called a rule of law guaranteeing privacy. The law of defamation has been effectively applied by the common law: it will cover, with the help of the innuendo, for practical purposes every injurious statement, by words, pictures, or otherwise, about a person. On the other hand, publicity in modern life is widespread; while many welcome it, some feel, or affect to feel, aggrieved at being described and portrayed in the popular press. But it is not likely that such matters can be prevented in England by any general law specifically directed to privacy. Many serious invasions of privacy may be left without protection; thus a man's garden or house may be overlooked, reporters may intrude at funerals or weddings, a man may be waylaid or beset on entering or leaving his house or business place by press photographers. I find it difficult to forecast the likelihood of any effective line of judicial or legislative measures to stop such inconveniences—if they do not involve trespass, or defamation, or indecency—however much I should welcome such measures. However, here again the maxim *solvitur ambulando*, which has been the sheet anchor of the common law, may apply: the future law will find a remedy for any mischief which is sufficiently serious.

Whether the common law will modify or change its views that any injury to a right of property, such as trespass to land, or goods, or person, is actionable *per se* without proof of damage[1] may be doubted. There is not likely to be any motive of social or economic policy involved, and the court has, and I suppose will continue to have, ways of discouraging frivolous actions. I cannot here discuss the many interesting problems which arise on the law of damages. I can only observe that I think the true rule has been now established in England that a tortfeasor is liable for the direct physical consequences of his tortious act, however improbable they might have appeared in prospect, subject only to the rule of remoteness.[2]

I shall now turn from the sphere of tort and consider

[1] *Nicholls* v. *Ely Beet Sugar Factory, Ltd.* [1936] Ch. 343.
[2] *Liesbosch Dredger* v. *Edison* [1933] A.C. 449.

some possible changes in the law of contracts. This is on the whole not so susceptible of the development of new rules as the law of tort. But there are many fundamental matters to be considered.

Consideration is perhaps the most characteristic and fundamental doctrine in the common law relating to contracts. Save in contracts under seal, no contract can be valid in law unless there is consideration. But some doubt may be felt as to its value when it is realized that it is peculiar to the common law. No other modern system has any such notion; the Code Civil does indeed provide for "cause" as a condition of contract, but it seems to be agreed that the provision is not practically significant: the Roman-Dutch law, the Scots law, know nothing of consideration; modern codes, the German and the Swiss, have disregarded the notion. Consideration is thus clearly no necessary part of a civilized law of contract. Its origin in the common law is obscure and due to a series of procedural accidents; it has had many vicissitudes in its history, and has become riddled with inconsistencies and anomalies. It has prevented the enforcement of many just contracts, and has led to misplaced ingenuity and chicanery. It is true to say that by reason of the technical rule of consideration, many common and essential operations of modern commerce are unenforceable in law, such for instance as bankers' commercial credits.

The scientific view is, in my opinion, as I have explained at length in a recent article in the *Harvard Law Review*,[1] that the sole condition of the enforceability of

---

[1] "Ought the Doctrine of Consideration to be Abolished from the Common Law?" *Ante*, pp. 287–326.

a contract, assuming the transaction to be free from illegality, fraud, mistake, or kindred defects, is that the parties should have intended to enter into binding relations of contract. I think this view should be accepted as the rule of the common law. It is true that in most cases of contract there is in fact consideration, and in any disputed case consideration would have the strongest evidential value as going to show the intention to make a binding contract. That is its true function; but that is a very different conception from the present common law, which treats it as the sole condition on which a contract can be valid at all. I do not see any difficulty in leaving it to the court (whether judge or jury) to decide on all the circumstances of the case whether or not in fact there was a serious intention to contract and, if they find there was, to give effect to that intention. *Pacta sunt servanda*. But it may be that such a change would involve too great a breach with so ancient a tradition. As a practical alternative I should propose that a promise should be enforceable as a contract if there be either (1) consideration, or (2) evidence in writing. That would in effect be to accept Lord Mansfield's ruling in *Pillans* v. *Van Mierop*,[1] but without his limitation of the rule to commercial contracts. I should apply it to contracts in general. Such an alternative would treat consideration as merely evidential. The alternatives of consideration and writing would be sufficient in practically every case of contract, and such a rule would agree with the practice of most countries in which consideration as understood at common law is unknown. In many jurisdictions a gratuitous promise

[1] (1765) 3 Burr. 1663 (K.B.).

is not enforceable without written evidence. I should also propose redefining consideration and removing some anomalies and absurdities from the idea. Thus I should abolish nominal or illusory consideration, though I should not require the court to pass on questions of adequacy if there is substantial consideration. Similarly the rule in *Foakes* v. *Beer*[1] should be abrogated; that is, the rule that acceptance of or a provision to accept a smaller sum in satisfaction of a larger sum is no consideration; and past consideration should be treated as sufficient consideration.

As a corollary to such a reform there should go, as I think, the repeal of Section 4 of the Statute of Frauds which deals with contracts, and Section 4 of the Sale of Goods Act, 1893. These sections have from the beginning proved unsatisfactory. They have led to untold chicanery and litigation; they have been restricted and explained away wherever possible; they have been the subject of unnumbered sophistries and evasions. I am not alone in believing that their removal from English law would be an unmixed blessing. If it is still thought necessary to have evidence in writing of a gratuitous contract, I should be content simply so to provide, leaving it to the judge to decide what writing in each case is sufficient.

A fundamental rule of the common law is that the meaning of a contract is to be ascertained by objective tests, that is to say the true construction of the words, written or spoken, actually used. A similar rule applies to the construction of statutes.[2] I disregard for this

---

[1] (1884) 9 App. Cas. 605. *Ante*, p. 293.
[2] *Inland Revenue Commissioners* v. *Duke of Westminster* [1936] A.C. 1.

purpose agreement evidenced on one side or the other by acts or conduct. That method of objective construction has been criticized but does not appear to me likely to be supplanted by a method based on evidence of mental intention. In any case of contested interpretation evidence of actual intention is likely to be conflicting; indeed it is always easy for any one to persuade himself that he had at a given moment a particular intention; self-sophistication is natural. However, where there has been an error in expression, the equitable relief of rectification gives the court a means to effectuate the real contract which has been erroneously expressed.[1]

English law will, I think, adopt in some form what the Scots lawyers call the *ius quaesitum tertio* and what United States lawyers call right of the "third party beneficiary". An English lawyer is so accustomed to the idea of privity of contract, to the idea that only a party to a contract can enforce it, and to the idea that consideration must proceed from the promisee, that he finds it hard to think in other terms. Yet equity has provided in England an artificial means of doing so, by applying the formula of *cestui que trust* and trustee; the benefit of the contract being regarded as a chose in action.[2] And just as assignment was made a legal concept, so a legal right of the third party to sue should be established. There are no doubt difficulties in a third party enforcing a contract between others, and it is possible that there may be questions of waiver or breach or enforcement of reciprocal conditions and similar questions, but these no doubt will be solved in England as in other countries. The

---

[1] *Inland Revenue Commissioners* v. *Raphael* [1935] A.C. 96.
[2] *Vandepitte* v. *Preferred Accident Insurance Corp. of New York* [1933] A.C. 70.

change is necessary among other things with a view to establishing the legal efficacy of many important commercial contracts, as, for instance, bankers' confirmed credits, which are now in strictness legally unenforceable.

Mistake or fundamental error sometimes raises a difficult problem in the law of contract, but though there have been difficulties I think the future will clear them up. The problem is rather to apply the principle to particular cases than to define it. It must be determined what is fundamental from the mutual standpoint of the parties, and then ascertained whether there was common error about that; that question is often complex and difficult to solve on the particular facts.[1]

The dissolution of a contract by the failure, impossibility, or illegality of a condition, which though fundamental is not expressed, has been explored in many cases. Here again the difficulties are in the application. But there is one matter on which, as I have explained, the English law should be changed; that is, the repayment of advance payments made under the dissolved contract.

In general, such cases of dissolution are said to be by virtue of an implied term in the contract between the parties. But that is a fiction. For the whole basis of this rule is that the parties did not contemplate and hence did not by contract provide for the happening of the resolutive condition. Hence it is not true in any case to treat it as an "implied" condition. Lord Sumner aptly said that the rule is adopted by the Court in order

---

[1] *Bell* v. *Lever Brothers, Ltd.* [1932] A.C. 161; *Norwich Union Fire Insurance Society, Ltd.* v. *Wm. H. Price, Ltd.* [1934] A.C. 455, 462.

to reconcile justice with the absolute contract. Law would be simpler,[1] as I have already stated, if the term "implied condition" or contract were not used except in cases where from the actual circumstances an actual intention is properly inferred or implied as a fact. What is so often called an implied term or a term implied by law simply means that there is no agreement or intention at all on the point, but the law imposes the term in order to do justice. This has often been pointed out by great judges. It is better and simpler expressly to recognize this; a failure to do so has sometimes led to confusion and error. Errors in language are apt to lead to erroneous conclusions in practice. In this, as in other respects, law will have to get its terminology right.

I need not repeat that many rules relating to contracts, especially commercial contracts, have been embodied in statutes. These are rules, in the main, of a kind not likely to be substantially changed in the near future; for instance, those relating to bills of exchange. No doubt, from time to time, difficulties of interpretation have to be solved and *casus omissi* have to be filled up, and what are called the gaps or interstices of the statutory provisions have to be made good by judicial action. Some of these are important, but not spectacular. One matter I may mention, viz. that the whole conception of contracts in restraint of trade is now undergoing, or has undergone, in practice, a complete change in unison with changing methods of industry and commerce; we live in days of conferences, marketing schemes, voluntary and compulsory combinations, international cartels; to say that such organizations, which necessarily involve

[1] *Hirji Mulji* v. *Cheong Yue S.S. Co.* [1926] A.C. 497, 510.

restraint of trade, are, unless effected by statutory authority, invalid and unlawful, is a mischievous figment. The legal rules of public policy must march with the times in actuality as they are supposed to do in theory.

In concluding, I feel how little I have really presented a forecast of the future of the common law. Will it change in the next hundred years as much as it has changed in the last hundred years, or perhaps more particularly the last seventy or eighty years? These last years have seen great developments in the mechanism of life, in commercial and industrial affairs, but still more in the transition from individualism to collectivism or, more correctly, to a policy not exactly of philanthropy but of what may be called social assistance and instruction and social regimentation. This aspect of policy which is public policy is outside the common law; it is effected by legislative measures, to some of which I have referred. But I have adverted to the enormous progress in the common law in respect to contract, tort, quasi-contract, and other spheres, and I have indicated some lines along which further progress may go. I have merely given examples. Many of these changes can be effected only by legislation; for instance, the alteration of the law of consideration; perhaps it may not be too late for the courts to redefine many portions of the law of negligence, such as that relating to trespassers; the House of Lords did clear away a mass of artificiality in the "Snail in the Bottle Case" and a little earlier in the important case of *Lloyd* v. *Grace, Smith & Co.*,[1] which defined a principal's liability in tort for his agent's fraud.

[1] [1912] A.C. 716.

But there is a greater mass of settled and defined rules than there was in 1830, and the scope of the court may prove to be more limited than it proved to have been in the years from 1830 till the present day. Yet it has been truly said that every half-century or so the law is recast and rewritten; at the risk of repetition I may refer to the constant process of erosion which is affecting the authorities. Thus in time, without any spectacular reversal, a rule of law may gradually, almost insensibly, become substantially changed so as to coincide with the changing needs and temper of the time. Authorities become obsolete. There are still many points to be decided. It is curious how even now a court finds itself in practice faced by a problem for which there is no authority or no authority which precisely fits. Then the court has to apply to the problem the dictates of justice while keeping as close as it can to the cases which appear most relevant. I am not afraid of being accused of sloppiness of thought when I say that the guiding principle of a judge in deciding cases is to do justice; that is, justice according to law, but still justice. I have not found any satisfactory definition of justice, but whatever it is, it is the quality of what is just. And what is just in any particular case is what appears to be just to the just man, in the same way as what is reasonable is what appears to be reasonable to the reasonable man. A judge applying the law as in duty bound may feel sometimes that he is doing what is unjust; when that happens it indicates a defect in the law. Perhaps it does not happen often; it certainly ought not to happen often. Mostly, but not always, a distinction can be found. There are cases in which the word "just" seems an inappropriate epithet to apply to the decision even if it is correct, as, for instance, in respect of the effect of a taxing statute, or a point in local government law, where the problem is technical and depends on the precise meaning of obscure and formal language and the question is rather of state or public policy. But in the range of what is specifically called the common law, that is, of individualistic justice, the primary object is to apply the rules which most nearly approximate to justice. The Reports carefully studied show how the judges, according to their powers and their capacity, have sought to do so. The progress of the common law is a record of what they have done, and I doubt not will continue to do, in ways and with results a few of which I may be able to forecast but most of which I cannot expect to foresee. That is the sphere of the common law which always must have an appeal to the lawyer. No one can feel an enthusiasm for rating law, or patent law, or tax law, or railway law, or perhaps even a base fee or a contingent remainder or an executory interest.

I suppose also that there will be an extension of what may be called administrative law, not in the sense of *droit administratif*, but in the sense of the settlement of disputes relating to the working out of administrative measures, where the statute provides for a special tribunal outside the ordinary courts of law. The common law has no concern with these matters, except to see that the statutory powers are not exceeded by regulations or references, and to see that rights of individuals are not infringed beyond what the statute permits. And as I have already said, the mass of legislation which annually appears interests the common lawyer only in so far as it affords scope for applying common-law principles of construction.

I feel sure that the future of the common law will lie in a truer humanity, and a more conscious adherence to practical exigencies. It will guard rights of property, but it will reconcile those rights with the rights of human beings. It will seek to abolish technicalities and rules which have no claim to exist except on grounds of antiquity. I may refer again by way of illustration to the proposals, already made, of the Law Revision Committee. It will seek to abolish fictions. Even in 1852, the Common Law Procedure Act, by Section 49, provided that it should no longer be necessary in pleading to state matters which need not be proved (i.e. which were not traversable), such as *assumpsit* in the *indebitatus* counts and losing and finding in trover. But bad traditions last long, and we still find people talking as if in quasi-contract there was still to be attributed some import to the idea of notional or imputed contract. Even before 1852 that had been recognized to be a fiction, and why should it be kept alive now, over fifty years after the forms of action were abolished? In fact, quasi-contracts are merely obligations to pay money which in certain events the law imposes and enforces, not because of the consent of the parties, but because of the actual facts. Equally the law says that in certain events a contract shall no longer bind: it does so, not because the parties have so agreed, but rather because they have not agreed at all about it. The contract has become inapplicable to the facts of the case. Why then call it an implied contract, a fiction which can serve no purpose and can only confuse? A fiction was adopted in the past merely as a device to justify a court in less enlightened days when it was applying a novel doctrine and was doing so on the analogy of, and by way of extending, a familiar rule. Hence the crop of absurd and outrageous fictions, now mostly forgotten, which it is almost indecent to exhume, fictions which can never have deceived anybody. A modern court should realize what is its ideal, that of doing justice according to the actual facts, though on the lines of established law. This can be illustrated by the case of *Donoghue* v. *Stevenson* (the "Snail in the Bottle Case"), already more than once referred to, where the House of Lords brushed aside technicalities and simply said that on the facts of the case there was a duty to take care and thus established a broad general rule of negligence.

If I may sum up what I have already said, the common law is a living organism and will, I believe, go on living and developing in the service of the cause of justice, maintaining its old tradition of deciding concrete cases on their merits and according to law on precedent or on the analogy of precedent except where a statute governs. That is what may be called the physiology of the living process as contrasted with the anatomy or organic structure—that is, the formal divisions or classifications which form the work of analytical jurisprudence. But law will become more and more self-conscious and self-critical. It will be less insular as it looks outside its own limits and considers how other countries proceed in solving the same problems as those which it has to deal with, and considers what guidance it can derive from them. It will dwell less on distinctions which have no realistic significance. It will be less concerned with the

Legal Essays and Addresses

literal interpretation and reconciliation, in a narrow and technical spirit, of decided cases. The judges will think more of the spirit of the decisions and will strive to mould and control them so as to serve the exigencies of social welfare and justice. In that great work all lawyers, academic and practising, bench and bar, will be proud to co-operate.

XIII

THE STUDY OF LAW[1]

THIS is a subject which admits of so many lines of approach and covers so large a field that it is rather appropriate to a treatise than a short address. I must be content to be impressionist rather than aim at being comprehensive or exhaustive.

In 1882 Sir Frederick Pollock in his inaugural address as Corpus Professor of Jurisprudence at Oxford, in speaking of his associates, Dicey, Bryce and Anson, described them as "fellow workers in a pursuit still followed in this land by few, scorned and depreciated by many, the scientific and systematic study of law". These were still the days of the case lawyer, who knew his reports and found his way about them partly by use and wont (as a salesman in a shop turns to the appropriate shelf or drawer), partly with the help of the *Digests* like Fisher's and precedent books like Bullen and Leake, in which you could find the cases you wanted by turning up the appropriate heading (as you would find a train in the ABC). I am not depreciating the great work done by the lawyers and judges in the long history of law in England. The judges have made the law which used to be spoken of as a sort of entity immanent in the breasts of the judges. They were law-givers, in whom was

---

[1] An address delivered to the University of London Law Society, at University College, on 24 October 1937. Published in 54 *Law Quarterly Review* (1938), 185–200.

reposed the power and duty of the King as the fountain of justice. Thus they held an independent authority and a responsibility which on the whole they admirably discharged. The raw material of the law consisted of their decisions given on concrete facts, supported by their reasons, broadening from precedent to precedent according to the principle of *stare decisis*. This characteristic feature of English law, too familiar to need discussion, explains the absence, which Pollock deplored, of a systematic and scientific study of law. It is contrasted with systems based on the Civil Law in which governing *a priori* principles have been expounded by commentators and institutional writers, cited in the Courts as authorities from which particular applications can be deduced by logic.

The English Law Reports still contain the raw material of law, growing and expanding from year to year as fresh cases or new facts call for decision. Principles follow from concrete decisions, in place of decisions following from principles. Only some judgments, it is true, are reported, because only a few embody a new principle (that is indeed rare in these days) or what is more frequent an extension or new application of an old principle. The practitioner or judge must still know his cases and how to use them, and how to reconcile with adherence to precedent such innovations as justice requires. What need then, it may be asked, is there for the scientific and systematic study of law? Is it still not enough to proceed from case to case, like the ancient Mediterranean mariners, hugging the coast from point to point, and avoiding the dangers of the open sea of system or science? Why contaminate enlightened common sense or rule of thumb, by principle or system? There may be many answers to this question. It may be that once a new discipline has been discovered, it supplants older and cruder methods. It may be that scientific methods are universal nowadays and invade even the privileged areas of the law. But most of all, I think there is both a practical and a theoretical purpose served by the new learning, if I may so call it. A constant process of innovation and amelioration is being carried on by the judges, as it has been through the long history of English law, with the help of the practitioners. It is better that they should understand the principles on which they are proceeding and work with enlightened consciousness. They can better deal with a case of negligence if they understand the true nature of that category of tort and the fundamental principles on which it is based: they can better deal with a case of mistake if they understand the principles on which mistake vitiates what appears to be agreement or a case of recovery of money paid under mistake if they understand the principles of unjust enrichment, or (as it has recently been called in America) restitution. Instances might be multiplied from every sphere of contract, tort, quasi-contract, property law, trust. English law is not static, but dynamic, it is a living system. There are those who are fortunate enough to have achieved a vision of its growth and development up to the time of Edward I and then up to the present day. That is not the lot of most of us. But every student of modern English law must know a great deal of its history in order to understand it as it is. Established rules which seem strange to scientific or foreign jurisprudence can be understood only by studying their historical origin, often based on procedural requirements, as for instance consideration, or on the acceptance (often almost fortuitous) of some maxim such as *actio personalis moritur cum persona*, or that every one is presumed to know the law (a rule traceable as far back as *Doctor and Student*,[1] which for obvious reasons may be necessary in the administration of criminal law, but is inapplicable in the sphere of civil law and untrue; yet it has been taken up and repeated by some judges though repudiated by others), or that there is no right of contribution between joint tortfeasors, or that the law does not give damages for the death of a human being. When the student is able to trace these *soi-disant* principles to their origin, they seem to lose their mystical authority. Hence the importance of the historical study of English law, as well as its systematic and scientific study. Indeed in one sense the scientific study of existing English law is impossible. Its growth has been determined in part by logic, it is true, but in part also by convenience, in part by artificial or procedural requirements, in part by the pressure of social ideas and conditions which have now ceased to exist, in part by pure accident, in part by the survival of primitive habits of mind. All this makes it all the more necessary to apply scientific method and to analyse out the elements which cannot fall into any scientific scheme, partly for theoretical, partly for practical, reasons. Anomalies can better be eliminated when they have been unmasked and marked down. It may be that some anomalies can be remedied by the judges when engaged at their daily task of deciding concrete cases, which is their normal

[1] Dialogue II, ch. XLVI.

The Study of Law

function of judicial legislation. Or it may be that the help of the other law-making body, Legislature or Parliament, may need to be invoked if there is to be a reform at all. Though the judges must be governed by precedent in their function as law-makers, since otherwise there would be no law at all, but merely *liberum arbitrium* or chaos, it is remarkable how, if a long period is taken, the law has changed. If I may misquote, *tempora mutantur, lex et mutatur in illis*. All this makes it seem doubtful how the words scientific or systematic can be applied to so amorphous and unstable a subject-matter. There is the further point that law in the juristic sense is not concerned with facts or observed sequences of cause and effect like what we call laws of nature, that is the generalized theories arrived at in the physical world as the result of observation and experiment of fact, but is normative or regulatory. It consists of mandates directed to achieving in the realm of human relations that ideal which we call justice. It involves a judgment as to right conduct which may be described as moral or ideal, not a mere theory of what happens in fact. It is based on moral values, though it is not true to say that law and morality coincide, because there are many duties which an ideal morality would exact, but which law is not able to prescribe, since law proceeds on a lower plane of practical obligation. The word science is used in so many different senses that I do not seek to define it here, but this much at least is clear, that if it is used in connection with law it is used in a special sense, viz. the reducing of a mass of heterogeneous precepts by analysis and synthesis into principles ascending from the lowest to the highest generalizations. In fact, English law is a study *sui generis*. A great American lawyer, no doubt impressed by these difficulties, defined its scope and object as prediction. The purpose of its rules was to enable the lawyer to predict what the Court, which enforces the law, would require to be done in the particular circumstances of any particular human relationship. This predictable quality of law, it is said, enables the lawyer to advise his client not merely what will be ordered if the matter comes before the Court, but what course he must take in the conduct of his affairs so that he can anticipate and obviate any danger of litigation. But this is scarcely a definition or even a description of law. Indeed law tested in this way would often seem both as a practical matter and a matter of theory to be a failure, when regard is had to the varying opinions of qualified lawyers and to the conflicting decisions of appellate Courts. Nor is this criticism met by the argument that in the great majority of cases the law does give reasonable certainty of prediction. Again, this way of looking at the thing demonstrates that law, if scientific at all, is not an exact science. It is a working body of rules directed to achieving justice, and so regarded might be conceived to be an art. There is indeed no such thing as abstract justice. It is an ideal which can be realized only in the concrete, and within such limits as the practical conduct of disputes in Courts of law permits. We are familiar with the poet's phrase, "the lawless science of the law".

These difficulties which I have so sketchily indicated may discourage the student and tempt him to think that, as for practical purposes of his profession, it is the predictable quality of law which matters, all he need study

The Study of Law

and understand is how to advise his client what his action should be to satisfy the law or what legal consequences will follow in any particular set of facts, and that systems, theories and principles may be disregarded. This has been the practical attitude of many successful lawyers in every branch of the law, certainly in the past, and even to-day. It was that conception which induced Sir Frederick Pollock's remark which I cited at the beginning of this address. But in the half-century since that was said things as well as ideas have unquestionably changed. It has been accepted that legal education is a necessity. Public men, whether lawyers or not, are interested in legal reform. Legal reform involves not merely the investigation of social, or industrial, or business conditions in human relationships, but also the nature of the existing legal rules, how they came to be as they are, how far they subserve social ends, how far they tend to fulfil the function of promoting justice. Hence the desire for legal education and for the study of law, which goes beyond the bare demands of vocational necessities. Legal education involves schools of law and professional teachers of law, who give their working life to the study of law, as a theoretical discipline, whether it is to be called science or not. Within the last half-century schools of law have multiplied and grown in this country. America had already led the way in this development. There are great law schools like Harvard, Yale and Columbia where the legal aspirant, mostly after a general university training, devotes three years to the study of law under a body of highly trained and highly specialized professors, most of whom have made important contributions to the academic study of whatever branch of law they have severally chosen as their special subject. The working lawyer cannot expect to achieve any such mastery of law. But he can profit by it in others, either in the course of his training or in later life by consulting the books or articles written by the experts. In England the development of the academic side of law is more recent and the status and value of professors has been perhaps less recognized, but it is being more and more realized how essential it is that they should be recognized. There have grown up many admirable schools of law, including that of this University, each with a faculty devoted to the study of law in all its aspects. There have been published many admirable books on the different branches of the common law and equity, on subjects like Conflict of Laws and International Law. There are well-known law journals, the *Law Quarterly Review*, the *Cambridge Law Journal*, and very recently another, the *Modern Law Review*. The great value of these journals is that they contain articles on special topics of law, often important contributions to jurisprudence, marked by learning, insight and originality. In addition to these English journals there are similar journals in the United States (such as the *Harvard Law Review*, the *Yale Law Journal* and many others), in Canada, in Australia and elsewhere. A working lawyer cannot expect to keep abreast of all this output of ideas, but he can at least study some portion so as to liberalize his views of law and to avoid the reproach of being a mere case lawyer. These journals also include notices and criticisms of current decisions, which are illuminating. And the last half-century has seen the publication of valuable treatises on law both here and in

America. It is sufficiently but not exactly accurate to treat as the first of these the classical works of Sir Frederick Pollock on Contract and on Torts, which sought to give a philosophic analysis of the principles of the subject, with a complete classification and collection of the relevant cases under the several principles. I need not refer to the various works of a similar character which have followed and which are available to the student and practitioner, or the various collections of essays on subjects of common law and equity which have appeared.

No doubt the lawyer must still know his cases, but there is all the difference between knowing them in a literal and mechanical fashion, and knowing them both synthetically and critically. In the latter case they are seen in the light of principle and not as dead precedents. The object of knowing cases is to apply them with understanding to the practical problems that arise. A set of facts may appear to be (in the slang phrase) on all fours with a decided case, and yet on a wider and truer view, such as a study of principles is calculated to give, it may become apparent that there are essential differences which lead to an entirely different conclusion. Thus a rule is differentiated and extended, its true nature and scope are better understood and the development of law goes on. One of the most important qualities of a working lawyer (whether at the bar or on the bench) is ability to make the proper use of authorities, to look at the rule as something alive, and not merely arbitrary and formal. And the lawyer must beware of what Lord Sumner once called the "will-o'-the-wisp" of the *obiter dictum*. How much bad law would have been avoided if *obiter dicta*, often unconsidered, of even eminent judges had been forgotten and disregarded, instead of being applied as has often happened, more or less blindly, to circumstances which the judges who uttered them never had in mind. Indeed there is often a danger in taking the statement of a rule by a judge as absolute and unqualified, whereas he made the statement only in view of the facts and questions he was considering. What he said, correct enough in its context, becomes misleading when torn from the context and applied to alien situations. Indeed the proper use of authority is a difficult art. These difficulties arise only in a system of case law, governed by the rule of *stare decisis*, such as ours. Even in English law it is different in that part of the law which is statutory. The judge's duty, his sole duty there, is to ascertain and to give effect to the intention of the Legislature; this he must do on the basis of the actual words of the statute, read in their place in the context, because the statute must be read as a whole. General principles of construction may sometimes help to solve the problem, but cannot determine it. It is sometimes said that a statute must be construed so as to depart as little as possible from the rules of common law or equity, and to make as little change as possible. But this is an unsafe guide in days of modern legislation, often or perhaps generally based on objects and policies alien to the common law. The construction of words in one statute may be no guide to the construction of similar words in another statute, even when all effect possible is given to the principle of *stare decisis*. The same words may take a different colouring from the different context in the statute in which they appear. I need not say that the

The Study of Law

idea that a Court is entitled to refuse to apply a statute if it appears clearly contrary to reason or the common law has long since been exploded. The doctrine of the supremacy of law is a cardinal doctrine of the English law and one aspect of its various meanings is that whatever Parliament enacts must receive effect in the Courts.

This is all I need say here about the statutory portion of law. Its bulk is now great and is growing, but such law is mostly for the specialist and has little interest for the student of law, save in so far as it illustrates principles of construction, or save in so far as it indicates trends of social thought and policy, which may have repercussions on the attitude of judges when they deal with common-law questions of kindred character. I should also in particular refer to those Acts which codify or consolidate portions of common law or equity, such as the Bills of Exchange Act, the Sale of Goods Act, the Marine Insurance Act, the Trustee Act, the Settled Land Act. Some Acts not merely consolidate but largely revolutionize a branch of law, like the law of Real Property. These are all Acts which must be mastered by the student if he is to learn the particular branch of law involved. Then there are special statutes like the Statute of Frauds and the Statutes of Limitation which are implicated in and interwoven with common law or statutory rights or remedies, or Acts which modify a rule of law, such as the Fatal Accidents Acts, which give a special remedy to certain persons for an individual's death, or the Employers' Liability Act, which gave a special exception, carefully hedged about, from the doctrine of common employment. While the great mass of legislation may be disregarded for purposes of this address, the student must have regard to statutes such as I have been particularizing.

I turn again to the study of the law which is found in the Reports and which is the typical English law, whether called common law or equity. As already pointed out its character is essentially empirical. It has grown through the centuries. It can be understood only by reference to history: I do not mean merely the history of the law itself, the influence of procedure, of the forms of action, of convenience in pleading. All these made it difficult and still often make it difficult to see the juristic conception under the procedural forms. But in a more substantial way we can see the influence of history, of current modes of social, moral, political and economic ideas—current, that is, among the classes from which the law-makers, judicial or legislative, were drawn. We can see often that a rule of law is based on or adapted to conditions and ideas that have become obsolete, and we have to consider whether it is possible to apply the maxim *cessante ratione legis cessat ipsa lex*. Let me take only two or three obvious examples from the last 100 years or so based on social ideas now out of date. The doctrine of common employment originated in the old Tory attitude to labour; later it was nurtured by the idea that everything is to be explained by implying a contract, however remote from actuality or from any thing the parties would be likely to have agreed; then, when there came changes in moral and social conceptions, this eminently unfair rule was saved from extinction by the Employers' Liability Act and Workmen's Compensation Acts, which latter Acts are in turn due to be

The Study of Law

reformed under more liberal ideas. The law of civil conspiracy has followed a somewhat analogous course, as ideas of repression and later of *laissez-faire* have given place to wider views as to the rights of concerted action. Then the strange rule that damage caused by the negligent killing of a human being could give no cause of action could not in its integrity survive the introduction of railways and the consequent increased risk to human life; public sentiment demanded at lowest the change embodied in the Fatal Accidents Act, and a recent Act has carried the process farther.[1] These are merely a few illustrations of the empirical character of English law and the changes to which it has been subject under the pressure of public opinion. It has reacted to the moral, social and political ideas and feelings of the time, which have profoundly and persistently affected not merely the Legislature, but also the judges. If we compare the tone of judgments delivered (say) in 1870 with those of to-day it is impossible not to observe the effect of changes in prevailing ideas.

But it may be asked how such a position is consistent with the doctrine of precedent or *stare decisis*. The answer is that English law in fact is always growing and has always been growing. A decision is an authority only for what it actually decides, and the same set of facts seldom repeat themselves. There is generally, though not always, enough difference to justify a strong and liberal-minded judge, if he feels that justice so requires, in distinguishing the case before him from the authority of the earlier cases cited as binding him. Thus what has been called a constant erosion of the existing authorities

[1] Law Reform (Miscellaneous Provisions) Act, 1934.

goes on, decisions seem to drop out of sight and become superseded, and old rules become changed or modified almost insensibly, sometimes beyond recognition. That great American lawyer, Mr Justice Holmes, said that every half-century the case law is rewritten so that earlier cases may be put aside. He meant, I take it, that the rules that survived from the earlier period can be found in the later cases. This is perhaps a paradox, but it is largely true. Law, of necessity, must adapt itself to current ideas and conditions. It would not be tolerated if it became out of harmony with them. There is no doubt throughout the ages a fundamental uniformity in method and ideas, reflecting the genius of the English race throughout the centuries, and the traditional ethos of common law and equity. Yet the changes and developments in judge-made law have been startling. Compare, for instance, the law of negligence a century ago with what it is to-day. Or take the rules as to the vicarious liability of an employer for the wrongful acts of his servants. In the time of Henry IV it was said that the employer could not be held liable for his servants' acts because they were not *his* acts. After the middle of the last century vicarious liability was becoming recognized as the general rule, but it was still said that the employer would not be liable for frauds of a servant even in doing the class of acts he was authorized to do, if he did them for his own personal advantage. That limitation was swept away twenty years ago by the House of Lords. The modern idea is that the employer, who employs his servant for his profit, should bear the loss caused to others by the servant's torts while apparently engaged about the employer's business just as much as if the employer himself was actually so engaged. Again, it used to be said that there could be no liability in tort without *culpa*. But that idea has long been implicitly disregarded and now it is explicitly disavowed, if by *culpa* is meant personal fault in performance. If, however, *culpa* means default in performance of an obligation which is personal to the defendant, then the default constitutes the *culpa*. Hence the cases of strict liability (*Rylands* v. *Fletcher*) and of breach of a statutory liability, and the cases of vicarious liability in respect of independent contractors or of specially qualified managers or shipmasters with whose management the employers are by law forbidden to interfere. It may, however, be said that the law never changes. The more it changes (or seems to change) the more it is the same thing. It is merely better understood. I regard this as a fiction and prefer to say that the law is a living organism, constantly growing, expanding, adapting itself, like a tree, which maintains its identity all the time, though in its full growth it looks very different from what it was when a sapling.

I have been dwelling on the historical aspect of English law. That is an aspect which can demand the devoted study of a lifetime. We have had the great work of Professor Holdsworth, which I understand will soon be carried on over the eighteenth century.[1] I need scarcely mention Pollock and Maitland's classic. But there is room for many labourers in the field of English legal history. Most of the Year Books still await editing, so as to bring about a knowledge and understanding of

[1] Vols. x, xi and xii of his *History of English Law* have since been published.

the medieval law. There is a great wealth of records to be studied and collated, so as to give a picture of the times. The exact position of Chancellors like Wolsey and Bacon in the history of equity can be ascertained only by minute research. We speak of Coke as marking the beginning of the modern law, but an elaborate monograph might well be written to explain precisely how he stands in relation to what is called the medieval law and to the law as it developed after him. Again, Blackstone's Commentaries form a landmark in the history of English law. It would be instructive to see how the centre of gravity of English law has changed since his day and also to observe the greater precision and elaboration in modern law of such rules as he deals with, so far as not obsolete, as contrasted with the indefiniteness which his classical style veils. But I must leave the fascinating subject of historical research.

The analysis and synthesis of the principles of English law and the liberal and enlightened criticism of its particular rules have been much advanced, but there is much still to be done. I am not here concerned with Jurisprudence or Comparative Law, though both studies are of great value in giving a wider outlook and in preventing an insular self-contentment. A great deal has been written, principally by continental jurists, on the fundamental principles and primary definitions of an abstract theory of law. I have not had the time or opportunity to get more than a fragmentary and superficial acquaintance with the elaborate philosophical and almost metaphysical disquisitions of this character. I must, I fear, leave it to others. Comparative law is certainly of great value to those who are considering

The Study of Law

particular rules of English law. It is helpful to see how other codes or systems deal with matters such as what we call contributory negligence, a most difficult subject, or the survival of a cause of action after death, or unjust enrichment, or the abuse of a right. But the general background of a foreign system is for the most part alien to the background of English law, so that caution is necessary in comparing them, and a foreign law must itself generally require for its understanding almost a lifetime of study and experience. However, on all sides of law the need is being realized of professional legal studies. There should be established an Institute of Legal Research which would supplement and aid the work of the Law Revision Committee.

Of the English civil law it now seems clear and is, I think, generally accepted that there are three principal categories, contract, tort, and quasi-contract, each of which deals with a characteristic relationship between the parties involved. In contract the relationship arises from consent, whether express or implied in fact; there is an intention to create that relationship. In tort and quasi-contract there is no intention to create the relationship. It arises by the operation of law on the facts of the case. Thus in quasi-contract the relationship which the law imposes arises from the fact that the defendant has been enriched or advantaged at the expense of the plaintiff under circumstances which make it just that he should make restitution to the plaintiff, so that it is unjust and a wrong to the plaintiff if he fails to do so. In tort the defendant has inflicted a wrong on the plaintiff under such circumstances that justice requires him to pay damages or make compensation for the wrong. In matters of contract there is generally no difficulty in defining the relationship, which is what is generally described as privity of contract. The trouble which has arisen has been because people have treated privity of contract as the norm for the other categories and have sought to find a sort of privity in the other two categories. Hence it has been said that in quasi-contract there can be no liability unless the law implies a contract. But that is a contradiction in terms because it is the parties who make the contract if there is a contract at all. The obligation really arises from the fact of unjust retention of what should be restored to the plaintiff. That is enough in law to constitute the nexus, if that term is to be used, though it is better to reject it altogether and to speak merely of the obligation arising in law from the actual facts. Equally in tort, it seems absurd to speak of privity when for instance a man negligently drives into another on the public highway. That in the old law would be trespass. It seems strange also to talk of privity in the case of a trespasser. But the vague idea of privity has had serious consequences in the law of negligence. Many of these have been swept away by the "Snail in the Bottle Case",[1] in which the House of Lords singularly performed its very important function of clearing up and simplifying a rule of law. The duty between the parties to take care in that case arose though the defendants, the manufacturers, did not know and had never heard of or dealt with the plaintiff. It arose simply because the defendants had been so negligent in preparing an article, which they sent out into the world to be used by some one, that it caused damage to the plaintiff

[1] *Donoghue* v. *Stevenson* [1932] A.C. 562.

who in the normal course used it. The obligation was imposed by law by reason of the facts, apart from any intention of the parties. In truth this has always been the basis of obligation both in tort and quasi-contract. But the use of fictions and vague phrases about privity and implied contract have obscured the simple principles, both in regard to the law of quasi-contract and of tort. If it be asked what practical value such analysis possesses, it may be answered, as I indicated before, that not only is accuracy of thought always good in itself, but it tends to the correct decision of actual cases. Wider generalizations have been suggested as co-ordinating the three great categories of the common law. It has been proposed as a general formula applicable to all that there is a cause of action wherever it is shown that damage has been done by the defendant to the plaintiff without just excuse. This might seem to shift the burden of proof or at least mean that the plaintiff completes his case by showing that he has been damaged by the act of the defendant, thereby putting on the defendant the burden of showing that there was a just excuse for what was done. Such a principle would be inconsistent with the ordinary rule of English law which requires the plaintiff to establish affirmatively his cause of action, just as the onus is always on the prosecution in criminal cases. That objection, however, would be met by construing the principle as meaning not only that the plaintiff must prove damage to himself, but absence in the defendant of just excuse, that is, must prove his whole cause of action, as is now the case. I question whether so general a principle is of any real significance. The plaintiff would have to prove in the case of a contract the contract and the breach, in the case of a tort the damage and the circumstances which showed that it was due to the wrongful act of the defendant, in the case of quasi-contract the circumstances from which in law the plaintiff's right of restitution arose. If the principle were extended to cover trusts, the plaintiff would similarly have to show the circumstances on which his beneficial interest was based and the breach of trust. In other words all that the generalization would mean would be that a right in law or equity had been infringed, and the problem of bringing the nature of the right and the circumstances of the case under the appropriate category would remain as before. In particular, in tort English law has insisted that the existence of a duty as between the plaintiff and defendant is essential to the cause of action. This has only led to trouble because sometimes an unduly narrow view has been taken of the circumstances out of which the duty may arise. In any event any general formula must be supplemented in any individual case by the application to that case of the appropriate particular rule to be found in the case law. General principles and particular case law must co-operate in the decision of any particular concrete problem. Each element has its proper place.

I have mentioned these great categories of law because they pervade the whole complex tissue of the daily life of each of us. Whether consciously or not we are always regulating our lives by law, just as we are always speaking prose (unless we are poets). Without this constant basis of law, civilized life could not go on. It is the basis of our social existence. It is generally plain or ascertainable what the law is in any particular circumstances, if not to the layman, at least to the lawyer whose advice he seeks

The Study of Law

or ought to seek if he feels doubt himself or wants to be safe. It is here that the ordinary practitioner of law is constantly effective. Hence those of you, possibly the majority of those here, must use your student days to master the subject. This is what may be called the vocational training. There are now admirable text-books on all the main branches of law, which you will study so as to be thoroughly conversant with the settled and established rules. The method of applying these rules in practice you will learn by studying the selected cases put before you by your teachers, and also by the moots which have become so valuable a part of the lawyer's training. In this way you will become fitted to help and advise your clients in the affairs of life and in all the normal questions which arise. Of course, you will have become familiar with the rules of procedure, in case your client's affairs render it necessary to have recourse to the Courts. But in most practising lawyers' experience, litigation will be rather exceptional. If clients are well advised by their lawyers, there will as a rule, given good will and honesty, be little occasion for litigation. Thus even the most important business transactions will be carried out with the help of legal advisers who will take care that every rule of law and practice is duly complied with. That may appear to be a counsel of perfection, but it holds in the vast majority of cases. It is true that facts are often disputed and obscure and that exceptional cases may present difficulties of law, in which the precise application of the law may not be clear and opinions may differ, so that the knot can be untied or cut only by a Court of law, perhaps only by the final Court. These may involve the most abstruse considerations of law, and the exercise of the greatest learning and experience. But whether the case is of the ordinary or the extraordinary type, you will be thankful for the complete grounding in law which you have received in your student days. Above all you will be thankful if you have acquired the legal aptitude, the habit of mind which makes you instinctively know what is the legal way of approaching the problem, of selecting the relevant facts, of appreciating the true lines of inquiry, and of knowing in what part of your library to turn for the guidance of authority. This is the vital part of the lawyer's equipment; without this live aptitude, mere accumulations of learning are little more than a dead weight. This habit of mind will make you grateful for the work of your teachers and prevent you from underrating the value of a scientific and systematic study of law, which in the fullest sense is only possible if you have in the Law Schools professors and teachers who make this study their life work. I do not mean that they are shut out from practical experience. Indeed that will help their study. The advice of the most highly specialized professors of law is constantly sought in most important affairs, and their services are constantly requisitioned by the State in advising and on committees and conferences. But the study and teaching of law constitute their primary avocation.

It is customary to conclude any address on the study of law with a panegyric of its excellencies, its high place and function. I have no intention of depreciating the pursuit to which I have devoted the greater part of my working life. But I should hesitate to call it, as Coke did, the perfection of human reason. Bacon must have known

The Study of Law

better, when he was writing the works which laid the foundation of modern experimental science. Science as a monument of the powers and range of the human mind, of observation and experiment, has a greatness to which law cannot aspire or approach. And the practical application of scientific ideas has revolutionized the whole mechanism of life. These things we all know. I have pointed out that law is not an exact science, that it is empirical in its growth and character, full of imperfections and anomalies. This is on its intellectual side. And its practical achievement in the service of man seems drab and poor when compared with the marvels of machinery, with aviation and radio or with the great healing work of the medical profession. Why then does law hold the place which, despite criticism and complaint, it unquestionably does in public esteem? It is true that lawyers have bulked large in the highest political and administrative positions, in the Cabinet, in the great public departments, in local government. This would seem to indicate the worth of a legal training. It is true also that law in its own way covers the whole range of human activity; there is no side of life which it does not touch. And the student of law must know the course of national history under which it developed, he must appreciate the affinity of its ideas with the social, moral and economic ideas alongside of which it developed. Law upholds the equality of all men, it impartially regards the proud and the lowly; humanity is its essential characteristic. These things would justify the esteem in which it is held. But I think that more vital than anything else is the nation's feeling that law is what holds the nation together, that it is the basis on which the whole superstructure rests. Justice is the foundation of the whole State. It resembles the foundations of physical structures, in that it is not always overtly thought of, but is taken for granted. But the nation, whether consciously or not, is aware of its vital importance. The root ideas of English law, such as the supremacy of law in that the order of the King or Government cannot justify an unlawful act, the independence and fairness of the judges, trial by jury, freedom from unlawful arrest or detention, the fairness of the criminal law, freedom of speech, are both the fruits and the nurturers of the British character. They justify the boast that the Common Law is the law of free peoples and the champion of democracy. It is on grounds of this nature and on the high character of lawyers, rather than on any technical perfection, that law and its practitioners and professors have their place in the public esteem. But we who have been admitted or are being admitted into the inner sanctuary of the law also feel for it a more intimate reverence and affection. Greater lawyers than ourselves have spoken reverently of their mistress the Common Law. This must seem to us to be no strange or artificial mode of speech, but a metaphor which embodies sober truth.

XIV

IN MEMORIAM

RIGHT HON.
SIR FREDERICK POLLOCK
Bart., K.C., D.C.L.

1845–1937[1]

IN the early part of last year I had occasion to quote in a judgment which I was delivering a passage from Pollock on Torts. In doing so I added that "fortunately" it was not a work of authority. Pollock, I was told, was charmed by this reference to him, partly because of that delicate sense of humour which was constantly coming out in conversation and even in his most serious works. Now his voice is silent. But his work remains. The object of this paper is to make a brief, necessarily superficial and imperfect, attempt to survey his influence in the age-long development of English law. The full valuation of that influence will need the considered judgment which in due course will be given by the legal world. This at least is clear, that he has vindicated to this generation the vital importance of extra-judicial writing in law. He was fond of distinguishing for purposes of English law between the written law, by which he meant statutory law, where the actual words of the Legislature are decisive, and unwritten law, as embodied in the

[1] First published in 53 *Law Quarterly Review* (1937), 151–167.

judgments of the Court, where what is decisive is the effect of the decision, not the language of the judge. The writings of a lawyer like Pollock, constantly cited in the Courts and quoted by the judges, are entitled to claim a place under his category of unwritten law, even in a system like ours, which does not normally seek its law from institutional writers.

When Pollock died a few weeks ago, at the great age of ninety-one but with his eager mind still vigorous to the last, there lay behind him a career of the most varied experience and vivid interest. But it may truly be said that the dominant motive and purpose throughout were the understanding and exposition of English law as viewed from every aspect. English law was to him no dead collection of mechanical rules or propositions, but a living system in which the sense of justice of a great people has sought realization. Hence his devotion to the understanding of the past; he traces the development of our law back to its earliest beginnings, not merely to Anglo-Saxon days but to its origins in days before they settled in this country; he seeks to follow its course through the ages because he finds throughout the same principles adapting themselves to changing conditions. He is an antiquarian, not for the sake of antiquarianism, but because it affords a fuller means of realizing English law as it is in its present form, which is seen thus as having evolved by a continuous process through the ages and as being still capable of continuing that process in time to come, over the wider areas in which it has ceased to be merely English law but has become the law of almost the whole of the English-speaking nations. In the understanding of English law he has further called

In Memoriam: Sir Frederick Pollock

to the aid of his studies Roman law, modern European law, and the great continental writers on jurisprudence.

To help to vitalize this mass of material he had his wealth of practical activities and experience and his wealth of general reading and scholarship. In one sense he was an academic lawyer, because his main legal work was done as professor, lecturer and writer. He did not practice in the ordinary sense of the word. Indeed no working lawyer, even though working 365 days in the year and twenty-four hours in the day, could have combined with his practice the study necessary to acquire Pollock's equipment. But Pollock was much more than an academic lawyer; in London, Cambridge, Oxford, in the United States, in India, in Paris and elsewhere in Europe, he saw men and cities. He was one of a family of great lawyers and judges. He was in touch with large affairs; he was active in many causes; he held one interesting, if not exacting, judicial office; he took an active part in the management of a great educational and professional society, Lincoln's Inn. Others will discuss in this number of the *Review* his many practical activities. I merely mention them as matters which were of service to him in his legal work. Others too will discuss his many-sided scholarship. He came to the law as a Fellow of Trinity, Cambridge (as in private duty bound I relate), after distinction both in Classics and in Philosophy, of which one fruit was his book on Spinoza. But he read widely all through his life; his reading extended even to Oriental languages, to which more than once in his legal writings he refers.

To understand the course of his legal development, it is necessary to say a word about the state of English law when he left Trinity and was called to the Bar in 1870, a topic to which he several times refers in his published writings. Legal education was then in a very poor way, indeed almost non-existent as a public discipline. Neither at the Universities nor at the Inns of Court was there any systematic teaching in English law, though there were about that time or shortly afterwards Chairs of Law occupied by most eminent men; for instance, at Oxford the teachers were Maine, Bryce, Holland, Markby, Anson and Dicey. At Harvard the Law School was already in full life, with Ames, Langdell, Thayer and Holmes, shortly after to be joined by Williston and Beale. A man who after going through the normal schools went from the University to the Bar, would generally go into a barrister's chambers and by reading his master's briefs and attending to hear his cases in Court would gradually imbibe an acquaintance with the reported cases, as Pollock tells us was the procedure adopted by his relation Baron Pollock. Pollock himself was fortunate enough to read with Lindley and to go as marshal with Willes. He often expresses his admiration for, and gratitude to, these great men. He tells us how lacking were any books expounding or analysing the principles of English law, which indeed was once described, as he quotes, as case law tempered by Fisher's *Digests*. But Lindley had published in the 'fifties the first edition of his great work on Partnership; in 1861 Maine published his lectures on Ancient Law, which Pollock always admired and, many years after, enriched with an illuminating Introduction and Notes. For Bentham and Austin Pollock had little sympathy or interest. The previous century had given the works of Blackstone; of him Pollock writes,

In Memoriam: Sir Frederick Pollock

speaking of things as at the eighteen-sixties, "there was much to be learnt (as there still is) from Blackstone, whose work was admirable in its day notwithstanding conspicuous faults of method and arrangement mostly not his own; but Blackstone had ceased to be read with attention even by lawyers and was not a safe guide for any period before the thirteenth century". Pollock was there primarily referring to English legal history which he says in the 'sixties "was only imperfectly known and what was known was concealed under huge masses of comparatively modern formation". This makes it astounding that by the 'nineties such a classic as Pollock and Maitland's *History of English Law* should have seen the light. Perhaps even more astounding was the publication in 1876 of the first edition of Pollock's *Principles of Contract*, of which the tenth edition, to which I shall refer in a little detail later, issued from the press last year (1936). That book is indeed a legal classic and heralds a new period of English legal study. So far as I know, there had been no books on the law of contract published in England, except those of Addison in 1847 and Leake in 1867. The work of Leake was excellent but not very inspired, and he is described by Pollock as a very sound and accurate writer. But Leake's book was for practitioners, while Pollock's book was for students of principles and legal thinkers. It is necessary to mention this in order to realize what a wealth of original thinking, as well as of industry and learning, went to that work of Pollock's. We take it now as a matter of course that there should be such expositions of the principles of English law, illuminated by accurate history, combining the philosophy of law with its practical aspects, wedding realism to speculation. There followed in 1887 the book on Torts, in some respects more brilliant than his *Principles of Contract*; the last edition by the author was published in 1929. Since then there have been many most important cases on the law of torts, and it is to be regretted that Pollock's final words on all these may not be forthcoming, though he has discussed some of the most important in various review articles.

The year 1881 also saw the publication on the other side of the Atlantic of O. W. Holmes' *The Common Law*, also an epoch-making work. I may here mention the long and close friendship existing between Holmes and Pollock right up to the date when Holmes died in 1934. Holmes had been Professor at the Harvard Law School before he became Chief Justice of Massachusetts and later an Associate Justice of the Supreme Court of the United States. In that great country there is not as here a deep gulf fixed between the professor's chair and the judicial seat on the bench. Save for occasional essays and lectures it was in the form of judgments that Holmes thereafter wrote on the law. But the two men were bound by ties of a devotion to the Common Law, and met from time to time either in England or the United States: they also wrote to each other and some day their correspondence, which is being collected by Mr Hale of Boston, may see the light.

Pollock indeed was deeply interested in the Common Law as developed in the United States. He favours citation by the Courts of the one country by the Courts of the other. He makes frequent citations in his own books of American authorities. He even ventured on the dream that one day there might be a combined sitting

In Memoriam: Sir Frederick Pollock

of Judges of the Supreme Court and House of Lords, a fascinating if Utopian picture. He gave two series of lectures in the United States which are published under the respective titles of the *Genius of the Common Law* and the *Expansion of the Common Law*. These are of great importance as illustrating Pollock's views on the broader aspect of the Common Law. So also are the articles which he contributed from time to time to the *Law Quarterly Review* (which he helped to found in 1885, along with Bryce, Holland, Markby, Dicey and others), to the *Harvard Law Review*, which was junior to the *Law Quarterly Review* by only two years, and to other periodicals, such as the *Journal of Comparative Legislation*. He published one collection of these essays in 1882 under the name of *Essays in Jurisprudence and Ethics*: this volume included essays on other than legal subjects such as on Mr Herbert Spencer's data of Ethics and on Marcus Aurelius and the Stoic Philosophy. A later collection entitled *Essays in the Law* was published in 1922 and included papers read in Oxford, London, Glasgow and the United States. I cannot forbear to mention his notice, reprinted in the *Essays*, from the *Cornhill Magazine*, of *Arabiniana*, or the sayings of Serjeant Arabin, who was a Judge in the Courts of the City of London from 1827 to 1841. The book is very rare. Pollock quotes many delightful passages. I have already mentioned his sense of humour, so familiar to those who met him. He must have enjoyed writing this little paper. Let me quote one short passage: the Serjeant is addressing a convicted prisoner. He says: "I have no doubt of your guilt; you go into a public-house and break bulk and drink beer; and that's what in law is called embezzlement." Since 1922 Pollock further contributed many papers to various journals.

I have mentioned the foundation of the *Law Quarterly Review*, which celebrated its Jubilee in 1935, when at the banquet presided over by the present Editor, Pollock delivered a most admirable speech. I cannot help ascribing to him the idea of a journal devoted to law, though he expressly disclaimed being sole founder, and indeed attributed the idea to Holland. This example has been followed not only by the *Harvard Law Review*, but by the Reviews published by the Law Faculties of many other Universities of the United States; there are also the *Canadian Bar Review*, the *Australian Law Journal*, the *Cambridge Law Journal* and others. No student of English law can realize the wealth of new ideas to be extracted from these journals unless he is careful to read them, or at least as much as his time will allow. In them also are to be found illuminating expositions and criticisms of current judgments of the Courts. These journals record the results of modern methods of the study of English law and owe much of their inception to Pollock.

These momentous services to the advancement of English law and of its study achieved within a period of less than fifteen years were followed by Pollock and Wright on *Possession in the Common Law*, in which Pollock collaborated with R. S. Wright, and by Pollock on Partnership which, published in 1877 as *A Digest of the Law of Partnership*, became in 1890 an annotated edition of the Partnership Act, 1890, drafted by Pollock himself. I shall have a little more to say of these works later.

In Memoriam: Sir Frederick Pollock

But Pollock's interest had been directed to law in India. In 1894 he delivered the Tagore Law Lectures at the University of Calcutta, the subject being the Law of Fraud in British India. Along with Fraud he dealt with Misrepresentation and Mistake, subjects which always interested him. He had, as he says, discussed these subjects as they appear in English law in his books already published and was content to restate the principles in the broadest and most general terms and then explain how they are applied in the Indian Acts. This work is most lucidly and accurately done.

Then in 1905 came an edition of the Indian Contract Act and Specific Relief Act, very fully annotated with references to English cases and also to the numerous cases in the Indian Courts. This book was produced in collaboration with that eminent Indian lawyer and judge with whom as a member of the Judicial Committee I had the honour to sit on Indian Appeals, the late Sir Dinshah Mulla. The sixth edition of this book was published in 1931, to a large extent without the benefit of Sir Dinshah's help, and involved the very laborious task of collecting relevant citations from the numerous Courts in the different States of British India. The multiplication of Law Reports in India involving the comparison of a vast number of authorities not always harmonious was a very heavy task. But it was well discharged. There are in the notes to the Contract Act many important observations on general principles of law, for instance on "Relations resembling those of Contract", which are sometimes called Quasi-Contract or Constructive Contract. There are some pungent criticisms of the Indian Contract Act which, passed in 1872, is said to have been originally based on a draft Civil Code of New York which was never enacted there. Pollock was always much interested in the extent to which and the manner in which English law had been adopted in British India. He refers to it more than once in his *Expansion of the Common Law*. Also between 1882 and 1886, on the instructions of the Government of India, he prepared a draft of a Civil Wrongs Bill: this was never enacted but it repays careful study: he has appended it with comments to his book on Torts.

I have yet to notice his *First Book of Jurisprudence for Students of the Common Law*, first published in 1896, a short but most illuminating study of the subject. In the Preface he acknowledges his indebtedness to Savigny, of the past generation, and to Maine, Ihering, and his friend Mr Justice Holmes. In his sixth edition, published in 1929, he pays a tribute to Sir William Holdsworth's *History of English Law*, "that great work" (*laudari a laudato viro*). Pollock was always generous to the younger generation. It would be tempting to analyse this comprehensive little book, with its precise and accurate definitions and statements of fundamental principles and simple summaries of recent research in early history. Let me instance the chapter on Law Reports. Pollock, as Editor of the Law Reports for forty years (he resigned in 1935), could not fail to be interested in law reporting, which after all is an essential condition of a law which, like the Common Law, depends on precedents; if cases were not properly reported, there could be no effective precedents. He begins this chapter by a humorous reference to Coke's suggestion that Moses was the first reporter. One delightful feature in that chapter is a

In Memoriam: Sir Frederick Pollock

comparison of three short passages of French as used in our law, the first being a specimen of living Anglo-Norman, A.D. 1292, the second of decaying Anglo-Norman, A.D. 1520, the third of degenerate law-French, seventeenth century. There are also two illuminating pages on the Year Books. He points out that a complete critical edition of the Year Books is much to be desired and would be a great help to the historical study of English law: some knowledge of them is needful, he says, for every one who wishes to know the law as a scholar and not merely as a practitioner. Perhaps some day this hope may be fulfilled with the help of generous benefactors and zealous scholars.[1] I cannot follow this interesting chapter farther. Law reporting also appears as the subject of one of the *Essays in the Law*, where there is reprinted a paper he read before the American Bar Association. He was interested not only in the early Reports, but also in original records, and constantly emphasized or illustrated a point by such references. For instance, in a note on alienation in early law (note Q in his 1930 edition of Maine's *Ancient Law*), he observes, to illustrate his point: "In fact I have seen in the Chapter library of Worcester a thirteenth-century deed in which the consent of the grantor's wife and his heir presumptive is expressed." Such things help to make the past law alive both to himself and his readers, and re-create its continuity. Closely akin to such questions are his references to pleading. I am tempted to quote a characteristic passage: "...in some things the whirligig of time has so brought us round that we are much nearer than

---

[1] The Rolls Series and the Selden Society have already done great service in this cause.

Blackstone was to our mediaeval ancestors. If Henry of Bratton could be taken through the rolls of the subsequent centuries he might well shake his head at the stiffening technicalities of the fourteenth century, grumble at the flamboyant over-subtlety of the sixteenth.... When he came to the latest forms of Common Law and Chancery pleading in the eighteenth century—the time when Blackstone thought everything almost perfect—he might peradventure break out, clerk in orders and archdeacon though he was, into such oaths as are reported a little after his time in the mouth of Hervey de Stanton, nicknamed 'Hervey the hasty'." But I cannot pursue the imaginary conversation with Henry de Bratton which follows.

Pollock, while deeply interested in the Year Book period, was of opinion that the nineteenth century was a period of great development of English law, though people were in the habit of saying that the capacity of English law to grow had been exhausted, and that the future of law rested in legislation. That it should be so is not surprising when it is realized that it had been an age of unexampled progress in industry and in social and political ideas. On the other hand, he found in the sixteenth and seventeenth centuries a period when the vitality of the law was depressed. His verdict on the two greatest Chief Justices was clearly expressed. He regarded Coke as a great working lawyer, but he lamented the pseudo-antiquarian pedantry of Coke; his mind, he said, was thoroughly unhistorical. For Mansfield he had a real admiration, being a judge who followed the tradition of cosmopolitan jurisprudence instead of being confined by the insular learning of the Inns of Court.

In Memoriam: Sir Frederick Pollock

He speculates what influence Mansfield might have exercised on the Common Law if he had lived two centuries before the age when he did; for instance, what effect his influence if exercised then would have had on the doctrine of Consideration. But Pollock does not fail to applaud the adoption of the law merchant under the directing genius of Mansfield; his judgments, he says, are classical. It was received into the Common Law in its mature form at the right moment when its customs had been improved by the experience of merchants and its errors largely corrected. Thus it was received under the influence of Mansfield, not as a fixed body of rules, but as a living body of custom. In that way it became an integral part of our law, though it had to pay as the price of being admitted the necessity of accommodating itself to the forms of the Common Law.

In this connection I may refer to Pollock's attitude towards Consideration. He sympathized with Mansfield's attempt to qualify it; the attempt, he said, came too late. But Pollock had a real belief in the bargain theory of contracts; what he deplored were the sophistries and refinements which gathered round it in the course of history. He once lamented to me the misfortune that the view had been adopted that the consideration must be simultaneous with the promise. He saw, however, the practical convenience of the bargain theory. He felt that in this as in so many other respects the Common Law did well to sacrifice some logic in the interests of convenience. And with all his passion for justice and for the reasonable—which he regarded as being one of the most essential elements of the Common Law—there went a conservative attachment to the old traditional tenets of the law. It was in this spirit that he had a sympathy with fictions. Some even of the more bizarre appealed to him, partly because of his historical or antiquarian sense, partly perhaps because of some humorous vein. He saw that they were useful to help the judges in their task of extending rules from case to case, by a sort of analogy, an "as if". They were to him, as he said, a kind of scaffolding. He pointed with satisfaction to a new and beneficent fiction even as late as the middle of the nineteenth century—the warranty of authority as agent. I am not sure that he would ever have agreed that a mature system of law should remove the scaffolding of fictions and state its rules simply as rules of positive law. With all his knowledge of other systems than ours, he was enamoured (as indeed every English lawyer must be) of our methods of case law. He can admire that great example of the case lawyer, Baron Parke. He quotes[1] with obvious enjoyment passages from the famous "Dialogue in the Shades" between Crogate and Baron Surrebutter as imagined by Hayes. But he is able to say that Parke, when not occupied with his technicalities, was a wise and enlightened judge, as most of us who have profited by his decisions fully realize. Lord Bramwell gives him an opportunity of making one of the profound observations which constantly recur in his writings. Bramwell's great idea, he says, was to reduce everything (or almost everything) to terms of contract, to apply the contract concept up to or beyond the bounds of possibility. That was Bramwell's justification of the doctrine of common employment which was said to be based on the implied terms of the workman's

[1] *The Genius of the Common Law* (1912), 27–37.

In Memoriam: Sir Frederick Pollock

engagement. Pollock from his earliest writings to the end abhorred that doctrine and never ceased to denounce it. Indeed it is striking to observe how certain cases met with his constant and reiterated disapproval. One such was the decision of the House of Lords in *Derry* v. *Peek*.[1] He stated the effect of that case to be that, save in exceptional cases and apart from duties incident to contract, English law does not recognize any duty whatever of taking any pains to ensure the accuracy of statements which one makes with the intent that others shall act on them, however mischievous the results, apart, that is, from the speaker's absolute want of belief in the truth.

One judge whom he could not suffer was Brougham, whose "omniscience" and "useful knowledge" offended Pollock's accurate and scholarly mind.

Another Common Law rule which roused his ire was the maxim, *Actio personalis moritur cum persona*. Pollock as an exact thinker in law reprobated what are called maxims; he reinforced the condemnation by a quotation from Paulus and another from Lord Esher. But of that particular maxim he said that its origin was obscure, that its meaning was uncertain, and that it was only made endurable by the exceptions which the judges had grafted upon it. The worst of these maxims is that it is so difficult to get rid of them. Like the forms of action their ghosts haunt us. With the kindred, though in truth different, rule in *Baker* v. *Bolton* he was little more in sympathy. But he said that as the decision of the House of Lords in *Admiralty Commissioners* v. *S.S. Amerika*[2] was final, no useful purpose could be served by further discussion.

[1] (1889) 14 App. Cas. 337.   [2] [1917] A.C. 38.

These examples of his critical boldness might be multiplied, if space permitted. But he had his favourite instances of what he called judicial valour evincing itself in a wise and bold decision, which evolves the solution of a problem out of a complicated tangle of decisions so simply, that, once the solution is given, it seems so clear that everybody wonders why there was any trouble. He found two such instances in Macnaghten's judgments; one was the *Nordenfelt Case*,[1] which decided that the reasonableness of an agreement limiting trade competition is to be determined on the merits of the case as a whole and not according to any formula. This phrase embodies, Pollock said, not merely a decision, but an ideal of general application. The other judgment of Macnaghten's which he cited was *Drummond* v. *Van Ingen*,[2] where Macnaghten released from its entanglement the broad general principle that on a sale of goods there is an implied condition that the goods are fit for a known purpose, and met the contention that the implied condition would hamper trade with the answer: "That is the stock argument in all these cases." Pollock, as I have already indicated, had a great admiration for the work of our judges in mercantile law. "The triumphs of their valour are written over the whole history of our mercantile law from the judgments of Mansfield to those of Macnaghten." He added his praise to our equity judges for the construction of partnership law. He described the doctrine of estoppel "as a simple and wholly untechnical conception, perhaps the most powerful and flexible instrument to be found in any system of Court jurisprudence". In another connection he found

[1] [1894] A.C. 535.   [2] (1887) 12 App. Cas. 284, 299.

In Memoriam: Sir Frederick Pollock

in "natural reason and just construction of the law, in the external standard of reasonableness, an idea which extends over the whole field of what we now call Quasi Contract". I confess I regret that Pollock did not find time to map out and delimit that still incompletely explored region. He was fully aware of its existence. His historical instinct, however, made him reluctant to dismiss the fiction of the implied contract; he compromised by proposing the name "Constructive Contract", though he has elsewhere pointed out the fallacy of seeking to reduce civil relations (excluding, or sometimes even including, torts) into the Procrustean bed of contract.

But I cannot here farther pursue such details. I have merely sought to illustrate Pollock's extraordinary freedom of mind, his penetrating insight, undimmed by his wealth of learning, his faculty of hitting off a simple and convincing solution of a problem, however complicated it might seem.

It might be wondered why the main devotion of his legal life was, as I think it was, to Common Law rather than to Equity. He went at first to read in Equity chambers. Perhaps the traditions of his famous family decided him. Perhaps his mind was essentially "reasonable" in the Common Law sense. He certainly was not attracted by the subtleties of conveyancing. He quotes, I think with approbation, Macaulay's lament over Fearne's devotion of a lifetime to "the barbarous puzzle of contingent remainders", though he admits that that subject appertains rather to Law than to Equity. He thought in early days that Equity was righteous overmuch and was setting a standard too high for mortal frailty. But whatever opinion he had of the technical rules of Equity, he found in Equity, in its broader and more enlightened aspects, the intelligent companion, not the arbitrary mistress, of the Common Law. Indeed, as he has pointed out, they are not separate systems but complementary parts of the same system of law. That he should have appreciated this, though he began his legal career before the Judicature Act, shows his independence of mind.

I have, I fear, little space for discussion of the great works which Pollock has left us, Contract, Torts, Possession, Partnership, and, jointly with his great friend Maitland, Pollock and Maitland on the *History of English Law*. The last mentioned of these books is too well known to need any detailed description here, even if it were possible. Pollock in a note appended to the preface says that "although the book was planned in common and has been revised by both of us, by far the greater share of the execution belongs to Mr Maitland, both as to the actual writing and as to the detailed research which was constantly required". I have been told by one who ought to know that about one-fifth of the actual writing was done by Pollock. Pollock says that the order of the names on the title page was "according to usage that of seniority at the bar". It was, as he states, "an attempt at a general reconstruction of the Common Law as Edward I found it". He adds that their main object was "to make our book a sure foundation for the next generation to build on and already it is fulfilling this purpose". That was written in 1907: now after nearly thirty years that fulfilment has been realized and is still being realized in fuller and fuller measure.

In Memoriam: Sir Frederick Pollock

I can pass to Pollock's great works on Contract and on Torts, the twin great branches of the Common Law. These books, which already rank as classics, inaugurated a new era in the literature of English law. The first edition of *Contract*, published in 1876, was a remarkable achievement for a young man only six years after his call to the Bar. It was planned to be, as he said, a treatise on the general principles which determine the validity and effect of contracts in their inception. Writing as he did two years after the Judicature Act, he sought to give "an equal and concurrent view of the doctrines of common law and equity". In the last (tenth) edition, published in 1936, he adhered to the original plan, though with much variation in detail, and enriched the book with all the added wealth of new law which had been evolved in more than half a century of busy legal development. The first edition ran to over 600 pages, the tenth to more than 700. He seeks throughout to give an analysis which, though neither term is strictly applicable, might be called philosophic or scientific of the fundamental principles of the subject and to combine with that object an examination of the detailed case law, arranged under the various heads under which he has divided and sub-divided the mass of material. He is fully conscious that in English law substantive or juristic principles are to be elicited from the procedural formulae in which, especially in the old law, they are apt to be embedded and obscured. He is also conscious, as he tells us, that the exclusive pursuit of the analytical method in dealing with legal conceptions always leads to straits and if the pursuit be obstinate lands us in sheer fictions. Where it seems necessary he may be historical or even antiquarian; but his main purpose is a realistic statement of the existing law; he looks backward only in order to look forward. In the main he is restrained in criticism or suggestions of reform. I had intended to quote a few passages in which Pollock expounds general principles so that I might illustrate the elegance and clarity of his style and the exactness of his analysis, but it seems impossible here. I may refer to the introductory pages of the tenth edition in which he analysed the fundamental conceptions of contract. It is interesting to compare these pages in the latest edition with the corresponding pages in the first edition and to note the changes in his more mature thought. He was a learner to the end. Nor can I examine the conceptions which underlie his classification of the enormous variety and complication of the subject. Perhaps the most interesting chapters are those which deal with Mistake, Fraud and Misrepresentation. But all through the book there is originality, comprehensiveness and acumen.

The same is true of the companion work on Torts, published eleven years after his *Contract*. Some have said that the later work shows more finish, the result of his increased experience in writing. I have been told by friends who teach law that they find *Contract* more difficult for students than *Torts*. The preface was addressed to Holmes and the book dedicated to Willes, who, he says, once and again had expressed his desire to see the law of obligations methodically treated in English. Pollock adds that it is a book of principles if it is any thing; details, he says, are used not in the manner of a digest, but so far as they seem called for in order to develop and illustrate the principles. I quote these words because I think they state succinctly the character of his work.

The thirteenth edition was published in 1929 and was the last that Pollock did. Since then there has been a considerable number of important cases on tort. So far as I know, Pollock had done no work on a new edition, though he had left with that object several notes on slips of paper.[1] He had, however, written some articles in the *Law Quarterly Review*, in particular on the important leading case, *Donoghue* v. *Stevenson*,[2] which he humorously describes as the "Snail in the Bottle Case", just as he headed a severe criticism of *Baker* v. *Snell*,[3] the dog-bite case, with the title, "The Dog and the Potman; or Go it, Bob!" He applauds the decision in *Donoghue* v. *Stevenson* in particular because it determines conclusively that what has sometimes been called "privity", a bastard brother of the contractual nexus, was not an essential element to constitute that duty which according to English law is a necessary condition of negligence. The analysis of negligence in his *Torts* embodies, at least implicitly, the same idea that found expression in *Donoghue* v. *Stevenson*, and in his article he points out that Lord Esher's famous *dictum* in *Heaven* v. *Pender*[4] has been in principle justified. He also wrote an illuminating paper on the scope of the duty towards trespassers, a topic which had been substantially elucidated in recent decisions. In this case also it is impossible here to analyse in detail the book itself. It is a model of comprehensiveness and analytical arrangement; it has all the charm of

[1] Preface to 14th edition (1939, by P. A. Landon), v–vi.
[2] [1932] A.C. 562.   [3] [1908] 2 K.B. 825.
[4] (1883) 11 Q.B.D. 503.

style which is characteristic of Pollock. It is original, independent and philosophical. He makes much use of decisions in the United States. Though in general he takes the detailed rules of law as he finds them in the cases, he can be scathing in criticism when he comes to the authorities like *Derry* v. *Peek*,[1] which he has always reprobated, and some newer ones as well.

But I must leave these two great books with the conviction that for generations to come they will influence the development of the Common Law and continue to be recognized as the classics which in truth they are.

Space does not allow me to do more than mention Pollock's edition of the Partnership Act. That Act is a model of draftsmanship; it was Pollock's own work. His notes are clear and concise and workmanlike. Another work which would call for a paper by itself is *Possession in the Common Law*. The book consists of two parts, the one dealing with possession for purposes of the civil law, which was written by Pollock himself, and the other dealing with possession in relation to the criminal law, written by R. S. (afterwards Mr Justice) Wright. It was a composite, not a joint work. Each part was the independent work of its particular author. Pollock says in the preface that while writing his book on Torts and considering questions of trespass, conversion and wrongs to property, he was led to inquire whether "a doctrine of possession did not exist in an implicit form in our authorities and what kind of doctrine it was". In the lectures on the Genius of the Common Law which he delivered at Columbia University in 1912 he reverted

---

[1] (1889) 14 App. Cas. 337.

to this book, claiming that out of the scattered English decisions arising out of the most varied circumstances, civil and criminal, there could be extracted a theory of possession consisting of a few comprehensive principles more elegant and in closer touch with actual conditions than could be extracted from the Roman jurists. He then proceeded to summarize them in four rules, which corresponded to the principles expounded at length with authorities in support, in his book, which is a masterpiece of original thinking and research.

I venture to hope that before long a comprehensive collection may be made of Pollock's articles, papers and lectures, and that it may be published, so that the vast scope of his learning and thought in law may be fully realized and made available for the service of lawyers.

Finally I quote two short passages to illustrate his actual method of writing. I feel some sense of temerity in doing so: there are so many others perhaps better adapted that I might have chosen.

The first quotation is from "Judicial Caution and Valour", *The Law Quarterly Review,* Vol. XLV, at p. 296:

The problem of judicial interpretation is to hold a just middle way between excess of valour and excess of caution. A too daring expounder is in danger of laying down sweeping rules without attending to the probable variations in the circumstances to which they will be applied; and then the application of his rule may have to be confined within tolerable bounds by a series of qualifications which leave it, to use a classical description, well nigh eaten up by exceptions. On the other hand, the pedestrian timidity that shrinks from hazarding any general conclusion will only land us in a still less desirable state, that of having no principle at all, but a heap of unrelated instances which those who come after may or may not find to be consistent with one another.

Doubtless it is very true that the more valiant judge runs the risk of his exposition being sooner or later disapproved by superior authority; while the more cautious one avoids that risk, but at the price of falling under a censure now familiar. Those who make no mistakes, it has been said, will never make anything; and the judge who is afraid of committing himself may be called sound and safe in his own generation, but will leave no mark on the law. Doubtless, also, caution has its proper place in resisting temptations to rash and premature definition, and especially to borrowing conceptions of foreign origin without adequately considering whether they are in harmony with the spirit of our own law. In short, discretion is good and very necessary, but without valour the law would have no vitality at all.

The second quotation is from *The Genius of the Common Law*, at p. 124:

For if there is any virtue in the Common Law whereby she stands for more than intellectual excellence in a special kind of learning, it is that Freedom is her sister, and in the spirit of freedom her greatest work has ever been done. By that spirit our lady has emboldened her servants to speak the truth before kings, to restrain the tyranny of usurping license, and to carry her ideal of equal public justice and ordered right into every quarter of the world. By the fire of that spirit our worship of her is touched and enlightened, and in its power, knowing that the service we render to her is freedom, we claim no inferior fellowship with our brethren of the other great Faculties, the healers of the body and the comforters of the soul, the lovers of all that is highest in this world and beyond. There is no more arduous enterprise for lawful men, and none more noble, than the perpetual quest of justice laid upon all of us who are pledged to serve our lady the Common Law.

In concluding a brief paper like this, I cannot help feeling that a catalogue of particulars is inadequate to give a vital picture of the man, just as a description of features and lineaments fails to give the impression of

In Memoriam: Sir Frederick Pollock

the living face. There are some men whose personalities transcend any particular things they have done. Some men are greater than their works or deeds, though these may have been great. There comes from such men an afflatus of impulse and inspiration. This is what we always felt with Pollock. There emanated from him a passion for the law, to the service of which he had devoted his powers. In reading that delightful book of autobiographical reminiscences, *For My Grandson*, written in 1929, we are conscious of the multiplicity of the points at which he touched life, of the breadth, the variety and the vividness of his interests. He might well have said that he had warmed both hands before the fires of life, that he had loved nature and, next to nature, art. But these interests, which would have been sufficient by themselves to have filled most men's lives, were to him only *parerga*. His real devotion was to law, in the service of which he spent his working life. He was proud of that service. For him there was nothing common or mean in law, which for him was the instrument of justice in human affairs. The embodiment of law which he loved was the Law of England, seen in all its amplitude in time and in space, progressing down the ages and expanding beyond England over the nations of the British Commonwealth, over India and over the United States; indeed he thought of the Common Law as the law of free nations and as the bond of union between the English-speaking peoples, on whichever side of the Atlantic or the Pacific their homes were. These were the causes for which he spent his life. His fruits will live after him.

INDEX OF MATTERS

Abuse of rights, 371–373, 403
Acceptance of goods, 230–231
Actio personalis moritur cum persona, 351, 390, 425
Addison on *Contracts*, 415
Administrative law, 194–195, 383
Agency, law of, 262–264, 361–362
Alibi, 177–178
American Bar Association, 421
American Bar Association Journal, 174 n.
American Restatement of Law of Contracts, 206, 214, 221, 290, 311, 320, 322; of Law of Restitution, 1, 3, 27–29, 34–65, 206; of Law of Torts, 119; on Conflict of Laws, 171, 346
Ames, Prof., 329, 358, 414
Animals, savage, legal liability for, 135 n., 136, 139–140, 141
Anson, Sir W., 287–288, 387, 414
Anticipatory breach of contract, 240–242
Arabiniana, 417
Assent in contracts, 209–211, 213
Assumpsit, 17, 18, 20, 30, 31, 38, 206, 207, 221, 305, 306, 307, 314, 356–357, 384
Aston J., 309
Atkin, Lord, 76, 164, 291
Atkinson, Lord, 6
Attornment, 270
Austin, John, 414
Australian Law Journal, 418

Bacon, Francis, 402, 408
Bailment, 236
Bankers and customers, 274–278
Bankers' confirmed credits, 319, 379
Bankes L.J., 270 n.
Bankruptcy, 252
Beale, Prof., 329, 346, 414

Benefits (in Restitution cases) conferred at request, 39, 49–50; lawfully acquired, 39, 52–53, 57; tortiously acquired, 39, 53–55, 57; voluntarily conferred, 39, 50–52
Bentham, Jeremy, 187, 198, 347, 359, 414
Bills of Exchange, 237, 265–267, 274–278, 317, 334, 380, 397
Bills of Lading, 238, 239, 263, 266, 269–271, 279–280, 334, 370
Birkenhead, Lord, 267 n.
Blackburn, Lord, 142, 253, 293–295
Blackstone, Sir W., 402, 414–415, 422
Bohm, E. M., 203
Bowen L.J., 109–110, 224
Bramwell, Lord, 78, 424
Bratton, Henry de, 422
Brougham, Lord, 74, 425
Bryce, Lord, 387, 414, 417

Cairns, Lord, 136
Cambridge Law Journal, 1 n., 394, 418
Camden, Lord, 67
Canadian Bar Review, 418
Cardozo C.J., 119
Carriage by air, 280–281
Carriers, transportation contracts of, 237–239, 265, 279–281, 283–286
Cattle trespass, liability for, 129, 135 n., 140
Causa in contract, 300–302, 303–304, 307, 323–324, 375
Chancery and King's Bench, functions of, 330–332, 335–336
Charities, promises to subscribe to, 321
Charter-parties, 266, 279–280

Index of Matters

Cheques, 274–278
C.I.F. sales, 269–271
Civil Wrongs Bill, 420
Cockburn C.J., 22, 267 n.
Codification of law, 190–191, 333–334, 338–341, 342
Coercion, 39, 46–49
Coke, Sir E., 295, 305, 347, 402, 408, 420, 422
Collins, Lord, 115–116
Columbia University Law School, 393, 432
Commercial Contracts, 265–268
Commercial Credits, 222, 235–236, 375
Commercial Law in the present century, 252–286
Common Law and Equity, definition of, 190, 328–329; distinguished from statute law, 334
Company Law, 252–253, 262–264, 335–336
Compositions with creditors, 317–318
Conflict of laws, 154–155, 158, 161–173, 339, 346; American Restatement on, 171, 346
Consideration in contract, 218–225, 227, 265, 287–326, 350, 375–377, 381, 390, 423
Contract, breach of, 50, 55, 98, 99, 101, 104–105, 121–123, 207, 233, 249–250, 254–262; implied in law, 2, 12, 15–16, 18, 20, 21, 22–24, 27, 29, 33, 34–36, 206, 357–359, 379–380, 384, 404–405, 427
Contractor, legal definition of, 142
Contracts, Law of, American Restatement of, 206, 214, 221, 290, 311, 320, 322; in relation to public policy, 66–95 pass.; relating to money or currency, 147–173 pass.; Williston on, 202–251
Conversion, Restitution in relation to, 53–54

Cotton L.J., 22, 205
County courts, 332
Cranworth, Lord, 135
Crompton J., 316
CurrencyJointResolution(U.S.A.), 161–162, 170
Currency problems, 147–173 pass., 244
Customer, definition of, 275

Damages, 96–123 pass., 243–245, 264–265, 404–406
Dangerous operations, definition of, 143–144
Davey, Lord, 263 n.
Debt, statute-barred, 220–221
Defamation, 370, 373
Denman, Lord, 312–313, 315
Deviation in transportation contracts, 239, 280
de Villiers A.J.A., 298–301, 324
Dicey, Prof. A. V., 164, 387, 414, 417
Dunedin, Lord, 2, 6, 9–10, 11, 12, 13, 14, 17, 19, 30, 289, 296–297, 324

Education, legal, 387–410 pass., 414–416
Ellenborough, Lord, 43
Employers' liability, 127–129, 141–146, 200, 361–363, 397, 398, 400
Enrichment, unjust, 1–33, 36–37, 39, 47, 52, 53, 54, 59–64, 206, 358, 360, 389, 403–404
Equity and Common Law, definition of, 190
Erle C.J., 308
Esher, Lord, 109, 425, 431
Estoppel, 214, 216, 426; promissory, 221, 321
Evidence, analysis of and scientific principles applicable to, 174–185 pass.; rules of, 338
Exchange, Bills of, 237, 265–267, 274–278, 317, 334, 380, 397

438

Index of Matters

Executive, legislative, and judicial powers, relation between, 193, 195

Factum probandum and *probans*, 176, 182, 183, 184
Fleming C.B., 67 *n*.
Fletcher Moulton L. J., 5, 15, 23
F.O.B. sales, 269
Foreseeability, in cases of negligence, 117, 120
Frustration of contracts; *see* Impossibility
Fry L.J., 205

General average, 55
Gold Clauses, 147–173
Goodhart, Prof. A. L., 118
Grand jury, 332
Grotius, 309
Guarantor, position of, in contract law, 227–228
Gutteridge, Professor, 319

Hague Rules, 279–280
Haldane, Lord, 6, 11–12, 17–18
Hale, Sir Matthew, 140
Halsbury, Lord, 76–77, 205, 249
Hamilton; *see* Sumner, Lord
Harvard Law Review, 34 *n*., 66 *n*., 287 *n*., 375, 394, 417, 418
Harvard Law School, 203, 393, 414, 416
Health Insurance, 194, 336, 362
Herschell, Lord, 110, 111, 352
Holdsworth Club, 252 *n*.
Holdsworth, Prof. Sir William, 253, 324–325, 401, 420
Holland, T. E., 414, 417, 418
Holmes J., 74, 89, 329, 371, 400, 414, 416, 420, 430
Holt L.C.J., 20, 97, 127, 224, 253, 267, 348

Illegality of contracts, 249, 287, 326, 379

Impossibility in contract law, 247–248, 254–262, 287, 304, 326, 360, 379
Indebitatus assumpsit, 18, 20, 30, 31, 37, 356–357, 384
Inference, application of to evidence, 176, 178, 184
Insanity, definition of, 337
Instalment contracts, 232, 259
Insurance, in Commercial Law, 281–285; in relation to suicide, 85–90; marine, 265–266, 269–271, 281–285, 334
Intention, in contract, 210, 215–217, 219, 220, 222, 233, 255, 258, 261, 269, 287–326 *pass.*, 376, 378, 403
Interest, recovery of, 352
International law, basis of, 188

Jackson, R. M., 35 *n*.
Jessel, Sir G., 68, 317
Journal of Comparative Legislation, 417
Judges, function and powers of, 191–194, 250, 328, 332, 333, 337, 340, 341–342, 349, 382–383, 388–391, 396
Judicial Committee of the Privy Council, duties of, 333
Judicial, executive, and legislative powers, relation between, 193, 195
Judicial proof, 174–185
Jury, function and value of the, 332

Keener on *Quasi-Contract*, 34, 35
Kent, 329
King's Bench and Chancery, functions of, 330–332, 335–336
King's Proctor, 80

Lading, bills of, 238, 239, 263, 266, 269–271, 279–280, 334, 370
Langdell, Prof., 329, 414
Law Quarterly Review, 394, 417, 418, 431, 433

Index of Matters

Law Revision Committee, 265, 325 n., 350, 355 n., 384, 403
Leake on *Contracts*, 34, 224, 415
Legal Education, 387–410 *pass.*, 414–416
Legislative, executive, and judicial powers, relation between, 193, 195
Liability, absolute or strict, 141, 361, 369, 401; employers', 127–129, 141–146, 200, 361–363, 397, 398, 400
Liberty of the subject, the, 195–196
Lien, equitable, 27, 28, 54, 58, 61
Lindley L.J., 22, 414
Lorenzen, Prof., 304, 324
Lunatics, contracts in relation to, 22–24, 52, 231
Lyndhurst, Lord, 74

Maasdorp J.A., 298
Macclesfield, Lord, 92
Mackenzie, Lord, 303
Macmillan, Lord 302
Macnaghten, Lord, 93, 263 n., 426
Magna Carta, 67
Maine, Sir H., 414, 420, 421
Maitland, F. W., 126, 401, 415, 428
Mansfield, Lord, 20, 39, 90, 219, 253, 267, 309–311, 314, 325, 348, 376, 422–423, 426
Markby, Sir William, 414, 417
Married women, legal rights of, 199, 231, 350, 353
Marshall on Insurance, 77
Martin B., 312
Mathew J., 252
Mental injury, 369–370
Misrepresentation, 246
Mistake, in contract, 39–46, 208–214, 217, 247, 260–263, 326, 379, 389
Modern Law Review, 394
Moulton, Lord, 138
Mulla, Sir Dinshah, 419

Negligence, 98–107, 116–120, 124–135, 139, 141–146, 200, 236, 264, 273, 275–278, 281, 284, 355, 360–369, 381, 385, 389, 400, 403, 404, 431
New Zealand Law Reports, 169
New Zealand Local Bodies Loans Act, 168
Nudum pactum, 293, 298–299, 309–310, 317, 318
Nuisance, 124, 126, 129, 130–131

Option, without consideration, 297–298
"Ordinary," meaning of, 110, 117, 136, 138

Parke, Baron, 3, 21, 24, 72–76, 312, 359, 424
Parker, Lord, 3, 6, 7, 9, 11, 13–15, 16, 19
Parliament, 189–193
Partnership, 252, 334, 418, 426, 432
Patents, 252
Pensions, old age, 194, 336, 362
Perpetuities, 77
Plesch, A., on *The Gold Clause*, 160 n.
Pollock C.B., 74, 75, 414
Pollock, Sir F., 15, 35, 208, 289, 329, 387–388, 393, 395, 401, 411–435
Poor Law, 336
Pound, Prof. Roscoe, 319, 324, 329
Precedent in English law, 192, 204, 388, 391, 395, 399, 420
Privacy, legal safeguards of, 373–374
Privity of contract, 26, 316, 322, 364, 378, 404–405, 431
Proof, Judicial, 174–185
Public Policy, 66–95; in relation to contracts, 249–250, 325
Puffendorff, 309

Quasi-contract, 2, 15–16, 17–18, 22, 25–27, 29, 32–33, 34–40, 50,

440

Index of Matters

53, 55, 60, 206–207, 231, 245–246, 248, 356–360, 384, 403–406, 427
Quasi-trust, 7

Real Property, law of, 397
Rectification in contract law, 212–213, 217, 378
Requisition Cases of contract, 256–257
Rescission of contracts, 235, 245–246
Restitutio in integrum, 102, 107–109
Restitution, American Restatement of Law of, 1, 3, 27–29, 34–65, 206; for breach of contract, 245–246
Roche, Lord, 76
Romilly, Lord, 162–163
Rules Committee, 339

Salvage, 51, 55
Scott, Prof. A. W., 37, 59
Scrutton L.J., 252 n., 270 n., 277 n.
Seavey, Prof. W. A., 37
Selborne, Lord, 162, 293–294, 300
Selden Society, 421 n.
Separation agreements, 84
Skynner L.C.B., 310
Solomon A.C.J., 298
Spencer, Herbert, 417
Star Chamber, 67
Stare decisis, principle of, 338, 341–345, 396, 399
Statutory powers as justification in defence, 132–134, 141
Sterling, meaning of, 147
Story J., 329
Subrogation, 9, 14, 46, 47, 58, 61
Suicide in relation to insurance, 85–90
Sumner, Lord, 3, 6, 8, 12, 16–17, 21, 23, 25–26, 32, 94, 99–102, 108, 221, 248, 255, 345, 358, 379, 395

Suretyship, 237

Tagore Law Lectures, 419
Tenterden, Lord, 20, 21, 315
Thayer, Dean, 329, 414
Third party beneficiary in contract, 378
Thompson, Prof. G. J., 202
Title paramount, 56
Tort, definition of, 403–406
Tortfeasors, contribution between joint, 352–353, 390; restitution to, 48–49
Torts, American Restatement of Law of, 119
Totalitarian government, 196
Tracing order, 2, 5, 8, 358
Trade, restraint of, 69, 77, 91–94, 380–381
Trade Unions, 195, 199
Trademarks, 252
Trafficking in honours, 71
Transportation contracts, 237–239, 265, 279–280, 283–286
Trespass, 124, 126, 129, 366–368, 374, 381, 404, 431–432
Trover, 30, 384
Trust, constructive, 7–8, 28, 37, 58–61, 62–64; express, 7, 60; resulting, 60
Trusts, Restatement of, 59–60

Ultra vires borrowing by company, 1–33 *pass.*, 45
Unemployment Insurance, 194, 336, 362
University College, London, 387 n.
Unrealized expectations (in Restitution cases), 44

Vinnius, 309
Vis major, 141, 170–171

Waiver of a condition, 320, 378
Walton, Dr F. P., 304–305
War risks, 284–285
Warranty, in English and American law, 235, 236, 239, 273

Index of Matters

Watson, Lord, 371
Wensleydale, Lord; *see* Parke, Baron
Westbury, Lord, 84
Wightman J., 316
Wigmore, Dean, on Judicial Proof, 174–185 *pass.*
Willes J., 414, 430
Williston, S., 37, 329, 414; on *Contracts*, 202–251

Wilmot J., 309, 315
Winfield, Prof. P. H., 35, 66 *n.*, 136 *n.*
Wolsey, Cardinal, 402
Wright, R. S., 418, 432

Yale Law Journal, 394
Yale Law School, 393
Yates J., 309
Year Books, the, 421

CAMBRIDGE: PRINTED BY W. LEWIS, M.A., AT THE UNIVERSITY PRESS